AF560313

URBAN PUBLIC SERVICES

PRICING AND SUBSIDY COMPONENT

Urban Public Services
Pricing and Subsidy Component

- Health and Security Services
- Infrastructural Services
- Environment Improvement Services

With Special Emphasis on Municipal Expenditure, Income from and Subsidy Element in Urban Services

Edited by

NAIB SINGH

Department of Geography,
B.S.C. Ji, Government College,
Sardargarh, Bathinda

Foreword by

DR. SURYA KANT

Reader, Department of Geography,
Panjab University, Chandigarh

DEEP & DEEP PUBLICATIONS PVT. LTD.
F-159, Rajouri Garden, New Delhi - 110027

URBAN PUBLIC SERVICES
PRICING AND SUBSIDY COMPONENT

ISBN 81-7629-824-7

Typeset by THE COMPOSERS,
260, C.A. Apt., Paschim Vihar, New Delhi - 110 063

Printed in India at NEW ELEGANT PRINTERS,
A-49, Phase-I, Mayapuri, New Delhi - 110 064

Published by DEEP & DEEP PUBLICATIONS PVT. LTD.,
F-159, Rajouri Garden, New Delhi-110 027
Phones : 25435369, 25440916.

E-mail: ddpbooks@yahoo.co.in • deep98@del13.vsnl.net.in
Showroom:
2/13, Ansari Road, Daryaganj, New Delhi-110002 • Telefax: 23245122

Contents

Foreword

Municipal bodies in India perform a variety of obligatory and non-obligatory functions, like water supply, sewerage and drainage, street lighting, public transport, fire brigade service etc., for the residents living under their respective jurisdictions. Poor state of municipal services in towns and cities in the country is a well recognised and documented fact. The National Commission on Urbanisation states, "urban centers have ... generated the most brutal and inhuman living conditions, with large sections of the citizens ... living in squatter settlements. The over crowding in slums and the desperate lack of water and sanitation leads not only to severe health problems but to the abject degradation of human life.... In the decades to come, who knows how much political tension and physical violence will be triggered off by the flagrant display of wealth which coexists with the rising expectations of the poor and with the appalling conditions of congestion and pollution which form their environment" (Vol. I, p. 1).

The malady seeks a diagnosis for its remedy. Analytical perspectives on the matter differ. One of the perspectives is that there is a reluctance to raise prices of services in face of sharp increase in expenditure on production, distribution and maintenance of these services in the wake of demographic growth, physical expansion of towns and cities along with rising cost of labour and material. The National Commission on Urbanisation also notes, "there is a universal complaint in India that local bodies, which are responsible for maintenance of existing services, are woefully short of resources, both for maintenance of existing services and for making the capital investment necessary for expansion" (Vol. II, p. 133). Deterioration in quality and availability of services is the natural outcome of all this. Less empowered social groups and peripheral localities do suffer the most in the process.

Although numerous studies are available on urban services and municipal finances yet seldom has been an attempt made to study the pricing mechanism of urban services so as to understand the bases on which urban services are subsidized and to find out a rational formula for their distribution. So far Indian Geography is considered, there is a complete dearth of such studies. The present book *Pricing of Urban Services—Pricing and Subsidy Component* by Naib Singh is a commendable exception. He is the first at least among the Indian geographers to take up this theme for innovative research.

A variety of questions raised in the book is very appropriate, timely and focused. Is there some basis for distribution of subsidies on urban services? Was there any social and or spatial discrimination in their distribution and what should be the rational approach to the subsidy element in the provision of urban services? In fact, the whole discussion in the book is centred around, how to build a sustainable system of urban services for towns and cities in India, which combines the virtues of service efficiency, social equity, operational effectiveness, dynamic growth and financial viability.

The job of finding answers to these questions has been handled with a fine research skill by Dr. Naib Singh. He picked up a case study of municipal towns in Bathinda district of Punjab. His personal knowledge on the working of services in the district, as he is settled in Bathinda city of the district, and extensive fieldwork conducted methodologically has been a great asset.

Some of the findings of his work deserve reproduction. Urban services in Punjab are highly subsidized. Only an amount of Rs. 32 18 million, making up only 8.0 per cent of total municipal expenditure (on average annual basis), is recovered; making less than 15 percent of total expenditure incurred by the municipalities on urban services. In other words, 85 paisa out of each rupee goes as subsidy. At the level of individual town, the large towns were guided by the principle of economic efficiency in spending on services in comparison to small towns, whereas the concept of equity prevailed over the efficiency criteria. In 1996-97, where per capita subsidy rose to its peak level of Rs. 38, inter-municipal variations were the least. It seems that there is threshold point beyond which the growth of subsidy has to be kept within limit.

Five out of eight urban services examined were fully subsidized, while remaining three were partially subsidized. Public health and sanitation received the highest amount of Rs. 15.30 million or about 30 per cent of total subsidy amount. Against this, the fire brigade services, received only Rs. 1.46 million or less than 3 per cent. Of all the services, three urban services viz., public health and sanitation, sewerage and roads cornered nearly 73 per cent of total subsidy amount during the period. Recovery rate varied from a high of about 46 per cent in case of water supply service to a low of less than 8 per cent in sewerage service.

Per capita amount of subsidy on urban services recorded strong positive association with all the attributes of towns, included in the analysis, but association was exceptionally strong with growth rate of population and per capita amount of expenditure. In other words, rapidly growing and high per capita spending towns provided very high per capita amount of subsidy on urban services.

In view of the high subsidy component in provision of urban services, there is a need for rationalization. The immediate solution that comes to mind is a hike in the tariff structure of urban services. Some of the core issues involved in the matter are: (i) Convincing people of the fact that they are getting highly subsidized urban services and that the poor quality of services being rendered is related largely to this fact; consequently he must pay for these services adequately, (ii) Working out a scenario in which the consumer is convinced that it is not the administrative mismanagement but the financial crunch which is more responsible for the prevailing situation, and (iii) preparing the local politician to cooperate by resisting the tendency towards populism and opposing it to encourage any rationalization of pricing of urban services. The situation is more favourable now than ever before. Already a favourable wind is blowing towards rationalizing of the prices of urban services. The urban-dwellers have also started getting a feel of it. Their mindset is now changing towards the content of emerging realities.

Such perceptive observations are a hallmark of Dr. Naib Singh's book. His entire work is noted for clarity of concepts, rigour of methodology, and depth of insights. He displays a remarkable capacity to draw incisive geographic inferences from his study.

He displays a slended commitment to objectivity while dealing with any issue. Fieldwork based observations and analysis further enhance the quality and objectivity of the work accomplished.

He has provided a model for others interested in similar themes. At the same time, it devolves upon dynamic and energetic Dr. Naib Singh that he continues exploring the hidden dimensions of this theme. Above all, the book contains several messages worthy of serious considerations by the audience in geography, economics, public administration, and urban and regional planning in addition to bureaucrats and policy planners, journalists, activists and an informed general audience. Dr. Naib Singh deserves our heartiest congratulations at accomplishing a singularly splendid job. I wish the book all success.

Chandigarh

Surya Kant

SURYA KANT
Reader
Department of Geography
Panjab University

Acknowledgements

Coming through the demands of research work, one is amazed by the reactions one may get from one's colleagues, friends, close associates and professionals. What I have found most wonderful is the unexpected inspiration and strength that came to me from unexpected quarters and made me all the more resolute in my purpose. I acknowledged that some Divine hand is quietly and resolutely guiding me on my way. I take this opportunity to give thanks to all those who contributed towards making the path easier and were my guiding lights in this research.

First and foremost, I would like to express my deepest gratitude to my Research Supervisor, Dr. Surya Kant, Reader in Geography, Panjab University, who unstintingly and dedicatedly devoted his time, efforts and resources to enable this project to take shape to its final fructification. I am also most grateful to Dr. Dhian Kaur, Reader and Chairperson, Geography Department, Panjab University for allowing me the use of the research facilities in the Department. I would like to thank Prof. Gopal Krishan, Senior Professor and Hony. Director, CRRID, Chandigarh, for cultivating my interest on this theme. Discussions with other faculty members in the Department have always been helpful in giving me clarity of thought on this theme.

I must give due acknowledgement for all the cooperation and help that was extended to me by the officials and employees of the eight municipalities. They helped me to obtain the desired information and requisite data. Further the Municipal Councillors and residents of all these municipalities deserve special mention for their aid in helping me to grasp the ground realities during the field survey. I must thank here, my friends, especially Sh. G.S. Dhindsa, DTP, Bathinda and Sh. K.S. Dhaliwal, DTP, Headquarters, Chandigarh for their sincere advice and help.

I would like to thank the Principal, colleagues and students of my college who were with me through all phases of the book.

I must give due credit to those who helped me give final shape to the book. They are Dr. Krishna Mohan and Dr. Prem Sagar, Geographers who took great pains. Sh. Mohan Singh, Cartographer, of the Department for his help in designing and drafting of maps and diagrams. I must thank Sh. Rakesh Arora who painstakingly worked on various drafts before finally arriving at this point. I thank Dr. R. Lamba for her editorial skills and suggestions.

I am indebted to my family especially my wife and my children for their patience and care that helped me persevere through the most difficult times.

Last but not the least I express my thanks to Shri G.S. Bhatia, Deep & Deep Publications Pvt. Ltd., New Delhi for cooperation and taking utmost care to achieve perfection to print and present the material in the book form.

Bathinda NAIB SINGH

SECTION I

1

Introduction

Urbanisation is an important phenomenon of the world today. With shifts in occupational categories the number of urban dwellers are rapidly increasing both in their actual numbers and share in total population. Of the 6.13 billion people in the world, 2.94 billion or 48 per cent were urbanites in 2001. The world, thus, has been going through a process of increasing number of urbanities with a newer set of priorities, needs and lifestyles.

The developed world became more urban than rural by the middle of the 19th century. The developing countries will achieve this status soon. The urban growth rate in the developing world is thrice that of the developed one. The developing countries will account for 93 per cent of the 2.06 billion increase in the global urban population between 1970 and 2020. Two out of three urban dwellers live in developing regions; by 2015 it will be more than three of the five (UNFPA, 1996, p. 1).

India is one of the developing nations. Urban development in India is presently going through a very dynamic stage. In the first 40 years of the 20th century, the country was still a fully agrarian society and its proportion of urban population was less than 12 per cent. However, the pace of urbanisation in India picked up pace after its Independence in 1947. Total urban population in India increased to 285 million in 2001 from 62 million in 1951, registering an increase of more than four and half times. During the 1971-81 decade urban growth was as high as 45 per cent. But the most relevant aspect is the rate of urban growth. Urban population is growing at a rate which is double that of the rural population. Among the urban areas, the small towns are somewhat stagnating. However, metropolitan cities stand out very prominently as they accommodate more than one-third of the total urban population of the country.

The most impressive of India's urban score is the size: about 218 million in 1991 which reached 285 million in 2001. It made about 28 per cent of the total population.

During 1901-2001, India's population increased four times: from 238 million in 1901 to 1027 million in 2001. Its urban population increased by more than ten times during the same period: from 26 million to 285 million. This was the outcome of massive rural-urban migration, in addition to the contribution made by the natural increase and reclassification of settlements. By 2020 more than 50 per cent of India's population is expected to live in urban areas, thus the age old image of India as a rural nation will most likely be relegated to the past.

As the population of urban places grows fast, the demand for urban services multiplies. There is an intensifying pressure on urban resources to cope up with the emerging situation. According to document entitled *The State of World Population,* the challenge of the future will be to sustain progress in social development in the face of unprecedented pressure to provide not only urban services but also to cater to the needs of under privileged sections of the society (UNFPA, 1996, p. 2). In most cases, the requisite funds would not be available and situations would tend to get aggravated.

The urban local bodies such as Municipal Corporations, Municipal Committees and Cantonment Boards/Notified Area Committees provide a variety of services, including water supply, public health and sanitation, education and others. These bodies are often incapable of handling the job satisfactorily. Hence, the state government departments such as Health and Education; and public corporations, such as water supply and sewerage board, have entered the field to do the needful. In principle, however, the municipal bodies are expected to perform these functions in the spirit of local self-government.

Functions performed by the municipal bodies in India can be classified into two categories: obligatory and discretionary functions.

Obligatory Functions

(i) *Civic functions:* Water supply, lighting of public streets, cleaning of public streets and places, disposing of nightsoil and rubbish, burial grounds, sewerage system, drainage, naming and numbering of streets and houses, washing places, etc.;

(ii) *Community functions:* Public vaccinations, registering births, deaths and marriages, prevention against infectious diseases, medical health and relief, etc.; and

(iii) *Regulatory functions:* Extinguishing of fires, regulating or abating offensive or dangerous trades or practices, prevention of adulteration of food, maintaining markets, etc.;

Discretionary Functions

(iv) Construction of new public parks and community halls, raising of gardens, maintaining libraries, museums and reading rooms;

(v) Detention of dogs and pigs;

(vi) Lodging and boarding houses, swimming pools, regulation of buildings, establishing *ashrams* for destitute, blind, crippled, lame and disabled persons; and

(vii) Poor houses, local natural disasters, control of beggary and shanties, holding fairs and exhibitions and management of public institutions.

In addition, some municipal enterprises including transport, public utilities, municipal trading, etc. are also run by the municipal bodies in India.

In Indian cities, the urban services provided by the Municipal Committees or Corporations are much below the mark. This is evidently clear in the limited and irregular hours of water supply, inefficient sewerage system and lack of sanitation. Fast and haphazard growth of cities/towns, administrative and financial mismanagement on the part of municipal bodies, lack of requisite funds for extension and maintenance of urban infrastructure and inadequacy of administrative and legal powers are some of the major reasons behind the malaise.

The inadequacy of funds is explained partly by the low pricing of different services under a spell of populism. These bodies are generally reluctant to raise the charges against water supply, or garbage disposal or any other service. On the other hand, the expenditure on the production, distribution and maintenance of these services is regularly increasing in the wake of demographic growth, physical expansion of cities and rising cost of labour and materials. An effort is made to fill this gap through the government grants received from time to time. Again, as these grants are grossly inadequate to meet the situation, the quality of services tends to deteriorate further. However, the mindset has started changing in the aftermath of macro-economic reforms initiated by the Indian government in 1991 and followed by the 74th Constitutional Amendment of 1992. Nevertheless, the change in ground realities is likely to take some more time before putting things in the right frame. The focus of the economic reforms agenda was to reduce the burden of subsidies on public goods and services while the Constitutional amendment was directed at making the urban local bodies stronger in democratic and financial terms.

As it emerges, people are not paying adequately for the services which they are enjoining. The cost of water supply may be 70 paise per kilolitre but they may be charged only 35 paise per kilolitre. Thus, they pay only half of what they should. This is known as the subsidy element which they enjoy, mostly being unaware of it. In fact, subsidy is the difference between what a consumer pays and what he should in the light of the provision costs of a service.

All this is bound to raise a number of questions pertaining to subsidy on urban services. Some of these questions are as follows:

1. Which of the urban services are provided by the municipal bodies to their residents?
2. What is the subsidy element in provision of the services and how it differs from one service to the other? Is there some objective basis for distribution of subsides on urban services?
3. Is there any spatial discrimination in distribution of subsidy? Do some parts of the towns benefit more than others from such subsidies? and
4. What should be the rational approach to the subsidy element in the provision of urban services?

Notwithstanding the significance attached to such and other related questions, very little attention has been paid to them in research. In particular, geographers ignored these issues, despite their crucial significance both to society and geographic research.

There are, however, several studies which deal with urban services and urban finances (NIUA, 1989; Krishnaswamy, 1958; Seth, 1965), but the subsidy element has escaped the attention of scholars as would be clear from the survey of literature, in the following.

Literature on Urban Services Subsidy Element

A review of the available literature on subsidy element in urban services exposes the lack of any substantive research by geographers on the theme. Having established the role of geography in the study of urban services, one may attempt to discern the contribution actually made by geographers in this field. This will help particularly in the identification of research gaps.

Literature regarding subsidy element in provision of urban services is not easily available. None the less, social scientists, such as anthropologists, economists, sociologists, those dealing with public administration and political science and experts from technical fields like, town planners and engineers, have conducted studies on the provision of urban services from different angles.

World Bank (1994), which devoted its Report of 1994 to 'Infrastructure for Development' provided only about two pages to the issue of subsidies. The report opines that 'subsidized provision of infrastructure is often proposed as a means of redistributing resources from higher income households to the poor. Yet its effectiveness depends on whether subsidies actually reach the poor, on the administrative costs associated with such targeting, and on the scope for allocating budgetary resources to this purpose without sacrificing other socially beneficial public expenditures'. It further added that the poor, who generally lack access to instructural facilities, do not get benefited, even from subsidized rates and these end up paying much higher prices for infrastructure services or their substitutes. Hence, the report suggested that 'subsidizing access to public infrastructure services is often more useful for the poor than price subsidies' (pp. 80-81).

In a study, conducted under the auspices of the HSMI-IHSP research cycle, Krishan and others (1994) examined the issues associated with the pricing of urban water supply, taking Ludhiana City in Punjab as a case study. The study, while recommending a hike in the existing structure of water pricing, noted that some basic issues, having profound impact on accessibility and quality of water supply service, were needed to be resolved before going ahead with the idea of changing the existing price structure. The following issues were listed: how to convince the people that they are getting a highly subsidized service and that the poor quality of services being rendered is related to this fact; they must pay for it adequately; how to workout a scenario in which the consumer is convinced that it is not the administrative mismanagement but financial crunch which is responsible for the prevailing situation; and how to prepare the local politician for resisting the tendency toward populism by opposing any rationalization of pricing of urban services?

On the issue of pricing of services, Sirken (1979) is of the opinion that if a cost has been incurred on the provision of a service, it should be recovered directly. Pricing of a commodity gives rise to a possibility of surplus reserves for extension of the system. It also gives an idea as to how much to produce and supply a given good or service. According to Sirken right price of a service is the one which leads to the production of the right amount of the service and its distribution to the right users in the right amounts and of right quality. The ideal price should provide an adequate return of revenue; guarantee a fair distribution of cost among consumers and lead to a justified use and discouragement of wastage (Bonbright, 1961).

Ironically, however, almost all the urban services in most of the developing countries including India are underpriced. As the tariff rates are kept low, the amount of subsidy keeps on increasing. For instance, water supply in almost all the towns in India is provided at highly subsidized rates. A study, conducted on pricing of water supply in Madras, found that water supply up to 30 kl. in the city is provided free of charge. Over this, the study (see Krishan, 1991) made a sarcastic remark, 'where is the water which can be supplied adequately'?

Human Settlement Management Institute (HSMI), New Delhi incollaboration with Institute for Housing and Urban Development Studies (IHUDS), Rotterdam, The Netherlands published two books to celebrate its tenth anniversary. One entitled Integrated Urban Infrastructure Development in Asia (Singh and others, 1996) emerged out of the papers presented at the International seminar held in February 1995 at New Delhi. It contained 22 papers in all but none of them focused on subsidy component in urban infrastructure services. In the introductory pages, the editors emphatically state that 'the management of urban growth should aim at achieving social justice, ecological sustainability, political participation, increased economic productivity and a culturally vibrant urban life. Promotion of new policies and strategies for managing urbanisation and integrated infrastructural development to improve the living environment and quality of life is of crucial importance (p. 3).

In this book, while a paper by Dharmarajan (1996, pp. 213-32) provided a critical assessment of the 15 years of experiences with Integrated Development of Small and Medium Towns (IDMST) scheme in India between 1980 and 1995, Krishan (1996, pp. 233-43) in another article presented a review of the IDSMT scheme in Punjab state.

Another volume entitled 'Urban India in Crisis' (Singh and Steinberg, 1996) containing 36 papers, divided into nine sections, examined various aspects related with urban services yet skipped the subsidy component in urban services.

In this book, in a paper on sanitation Sarma and Jansen (1996, pp. 133-44) stated that it is a perennial urban problem in India. In the absence of toilet facility, millions of people in various urban centres in the country are compelled to defecate in the open. In another paper, Rana (1996, pp. 99-108) identified four services, namely, public transport, water supply and sanitation, power supply and communication as the major infrastructures, forming the backbone of urban development. Hence, he pleased for integration of their planning and development. While Sharma (1996, pp. 121-32) advocated for harmonizing the relationship between urban planning and the natural processes. He lamented the tendency in contemporary town planning practices to subjugate the natural systems to human needs. In his view irrational engineering practices dislocate drainage and large sewers dislocate recharging of ground water. Sewers should run along *nalas* and be designed as local sewers carrying only black water for root zone treatment at suitable locations within the city. Solid waste should be segregated at source and treated as a resource rather than a liability.

In another article, Kundu (1996, pp. 191-206) examined the changing policy perspective in the context of basic amenities, such as shelter, water supply, sewerage and sanitation, health care and public distribution system of foodgrains, provided by the government under various beneficiary schemes. In his opinion, accessibility and affordability of the urban services have been the two major issues. This is the reason that the poor have been able to avail only a small share of these amenities and facilities, while higher income groups obtained the better quality and higher order services.

In a book entitled "Great Cities of the World", Robson (1954) focused attention on the problems which the municipal bodies have to face in delivering different urban services.

Bhourasarkar (1954) in his study of municipal finances in major states of India also provided some space to a discussion on the scope of municipal functions and the problems of the municipalities regarding provision of urban service.

Heggade (1998) has expressed the view that urban water supply, sewerage and sanitation system in India is highly neglected. The financial allocation from the state governments is highly inadequate.

Datta (1970), in a pioneer work, discussed the need for subsidy in provision of urban services, such as water supply and sanitation. Mishra (1986) discussed public health, sanitation, road, public safety and medical relief, etc. performed by the Cuttack municipality without touching upon the issue of subsidy element in urban services. In a book on 'Government in Crisis', Robson (1966) highlighted the inadequacy of various urban services. Ghosh (1964) discussed the expenditure pattern of Calcutta Municipal Corporation. Krishan (1990) in an article on "Privatisation of Urban Service Provision: The Case Study of India", stressed upon the role of private sector in the field of service provision.

Planning Commission, Government of India, in its national Human Development Report, 2001, revealed that major problem in urban solid waste management relates to sewage disposal and a large number of towns are without sewage system (Government of India, 2002, p. 40).

In the same it asserted that millions of people in the country suffer from water borne diseases on account of lack of access to safe drinking water. It is the poor who suffer from higher prevalence of disease as compared to the rich (Government of India, 2002, p. 41).

It is evidently clear from the above review of literature that there is virtually a complete dearth of systematic studies on subsidy element in the provision of urban services in the existing literature. This is true despite both academic and applied significance of the theme. The present book proposes to fill up the existing gap through a case study of towns of Bathinda district of Punjab in India with the following objectives:

(i) To know the number and nature of services provided by the municipal bodies in the district;
(ii) To understand the subsidy element in provision of urban services and to examine inter-service and inter-municipal variations in it;
(iii) To identify spatial discrimination, if any, in the distribution of subsidy on different urban services; and
(iv) To suggest an approach for rationalization of the subsidy element in urban services.

A number of research questions could be raised in this context:

(i) What is the role of location, size and functions in differentiating expenditure patterns of municipal bodies on various urban services?
(ii) How the role of location differs from that of size and function?
(iii) How the municipal expenditure on income from and subsidy element in urban services differs within the district, and
(iv) How it differs within towns?

As is evident from the nature of above stated research questions, it is clear that a consistent approach and methodology from the geographic perspective was to be used to conduct the present study. This is to ensure geographic character of the study so as to make it distinctive from studies done in other disciplines like economics or public administration.

Related to the questions raised that prompted this work, some hypotheses have been framed for testing. These may be stated as follows:

(i) Administrative and civic status of a town plays a significant role in generation of municipal income and its spending on various urban services. For their higher spending capacity, higher placed civic and administrative towns will provide higher amount of subsidy on urban services. Hence, higher the status of a town greater would be the amount and share of subsidy element in urban services provided to its residents.

(ii) The component of subsidy on urban services will differ from service to service and town to town. Services such as street lighting and sanitation will be more subsidized than water supply and sewerage. Similarly, fast growing and dynamic towns will provide larger amount of subsidy on services than slow growing and stagnant ones.

(iii) There would be inter and intra-municipal town discriminations in distribution of subsidy on various urban services. Localities having central location and resided in by citizens having higher economic, political and social status would benefit more from the subsidies than those having peripheral locations and resided in by the socio-economically and politically weaker sections of humanity. However, such a discrimination will be more in case of big towns in comparison to small towns.

The Study Area

With per capita income of Rs. 21,184 in 1998-99 (at current prices) Punjab was placed at the top among 16 major states of India. Agriculturally, it is the most prosperous state in India. As per 2001 Census, the state had a population of 24.29 million making up 2.35 per cent of the total Indian population. Also 8.26 million or 34 per cent of Punjab's population was living in urban areas and this was higher than the national average of 28 per cent.

As per 2001 Census, the urban population of the state is distributed among 157 towns/urban agglomerations of varying size and importance. Fourteen towns had population more than one lakh each. Together they accommodated half the total urban population of the state. Ludhiana, with a population of over one million, is the largest urban centre in the state. On the other side of the scale is Sangat town (Bathinda district) having only 5396 persons.

Bathinda, one of the 17 districts in the state (Map 1.1), is an agriculturally developed district, having commercialisation in cotton cultivation. There are 8 towns in the district, almost all functioning as market 'mandi' towns to deal with the agricultural produce. They accommodate 352 thousand persons making 4.26 per cent of the total urban population in the State. Urban population stood at about 30 per cent which is quite lower than the State average of 34 per cent. It is, thus, a low urbanized district in the state.

Map 1.1

BATHINDA DISTRICT
The Study Area

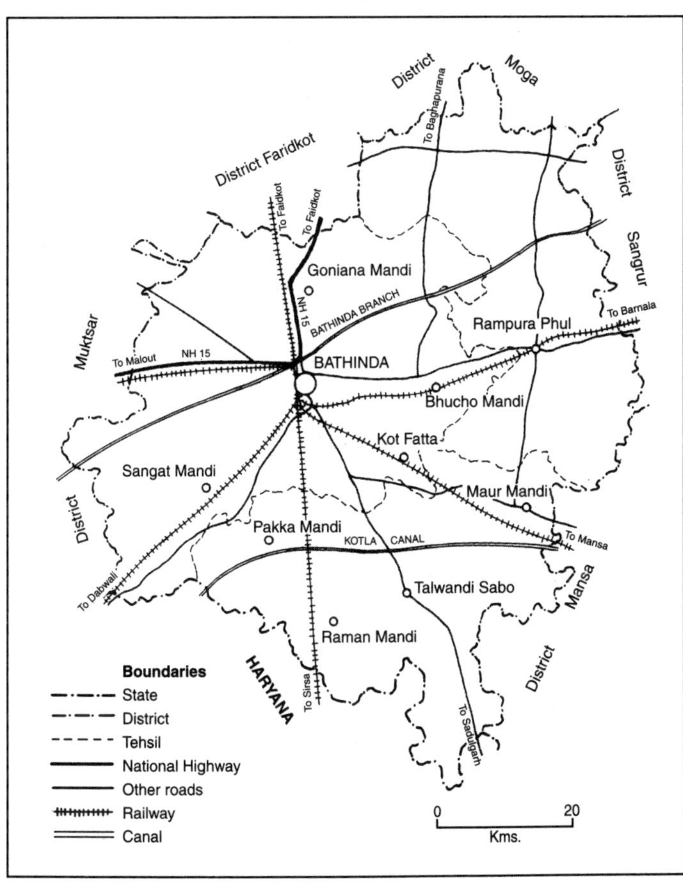

Bathinda, which enjoys the status of being a district headquarters is the largest urban centre in the district. It had a population of 2,17,389 persons in 2001. On the other side of the scale is Sangat having a population of only 5396.

Eight major urban services, provided by municipal towns in Bathinda district, included water supply, sewerage, public health and sanitation, drainage, roads, street lighting, fire services and recreational services. While Bathinda and Rampura Phul municipalities run all the eight services, Kot Fatta renders only four services (Table 1.1). Five of the eight services were fully subsidized in the district, remaining three have been partially subsidized (Table 1.2).

TABLE 1.1

Bathinda District: Availability of Urban Services by Municipalities, 2002

Name of town	*Name of municipal service*							
	Water supply	*Sewer-age*	*Public health & sanitation*	*Drain-age*	*Roads*	*Street lighting*	*Fire services*	*Recreational facilities*
Bathinda	■	■	■	■	■	■	■	■
Rampura Phul	■	■	■	■	■	■	■	■
Maur Mandi	■	■	■	■	■	■	□	□
Raman Mandi	■	■	■	■	■	■	□	■
Goniana Mandi	■	■	■	■	■	■	□	■
Bhucho Mandi	■	■	■	■	■	■	□	■
Kot Fatta	■	□	■	■	■	□	□	□
Sangat Mandi	■	□	■	■	■	■	□	□

■ Available □ Non-available

As revealed in per capita expenditure on urban services, level of services in Bathinda district is almost at the same level as in Punjab as a whole. Against the per capita expenditure of Rs. 1017 (on current prices) on urban services in the Punjab as a whole it was 919 in Bathinda in 2001. Earlier in 1993-94, the situation was not much different. As against the per capita expenditure of Rs. 475 on urban services in the Punjab as a whole it was Rs. 476 in Bathinda.

Within the district, per capita expenditure on urban services ranged from a high of Rs. 356 in Bathinda City to a low of only

TABLE 1.2

Bathinda District: Extent of Subsidy Element in Municipal Services

Name of town	Name of municipal service							
	Water supply	*Sewer-age*	*Public health & sanitation*	*Drain-age*	*Roads*	*Street lighting*	*Fire services*	*Recreational facilities*
Bathinda	●	●	■	■	■	■	■	●
Rampura Phul	●	●	■	■	■	■	■	■
Maur Mandi	●	●	■	■	■	■	□	□
Raman Mandi	●	●	■	■	■	■	□	■
Goniana Mandi	●	●	■	■	■	■	□	■
Bhucho Mandi	●	●	■	■	■	■	□	■
Kot Fatta	●	□	■	■	■	□	□	□
Sangat Mandi	●	□	■	■	■	■	□	□

■ Fully subsidized ● Partially subsidized □ Non-available

Rs. 47 in Kot Fatta. The average for all the municipalities in the district has been Rs. 278. This is bound to influence the quality as well as quantity of urban services provided by these municipalities. The subsidy element also differed between municipalities and services provided by them.

Organisation of Study

In line with the objectives of the study, the discussion has been organized into three sections which are further divided into eight chapters. Section I contains two chapters, dealing with conceptual framework and methodology with a brief introductory background of the municipal towns in Bathinda district. Section II contains four chapters, dealing with municipal services and finances in different districts of Punjab, distribution of expenditure and subsidy on infrastructural services, public health and security services, environment and health improvement services in sequential order. Section III consolidates the picture of subsidy component in different urban services and suggests the ways and means of rationalizing the subsidy component on them in Chapter VII. Finally, the summary of conclusions is presented in Chapter VIII.

2

Profile of Towns

INTRODUCTION

The district derives its name from its present headquarters, Bathinda, which is a historical town. It is said that Bathinda derives its name from a combination of the names of two great personalities, the Rajput ruler, Binai Pal, and his *vazir*, Thanda Ram. Later on the town was conquered by Maharaja Ala Singh (about 1754 AD), and shared the history of the erstwhile princely state of Patiala. With the dawn of independence and merger of Patiala and East Punjab States into a union, styled as PEPSU, Bathinda[1] became a full-fledged district in 1948, a status that has continued even after the merger of PEPSU with the Punjab state in 1956.

Bathinda, one of the southern districts of the Punjab state, lies in the West Indo-Gangetic Plain. The district is situated in the northwestern dry region of the Punjab. The Rajasthan desert, not far from the district, has a lasting impact on its climate. Climatically therefore, the district, has a very hot summer, a short rainy season and a dry but bracing winter.

Nearly 30 per cent of the population of the district lives in urban areas compared to 34 per cent in the state as a whole. In all, there are eight urban centres in the district. These differ widely in area and population sizes. Bathinda, the largest town in the district shares more 70 per cent of the area and 62 per cent of the total urban population of all towns. In contrast, Sangat Mandi, the smallest town, shares less than one per cent of area and two per cent of population (Map 2.1A & 2.1B). In literacy, it stands at

1. The spellings have been recently revised from 'Bhatinda' to 'Bathinda' on the authority of the Survey of India to conform to the Colloquial phonetic expression as locally accepted and popular.

Map 2.1

Distribution of Urban Centres in Bathinda District, 2001

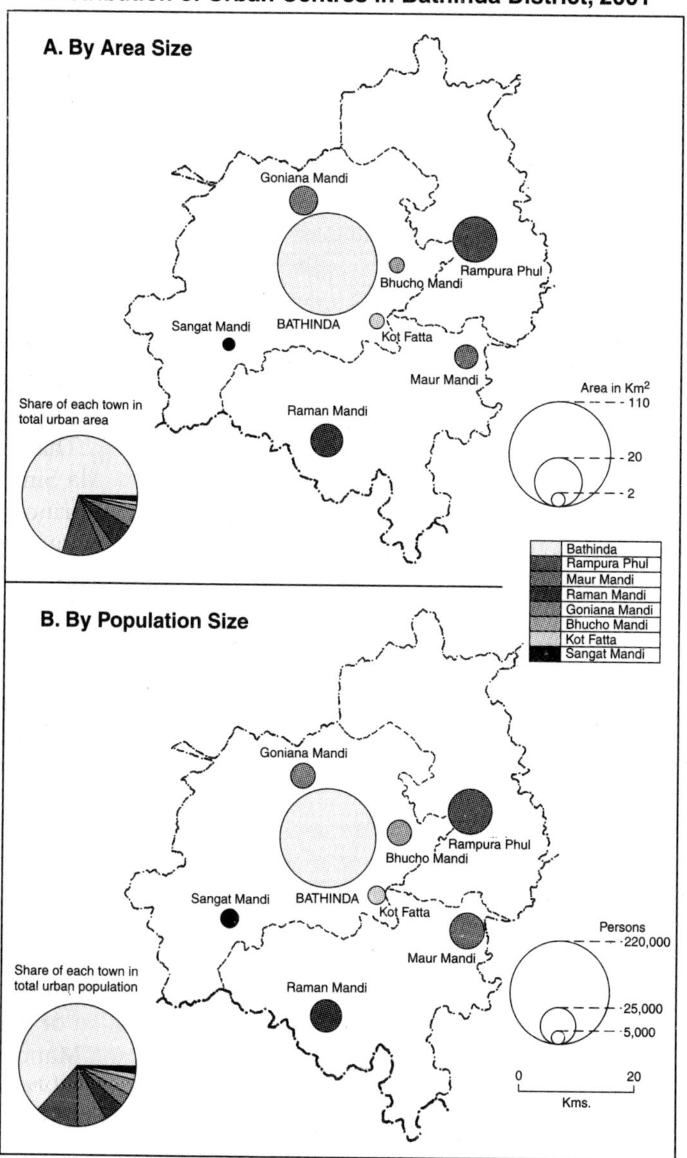

the lowest level among all the districts in the State. Only about 62 per cent of the population of the district is literate as against the state average of 70 per cent in 2001. Workers constitute 31 per cent of the total population. Of the working force, more than three-fourths are engaged in agriculture as cultivators and agricultural labourers.

About 90 per cent of the total reported area of the district is under cultivation and 56 per cent of this area is irrigated. Canals and tubewells are the main source of irrigation. The principal crops are wheat and cotton. Among the commercial crops, cotton is extensively cultivated in this district. Cotton production in large quantities has been in turn responsible for the establishment of a number of cotton ginning and pressing factories which are located at Bathinda, Raman Mandi and Rampura Phul.

The district is famous for a number of historical places, associated with the Sikh religion. Talwandi Sabo, which has a historic Gurdwara and Damdama Sahib, which is the venue of the famous Baisakhi fair, held annually are two such places of pilgrimage. Bathinda has an old fort with a Gurdwara named after Guru Gobind Singh located inside.

In the following the geography of different towns in the district will briefly be discussed to understand their location, history, functions and factors responsible for their growth and development.

BATHINDA CITY

Bathinda, the headquarters of the district by the same name, is located at a distance of 157 kms. from Patiala, capital of the erstwhile Patiala State and about 210 kms. from Chandigarh, the capital headquarters of Punjab State. It lies at 30° 13′ North latitude and 57° 0′ East longitude. A prominent cantonment and a thermal plant are located here. Bathinda is the biggest railway junction of North India, with seven railway lines converging at it. These are the Rajpura, Firozepur, Fazilka, Ganganagar, Hanuman Garh, Rewari and Delhi lines. It is located on the Delhi-Firozepur national highway. Its road links with the neighbouring towns are also direct and strong. All the railway and road routes going to western Rajasthan and northwestern Haryana pass through Bathinda city, giving it a nodal location.

The area around the town is sandy having an undulating topography with semi-desert conditions. The sub-soil water is saline, not suited for drinking purposes. It has a very hot stormy summer season, a mild rainy season and dry but bracing winter. Well developed canal irrigation around Bathinda has given rise to intensive commercial cultivation of cotton and wheat in its surrounding area. Bathinda has thus emerged as a major agricultural market centre of the State.

Historical Background

Bathinda, a historical city, has its origin in the medieval period of Indian history. The nomenclature has been derived from the names of a Rajput ruler, Binaipal, and his minister, Thanda Ram. According to Khalifa Muhammad Hassan, author of the history of Patiala State, its original name had been Bikramgarh. According to Ibn Batuta (1304-1368 A.D.) it was known as Batrind. According to 'Ainai-Barar Bans', Bathinda was built by Bhati Rao, son of Bal Band, who became the ruler of Punjab in 336 *Bikrami Samvat*. He also founded Bhatner. It was also called Whatinda and Bitunda, before it came to be known as Bhatinda. Now, its name has been changed to Bathinda on the authority of the Survey of India, to conform to the colloquial phonetic expression, as locally pronounced.

The town had a 'fort' at its nucleus. After annexation by Maharaja Ala Singh in 1754, the city became a part of Patiala State. The setting up of Rajendra Ganj Mandi in 1835 (presently known as Sattar Bazar, Kikkar Bazar and Sirki Bazar) and construction of the first meter guage railway line to Hisar in 1890 delineated its rudimentary form. With construction of Civil Lines, comprising District courts, Police lines and Central Jail in 1953 as well as Civil Hospital in 1956, its boundaries further extended. In 1970 came the two important public sector units, a thermal power plant and a fertilizer plant, which added to the industrial prestige of the city. The establishment of the Government Rajendra College in 1950 and the Engineering College in 1989 raised its prestige as an educational centre. This dynamic city has been growing fast since 1971.

Physical and Demographic Growth

The gradual physical growth of the city called for periodic extension of its territorial limits. The city spread over 8.85 km^2 till 1971, expanded to 20 km^2 in 1976 and further to 36.68 km^2 by 1981. The municipal limit was further extended to 97 km^2 by 1991 and then on to 110 km^2 in 2001 (Table 2.1). In 2001, the city was divided into 35 municipal wards for provision of municipal services and municipal elections (Map 2.2).

TABLE 2.1
Bathinda District: Some Demographic Characteristics of Towns

Name of town	*Civic status*	*Area in km^2 2001*	*Population 2001*	*Annual growth rate in %age (1971-2001)*	*Literacy in %age 2001*	*Density (person/km^2)*	*Main functions*
Bathinda	I	110	217389	4.1	79	1976	Administrration, Trade & Commerce, Industry
Rampura Phul	III	18	44661	2.2	74	2481	Trade, Administration
Maur Mandi	III	4.80	27531	2.4	67	5736	Trade in Agricultural produce
Raman Mandi	IV	9.90	19549	1.8	67	1975	Trade in Agricultural produce
Goniana Mandi	IV	8.00	12812	2.3	80	1602	Trade in Agricultural produce
Bhucho Mandi	IV	2.20	13183	5.1	73	5992	Trade in Agricultural produce
Kot Fatta	V	1.60	6493	1.4	59	4058	Trade in Agricultural produce
Sangat Mandi	V	1.28	5396	1.4	60	4216	Trade in Agricultural produce
Total		**155.78**	**347014**				—

Source: Calculated from Census of India, *Town Directory, Punjab, 1991*, and *Urban-Rural Distribution, 2001*, Directorate of Census Operations, Punjab, Chandigarh.

Map 2.2

Bathinda Municipality

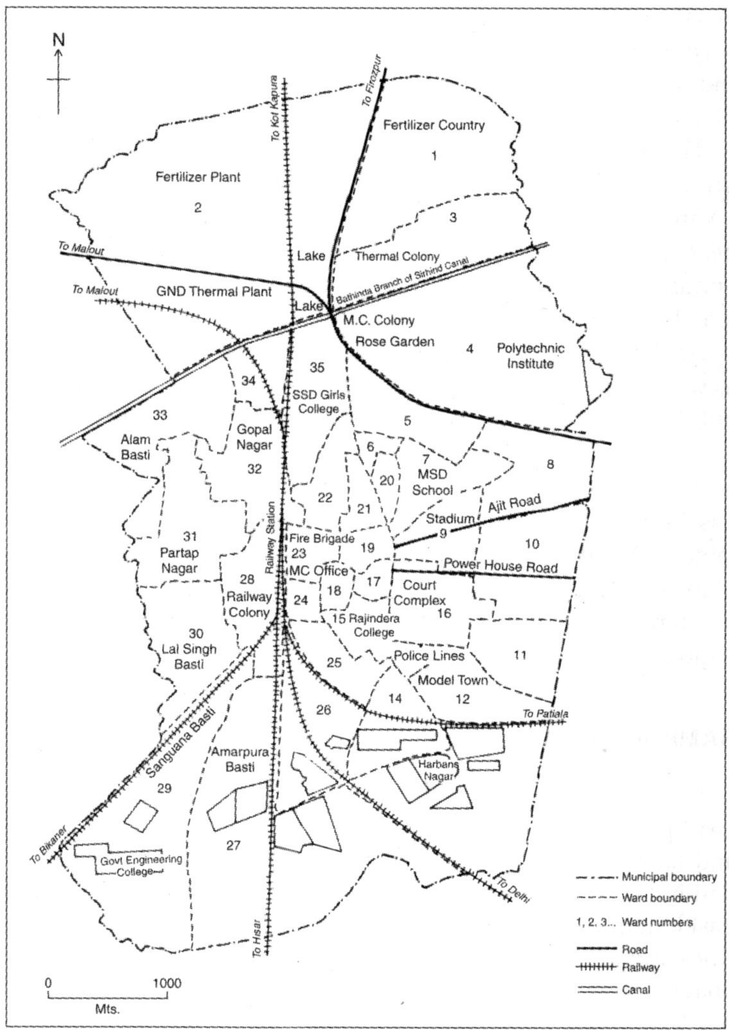

Bathinda is a multifunctional city having various functions of the administrative, commercial, defence and within its precincts education. It is a famous cloth market, serving southern Punjab, northern Haryana and parts of Rajasthan. It is an important centre for distribution of agricultural inputs and collection of agricultural produce. The Civil Hospital provides medical facilities to the city and its surrounding area. The emergence of the Thermal Plant, Fertilizer Plant, Milk Plant, Spinning mills, Cement factory and several other units have put the city on the industrial map of India. The establishment of the Military cantonment over an area of about 62 kms^2 has made a strong impact in its growth.

The Bathinda city had a population of only 34,991 in 1951. It grew to 2,17,389 by 2001 in the span of about 50 years, registering an annual growth rate of 3.72 per cent. The period from 1971 has been of fast growth. The population grew by 4.1 per cent per annum during 1971-2001 (Table 2.1). In 2001, population density was 1976 persons/km^2.

As Bathinda city is growing fast, the pressure on services such as water supply, sewerage, sanitation, road maintenance and street lighting provided by the municipal committee of Bathinda is intensifying. Extensive physical expansion of the city has had additional implications for provision of urban services. The task has been further complicated by an alarming rise in the water table of the city in recent years. This could have been the outcome of the intensive canal irrigation to grow commercial crops without much respect for the ecological existence and perpetuation of the region.

RAMPURA PHUL

Rampura Phul, a second ranking town and sub-divisional headquarters, is located on the Bathinda-Sangrur State Highway and Bathinda-Ambala railway line at a distance of 32 kms. from Bathinda city. It is located at 30° 15′ North latitude and 75° 15′ East longitude. Rampura Phul is also linked with other important cities and villages, i.e. Patiala, Chandigarh, Mansa, Maur Mandi, Bhagta, Nihal Singh Wala, etc. by road routes. It is made up of two twin towns namely Rampura and Phul. Phul, bearing a more or less rural character, is located at a distant of three kms from Rampura. For both, however, a single municipality has been established for urban administration.

The area around the town is sandy having semi-undulating topography and desertic climate. Gradually, it has largely been made a leveled plain by the farm community in the area.

Nevertheless, sand dunes are seen towards Lehra Bega and Mehraj villages. The sub-soil water, which is saline, has been unfit for drinking purposes. Its climate is like that of Bathinda. It has summer season from mid-April to mid-July and winter season remains from mid-November to mid-February. It has monsoonal climate, receiving rainfall for two months from middle of July to middle of September. Also it has both autumn and spring seasons. The surrounding area has intensive commercial cultivation in cotton and wheat. So it is emerging as a centre for agricultural inputs and trade in agricultural produce.

Historical Backgrounds

Historically, it is linked with the fort of Phul, located in the centre of Phul township and built by Maharaja Nabha nearly 200 years ago. Phul had been the military training centre and headquarters of Nabha princely state upto 1949. After the formation of the PEPSU state in 1949, Phul became a part of the newly born Punjab state. However, Rampura Phul together were declared as forming the Town Area Committee precincts by the British Government in 1920, thereafter it was raised to the status of Municipal Committee in 1950, still including both Rampura and Phul.

Physical and Demographic Growth

Rampura Phul Mandi is an important centre for distribution of agricultural inputs and trade in agricultural produce. More than 20 factories associated with cotton ginning and processing of oil were established between 1975 and 1992 on different roads linking the town to other places in the region. It has the provision of railway station, Post office and Police station. The Civil Hospital provides necessary medical facilities to the Mandi township and its surrounding areas. It also has educational facilities upto the college level. It is, however, lacking in professional and technical education institutions.

Rampura Phul had a population of only 14,408 in 1951. It grew to 19,700 in 1961 to 23,406 in 1971 and to 44,661 in 2001. The population size has been growing relatively faster after 1971, and can be attributed to increased productivity and commercialisation after 1966. Population grew by 2.2 per cent per annum during 1971-2001. Density of population at 2481 person/km^2 in 2001, was quite higher than that of Bathinda city. The town was divided into 17 municipal wards (Map 2.3) as

Map 2.3

Rampura Phul Municipality

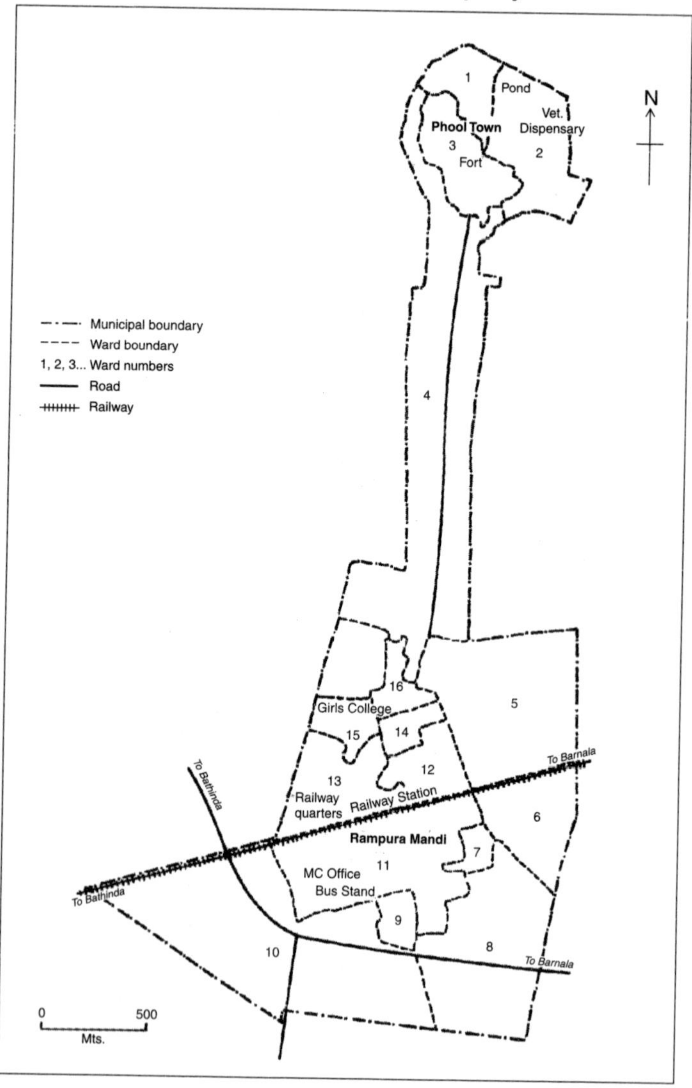

Rampura Phul is a growing town. With growth in population and physical expansion the demand for urban services has been increasing. It has intensified the pressure on services such as water supply, sewerage, sanitation, road maintenance and street lighting provided by the municipal committee of Rampura Phul. This may also be due to the combined effect of physical expansion of the Mandi area, narrow streets and growth of population and increased number of factories.

MAUR MANDI

Maur, an important town of Talwandi Sabo sub-division, is located on the Bathinda-Delhi railway line at a distance of 34 km. South-East of Bathinda. It lies at 30°13′ North latitude and 70°15′ East longitude. Maur Mandi is linked by road with other important towns in the region. These include Chandigarh, Patiala, Bathinda, Mansa, Rampura and Sunam. In 2001, it had an area of 4.80 km^2 and a population of nearly 28 thousand persons, giving a population density of 5736 persons/km^2. This is the second highest density of population after Bhucho Mandi town in the district.

Topography around the town is plain with occasional undulations. The quality of the sub-soil water differs in micro-space. At some places, water is less saline, hence suitable for drinking. While in some other locations, it contains high salinity and is unfit for drinking. Climatically, it resembles with whole of Malwa region. Here summers are hot and winters cold. Annual average temperature ranges between 1 degree and 44.5 degree centigrade. It reveals that winter and summer temperatures differ widely. Even the minimum and maximum temperatures differ considerably on daily basis. It receives an average rainfall of 50 cms., which is quite deficient to grow commercial crops such as cotton, rice and wheat. Canal and tubewell irrigation has come up in this area in a big way to supplement deficiency of rainfall. As the name itself suggests, Maur Mandi is a town which has a thriving trade in agricultural produce.

Historical Background

Mandi town does not have any significant historical or religious background. Established during the British rule, under the small town committee scheme in the first quarter of the 20th century, it was raised to the status of Municipal Committee after Independence. Its development began only after it was raised to the status of Municipal Committee in 1951.

Physical and Demographic Growth

The gradual physical growth called for periodic extension of its territorial limits. The Mandi was spread over less than one square kilometer till 1974. In 2001, it spread to over 4.8 km^2 area, registering an increase of about five times.

Maur Mandi is an important centre for distribution of agricultural inputs and collection of agricultural produce. About 15 factories associated with cotton ginning and oil processing were established from 1977 to 1996 on Kube road, popularly known as Factory road. It has a railway station, post office and police station from the very beginning and a civil hospital came up in 1961-62. Now it has all the basic facilities including school education upto 10+2 level. A big cattle fair, held here four times a year, attracts cattle traders from several parts of North India. Most of the cattle trade is facilitated through Maur Mandi railway station. From here wagons loaded with cattle go to different centres distributed in all the states of North India.

Maur Mandi had a population of only 13,407 persons in 1971. It increased to 27,531 persons in 2001, doubling in 30 years. Growth rate of population was the fastest during 1971-81. Notably, area of the town grew by 140 per cent during 1974-2001. During 1971-2001, population grew at the annual rate of 2.4 per cent. In 2001, the town was divided into 15 municipal wards (Map 2.4).

Maur Mandi is a growing town. Here, density of population is quite high. Its population density of 5736 persons/km^2 is second highest after Bhucho Mandi among all the eight towns in the district. The pressure on urban services such as water supply, sewerage and sanitation, road maintenance and street lighting provided by the municipal committee of Maur Mandi has gradually been intensifying. There is a mis-match between the

Map 2.4

Maur Mandi Municipality

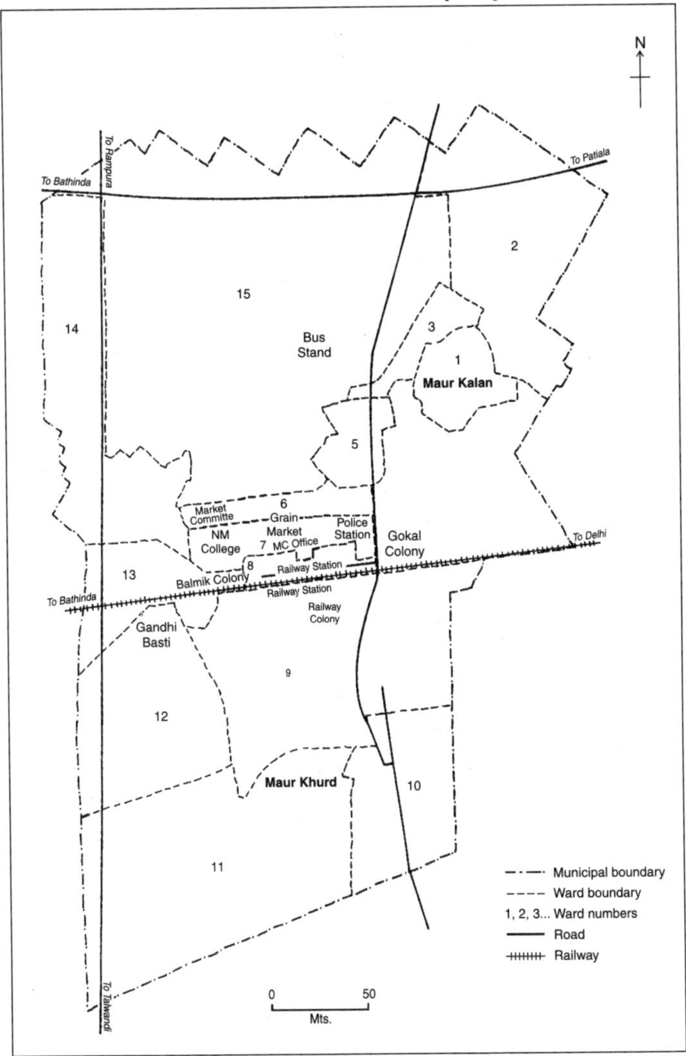

areal extent and growth of population, on one hand, and increase in civic amenities in the town, on the other hand. Moreover, resolution of hopes and aspirations of town dwellers for a good living has been increasing in recent years.

RAMAN MANDI

Raman Mandi, an important town of the district, is located on the Sirsa-Bathinda railway line at a distance of 40 kms. South of Bathinda city. It lies at 29° 57′ North latitude and 74° 56′ East longitude. Raman Mandi is linked with other important towns such as Maur, Talwandi Sabo, Kalayanwali, Dabwali and Sangat by road routes. The area around the town has sandy soils and the topography is a mix of undulation with plain areas. The sub-soil water is both saline and sweet, depending on location. Its climate resembles that of South Punjab, having hot summers and cold winters. It receives rainfall through monsoonal winds. The canal irrigation is well developed in areas around the town area. This has given rise to intensive commercial cultivation of cotton and wheat. Now it is emerging as an agricultural market centre.

Historical Background

Raman Mandi town does not have any particular historical or religious background. Established during the British rule, under the small town committee scheme on the land acquired from Raman village in the first quarter of 20th century, it got the status of sub-tehsil headquarters before 1949. It was declared Raman Mandi Municipal Committee in 1956, leading to its faster growth.

Physical and Demographic Growth

To begin with, Raman Mandi town established on fifty acres of land area, doubled in size by 1960-61. In 1982, it registered an increase of more than twelve times to acquire an area of 1210 acres or 5 kms^2. In 2001, its jurisdiction was further extended to reach 9.90 kms^2. It has now the third largest jurisdiction after Bathinda and Rampura Phul towns.

Raman Mandi has eight main factories, cotton ginning mills being the most important ones. Two of the cotton ginning mills were established as early as in the 1930s. Others came up between 1975 and 1982. The Road going towards Talwandi Sabo has the maximum number of factories. Raman Mandi had a Railway Station, Post office and Police station since its inception. The Civil Hospital was established in 1970 to cater to the medical needs of the town dwellers and villagers in the vicinity. It has schooling facilities upto 10+2 level thereafter students go for a college education to Bathinda city.

Raman Mandi had a population of only 11,574 persons in 1971. It grew to 19,549 persons in 2001, registering an increase or more than two-thirds in 30 years. It is a slow growing town of the district. Its population grew by 1.8 per cent per annum during 1971-2001. In 2001, it was divided into 13 municipal wards (Map 2.5). Its main importance lies in its being a Mandi town where trade in agricultural products predominates.

GONIANA MANDI

Goniana, a small Mandi town of the district, is located on the Bathinda-Firozpur railway line at a distance of 13 kms. North from Bathinda city. It lies at 30° 20′ North latitude and 74° 55′ East longitude. Goniana Mandi is linked with other important towns including Bathinda, Faridkot and Firozepur by roads routes.

The area around the town is fertile and has a plain topography. The sub-soil water is both saline and sweet. Wherever the water is sweet, it is fit for drinking. Its climate resembles that of Bathinda city. It has the summer season from the middle of April to mid-July and the winter season from middle of November to middle of February. It gets seasonal rain from monsoonal winds for two months from mid-July to mid-September. It has, both Autumn and Spring seasons. In its surrounding areas, cotton and wheat are the main commercial crops. But, the town is not developing fast. In all probability its proximity to Bathinda city, which had been working as a backwash effect, could be a hindrance in its development.

Historical and Religious Background

Like Raman Mandi, Goniana Mandi also does not have any particular historical background. Established in 1890, on the land from Nahiawala and Bullar villages, it was called Balbir Mandi during the reign of the Maharaja of Faridkot. In the beginning, it was popular for grinding of pulses. It got its present name of Goniana Mandi after the reign of Maharaja Faridkot was over in

Map 2.5

Raman Mandi Municipality

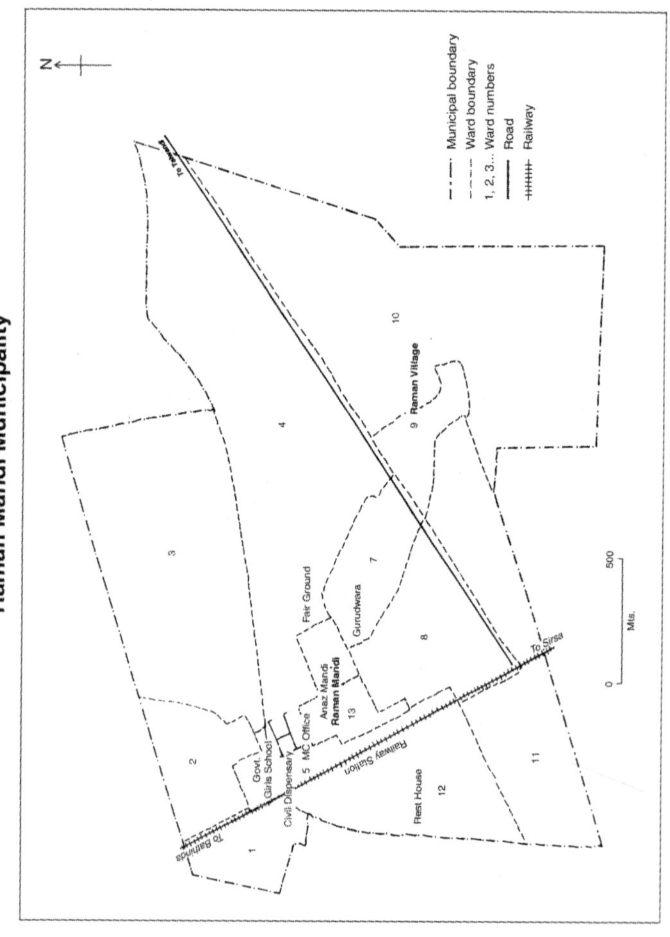

1948. It was declared as a municipal town in 1952 with the establishment of Municipal Committee for its civic administration.

A Gurdwara named after Tikana Bhai Jagata Ji Sahib is a religious place of pilgrimage of this Mandi town. Built in 1950 the Gurdwara belongs to the Bhai Kanhaiya Gaddi. Bhai Asa Singh was the head at that time. Now, Bhai Tirth Singh looks after it. The Gurdwara is visited by devotees belonging to both the Hindu and Sikh religions. A number of educational institutions are run from within the Gurdwara premises. A college for girls, a computer centre, a government high school for girls, and a public school all are located inside the Gurdwara. The Gurdwara has its own printing press, which is unique in itself. The Gurdwara has a large library which is named after Guru Nanak.

Due to its religious significance the Punjab Mail train, running between Firozepur city and Mumbai, stops on *'Sangrand'* or Sankranti day (about 10 times a year) at this station. Several well known doctors, on grounds of charity make special visits for the medical checkup of patients at the Gurdwara health camps. A dispensary for free distribution of medicines among patients is also located within the Gurdwara.

Physical and Demographic Growth

The gradual physical growth called for periodic extension of its territorial limits. In the beginning, it extended to about 20 acres of land. But with an increase in population and functions, its areal extent was reaching upto 8 kms^2 in 2001, making it the fourth largest town area-wise in the district. In 2001, it was divided into 13 municipal wards (Map 2.6).

Goniana Mandi, an important centre for distribution of agricultural inputs and extension services along with trade in agricultural produce, has more than 10 factories associated with cotton ginning, and rice shelling. These were established here between 1975 and 1982. A public sector cable wire factory is also located here. It had a railway station, post office and police station since inception but the Civil Hospital was established in 1970. It caters to the medical needs of Mandi town and its surrounding areas.

Map 2.6
Goniana Mandi Municipality

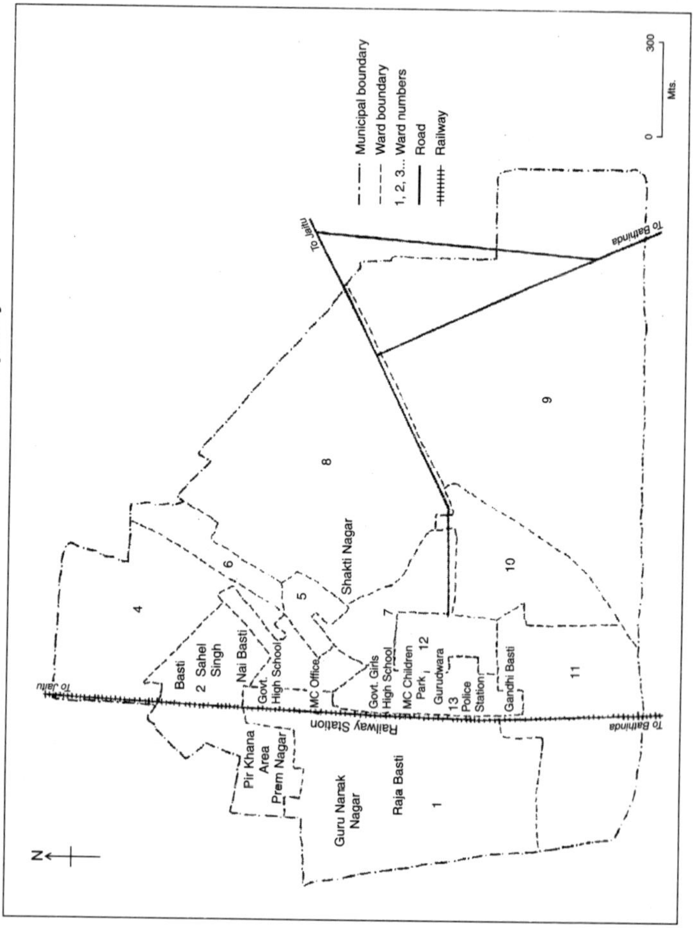

Goniana Mandi had a population of only 6408 in 1971 which increased to 12,812 persons in 2001. It nearly doubled in 30 years. It has a population density of 1602 persons per square kilometer, which is the lowest average for any town in the district.

Due to the increase in population and its physical expansion the pressure on various services provided by the municipality is intensifying. The situation has been further complicated by the lack of desired investment in urban services which in turn was due to weak financial health of the municipal government in the town.

BHUCHO MANDI

Bhucho Mandi town is located on the Bathinda-Ambala Railway line at a distance of 17 kms East from Bathinda city. Its latitudinal and longitudinal extents are 30° 14′ North and 75° 07′ East respectively. Bhucho Mandi is well linked with Bathinda, Barnala and Rampura Phul towns by road and rail routes.

The area around the town has sandy soils and the topography is undulating. However, a large part of the land has now been leveled by farmers. Now only a few small sand dunes can be seen towards Lehra Bega village. The sub-soil water is both saline and sweet, depending on location.

Its climate resembles that of Bathinda city. Here, summer season extends from middle of April to middle of July and the winter season from middle of November to mid-February. It receives rainfall from monsoonal winds for two months from middle of July to middle of September. Likewise it has both autumn and spring seasons. Cotton is grown as the most important crop in this area. Bhucho Mandi town acts as a centre for trade in agricultural produce.

Historical Background

In 1908, the District Board, Firozepur decided to establish a new grain market near Bhucho Kalan village. A piece of 100 acres land from Bhucho Khurd was acquired for the purpose. In 1920, this grain market was upgraded to Town Area Committee which became the Notified Area Committee in 1940. It was declared

Municipal Committee in 1952 and the first election was held in that very year. Gradually, its growth picked up, necessitating extension of its limits. In 1976, its limits extended over 200 acres. For this purpose, land was acquired from Kahan Singh Wala, Station Wala and Ram Bilas. In 2001, it covered an area of 2.20 km^2 and was divided into 13 municipal wards (Map 2.7).

Physical and Demographic Growth

Bhucho Mandi has more than 11 factories associated with cotton ginning, rice shelling and manufacturing of steel. The first cotton ginning factory was established in 1954-55 and the first rice sheller in 1985-86. Four factories have been located on the main road linking Bathinda with Barnala. It has a medical dispensary, which had been established in 1945-46. There had been a post office here even before the partition in 1947. A police post was added thereafter. Besides, there is one senior secondary school for boys and a High school for girls, established in 1960. It had a railway station from the very beginning.

Bhucho Mandi had a population of only 2945 persons in 1971, which grew to 13,183 in 2001. It is the fastest growing town in the district. Its population grew at the annual growth rate of 5.1 per cent during the 30 years between 1971-2001. Its population density of 5992 persons/km^2 is the highest of all the towns in the district. Further, it is considered the richest municipal town of the district. The municipality has land under its control which is sold from time to time to earn extra income.

KOT FATTA

Kot Fatta, a very small township is located at a distance of 18 kms. East of the Bathinda-Delhi railway line. It lies at 30° 07′ North latitude and 70° 06′ East longitude. Kot Fatta is linked with other important towns like Bathinda, Maur, and Bhucho by road.

The area around the town has sandy soils and undulating topography mixed with plains. The sub-soil water is saline at some places, while it is sweet at some other locations. Its climate resembles that of South Punjab. It is hot in the summers and cold

Map 2.7

Bhucho Mandi Municipality

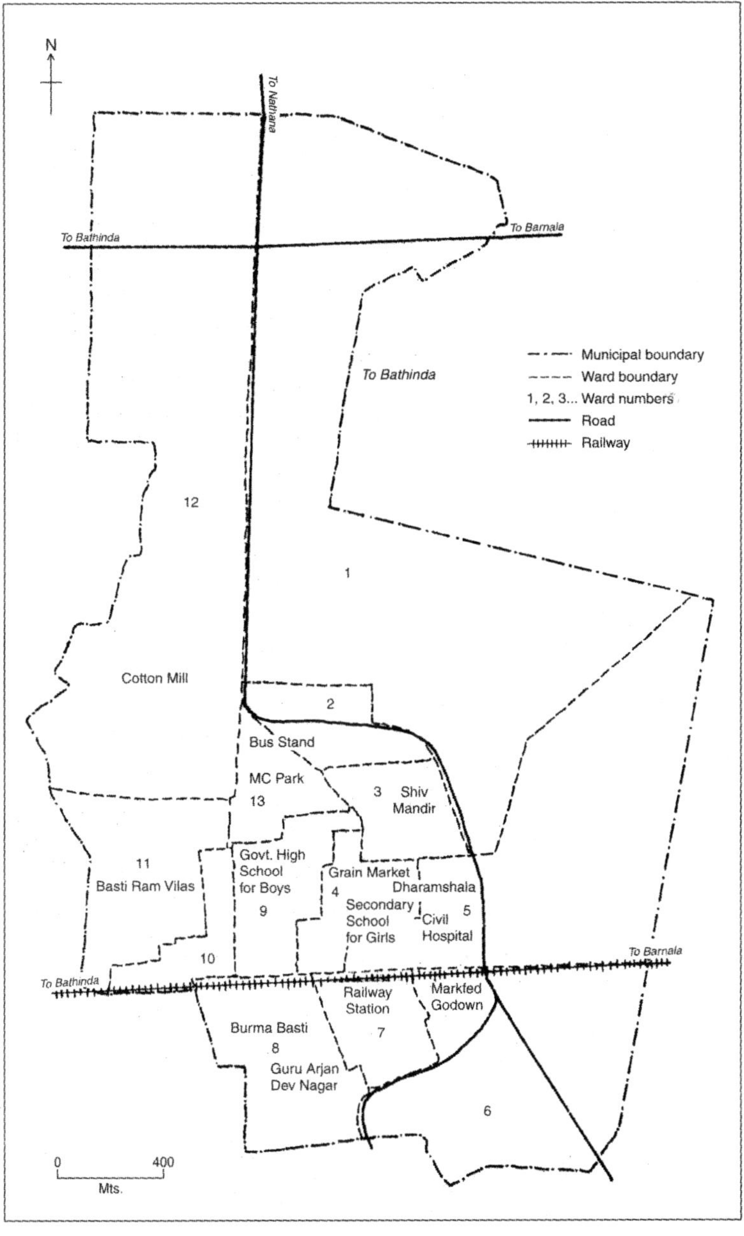

in winters. In summers the temperatures go quite high in the months of May and June. Cotton and wheat are the two main crops grown here.

Historical Background

The town has an important religious 'dera' or centre named after the religious head Baba Basus Das Ji Khadesari. The dera established around 1750, is about 3 kms away from the town. Baba Basau Ji, a religious saint, kept standing in penance for a long period of 24 years. Baba Basau took birth in a Hindu family of Kot Fatta. The Dera, which spreads over an area of 34 acres, is the foundation and head quarters of several such deras located in Delhi, Mumbai and Jaipur cities. Devotees from different parts of Punjab as well as from Haryana, Himachal Pradesh, Delhi, Uttar Pradesh and Rajasthan come in large numbers on every tenth night of the full moon.

Physical and Demographic Growth

During the British rule, a Town Area Committee was established here in 1939. This was done to make arrangements for the devotees visiting the place in large numbers. Initially, its area was about half a square kilometre. It was declared as a municipal town in 1956-57 under PEPSU administration. In 2001, its jurisdiction had been increased to 1.60 km^2 and was divided into 11 municipal wards (Map 2.8). It has the second smallest area size among the towns and ranks only after Sangat Mandi.

This small township is significant as a market town for trade in agricultural produce. There is no important manufacturing unit in the town except six flour mills. An Ayurvedic dispensary was established in 1962-63. The town has one Govt. High School, which had been established in 1962-63. Besides, there are three Government Primary Schools established in 1942-43. One sub-post office and police station was established in 1940-41 and 1955-56 respectively. It has also two bank branches to provide banking facilities. It has three Gurdwaras, two Hanuman Temples, one Ravidas temple and one Mata Durga temple. In this way, Kot Fatta makes for a religious confluence of communities.

Map 2.8

Kot Fatta Municipality

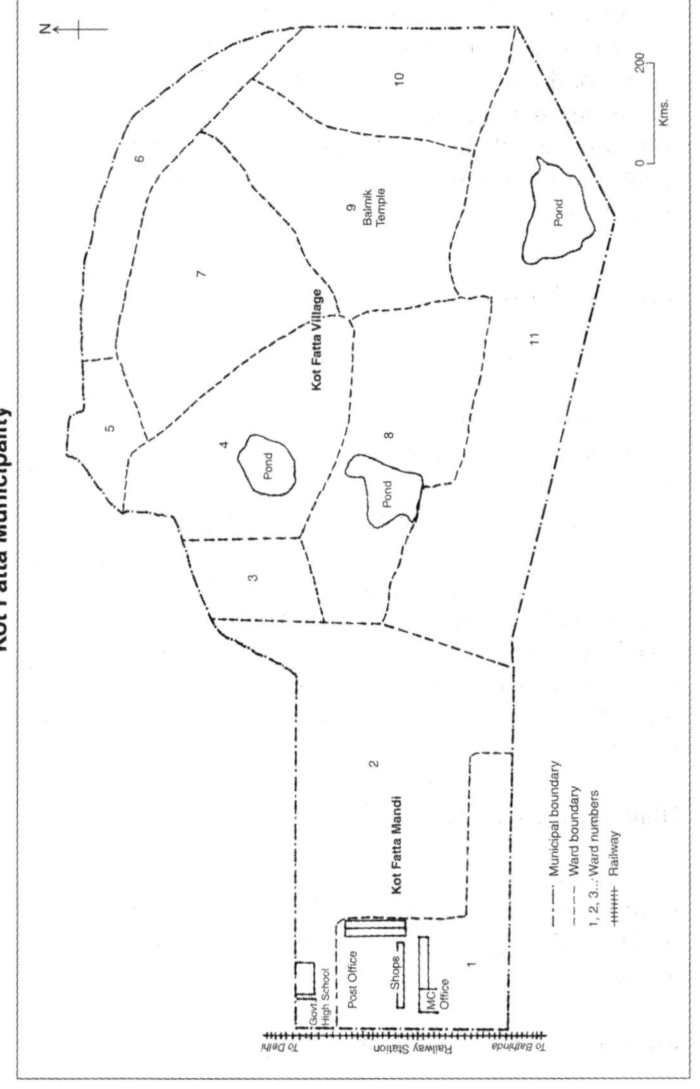

Kot Fatta town had a population of 4308 in 1971. It grew to 6493 in 2001, registering an annual growth rate of 1.4 per cent in 30 years. It is the slowest growing town in the district. Density of population has been 4058 persons/km^2, which is quite high.

As Kot Fatta is a very small town with meagre income sources it cannot do justice as far as making adequate provision for basic urban services is concerned. The municipal administration here provided only the two services, i.e., street lighting which is quite poor and sanitation till the early 90s. In 1994, tap water supply was added as a third municipal service.

SANGAT MANDI

Sangat, a small town, is located on the Bathinda-Bikaner railway line at a distance of 17 kms. from Bathinda city. It lies at 30° 05′ North latitude and 74°-50′ East longitude. Sangat Mandi is linked with several important towns including Bathinda, Rama, Dabwali and Giddarbaha.

The area around the town has sandy soils and undulating topography. The sub-soil water is not so brackish, hence is suitable for drinking purposes. Its climate resembles that of South Punjab. The summer season is quite hot and the winters are cold. It receives 50 cms average annual rainfall. In this rain deficient area, canal irrigation is well developed. This has given rise to intensive commercial cultivation of cotton and wheat crops in its surrounding areas.

Historical Background

A small village of Sangat was designated as Town Area Committee during the British rule in 1939. Thereafter, it was declared Municipal Committee in 1957. Nevertheless, it has been a slow growing town.

Physical and Demographic Growth

The Mandi township from the very beginning has been covering an areal jurisdiction of 1.28 km^2. In this way, no change has occurred in its jurisdiction over a period of more than six decades.

Following the spread of Green Revolution in this area, Sangat Mandi town has been emerging as a trade centre in foodgrains and other commercial crops grown in the area. Over the period, two processing units, one associated with cotton ginning and other with processing of oil have come here. The former was established in 1960 and the latter in 1991. It has a railway station, post office and police station. A civil hospital established in 1952, falls under the revenue boundaries of Sangat Kalan village, outside the boundaries of the Municipal Committee. It caters to the medical needs of Mandi township as well as the surrounding area. It has educational institutions up to senior secondary level. Banking facilities are also available here.

Sangat Mandi had a population only 3531 in 1971 which increased to 5396 in 2001, registering an annual growth rate of 1.4 per cent in 30 years. The population, infact, declined during the 1971-91 period, as it came down to 2731 persons in 1991 from 3531 persons in 1971. In 2001, the population density was 4216 persons/km^2 and was divided into 11 municipal wards (Map 2.9). The municipal administration has weak financial background, as its revenue income sources are highly limited. It has to depend on government grants which are not only inadequate but also received irregularly.

Main Highlights

The following points emerge quite strongly out of the preceding discussions:

- The fate of dominant majority of towns in Bathinda district is closely linked with trade in agricultural surplus. Majority of them evolved as market towns during the British rule and as collection and disposal centres of agricultural produce especially cotton. Locationally, these were established on rail routes by ensuring railway stations for them.
- In post-Independence period administrative and developmental services became the additional activities. However, the success of the Green Revolution in Punjab brought a dynamic change in role and importance of towns in the district. Under the impact of the Green Revolution, there has been not only many-fold increase in the marketable surplus from agricultural sector but also outside needs of

Map 2.9

Sangat Mandi Municipality

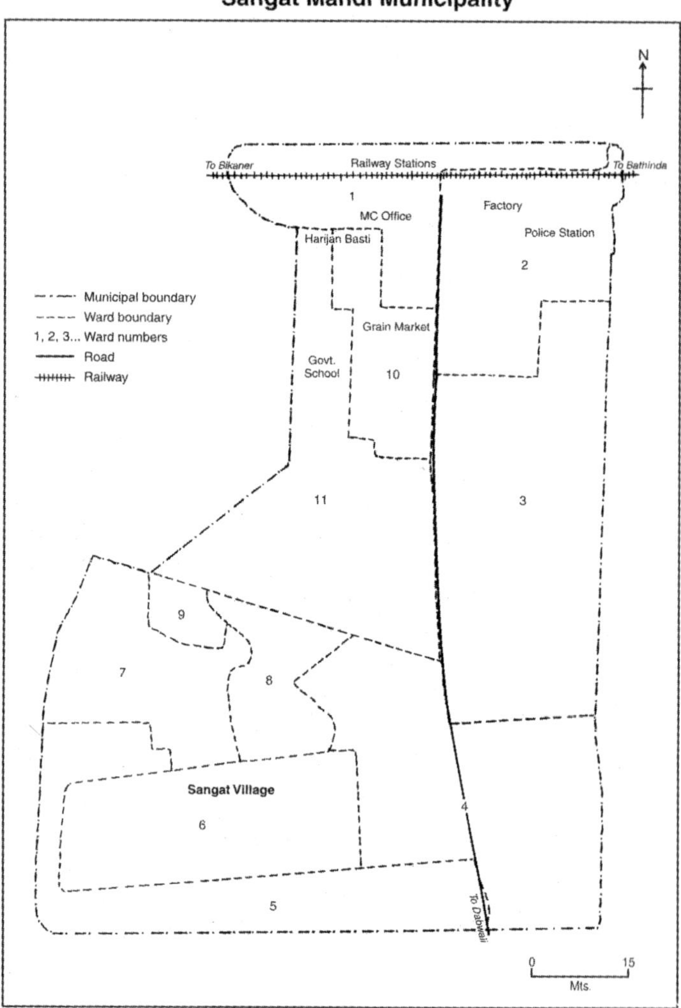

the farm sector have enlarged. Towns in the district started acting as suppliers of agricultural inputs such as chemical fertilizers, new variety of seeds and implements and market for marketable surplus generated from the farm sector. With increased interaction with the hinterland, depending on location and agricultural development in the hinterland, towns in the district grew fast especially after 1971.

- As the trade in agricultural produce is the dominant function of almost all the towns in the district, five of eight towns in the district are denoted as 'Mandi' which in turn denote market township. These are Maur Mandi, Raman Mandi, Goniana Mandi, Bhucho Mandi and Sangat Mandi. Of all the towns in the district, Bhucho Mandi, Bathinda city and Maur Mandi are the fastest growing towns, while Kot Fatta and Sangat Mandi are almost stagnant towns.
- During the last three decades (1971-2001), population of Bhucho Mandi town has grown by about three and a half times. In contrast, the population of Kot Fatta and Sangat Mandi towns grew only by about half its size during the same time. Bathinda city is the largest town and Sangat Mandi, the smallest town, in the district both in terms of area and population. In terms of population density, Bhucho Mandi has the highest population density of 5992 persons/km^2 and Goniana Mandi had the lowest density of 1602 persons/km^2. With more than 80 per cent literacy rate Goniana Mandi is the most literate town in the district and Kot Fatta is the least literate town with 59 per cent literacy rate.
- With growth of population and physical expansion of towns, the pressure on urban services such as water supply, sewerage, sanitation, and maintenance of roads, provided by municipal bodies has been intensifying in almost all the towns in the district. Emergence of slums, traffic congestion, air and water pollution were gradually coming up as the serious challenges before the municipal bodies. This has been further complicated by lack of finances and limited revenue income generation sources with the municipal bodies in the district.

3

Municipal Income and Expenditure

Before proceeding further into the study of municipal expenditure on services and the subsidy element in it, we attempt a brief overview of the municipal finances of Punjab, its different districts and municipalities. This would present the comparative picture of municipal finances in Bathinda district *vis-à-vis* other districts in the state.

Notwithstanding the long history of municipal administration in India, modern municipal administration was introduced during the British rule. It was first introduced in the late 17th century in Madras. Since, Punjab came late under the British rule in the 1840s, the first municipality in Punjab was established in 1862 at Jalandhar. The first Municipal Bodies law was enacted in 1867 with the introduction of Act XV of 1867. By the end of the 19th century there were 28 municipalities in Punjab. In the year 1911 came a comprehensive municipal Act, the Punjab Municipal Act, (PMA) of 1911, which provided the detailed foundation of municipal administration in the state. Since then, the Act has been modified a number of times and even though some other new acts have also been introduced thereafter yet the PMA (1911) remains the basic structure for municipal administration in Punjab.

At the time of Independence, the number of municipalities in Punjab had been fifty. This rose to 103 in 1965-66 when Punjab was reorganized into a Punjabi speaking state in 1966 and took the present shape. Currently, the number of municipalities in the state is 132, distributed in 17 districts. Five of these have the status of municipal corporation, the rest are municipal committees. They differ widely in their geographical distribution, population size, civic status and functions. All these factors play a vital role in their income and expenditure levels.

The major sources of municipal income in Punjab include octroi, house and land tax, and grants from the government. On the other hand, the main expenditure heads include the establishment, salary of the municipal staff, municipal services such as water supply, electricity supply, sanitation, construction and maintenance of roads, parks, etc. and the repayment of loans and interest on loans. In the financial year 1997-98, total municipal income in Punjab had been Rs. 4188.01 million, against an expenditure of Rs. 3996.23 million. Earlier in 1965-66, total municipal income had been Rs. 144.85 million, against an expenditure of Rs. 136.90 million. In fact, there is tradition to keep a surplus budget by the municipal administration.

However, an examination of the aggregate picture of municipal income and expenditure in Punjab during the period 1980-98 revealed that during this period six financial years had deficit budgets. In the beginning of the eighties, municipal budgets had been in the deficit for four consecutive years, but after 1989-90 it has always been in surplus. However, this surplus amount has been fluctuating highly over the financial years. For example, the surplus amount has been only Rs. 4.34 million during 1995-96, but it rose to Rs. 191.8 million later in response to a dominant tendency of keeping a surplus budget by all these cash-starved municipal bodies, in general.

Aggregate municipal income, from all sources, increased by more than eight times (8.27 times) during 1980-98 in the state of Punjab. Against this, increase in expenditure was of less than eight times (7.57 times) during the same time (Table 3.1). It seems that the tendency to keep a surplus budget has been responsible for this. Increase in municipal income and expenditure, if seen in per capita terms, is rather disappointing. In per capita terms, income increased by about six times (5.87 times) and expenditure by 5.37 times during 1980-98. During this period, wholesale price index (WPI) increased by about four times. However, it must be noted that there has been a rapid increase both in income and expenditure of municipalities in the state after the Indian Parliament passed the 74th Amendment to provide constitutional safeguards to their financial, functional and democratic character in 1992 and thereafter enactment of Municipal Act by Punjab government in 1994. The quantum of grants from the government has increased substantially after 1992-93. Per capita municipal income which was Rs. 395 in 1992-93 increased to Rs. 497 in 1993-94 and to Rs. 612 in 1994-95. It rose to Rs. 687 in 1997-98. Similarly, per capita expenditure rose from Rs. 383 to Rs. 475, then to Rs. 595 and finally to Rs. 655 during the same period. Municipal budgets recorded the maximum surplus in 1997-98 against a maximum deficit in 1982-83 (Table 3.1 and Fig. 3.1).

TABLE 3.1
Punjab: Trends in Municipal Income and Expenditure, 1980-98

(Figures in 000 Rs.)

Year	*Income*	*Expenditure*	*Balance*
1980-81	506184 (117)	527717 (122)	-21533
1981-82	643181 (149)	646473 (150)	-3292
1982-83	818732 (190)	843315 (195)	-24583
1983-84	870580 (201)	873407 (202)	-2827
1984-85	967631 (221)	947607 (216)	20024
1985-86	1171303 (267)	1145525 (261)	25778
1986-87	1287987 (292)	1283344 (291)	4643
1987-88	1340684 (305)	1353076 (307)	-12392
1988-89	2324361 (528)	2262543 (514)	61818
1989-90	1648256 (374)	1712619 (389)	-64363
1990-91	1894312 (430)	1776873 (404)	117439
1991-92	2083083 (473)	2032972 (462)	50111
1992-93	2321678 (395)	2250121 (383)	71557
1993-94	3006084 (497)	2875293 (475)	130791
1994-95	3713748 (612)	3608905 (595)	104843
1995-96	3753663 (618)	3749320 (618)	4343
1996-97	4066964 (667)	4030958 (661)	36006
1997-98	4188010 (687)	3996232 (655)	191778
1998-99	5132068 (841)	5022699 (823)	-109369
1999-00	6730709 (1096)	6477989 (1055)	252720
2000-01	7356912 (1198)	7357000 (1198)	-88

Note: Figures in parenthesis indicate per capita income/expenditure in rupees. It has been calculated on the basis of population figures available from *Statistical Abstract of Punjab*, Economic Adviser to Government of Punjab, Chandigarh, for different years.

PER CAPITA MUNICIPAL INCOME AND EXPENDITURE: INTER-DISTRICT COMPARISON

There were wide inter-district and inter-municipal variations in municipal income and expenditure in Punjab. For a more realistic

Fig. 3.1

A. Punjab: Municipal Income and Expenditure by Districts, 1997-98

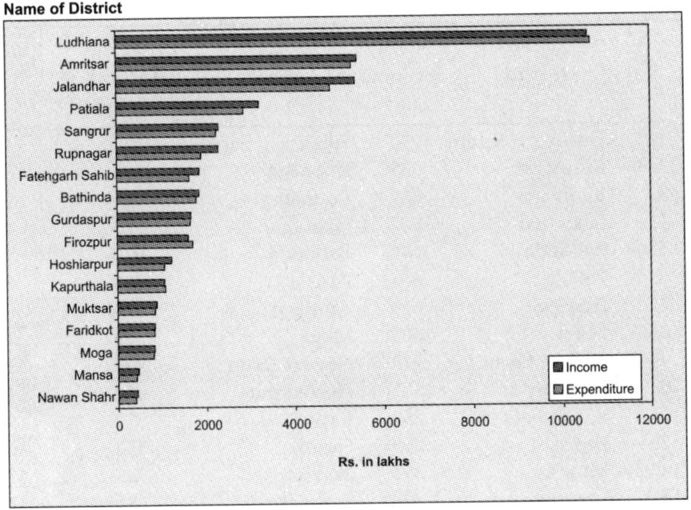

B. Punjab: Per Capita Income and Expenditure by Districts, 1997-98

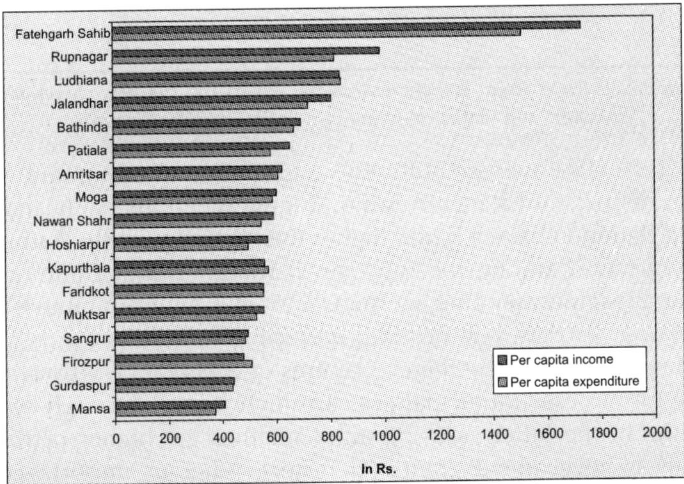

comparison, district-wise municipal income and expenditure has been calculated on per capita basis.

During 1997-98, per capita municipal income varied from a high of Rs. 1730 in Fatehgarh to a low of Rs. 408 in Mansa (Table 3.2) giving a ratio of 1:4.2 between the two.

TABLE 3.2
Punjab: Inter-district Comparison of Per Capita Municipal Income and Expenditure, 1997-98

Sr. No.	Name of District	Income Per Head (in Rs.)	Name of District	Expenditure Per Head (in Rs.)	Ranking
1.	Fatehgarh Sahib	1730	Fatehgarh Sahib	1510	1
2.	Rupnagar	989	Rupnagar	819	3
3.	Ludhiana	839	Ludhiana	844	2
4.	Jalandhar	807	Jalandhar	723	4
5.	Bathinda	696	Bathinda	670	5
6.	Patiala	654	Patiala	583	8
7.	Amritsar	626	Amritsar	610	6
8.	Moga	605	Moga	589	7
9.	Nawan Shahr	592	Nawan Shahr	547	11
10.	Hoshiarpur	571	Hoshiarpur	499	14
11.	Kapurthala	559	Kapurthala	572	9
12.	Faridkot	555	Faridkot	554	10
13.	Muktsar	554	Muktsar	527	12
14.	Sangrur	496	Sangrur	485	15
15.	Firozepur	479	Firozepur	509	13
16.	Gurdaspur	442	Gurdaspur	438	16
17.	Mansa	408	Mansa	373	17
18.	Punjab	687		655	

Source: Calculated from *Statistical Abstract, Punjab* for 1997-98, Directorate of Economic and Statistical Organisation, Punjab, Chandigarh.

If the state average of Rs. 687 is taken as a dividing line, only five districts of Fatehgarh Sahib, Rupnagar, Ludhiana, Jalandhar and Bathinda have a figure higher than this. Evidently, Bathinda district was among the top five districts, having a per capita municipal income of higher than the state average. In all five top-ranking districts, one or more municipal towns have either big urban-industrial/commercial centres or a famous Gurdwara. In the former case municipalities earn high income through octroi, while in the latter case the municipalities get higher octroi as well as government grants for historic-religious importance of such towns. Fatehgarh Sahib municipal town, in Fatehgarh Sahib district, where two sons of Guru Gobind Singh Ji were cemented alive in a wall of the fort during the Muslim rule (1206-1757) in India, receives a handsome amount of government grants and earns octroi as a toll tax on entry of non-local vehicles into the town. Here, a historical Gurdwara has been constructed at the place of sacrifice. Per capita municipal income in Fatehgarh Sahib district was higher by 75 per cent than that of the second ranking district in this context (i.e. Rupnagar) and was higher by 424 per cent of that of the lowest per capita municipal income district of Mansa.

On the other side of the scale, in four districts of Sangrur, Firozepur, Gurdaspur and Mansa, per capita municipal income was less than Rs. 500. None of these four districts, having a border location, have either any municipal town of industrial/commercial importance nor are of great historic or religious significance.

Like the municipal income, municipal expenditure too differed widely among the districts. It ranged from a high of Rs. 1510 in Fatehgarh Sahib district to a low of Rs. 373 in Mansa district, giving a difference of 4 times, i.e. a ratio of 1:40. Earlier, in the case of municipal income this ratio was slightly higher (4.24 times) than that of expenditure. Bathinda district with a per capita municipal expenditure of Rs. 670 was placed fifth from the top among all the seventeen districts in the state. In line with its position among top five municipal income districts in the state it was again placed in five top districts of Fatehgarh Sahib, Rupnagar, Ludhiana, Jalandhar and Bathinda. The same districts featured earlier in the top five high income municipal districts. This means, higher the per capita municipal income in a district higher is its per capita municipal expenditure. Some notable exceptions in this context are Ludhiana, Amritsar, Kapurthala and Firozepur which rank in municipal expenditure than in income. The case with Patiala, Hoshiarpur, Nawan Shahr and Sangrur districts is just the reverse.

On the basis of per capita municipal income and expenditure, districts have been grouped into three categories of high, moderate and low. On the whole, there is high degree of correspondence between income and expenditure categories of the districts (Table 3.3).

TABLE 3.3

Punjab: Classification of Districts According to Per Capita Municipal Income and Expenditure, 1997-98

Sr. No.	Income category (in Rs.)	Income level	Name of Districts
		A. Income	
1.	More than 700	High	Fatehgarh Sahib, Rupnagar, Ludhiana, Jalandhar = 4
2.	500-700	Moderate	Bathinda, Patiala, Amritsar, Moga, Nawan Shahr, Hoshiarpur, Kapurthala, Faridkot, Muktsar = 9
3.	Less than 500	Low	Sangrur, Firozepur, Gurdaspur, Mansa = 4
		B. Expenditure	
1.	More than 700	High	Fatehgarh Sahib, Rupnagar, Ludhiana, Jalandhar = 4
2.	500-700	Moderate	Bathinda, Patiala, Amritsar, Moga, Nawan Shahr, Firozepur, Kapurthala, Faridkot, Muktsar = 9
3.	Less than 500	Low	Sangrur, Hoshiarpur, Gurdaspur, Mansa= 4

INTER-DISTRICT VARIATIONS IN SHARE OF MUNICIPAL INCOME AND EXPENDITURE

Districts differ widely in the proportional shares of municipal incomes and expenditures in 1997-98. The income share varied from a high of 25.31 per cent in Ludhiana district to a low of 1.03 per cent in Nawan Shahr district (Table 3.4). Three districts of Ludhiana, Amritsar and Jalandhar, each having one of the three municipal corporation towns in the state, receive, in combination, more than half (51.1 per cent) the total municipal income in Punjab. Against this, their combined population against the total population of municipal towns in the state was less than half (45.83 per cent). Evidently, districts having big municipal towns get high income in comparison to their population shares in urban population in the state. This may be explained by a variety of factors including higher income generating capacity of big urban industrial and commercial towns in the forms of octroi, market fee and tax on houses and property besides getting higher grants from the government under various schemes such as slum up-gradation, etc. Against this, eight districts, namely, Firozepur, Hoshiarpur, Kapurthala, Muktsar, Faridkot, Moga, Mansa and

Nawan Shahr had a combined share of only 17.44 per cent in the total municipal income in the state. Against this, their combined share in total urban population in the state came to 22.43 per cent. In this way their combined population comes to, more than one-fifths in total urban population against only about one-sixth of the total municipal income in the state. Obviously, there is a mismatch between the shares of municipal income and urban population of different districts in the state.

TABLE 3.4

Punjab: District-wise Share in Total Municipal Income and Expenditure, 1997-98

(Figures in %)

Sr. No.	*Name of district*	*Income share*	*Expenditure share*	*Population share*
1.	Gurdaspur	3.96	4.11	6.16
2.	Amritsar	12.94	13.23	14.20
3.	Kapurthala	2.52	2.70	3.10
4.	Jalandhar	12.83	12.04	10.91
5.	Nawan Shahr	1.03	1.00	1.20
6.	Hoshiarpur	2.90	2.66	3.49
7.	Rupnagar	5.48	4.76	3.80
8.	Ludhiana	25.31	26.69	20.72
9.	Firozpur	3.81	4.25	5.47
10.	Muktsar	2.11	2.11	2.62
11.	Moga	1.98	2.02	2.24
12.	Bathinda	4.42	4.46	4.36
13.	Faridkot	1.99	2.08	2.46
14.	Mansa	1.10	1.05	1.85
15.	Sangrur	5.49	5.61	7.59
16.	Patiala	7.69	7.18	8.07
17.	Fatehgarh Sahib	4.43	4.06	1.76
	Punjab	100.00	100.00	100.00

A similar tendency, though in a more accentuated form, has been noticed in the case of municipal expenditure. The combined municipal expenditure of the top three districts of Ludhiana, Amritsar and Jalandhar made up more than half or about 52 per cent against their total combined income of 51 per cent and combined urban population of about 46 per cent. Against this, the combined municipal expenditure of eight bottom ranking districts, namely, Fatehgarh Sahib, Kapurthala, Hoshiarpur, Muktsar, Faridkot, Moga, Mansa and Nawan Shahr made up only about 18 per cent of the total municipal expenditure in the state. Their combined income share was 18.1 per cent and population share was about 19 per cent. At the level of individual districts, there are at least four districts, namely, Gurdaspur, Firozpur, Mansa and Sangrur, where population shares are much higher than their respective shares in total municipal income and expenditure of the State. In contrast, the case of Fatehgarh Sahib, Jalandhar, Ludhiana and Rupnagar districts was at first the reverse. While, Nawan Shahr and Bathinda districts were a case of near correspondence among their respective shares of income, expenditure and population.

MUNICIPAL INCOME BY SOURCES: INTER-DISTRICT COMPARISON

Octroi is the major source of municipal income in Punjab. In 1997-98, nearly 58 per cent of total municipal income came from this source. There were, however, wide inter-district variations. It varied from a high of about 80 per cent in Rupnagar district to a low of about 37 per cent in Muktsar district (Table 3.5). In Bathinda district, octroi contributed two-thirds or 66.7 per cent of the total municipal income. The share of octroi in income of municipalities in Bathinda district has been higher than the state average. In fact, Bathinda ranks next only to Rupnagar, the highest ranking district in this context. There are seven other districts, including Bathinda district, where octroi contributes higher than the state average.

In four districts, namely, Rupnagar, Bathinda, Gurdaspur and Jalandhar octroi contributed more than three-fifths of the total municipal income. On the other hand, in seven districts of Muktsar, Firozpur, Nawan Shahr, Mansa, Fatehgarh Sahib, Faridkot and Hoshiarpur octroi contributed less than half the total municipal income. Obviously, the dependency of municipal bodies in these districts increased on government grants which are, in general, an irregular source of income. Whereas, the octroi makes a regular as well as independent source of municipal income.

The next important source of municipal income in Punjab is the income from 'other' taxes. 'Other' taxes which include a large

TABLE 3.5

Punjab: Inter-district Variations in Municipal Income by Income Sources, 1997-98

(Income figures in Lakh Rupees)

Sr. No.	*Name of District*	*Total income*	*Income from octroi*	*Share in %*	*Income from house and land taxes*	*Share in %*	*Income from other taxes*	*Share in %*	*Income from grants*	*Share in %*	*Income from miscellaneous sources*	*Share in %*
1.	Gurdaspur	1658.45	1032.44	62.25	66.53	4.01	263.71	15.90	252.67	15.24	43.10	2.60
2.	Amritsar	5420.19	3187.06	58.80	302.01	5.57	1087.18	20.06	843.94	15.57	—	—
3.	Kapurthala	1057.14	558.12	52.80	101.66	9.62	299.14	28.30	46.69	4.42	51.53	4.87
4.	Jalandhar	5373.45	3320.41	61.79	378.02	7.03	958.76	17.84	702.10	13.07	14.16	0.26
5.	Nawan Shahr	431.67	173.79	40.26	35.86	8.31	65.31	15.13	72.06	16.69	84.65	19.61
6.	Hoshiarpur	1215.46	592.06	48.71	91.64	7.54	292.32	24.05	218.93	18.01	20.51	1.69
7.	Rupnagar	2296.59	1824.62	79.45	62.80	2.73	361.25	15.73	45.43	1.98	2.49	0.11
8.	Ludhiana	10598.82	6321.21	59.64	1495.50	14.11	2384.22	22.50	288.19	2.72	109.20	1.03
9.	Firozpur	1597.08	629.07	39.39	102.11	6.39	482.15	30.19	336.69	21.08	47.06	2.95
10.	Faridkot	832.09	366.14	44.00	34.87	4.19	189.21	22.74	208.30	25.03	33.57	4.03
11.	Muktsar	884.02	326.38	36.92	31.07	3.51	118.25	13.38	341.42	38.62	66.90	7.57
12.	Moga	828.19	491.54	59.35	54.95	6.63	210.50	25.42	32.20	3.89	39.00	4.71
13.	Bathinda	1850.61	1232.81	66.62	70.37	3.80	290.08	15.67	228.24	12.33	29.11	1.57
14.	Mansa	460.13	189.69	41.23	32.34	7.03	171.38	37.25	66.72	14.50	—	—
15.	Sangrur	2298.75	1244.04	54.12	160.96	7.0	488.08	21.23	217.33	9.45	188.34	8.19
16.	Patiala	3220.24	1795.39	55.75	339.12	10.53	673.63	20.92	412.03	12.80	0.07	2.17
17.	Fatehgarh Sahib	1857.22	888.44	47.84	89.65	4.83	170.92	9.20	151.74	8.17	556.47	29.96
	Punjab	41880.10	24173.21	57.72	3449.46	8.24	8506.59	20.31	4464.68	10.66	1286.16	3.07

Source: Calculated from *Statistical Abstract*, Punjab for 1997-98, Directorate of Economic and Statistical Organisation, Punjab, Chandigarh.

variety of revenue sources such as revenue earnings from water and electricity supply, conservancy, sales proceeds of land, receipts from markets and slaughter houses and fees from institutions including the educational. More than one-fifth or 20.3 per cent of total municipal income comes from this source. In this way municipal bodies in Punjab earn more than three-fourths of their total revenue income from octroi and other taxes (Map 3.1).

Map 3.1

PUNJAB
Composition of Municipal Expenditure 1997-98

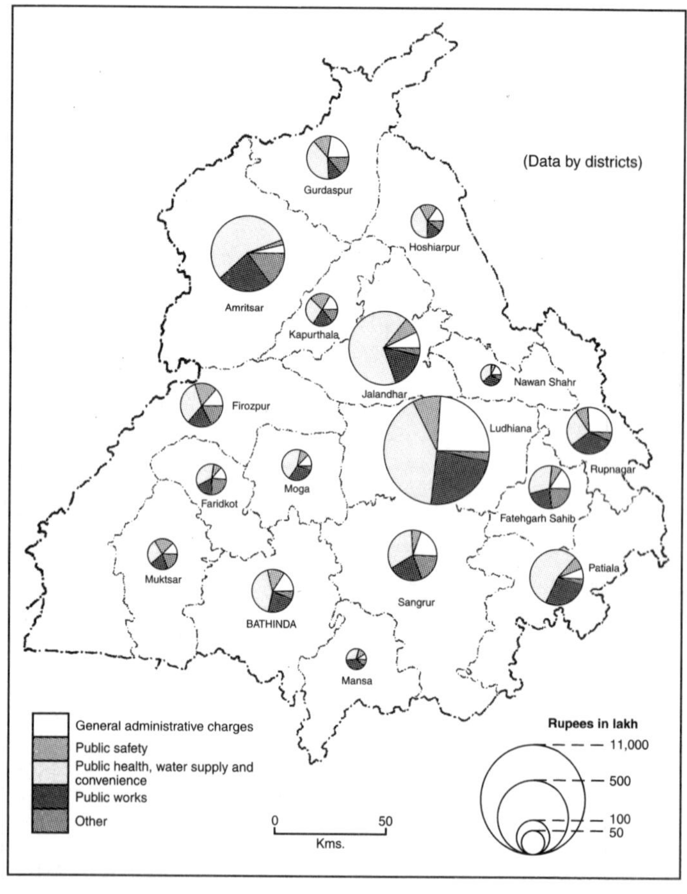

However, income from 'other taxes' differs significantly at district level. It varied from a high of 37.3 per cent in Mansa district to a low of 9.2 per cent in Fatehgarh Sahib district. In ten districts, namely, Mansa, Firozpur, Kapurthala, Moga, Hoshiarpur, Faridkot, Sangrur, Patiala, Amritsar and Ludhiana this proportion was higher than the state average. In other words, half the districts in the state have this proportion higher than the state average.

Moga and Mansa, where the proportional share of 'other' taxes in municipal income is quite high, are newly formed districts. On the other side of the scale, Fatehgarh Sahib and Muktsar are the two districts where 'other' tax contributes very less to the municipal income. Fatehgarh Sahib is such a district where this proportion is even less than half of the state average. Other districts having low proportion of 'other' taxes in total municipal income are Nawan Shahr, Rupnagar, and Bathinda.

Grants from government and local funds, make the third important source of municipal income in Punjab. It contributed 10.7 per cent or more than one-tenth of the total municipal income. Among the districts, it varied from a high of 38.6 per cent in Muktsar to a low of 2 per cent in Rupnagar. In seven districts, namely, Muktsar, Faridkot, Firozpur, Hoshiarpur, Nawan Shahr, Amritsar and Gurdaspur the grants contribute more than 15.0 per cent in total municipal income. In five of these districts, namely, Muktsar, Faridkot, Firozpur, Hoshiarpur and Nawan Shahr octroi contributes quite low in municipal income, increasing their dependency on grants received from the government.

On the other hand, districts where grants contribute less towards municipal income are Kapurthala, Rupnagar, Ludhiana, Moga, Sangrur and Fatehgarh Sahib. Bathinda district makes an interesting case. Here, octroi contributes two-thirds towards total municipal income. This makes Bathinda rank second among all the districts in the state. Nevertheless, contribution of government grants in municipal income was higher than the state average.

Tax on houses and land contributes another 8 per cent to municipal income in Punjab. Ludhiana district, having the largest city, Ludhiana, in the state, had the highest proportion (14.1 per cent) of municipal income from this source. Next was Patiala district with 10.5 per cent of total municipal income, Kapurthala and Nawan Shahr were the other two districts where this proportion was higher than the state average. In contrast, in five districts of Gurdaspur, Rupnagar, Faridkot, Muktsar and Bathinda, the share of income from this source was less than half the state average.

Income from 'miscellaneous' sources such as realization of sinking funds, advances, deposits, etc., contributed remaining about 3 per cent of the municipal income in the state. Among districts, share of income from this source varied from a high of about 30 per cent in Fatehgarh Sahib to zero in Amritsar and Mansa districts. In two other districts, contribution of this source to municipal income was almost negligible. These districts were Jalandhar and Rupnagar. In three districts, namely, Hoshiarpur, Ludhiana and Bathinda this proportion was less than 2 per cent.

Besides Fatehgarh Sahib, other districts where income from 'miscellaneous' sources contributed significantly included Nawan Shahr (19.6 per cent), Moga (8.2 per cent), Sangrur (8.2 per cent), Muktsar (7.6 per cent) and Kapurthala (4.9 per cent).

In brief, octroi forms the most important source of municipal income in Punjab. It contributes more than half the total municipal income in the state. There are wide inter-district variations in this regard. In districts where important industrial and business centres are located, higher proportion of municipal income from this source is received. Among such districts are Rupnagar, Jalandhar, Ludhiana, Moga and Bathinda. Districts where income from octroi does not contribute significantly to municipal income have to depend on grants from the government and other sources as a major source of the municipal income. Such grants are received neither regularly nor in the desired quantity. Moreover, such grants remain tied up with certain conditions. Against this, municipal income from octroi is not only a regular but also an independent source of income. Muktsar, Faridkot, Firozpur, Hoshiarpur and Nawan Shahr are the districts where the dependency of municipal income on grants has been quite high.

Interestingly, in the case of Fatehgarh Sahib and Nawan Shahr districts income from 'miscellaneous' sources such as realization of sinking funds, advances, deposits, etc. contributed significantly to municipal income. In Bathinda district, where octroi contributed two-thirds of the total municipal income, ranked second after Rupnagar in this regard in the year 1997-98. In this district, 'other' taxes and grants made the second and third important sources of municipal income, respectively.

INTER-DISTRICT VARIATIONS IN MUNICIPAL EXPENDITURE BY EXPENDITURE HEADS

Before we proceed to examine inter-district variations in municipal expenditure on different heads of expenditure, it is imperative to have an assessment of the overall picture of the state as a whole at the outset. Of the six major urban services, rendered by municipalities in Punjab, water supply is the most important expenditure head. During 1980-98, its share ranged between 26 and 43 per cent in total municipal expenditure on major urban services. While the share of water supply was as high as 43.3 per cent in 1981-82, it came down to only 25.7 per cent in 1984-85 (Table 3.6).

Next important expenditure head is the sanitation service, consuming another significant slice, which ranged between 18 and 34 per cent during 1980-98. Its share was as high as 33.6 per cent in 1992-93 and as low as 18.2 per cent in 1982-83. Water supply combined with sanitation consumed more than half the total municipal expenditure on urban services in Punjab.

Construction and maintenance of municipal roads is the third major expenditure head of municipal expenditure on urban services in the state. Its share in total municipal expenditure on major urban services ranged from a minimum of 12.8 per cent in 1989-90 to a maximum of 23.4 per cent in 1994-95. Drainage is an almost equally important head of municipal expenditure in the state. Its share in total municipal expenditure on major urban services ranged from a low of 7.8 per cent in 1989-90 to a high of 17.9 per cent in 1980-81. It shows that expenditure priorities of municipalities, as regards the urban services, are quite justified. This is mainly because, water supply, sanitation and municipal roads form the dominant expenditure heads of municipal expenditure in the state (Map 3.2).

In terms of expenditure, street lighting, consuming between five and sixteen per cent of municipal expenditure on major urban services, comes fifth among six major urban services. Its share in municipal expenditure on major urban services in the state ranged from a low of 4.6 per cent in 1981-82 to a high of 15.6 per cent in 1984-85. Fire services, managed and maintained by only some municipal bodies, consumed between one to four per cent of municipal expenditure on major urban services in the state. Its share ranged from a low of 1.4 per cent in 1982-83 to a high of 3.4 per cent in 1992-93.

TABLE 3.6

Punjab: Trends in Municipal Expenditure on Different Urban Services, 1980-98

(*Rs. in lakhs*)

Year	*Water supply*	*Street lighting*	*Sanitation*	*Roads*	*Drainage*	*Fire services*	*Total expenditure*
1980-81	972.10	157.42	645.95	612.79	533.23	59.64	2981.13
	(32.60)	(5.28)	(21.67)	(20.56)	(17.89)	(2.00)	(100)
1981-82	1768.94	186.82	790.48	700.39	565.25	70.71	4082.59
	(43.33)	(4.58)	(19.36)	(17.16)	(13.85)	(1.73)	(100)
1982-83	1693.68	433.79	775.31	715.01	585.48	59.77	4263.04
	(39.73)	(10.18)	(18.19)	(16.77)	(13.73)	(1.40)	(100)
1983-84	1263.07	546.75	773.36	805.80	730.03	67.45	4186.46
	(30.17)	(13.06)	(18.47)	(19.25)	(17.44)	(1.61)	(100)
1984-85	1041.00	632.82	919.08	836.56	542.51	80.97	4052.94
	(25.69)	(15.60)	(22.68)	(20.64)	(13.39)	(2.00)	(100)
1985-86	1321.87	686.56	1160.68	1039.22	675.60	101.18	4985.11
	(26.52)	(13.77)	(23.28)	(20.85)	(13.55)	(2.03)	(100)
1986-87	1909.34	445.76	1338.63	1095.97	651.70	107.34	5548.74
	(34.41)	(8.03)	(24.12)	(19.75)	(11.75)	(1.94)	(100)
1987-88	1434.74	508.78	1706.61	983.69	750.11	144.24	5528.17
	(25.95)	(9.20)	(30.87)	(17.79)	(13.57)	(2.61)	(100)
1988-89	2443.14	573.87	1998.60	1281.87	753.11	182.32	7232.91
	(33.78)	(7.93)	(27.63)	(17.72)	(10.41)	(2.53)	(100)
1989-90	3732.06	861.86	1992.81	1099.66	669.76	237.35	8593.50
	(43.43)	(10.03)	(23.19)	(12.80)	(7.79)	(2.76)	(100)
1990-91	2014.28	673.46	2344.98	1284.43	773.72	245.63	7336.50
	(27.46)	(9.18)	(31.96)	(17.50)	(10.55)	(3.35)	(100)
1991-92	2390.44	732.10	3061.32	1673.97	1073.64	299.01	9230.48
	(25.90)	(7.93)	(33.17)	(18.14)	(11.63)	(3.25)	(100)
1992-93	2948.39	889.59	3638.55	1880.17	1107.29	363.86	10827.85
	(27.23)	(8.22)	(33.60)	(17.36)	(10.23)	(3.36)	(100)
1993-94	4386.74	1036.24	3853.84	2441.49	1541.44	361.93	13621.68
	(32.20)	(7.61)	(28.29)	(17.92)	(11.32)	(2.66)	(100)
1994-95	5103.17	1443.37	3186.25	3768.39	2124.25	411.08	16036.51
	(31.82)	(9.00)	(19.87)	(23.50)	(13.25)	(2.56)	(100)
1995-96	6433.11	1852.83	5303.13	5233.48	3060.81	509.16	22392.52
	(28.73)	(8.27)	(23.68)	(23.37)	(13.67)	(2.27)	(100)
1996-97	6846.46	1930.56	5965.00	4878.70	2453.02	514.81	22588.55
	(30.31)	(8.55)	(26.40)	(21.60)	(10.86)	(2.28)	(100)
1997-98	7094.46	1919.58	5494.73	4322.80	2763.28	596.79	22191.64
	(31.97)	(8.65)	(24.76)	(19.48)	(12.45)	(2.69)	(100)

Note: Figures in parenthesis indicate percentage in total expenditure on services.

Source: Calculated from *Statistical Abstract, Punjab* for 1997-98, Directorate of Economic and Statistical Organisation, Punjab, Chandigarh.

Map 3.2

PUNJAB

Composition of Municipal Income 1997-98

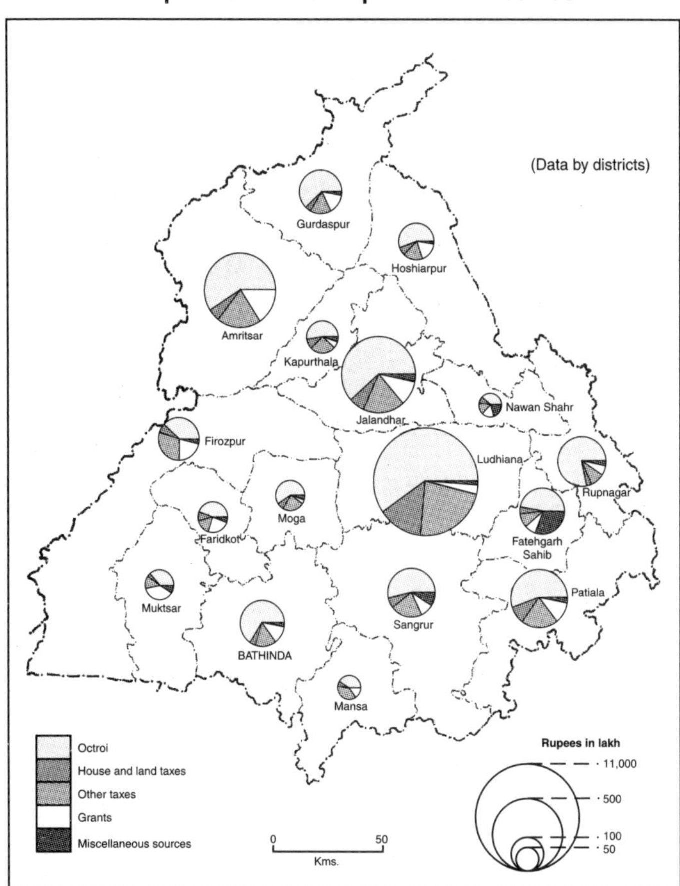

In this way, water supply followed by public health services (sanitation and drainage) and municipal roads have been expenditure heads that consumed the dominant share of municipal expenditure on major urban services in the state. There were, however, wide inter-district and inter-municipal variations in this regard.

It varied from a high of nearly 65 per cent in Jalandhar district to a low of about 25 per cent in Rupnagar (Table 3.7). In other

TABLE 3.7

Punjab: Inter-district Variations in Municipal Expenditure by Expenditure Item, 1997-98

(Expenditure figures in Lakh Rupees)

Sr. No.	Name of District	Total Expenditure	Amount spent upon general administrative charges	Share in %	Amount spent upon public safety	Share in %	Amount spent upon public, health, water supply and convenience etc.	Share in %	Amount spent upon public works	Share in %	Amount spent upon others	Share in %
1.	Gurdaspur	1644.34	385.48	23.44	223.96	13.62	647.16	39.36	159.39	9.69	228.35	13.89
2.	Amritsar	5287.16	200.92	3.80	84.51	1.60	2974.86	56.27	1228.28	23.23	798.59	15.10
3.	Kapurthala	1080.76	179.93	16.65	234.90	21.73	306.57	28.37	194.66	18.01	164.70	15.24
4.	Jalandhar	4813.33	364.06	7.56	410.78	8.53	3124.23	64.91	779.62	16.20	134.64	2.80
5.	Nawan Shahr	399.04	67.71	16.97	22.28	5.58	157.26	39.41	126.57	31.72	25.32	6.35
6.	Hoshiarpur	1061.76	162.77	15.33	181.65	17.11	462.05	43.52	142.12	13.39	113.17	10.66
7.	Rupnagar	1901.56	511.97	26.92	169.15	8.90	478.07	25.14	628.69	33.06	113.68	5.98
8.	Ludhiana	10665.27	2564.16	24.04	897.04	8.41	4427.87	41.52	2493.30	23.38	282.90	2.65
9.	Firozpur	1696.76	219.60	12.94	292.52	17.24	590.77	34.82	312.24	18.40	281.63	16.60
10.	Faridkot	830.15	129.09	15.55	62.12	7.48	280.88	33.83	151.10	18.20	206.96	24.93
11.	Muktsar	841.77	99.30	11.80	190.50	22.63	229.07	27.21	140.84	16.73	182.06	21.63
12.	Moga	806.45	106.40	13.19	71.17	8.83	353.54	43.84	247.02	30.63	28.32	3.51
13.	Bathinda	1781.16	275.37	15.46	232.43	13.05	783.34	43.98	383.43	21.53	106.59	5.98
14.	Mansa	419.94	32.27	7.68	52.59	12.52	135.38	32.24	155.63	37.10	44.07	10.49
15.	Sangrur	2243.83	453.66	20.22	125.21	5.58	767.13	34.19	490.23	21.85	407.60	18.17
16.	Patiala	2867.44	169.27	5.90	215.43	7.51	1586.53	55.33	810.40	28.26	85.81	2.99
17.	Fatehgarh Sahib	1621.60	270.18	16.66	111.02	6.85	515.68	31.80	356.60	21.99	368.12	22.70
	Total	39962.32	6192.14	15.49	3577.26	8.95	17820.39	44.59	8800.12	22.02	3572.51	8.94

Source: Calculated from *Statistical Abstract, Punjab* for 1997-98, Directorate of Economic and Statistical Organisation, Punjab, Chandigarh.

words, it ranged from about two-thirds to one-fourth of the total municipal expenditure. In three districts of Jalandhar, Amritsar, Patiala expenditure on the item made up for more than half the total municipal expenditure. In four other districts, namely, Hoshiarpur, Ludhiana, Moga and Bathinda, this proportion ranged between 40 to 50 per cent. Notably, majority of the districts incurring 40 per cent plus expenditure on public health, water supply and public conveniences, etc. are possessed of atleast one municipal town which is an important urban-industrial and sub-regional centre.

On the other hand, in the three districts of Rupnagar, Muktsar and Kapurthala the expenditure on this head was less than 30 per cent of the total municipal expenditure. In remaining seven districts, this proportion ranged between 30 to 40 per cent. On the whole, majority of the districts in the state incurred expenditure on public health, water supply and public convenience which was lower than the state average.

More than one-fifth (or 22 per cent) of the total municipal expenditure goes to public works, including construction and maintenance of municipal roads, buildings, establishments and stores as well as miscellaneous works. There were wide inter-district variations in this regard also. It varied from a high of 37 per cent in Mansa district to a low of about 10 per cent in Gurdaspur district. In five districts, namely, Nawan Shahr, Rupnagar, Moga, Mansa and Patiala the share of public works in total municipal expenditure made up for more than 25 per cent or one-fourth of the total. In five other districts, namely, Amritsar, Ludhiana, Bathinda, Sangrur and Fatehgarh Sahib this proportion ranged between 20 and 25 per cent. On the other side of the scale, in Hoshiarpur and Gurdaspur its share was less than 15 per cent of the total municipal expenditure.

The third important expenditure head was the general administration charges including the salaries and perks of the heads of committees/corporations, executive officers, secretaries and their supporting staff, taxes on vehicles, maintenance of buildings, etc. It is to be noted here that it does not include the salary paid to the municipal staff, employed to impart different municipal services. For example, salary of the staff employed for sanitation work or water supply form an integral part of the budget head of the respective departments of the municipal government. In this way, expenditure on general administration included only the salary of general staff. More than one-seventh or 15.5 per cent of the total municipal expenditure was incurred on this item in 1997-98. Among the districts, it varied from a high of about 27 per cent in Rupnagar to a low of about 4 per cent in Amritsar. In four districts of Rupnagar, Ludhiana, Gurdaspur and Sangrur this proportion was more than one-fifth or 20 per cent. In another six districts, this proportion ranged between 15 to 20 per cent. Three districts, namely, Amritsar, Jalandhar and Ludhiana, each having one municipal town with the status of municipal corporation, present a contrasting picture. In such municipal bodies, the general purpose administrative staff is not only numerically large but also paid higher. In Ludhiana district, which is the largest municipal town of the state, expenditure on general administration was as high as 24 per cent in the total municipal expenditure.

In four districts of Amritsar, Jalandhar, Mansa and Patiala this proportion was less than one-tenth or 10 per cent. In the three districts, namely, Firozpur, Muktsar and Moga this proportion was between 10 to 15 per cent. In fact, in half of the districts the share of this expenditure in total municipal expenditure was less than the average for the state.

Public safety including street lighting, fire service and 'miscellaneous' services accounted for about 9 per cent. It ranged from a high of about 23 per cent in Muktsar to a low of less than 2 per cent in Amritsar district. In seven districts, this proportion was more than 10 per cent. In all, more than half the districts have a share more than the average. In contrast, in three districts of Amritsar, Nawan Shahr and Patiala the share of this expenditure head has been less than 6 per cent of the total municipal expenditure.

Remaining about 9 per cent of the total municipal expenditure was incurred on 'other' items including general purpose, payment of interest on loans, investment, payment of sinking funds, repayment of loans, etc. There were wide inter-district variations in this regard too. It varied from a high of about 25 per cent in Faridkot to a low of less than three per cent in Jalandhar and Patiala districts.

In three districts, namely, Faridkot, Muktsar and Fatehgarh Sahib this share was more than one-fifth or 20 per cent. In another seven districts, it ranged between 10 and 20 per cent. On the whole, 10 districts had this proportion higher than the average.

On the other side of the scale, in four districts, namely, Jalandhar, Ludhiana, Moga and Patiala this share was less than 5 per cent. Bathinda district with a proportional share of about 6 per cent was below the state average.

Briefly, urban services including public health, public works and public safety consume the dominant share of municipal expenditure in Punjab. The combined share of these services made up for three-fourths of the total municipal expenditure. Public health, water supply and convenience alone consume nearly 45 per cent. Another 22 per cent goes to public works. Public safety consumes remaining 9 per cent. General administrative services consume about 16 per cent of the total municipal budget. It includes salaries only to general staff of municipalities as well as maintenance of building, payment of rent on land and building and maintenance of vehicles. The salaries of municipal staff employed for various urban services such as water supply, sanitation, street lighting, etc. are not included.

There were wide inter-district variations under each of the expenditure heads of municipal expenditure. In three districts of Amritsar, Jalandhar and Patiala expenditure on public health, water supply and conveniences made up for more than half of the total municipal expenditure, in contrast it was less than one-third in the five districts: Kapurthala, Rupnagar, Muktsar, Mansa and Fatehgarh Sahib. Similarly, expenditure on public works was as high as 37 per cent in Mansa district and as low as less than 10 per cent in Gurdaspur district. Expenditure shares of almost all the heads of municipal expenditure in Bathinda district were almost equal to the state averages.

INTER-MUNICIPAL VARIATIONS IN INCOME

After an examination of municipal income and expenditure at the district level, we analyse, in the following, the pattern of municipal income and expenditure at the level of municipalities. Beginning with the municipal income, it comes to notice that the municipal income varied widely among municipalities also. Municipal towns differ widely in terms of their location, municipal status, population size and administrative status. These factors contribute individually as well as collectively to variations in municipal income. Calculated on per capita basis, municipal income differed from a high of Rs. 3857 in Mandi Gobindgarh to a low of Rs. 37 in Khomano (both in Fatehgarh Sahib district). It gives a ratio of 104 between the two. Gobindgarh town is a well known industrial township of North India that is renowned for manufacturing steel from imported scrap. Municipality earns huge income from the octroi, as on an average thousands of trucks, loaded with steel scrap enter the town per month. Against this, Khomano is a small service town without any important industrial or trading enterprise.

There are six municipalities, namely, Gobindgarh, Derabassi, Mohali, Nangal, Rajpura and Doraha where per capita municipal income was more than Rs. 1000. All these towns have important industrial estates in or around them. Interestingly none of these towns have the administrative status of district headquarters. However, locationally all of them fall on important transport nodes. Municipalities earn handsome amount as octroi from vehicles loaded with goods. In all, 13 municipal towns fall in the high income category where per capita municipal income is higher than Rs. 800. Bathinda (Bathinda district) falls in this category of municipal towns (Table 3.8).

In another 24 municipal towns, making up less than one-fifth of all the municipal towns, per capita municipal income ranged between Rs. 600 to 799, categorized as moderately high per capita municipal towns. They are widely distributed in different parts of the state and were mostly medium population sized towns. This category, however, included Amritsar and Moga municipal towns which had the status of district headquarters. The municipal body of Amritsar has the status of municipal corporation.

On the other side of the scale, there were nine towns where per capita municipal income was less than Rs. 200. These include Bhadaur, Handiaya (Sangrur district), Majitha, Khem Karan, Ramdas (Amritsar district), Malaud (Ludhiana), Kot Fatta (Bathinda), Sardulgarh (Mansa) and Khomano (Fatehgarh Sahib). Evidently, five of them were from two districts of Amritsar and Sangrur. Notably, one of them fell in Bathinda district. These have been categorized as very low per capita income municipalities.

TABLE 3.8
Punjab: Classification of Municipalities According to Per Capita Municipal Income, 1997-98

Sr. No.	Income Category (Rs.)	Income Level	Name of Municipalities
1.	More than 800	High	Gobindgarh, Derabassi, Mohali, Nangal, Rajpura, Doraha, Giddarbaha, Sahnewal, Ludhiana, Jalandhar, Bhogpur, Bathinda, Garhshankar **= 13**
2.	600-799	Moderately High	Goraya, Jalalabad, Patran, Guru Har Sahai, Banga, Khanna, Kot Kapura, Amritsar, Ahmedgarh, Nawan Shahr, Kapurthala, Noor Mahal, Banur, Barnala, Moga, Mahil Pur, Begowal, Bhawanigarh, Mukerian, Dina Nagar, Kurali, Bagha Purana, Machhiwara, Sultanpur Lodhi **= 24**
3.	400-599	Moderate	Sangrur, Hoshiarpur, Mullanpur, Tappa, Bhucho Mandi, Khanauri, Raman Mandi, Shah Kot, Nakodar, Patiala, Samrala, Phillaur, Pathankot, Morinda, Nabha, Gardhiwala, Goniana Mandi, Sunam, Dhariwal, Muktsar, Phagwara, Urmar Tanda, Jaitu, Raikot, Dhilawan, Abohar, Rampura Phul, Cheema, Mansa, Jagraon, Samana, Rahon, Maler Kotla, Fazilka, Ghagga, Fatehgarh Churian, Sirhind, Amloh, Gurdaspur, Lehra Gaga, Budhlada, Dharam Kot, Kharar **= 43**
4.	200-399	Low	Malout, Dasua, Hariana, Dirba, Faridkot, Sangat Mandi, Zira, Firozpur, Dhuri, Baretta, Alawalpur, Moonak, Adam Pur, Rup Nagar, Dera Baba Nanak, Batala, Ajnala, Ghanaur, Bhikhi, Jandiala, Bhulath, Anandpur Sahib, Kartarpur, Maur Mandi, Rayya, Dhanaula, Bhikhiwind, Balachaur, Payal, Bassi Pathana, Sujanpur, Bariwala, Patti, Tarn Taran, Kadian, Badhni Kalan, Shri Har Gobindpur, Lohian, Longowal, Makhu, Talwandi Bhai, Sanaur, Shamchaurasi **= 43**
5.	Less than 200	Very Low	Bhadaur, Ramdas, Sardul Garh, Majitha, Handiaya, Malaud, Khem Karan, Kot Fatta, Khamano **= 9**

Of the total 43 municipalities where per capita income ranged between Rs. 200 and Rs. 399 have been categorized as low income municipalities. Except Faridkot and Firozpur all were small and medium class towns and majority of them have a limited industrial or commercial base. Most of them were functioning as service towns. Two of these municipalities, namely, Sangat Mandi and Maur Mandi fall in Bathinda district. In this way, three of eight towns in Bathinda district fall in the low to very low per capita income category of municipal towns.

Remaining, 43 towns, making up about one-third of all the towns in the state, have per capita income ranging between Rs. 400 and Rs. 599, categorized as moderate income municipal towns. Six of them namely, Sangrur, Hoshiarpur, Mansa, Patiala, Muktsar and Gurdaspur function as district headquarters. Half the towns in Bathinda district fall in this category.

Briefly, there are wide inter-municipal town variations in municipal income in Punjab. The highest per capita municipal income municipal town (Gobindgarh in Fatehgarh Sahib district) has a per capita income (Rs. 3857) which is 104 times higher than that of the towns whose income is placed at the lowest rank (Khomano in the same district). Industrial and/or commercial base and nodal location played a significant role in per capita income of municipal towns. Administrative status of a municipal town has a limited role in this regard as 28 municipal towns out of a total of 132 such towns in the state have high per capita income. Against this, 52 towns, making about two-fifths of the total municipal towns, have low to very low per capita municipal income. Only half of the 8 municipal towns in Bathinda district fall in moderate category (between Rs. 400 and Rs. 599) of per capita municipal income. Bathinda town falls in the high per capita municipal income category and remaining three fall in low to very low income category. Evidently municipal towns in Bathinda district fell in all the three municipal income categories.

INTER-MUNICIPAL VARIATIONS IN MUNICIPAL EXPENDITURE

Like income, there are wide inter-town disparities in municipal expenditure in the state. In 1997-98, it varied from a high of Rs. 3299 in Gobindgarh municipal town (Fatehgarh Sahib district) to a low of Rs. 37 per capita in Khomano municipality in the same district making a difference of 89 times between the highest and the lowest per capita expenditure municipalities. Earlier, the difference was 104 times between the highest income and lowest income municipalities. Evidently, inter-town disparities in per capita municipal income were higher than in per capita municipal expenditure.

Per capita income as well as expenditure of Khomano municipality, at the lowest level, were the same (Rs. 37). But the per capita expenditure of Mandi Gobindgarh town, the highest per capita spending municipality, was only about 86 per cent of its per capita income. In 10 out of 132 municipal towns in the state, per capita municipal expenditure was more than Rs. 800, categorized as high spending municipalities (Table 3.9). These included Gobindgarh, Derabassi, Mohali, Nangal, Rajpura, Doraha, Giddarbaha, Ludhiana, Jalandhar and Bathinda.

Earlier, all these were placed in the high per capita income category, indicating a broad conformity between per capita municipal income and expenditure of towns. Earlier in per capita income, the high income category included 13 towns. Municipal towns which failed to find a place in the 'high expenditure' category but were earlier in the 'high income' category included Sahnewal (Ludhiana district), Bhogpur (Jalandhar district) and Garh Shankar (Hoshiarpur district). Obviously, the municipalities in these towns earned more to spend less.

In another 21 municipalities, per capita municipal income ranged between Rs. 600 and Rs. 799, categorized as moderately high expenditure towns. In all, 31 municipal towns making up less than one-fourth of all municipal towns fall in the high to moderately high category of expenditure. Earlier, in per capita income the number of such towns was 37. Notably, municipal towns such as Goraya, Bhogpur and Sahnewal which were earlier in high or moderately high per capita income category, fall now in 'low' or 'very low' category of per capita expenditure. Khanna and Sultanpur Lodhi also came down to 'moderate' category of per capita expenditure from 'moderately high' category of per capita income.

The 47 towns, where per capita expenditure falls between Rs. 400 and Rs. 599, have been categorized as 'moderate' expenditure municipal towns. The number of such towns was 43 earlier.

TABLE 3.9

Punjab: Classification of Municipalities According to Per Capita Municipal Expenditure, 1997-98

Sr. No.	Expenditure Category (Rs.)	Expenditure Level	Name of Municipalities
1.	More than 800	High	Gobindgarh, Derabassi, Mohali, Nangal, Rajpura, Doraha, Giddarbaha, Ludhiana, Jalandhar, Bathinda **= 10**
2.	600-799	Moderately High	Jalalabad, Bhucho Mandi, Patran, Guru Har Sahai, Kot Kapura, Garhshankar, Dina Nagar, Amritsar, Ahmedgarh, Nawan Shahr, Banga, Banur, Sunam, Mahil Pur, Moga, Begowal, Morinda, Kurali, Barnala, Kapurthala, Machhiwara **= 21**
3.	400-599	Moderate	Bhiwanigarh, Phagwara, Mullanpur, Mukerian, Raman Mandi, Gardhiwala, Tappa, Noor Mahal, Sangrur, Samrala, Dhilwan, Patiala, Bagha Purana, Khanauri, Goniana Mandi, Pathankot, Abohar, Shah Kot, Raikot, Hoshiarpur, Rampura Phul, Jagraon, Khanna, Sultanpur Lodhi, Fazilka, Jaitu, Kharar, Fatehgarh Churian, Cheema, Urmar Tanda, Nabha, Nakodar, Dhariwal, Mansa, Amloh, Gurdaspur, Muktsar, Phillaur, Malerkotla, Sirhind, Lehragaga, Budhlada, Firozpur, Zira, Rahon, Faridkot, Dasuya **= 47**
4.	200-399	Low	Malout, Bariwala, Samana, Bhikhi, Dhuri, Baretta, Rup Nagar, Ajnala, Dharamkot, Sangat Mandi, Batala, Anandpur Sahib, Hariana, Ghanaur, Dirba, Moonak, Dhanaula, Maur Mandi, Bhikhiwind, Rayya, Ghagga, Balachaur, Jandiala, Dera Baba Nanak, Makhu, Talwandi Bhai, Bhulath, Bassi Pathana, Adampur, Goraya, Payal, Shri Har Gobindpur, Kartarpur, Patti, Qadian, Tarn Taran, Alawalpur, Bhadaur, Sujanpur **= 39**
5.	Less than 200	Very Low	Badhani Kalan, Longowal, Ramdas, Bhogpur, Lohian, Majitha, Sangrur, Shamchaurari, Malaud, Sahnewal, Khem Karan, Handiaya, Kot Fatta, Sardul Garh, Khamano **= 15**

As many as eight municipal towns, namely, Sangrur, Patiala, Hoshiarpur, Mansa, Gurdaspur, Muktsar, Firozpur and Faridkot have the administrative status of district headquarters. Six of them, namely, Sangrur, Patiala, Hoshiarpur, Mansa, Gurdaspur, Muktsar were earlier in the same category of per capita municipal income. Remaining two, Firozpur and Faridkot, which now fall in 'moderate' category of per capita municipal expenditure, were earlier in the 'low' category of per capita municipal income. Conclusively, they spend more but earn less. Three of the eight municipal towns in Bathinda district fall in the 'moderate' category of per capita expenditure municipal towns. Earlier, the number of such towns was four in per capita municipal income. Bhucho Mandi town, which was earlier in this category, now falls in the 'moderately high' category of per capita expenditure.

In the remaining 54 towns, making two-fifths of the total municipal towns in the state, where per capita expenditure has been less than Rs. 399, the ranking is 'low' to 'very low'. Earlier, the number of such towns was 52. It is surprising to note that municipal towns such as Goraya, Bhogpur and Sahnewal, earlier falling in 'high' or 'moderately high' category had now fallen to the 'low' or 'very low' category of per capita municipal income. On the whole, there has been a broad correspondence between the per capita income and expenditure of municipal towns.

Three of eight towns in Bathinda district fall in the 'low' or 'very low' category of per capita municipal expenditure. Earlier, the same pattern was observed in the case of per capita municipal income. Bhucho Mandi, which was in the 'moderate' category of per capita income and had moved up to the 'moderately high' category of per capita expenditure, was the only exception.

After having an overview of municipal income and expenditure patterns in Punjab at the aggregate level, district level and municipal level, we examine the pattern of subsidy on urban services at all these hierarchical levels.

SUBSIDY ON URBAN SERVICES: COMPARATIVE PICTURE

Municipal bodies in Punjab having different civic and administrative status, size, functions and locations perform a variety of services for the residents under their respective jurisdictions. Some of the municipal services are obligatory in nature, while others are discretionary. The municipal bodies incur huge sums on account of these services. Only a small proportion of this amount is received back by the municipality as income from all such services. The remaining balance, which is a huge amount, is considered as subsidy on municipal or urban services.

During 1995-98, on average annual basis municipal bodies in Punjab incurred an amount of Rs. 2239.03 million on urban services, making up more than 57 per cent of the total municipal expenditure (Rs. 3925.6 millions) during this period. In other words, fifty-seven paisa out of every rupee spent by municipalities in Punjab went to urban services. Rest of the money was incurred on the maintenance of establishment, payment of salaries to the staff, repayment of loans, interest on loans and other miscellaneous items. In this way, while the major share of the municipal expenditure in Punjab went to running and maintaining of urban services, the share and amount of non-developmental expenditure, incurred on establishment, salaries of staff and repayment of loans and interests was no less significant.

The revenue earned by municipal bodies in Punjab for rendering urban services was Rs. 321.8 million during the same period. This made only 8 per cent in total municipal income (average annual) of Rs. 4002.9 million. In other words, only eight paisa out of each rupee earned by municipalities in Punjab through various sources came as revenue income from the urban services. As stated before, the major municipal income sources in Punjab are octroi, tax on houses and lands and grants from the government, rather than income from urban services.

The income earned as revenue on the provision of urban services made for less than 15 per cent of the total municipal expenditure on services. On average annual basis, the income earned during 1995-98 made only Rs. 321.8 million against an expenditure of Rs. 2239.03 million (Table 3.10). In other words, more than 85 paisa of each rupee spent by municipalities in Punjab on urban services during 1995-98 has been the subsidy element. Evidently, urban services are highly subsidized in Punjab. Of course, there are wide inter-district and inter-municipal variations in this regard.

TABLE 3.10
Punjab: Subsidy in Municipal Services by Districts, 1995-98*

Name of the district	*Expenditure on municipal services*	*Income from municipal services (Rs. in lakh)*	*Subsidy on municipal services (Rs. in lakh)*	*Subsidy as % in total expenditure on services*	*Subsidy per capita (in Rs.)*
Gurdaspur	709.04	90.96	618.08	87.17	165
Amritsar	2665.07	605.11	2059.96	77.29	238
Kapurthala	495.26	130.62	364.64	73.63	193
Jalandhar	3468.09	427.94	3040.15	87.66	451
Nawan Shahr	179.06	17.94	161.12	89.98	221
Hoshiarpur	581.43	91.57	489.86	84.25	230
Rupnagar	713.38	76.28	637.10	89.30	274
Ludhiana	6756.29	780.16	5976.13	88.45	473
Firozpur	769.60	154.35	615.25	79.94	184
Faridkot	487.89	28.14	459.75	94.23	307
Muktsar	415.87	37.75	378.12	90.92	237
Moga	492.04	87.98	404.06	82.12	295
Bathinda	1094.11	94.99	999.12	91.32	376
Mansa	183.00	27.65	155.35	84.89	145
Sangrur	1124.71	181.99	942.72	83.82	204
Patiala	1524.28	318.60	1205.68	79.10	245
Fatehgarh Sahib	731.18	66.02	665.16	90.97	659
Punjab	22390.30	3218.05	19172.25	85.63	315

* Expenditure and income figures on municipal services are annual averages for the three years 1995-98.

Source: Calculated from *Statistical Abstract, Punjab* for 1997-98, Directorate of Economic and Statistical Organisation, Punjab, Chandigarh.

INTER-DISTRICT VARIATIONS IN SUBSIDY SHARE

As stated above, on an average more than 85 per cent or Rs. 321.8 million of the total annual municipal expenditure (Rs. 2239.03 million) on urban services went as subsidy element in Punjab during 1995-98. Among districts, it varied from a high of 94.2 per cent in Faridkot district to a low of 73.6 per cent in Kapurthala district.

Nine of the seventeen districts in Punjab have this share higher than the average (85.6 per cent) for all the municipal towns in Punjab (Table 3.11). This included Gurdaspur, Jalandhar, Nawan Shahr, Rupnagar, Ludhiana, Faridkot, Muktsar, Bathinda and Fatehgarh Sahib. Districts falling in this category belong to all parts of the state. It is, however, to be noted that three (Faridkot,

TABLE 3.11

Punjab: Districts Classified According to Share in Subsidy on Total Expenditure for Urban Services, 1995-98*

Sr. No.	*Subsidy Share in Percentage*	*Name of the District*	
1.	Above 85	Gurdaspur, Jalandhar, Nawan Shahr, Ludhiana, Faridkot, Muktsar, Bathinda, Fatehgarh, Rupnagar	= 9
2.	80-85	Hoshiarpur, Moga, Mansa, Sangrur	= 4
3.	Below 80	Amritsar, Kapurthala, Firozpur, Patiala	= 4

* Three years average.

Bathinda and Muktsar) of the four top ranking districts (fourth one being Fatehgarh Sahib) in this regard, each having more than 90.0 per cent subsidy share, fall in South-West Punjab. In these districts, municipal bodies have to incur relatively large amounts on water supply especially for developing and maintaining water pipelines brought from canals, located distantly from towns and to conserve water due to near aridic conditions. The underground water in this part of the state is brackish, hence unfit for drinking purposes. At the same time, water requirement for drinking and other purposes here is relatively higher than other parts of the state due to the arid climate.

In four districts, percentage of subsidy on urban services varied between 80-85 per cent. These included Hoshiarpur, Moga, Mansa and Sangrur districts. Again, three of the four districts in this category fall in south-western Punjab, having high aridity conditions and brackish water in acquifer. Provision of drinking water, which is one of the obligatory functions of municipalities in Punjab as well as in other parts of the country, need high capital investment. As it is a basic necessity of life, domestic water supply rates are kept low. In addition, drinking water supply at public places and slum colonies is free of cost. Even the cost involved in providing water supply is not fully charged. The ultimate result is a high degree of subsidy on supply of water by the municipalities to their residents. Thus, greater the consumption of water available from municipal sources in a town, higher is the subsidy element on water supply.

Remaining four districts of Amritsar, Kapurthala, Firozpur and Patiala have the subsidy proportion less than 80 per cent. Among these, Kapurthala provided the lowest and Firozpur the highest share. Firozpur, a district sharing an international border with Pakistan, has arid climate. In this region, ground water being unfit for human consumption, canal water is transported over long distances before it is supplied to different parts of the towns in the region.

Briefly, urban services in Punjab are highly subsidized. Only an amount of Rs. 321.8 million, making only 8.0 per cent of total municipal expenditure (on average annual basis) and less than 15 per cent of total municipal expenditure on urban services, is recovered by the municipalities. In other words, 85 paisa out of each rupee spent by municipal bodies on urban services goes in subsidy. However, there were wide inter-district variations in this regard. In general, municipal bodies in districts falling in South-West Punjab provided higher proportion of subsidy on urban services. For ecological reasons, per head cost of providing urban services, which in turn are highly subsidized, are much higher in this part of the state. Bathinda district is ranked second among the 17 districts in the state in terms of the subsidy element in urban services.

INTER-DISTRICT VARIATIONS IN PER CAPITA SUBSIDY ON SERVICES

Inter-district disparities in subsidy element on urban services gets more accentuated in per capita terms than in proportional share. Against the state average of Rs. 315 per capita per annum subsidy on urban services, it ranged from a high of Rs. 659 in Fatehgarh Sahib district to a low of only Rs. 145 in Mansa district. It gave a ratio of 1:4.5 between the highest and lowest values. Earlier, this ratio was only 1:1.3 in case of proportional share of subsidy on various urban services.

In five districts, namely Fatehgarh Sahib, Ludhiana, Jalandhar, Bathinda and Faridkot per capita subsidy on urban services was more than Rs. 300. Two of them (Jalandhar and Ludhiana) are high developed, one (Faridkot) is moderately developed and remaining two (Fatehgarh Sahib and Bathinda) are lesser developed districts in Punjab. In this way, municipal bodies in more developed districts provided higher per capita subsidy on urban services than those in the lesser developed districts. Municipal bodies in highly developed districts have higher revenue generation capacity in comparison to those in the lesser developed districts. For this reason, municipal bodies in developed districts incurred higher capita expenditure on different urban services than those in the lesser developed districts. That is the reason for a strong positive correspondence between per capita income and expenditure of municipalities at the district level (Map 3.3). Per capita municipal income and expenditure of municipalities at the district level finds a strong association,

Map 3.3

PUNJAB
Spatial Correspondence between Municipal Income and Expenditure 1997-98
(Data by districts)

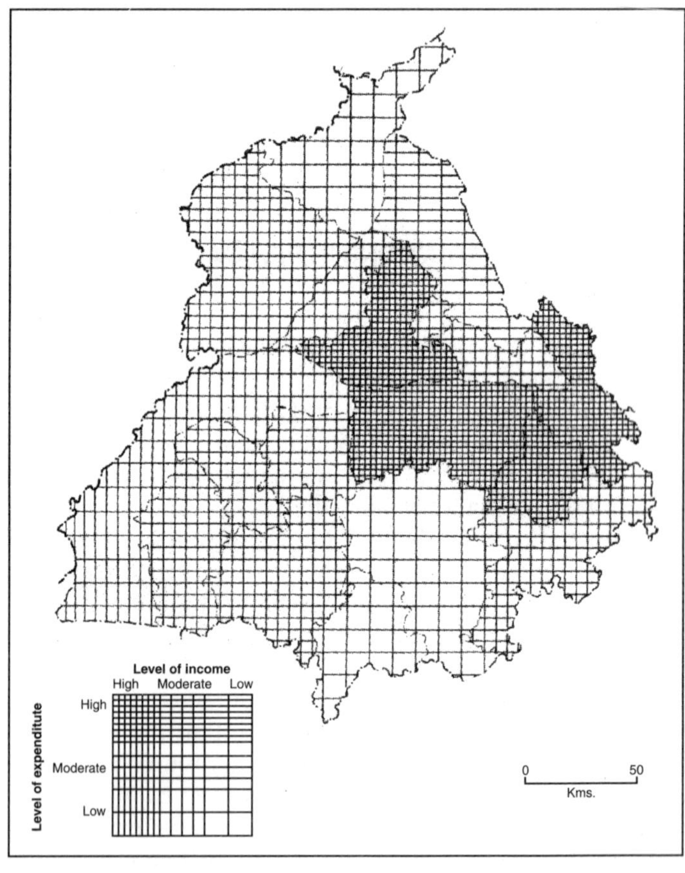

co-efficient of rank correlation value being r = 0.86 (Table 3.12). Association between municipal per capita municipal expenditure and subsidy was still stronger (r = 0.88).

TABLE 3.12

Punjab: Association between Per Capita Municipal Income and Per Capita Subsidy on Municipal Services by Districts, 1997-98

		Ranking of districts in per capita municipal		
S. No.	*Name of district*	*Subsidy on service*	*Income*	*Expenditure*
1.	Fatehgarh Sahib	1	1	1
2.	Ludhiana	2	3	2
3.	Jalandhar	3	4	4
4.	Bathinda	4	5	5
5.	Faridkot	5	12	10
6.	Moga	6	8	7
7.	Rupnagar	7	2	3
8.	Patiala	8	6	8
9.	Amritsar	9	7	6
10.	Muktsar	10	13	12
11.	Hoshiarpur	11	10	14
12.	Nawan Shahr	12	9	11
13.	Sangrur	13	14	15
14.	Kapurthala	14	11	9
15.	Firozpur	15	15	13
16.	Gurdaspur	16	16	16
17.	Mansa	17	17	17

Notes: (i) Rank correlation value between municipal income and subsidy = 0.856.
(ii) Rank correlation value between municipal expenditure and subsidy = 0.878.

In other words, higher the per capita municipal income in a district higher would be the amount of per capita subsidy given by municipalities in that district on urban services. Similarly, higher the per capita earnings of a municipality, higher is their spending on urban services. Since, urban services are highly subsidized, more the expenditure of a municipality on urban services more is the per capita amount of subsidy it provided on urban services to its residents.

On the whole, municipalities in four districts provided higher per capita amount of subsidy on urban services than the state average. Against this, there has been a district (Mansa) where per capita subsidy on urban services was less than half of the state average of Rs. 315. In fact, there are at least four districts, namely, Mansa, Gurdaspur, Firozpur and Kapurthala where per capita amount of subsidy on urban services was less than Rs. 200 (Table 3.10).

Briefly, inter-district variations in per capita amount of subsidy on urban services were more pronounced than in proportional shares of subsidy. Ratio between the highest and the lowest per capita amount of municipal subsidy at district level was 1:4.5 against this the ratio between the highest and the lowest share of municipal subsidy was 1:1.3.

Per capita amount of municipal subsidy on urban services in the district finds a strong positive association with the development of the districts. In developed districts, municipalities tend to generate high income from their revenue sources which enhance their capacity to spend on urban services. Since most of the urban services are highly subsidized, the amount of subsidy, both in proportional and per capita terms, gets increased in such districts. This is probably the reason why there is a still higher association between the per capita municipal expenditure and per capita municipal subsidy of districts in the state.

MAIN HIGHLIGHTS

- The major sources of municipal income in Punjab include octroi, house and land tax, and grants from the government. On the other hand, the main expenditure heads include the establishment, salary of the municipal staff, municipal services such as water supply, electricity supply, sanitation, construction and maintenance of roads, parks, etc. and the repayment of loans and interest on loans. In the financial year 1997-98, total municipal income in Punjab had been Rs. 4188.01 million, against an expenditure of Rs. 3996.23 million. Earlier in 1965-66, total municipal income had been Rs. 144.85 million, against an expenditure of Rs. 136.90 million. Evidently, there is a tradition to maintain a surplus budget by the municipal administration in the state.
- Aggregate municipal income, from all sources, increased by more than eight times during 1980-98 in the state of Punjab. Against this, increase in expenditure was of less than eight times during the same time. It seems that the tendency to

keep a surplus budget has been responsible for this. Increase in municipal income and expenditure, if seen in per capita terms, is rather disappointing. In per capita terms, income increased by about six times and expenditure by more than five times during 1980-98.

- The quantum of grants from the government has increased substantially after 1992-93. Per capita municipal income which was Rs. 395 in 1992-93 increased to Rs. 497 in 1993-94 and to Rs. 612 in 1994-95. It rose to Rs. 687 in 1997-98. Similarly, per capita expenditure rose from Rs. 383 to Rs. 475, then to Rs. 595 and finally to Rs. 655 during the same period. Municipal budgets recorded the maximum surplus in 1997-98 against a maximum deficit in 1982-83.
- Like the municipal income, municipal expenditure too differed widely among the districts. It ranged from a high of Rs. 1510 in Fatehgarh Sahib district to a low of Rs. 373 in Mansa district, giving a difference of 4 times, i.e. a ratio of 1:40. Earlier, in the case of municipal income this ratio was slightly higher (4.24 times) than that of expenditure. Bathinda district with a per capita municipal expenditure of Rs. 670 was placed fifth from the top among all the seventeen districts in the state. In line with its position among top five municipal income districts in the state it was again placed in five top districts of Fatehgarh Sahib, Rupnagar, Ludhiana, Jalandhar and Bathinda.
- The combined municipal expenditure of the top three districts of Ludhiana, Amritsar and Jalandhar made up more than half or about 52 per cent against their total combined income of 51 per cent and combined urban population of about 46 per cent. Against this, the combined municipal expenditure of eight bottom ranking districts, namely, Fatehgarh Sahib, Kapurthala, Hoshiarpur, Muktsar, Faridkot, Moga, Mansa and Nawan Shahr made up only about 18 per cent of the total municipal expenditure in the state. Their combined income share was 18.1 per cent and population share was about 19 per cent.
- Octroi is the major source of municipal income in Punjab. In 1997-98, nearly 58 per cent of total municipal income came from this source. There were, however, wide inter-district variations. It varied from a high of about 80 per cent

in Rupnagar district to a low of about 37 per cent in Muktsar district. In Bathinda district, octroi contributed two-thirds or 66.7 per cent of the total municipal income. The share of octroi in income of municipalities in Bathinda district has been higher than the state average. In fact, Bathinda ranks next only to Rupnagar, the highest ranking district in this context. There are seven other districts, including Bathinda district, where octroi contributes higher than the state average.

- Three urban services, namely, public health, public works and public safety consume the dominant share of municipal expenditure in Punjab. The combined share of these services made up for three-fourths of the total municipal expenditure. Public health, water supply and conveniences alone consume nearly 45 per cent. Another 22 per cent goes to public works. Public safety consumes another 9 per cent. Besides, general administrative services consume about 16 per cent of the total municipal budget. It includes salaries only to general staff of municipalities as well as maintenance of building, payment of rent on land and building and maintenance of vehicles. The salaries of municipal staff employed for various urban services such as water supply, sanitation, street lighting, etc. are not included.
- There were wide inter-district variations under each of the expenditure heads of municipal expenditure. In three districts of Amritsar, Jalandhar and Patiala expenditure on public health, water supply and convenience made up for more than half of the total municipal expenditure, in contrast it was less than one-third in the five districts, Kapurthala, Rupnagar, Muktsar, Mansa and Fatehgarh Sahib. Similarly, expenditure on public works was as high as 37 per cent in Mansa district and as low as less than 10 per cent in Gurdaspur district. Expenditure shares of almost all the heads of municipal expenditure in Bathinda district were almost equal to the state averages.
- There are wide inter-municipal town variations in municipal income in Punjab. The highest per capita municipal income town (Gobindgarh in Fatehgarh Sahib district) has a per capita income (Rs. 3857) which is 104 times higher than that of the towns whose income is placed at the lowest rank

(Khomano in the same district). Industrial and/or commercial base and nodal location played a significant role in per capita income of towns. Administrative status of a municipal town has a limited role in this regard as 28 municipal towns out of a total of 132 such towns in the state have high per capita income.

- Like income, there are wide inter-town disparities in municipal expenditure in the state. In 1997-98, it varied from a high of Rs. 3299 in Gobindgarh municipal town (Fatehgarh Sahib district) to a low of Rs. 37 per capita in Khomano municipality in the same district making a difference of 89 times between the highest and the lowest per capita municipal expenditure. Earlier, the difference was 104 times between the highest income and lowest income municipalities. Evidently, inter-town disparities in per capita municipal income were higher than in per capita expenditure.
- Three of eight towns in Bathinda district fall in the 'low' or 'very low' categories of per capita municipal expenditure. Earlier, the same pattern was observed in the case of per capita municipal income. Bhucho Mandi, which was in the 'moderate' category of per capita income and had moved up to the 'moderately high' category of per capita expenditure, was the only exception.
- During 1995-98, on average annual basis municipal bodies in Punjab incurred an amount of Rs. 2239.03 million on urban services, making up more than 57 per cent of the total municipal expenditure (Rs. 3925.6 millions) during this period. In other words, fifty-seven paisa out of every rupee spent by municipalities in Punjab went to urban services. Rest of the money was incurred on the maintenance of establishment, payment of salaries to the staff, repayment of loans, interest on loans and other miscellaneous items. In this way, while the major share of the municipal expenditure in Punjab went in to running and maintaining of urban services, the share and amount of non-developmental expenditure, incurred on establishment, salaries of staff and repayment of loans and interests was no less significant.
- Urban services in Punjab are highly subsidized. An amount of Rs. 321.8 million, making only 8.0 per cent of total

municipal expenditure (on average annual basis) and less than 15 per cent of total municipal expenditure on urban services, is recovered by the municipalities. In other words, 85 paisa out of each rupee spent by municipal bodies on urban services goes in subsidy. However, there were wide inter-district variations in this regard. In general, municipal bodies in districts falling in South-West Punjab provided higher proportion of subsidy on urban services. For ecological reasons, per head cost of providing urban services, which in turn are highly subsidized, are much higher in this part of the state. Bathinda district is ranked second among the 17 districts in the state in terms of the subsidy element in urban services.

- Inter-district disparities in subsidy element on urban services gets more accentuated in per capita terms than in proportional share. Against the state average of Rs. 315 per capita per annum subsidy on urban services, it ranged from a high of Rs. 659 in Fatehgarh Sahib district to a low of only Rs. 145 in Mansa district. It gave a ratio of 1:4.5 between the highest and lowest values. Earlier, this ratio was only 1:1.3 in case of proportional share of subsidy on various urban services.
- Per capita amount of municipal subsidy on urban services in the district finds a strong positive association with the development of the districts. In developed districts, municipalities tend to generate high income from their own income sources which enhance their capacity to spend on urban services. Since most of the urban services are highly subsidized, the amount of subsidy, both in proportional and per capita terms, gets increased in such districts. This is probably the reason why there is a still higher association between the per capita municipal expenditure and per capita municipal subsidy of districts in the state.

4

Public Health and Security Services

WATER SUPPLY

The supply of safe drinking water has been listed among the statuary functions of municipal bodies in India, recognizing the essentiality of water as one of the basic needs of life. However, neither do all the municipalities provide this service to their residents nor is the coverage universal among towns, which are providing this service. In 1991, about one-fourth of the total urban population of the country was still left unserved by safe drinking water facility. Also, there were wide regional variations. In 1991, population coverage under safe drinking water supply at the national level ranged from a high of 93 per cent in Himachal Pradesh to a low of only 33 per cent in Assam. In Punjab, 53 per cent of the total urban population was covered under the safe drinking water supply scheme.

In Punjab, a medium sized state, the wide variations in physiography plays a significant role in determining the need and availability of drinking water in its different parts. In the semi-desertic south-western Punjab, the requirement for water is more than what is available from local sources. Against this, in the well drained loamy soil areas of the Sutlej-Beas divide, popularly known as the 'Doaba' region, the availability of water is adequate.

Bathinda district, situated in semi-desertic south-western Punjab, has distinct physiographic personality. Major parts of the district have sandy soils and brackish underground water. Thus, not only is availability of underground water scarce but it is also nearly unfit for human consumption. Hence, the government has to arrange alternative sources of drinking water in the district. In urban areas, municipal bodies are responsible for supplying water to their residents, while, in rural areas, the rural wing of the Public Health Engineering Department (PHED) of the Punjab Government performs the job.

This chapter attempts to study the changes in spatio-temporal distribution of water supply network, the municipal income and expenditure as well as the subsidy component on water supply in municipal towns of Bathinda district. The basic objective is to understand and compare the subsidy component in water supply services by the municipalities in Bathinda.

Sources and Coverage

The available underground water in the district being almost unfit for the human consumption, the surface water has been the main source of drinking water. The water from the Sirhind Canal, which passes through this district, is supplied for drinking purpose. Piped water connections and hand pumps, the two main methods of water supply, are used by the municipalities for the purpose. Water taps are used for water supply to individual households, while stand posts and hand-pumps are placed at public places.

The canal or surface water is the dominant source of`water supply in urban areas of Bathinda district. This is mainly because the ground water is brackish in major parts of the district, and unfit for human consumption. However, in towns where ground water is palatable it is used for water supply. In four municipalities, surface or canal water is the exclusive source of water supply. In Goniana Mandi and Bathinda, both surface water and ground water are used for water supply. Goniana Mandi mixes surface water with ground water before supplying. Bhucho Mandi and Rampura Phul, the remaining two municipalities, depend mainly on ground water. It is only in the case of emergency that Rampura Phul municipality uses canal water. Bhucho Mandi, located about four kilometers from the canal has sweet drinkable ground water as the main source of supply.

With the exception of Raman Mandi, the municipalities in the district use both piped and non-piped modes of supplying water. In Raman Mandi, the domestic connection is the only source of water supply. The domestic connections and stand posts are the piped water sources, while the hand-pump is a non-piped source. The municipalities install domestic connections on demand, while stand-posts and hand pumps are placed at important public places like the markets, public library, and government offices. The former may be termed as 'demand' based and the latter as 'need' based source of water supply. It is the 'demand' based source that fetches revenue for the municipalities while the rest is free of cost.

Before 1980-81, there were about 13 thousand water tap connections in the municipal towns of the district and these were available only in six towns then. In two municipal towns, namely, Sangat Mandi and Kot Fatta[1] tapped water supply was not available (Table 4.1). The number of water tap connections rose to more than 30 thousand by 1997-98, registering an increase of 133 per cent in eighteen years. The Bathinda municipal committee, having the largest number of water connections (7443) before 1980-81, had the majority (58 per cent) of all connections in towns of the district. Even in 1997-98, the share of Bathinda (M.C.) was 56 per cent. Bathinda town has the status of district headquarters and is the largest town in the district. Rampura Phul, the second largest town in district, had another 14 per cent of total connections in 1997-98. Remaining 30 per cent water connections were in the towns of Maur Mandi, Raman Mandi, Goniana Mandi, Bhucho Mandi, Sangat Mandi and Kot Fatta. In 1991, their combined population made up about 27 per cent of the total urban population in the district. Against this, Bathinda town had a share of 60 per cent of total urban population in the district. Thus, small-sized towns were better placed in this regard.

The number of tap water connections grew faster in municipalities where the number of such connections was small at the base year. Index numbers, calculated for a better understanding of the progress in the tap water supply connections, reveal that Kot Fatta, where water connection service was introduced as late as in 1994-95, had an index number which registered the highest increase from 100 in 1994-95 to 361 in 1997-98. On the other hand, Raman Mandi registered the lowest increase of 77 with index number moving from 100 to 177 during

1. In Sangat Mandi town water connections were introduced in 1985-86 and in Kot Fatta town in 1994-95. Prior to that, the hand pump remained the only source of water supply.

TABLE 4.1

Bathinda District: Progress in Water Connections by Municipalities, 1980-98

Financial year	*Bathinda*		*Rampura Phul*		*Maur Mandi*		*Raman Mandi*		*Goniana Mandi*		*Bhucho Mandi*		*Sangat Mandi*		*Kot-Fatta*		*All Towns*	
	Cumulative numbers	*Index number*	*Cumulative numbers*	*Index number*	*Cumulative numbers*	*Index number*	*Cumulative numbers*	*Index number*	*Cumulative numbers*	*Index number*	*Cumulative numbers*	*Index number*	*Cumulative numbers*	*Index number*	*Cumulative numbers*	*Index number*	*Cumulative numbers*	*Index number*
Before 1980-81	7443	100	1657	100	950	100	1350	100	966	100	571	100	—	—	—	—	12937	100
1980-81	7668	103	1707	103	1034	108	1400	103	1009	104	585	102	—	—	—	—	13403	104
1981-82	8048	108	1747	105	1104	116	1449	107	1053	109	621	108	—	—	—	—	14022	105
1982-83	8606	116	1807	109	1168	122	1500	111	1079	112	730	127	—	—	—	—	14890	106
1983-84	9037	121	1905	114	1227	129	1551	114	1107	115	896	157	—	—	—	—	15723	106
1984-85	9629	129	1990	120	1293	136	1611	119	1139	118	947	166	—	—	—	—	16609	106
1985-86	10194	137	2092	126	1329	139	1651	122	1155	120	1005	176	147	100	—	—	17573	106
1986-87	10726	144	2362	142	1403	147	1692	125	1227	127	1095	192	193	131	—	—	18698	106
1987-88	11234	151	2512	151	1458	153	1755	130	1283	132	1176	206	226	153	—	—	19644	105
1988-89	11600	156	2700	168	1519	159	1805	133	1326	137	1241	217	270	183	—	—	20461	104
1989-90	12012	161	2950	178	1589	167	1861	137	1380	143	1290	226	293	199	—	—	21375	104
1990-91	12457	167	3236	195	1632	171	1914	141	1416	147	1360	238	307	208	—	—	22322	104
1991-92	12980	174	3367	203	1685	177	1959	145	1453	151	1411	247	318	215	—	—	23173	104
1992-93	13561	182	3501	211	1750	184	2019	149	1476	153	1464	256	328	222	—	—	24099	104
1993-94	14751	198	3648	220	1808	190	2093	155	1515	157	1578	275	363	246	—	—	25756	107
1994-95	15435	207	3881	234	1879	197	2162	160	1582	164	1672	292	460	312	150	100	27221	106
1995-96	15865	213	4046	244	1945	204	2262	167	1627	169	1743	308	474	322	483	322	28445	105
1996-97	16209	218	4130	249	2017	212	2312	171	1692	176	1847	323	490	333	497	331	29194	103
1997-98	16732	225	4225	255	2079	217	2401	177	1756	183	1899	332	507	345	547	361	30146	103

Note: To calculate index numbers, the number of connections at the base is taken as 100.
Source: Data calculated from *The Water Supply Register* of different municipalities for various years.

1980-1998. Remaining municipalities fall in between the two extremes (Table 4.1 and Fig. 4.1). Notably, tap water connections service is a recent introduction in Kot Fatta.

Fig. 4.1

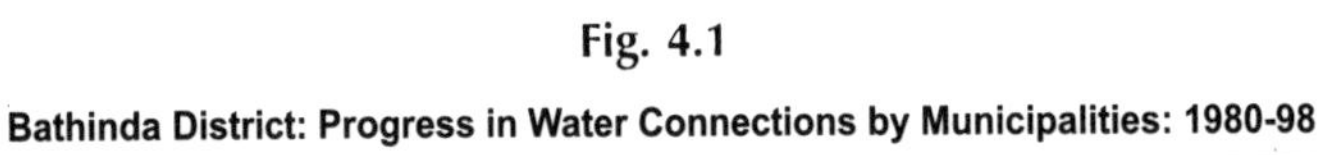

Bathinda District: Progress in Water Connections by Municipalities: 1980-98

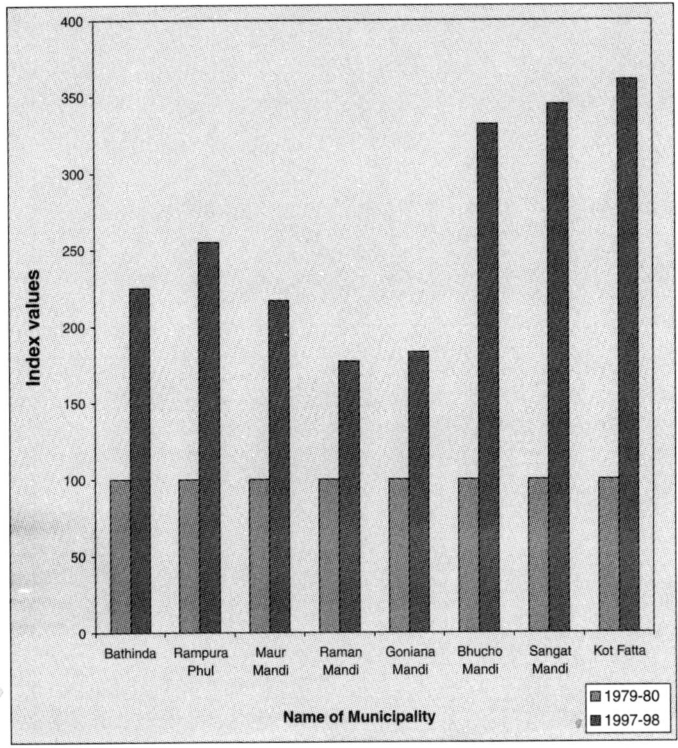

Note: In Sangat Mandi, tap water supply started late in 1985-86 and in Kot Fatta in 1994-95. Hence, the respective base year for these towns are 1985-86 and 1994-95, respectively.

The period from 1985 to 1989 is marked with rapid expansion in the number of tap water connections in Rampura Phul. In Bhucho Mandi, such a situation existed from 1982 to 1989. Also the numerical growth of water connections in different towns of the district coincided with the receipt of grants received from various sources to augment water supply (see Maps 4.1 to 4.8).

In brief, while Bathinda (M.C.) tops in total number of tap water connections, Kot Fatta Mandi recorded the highest growth in this regard.

Map 4.1

Bathinda Municipality
Water Supply : Spatial Expansion and Coverage

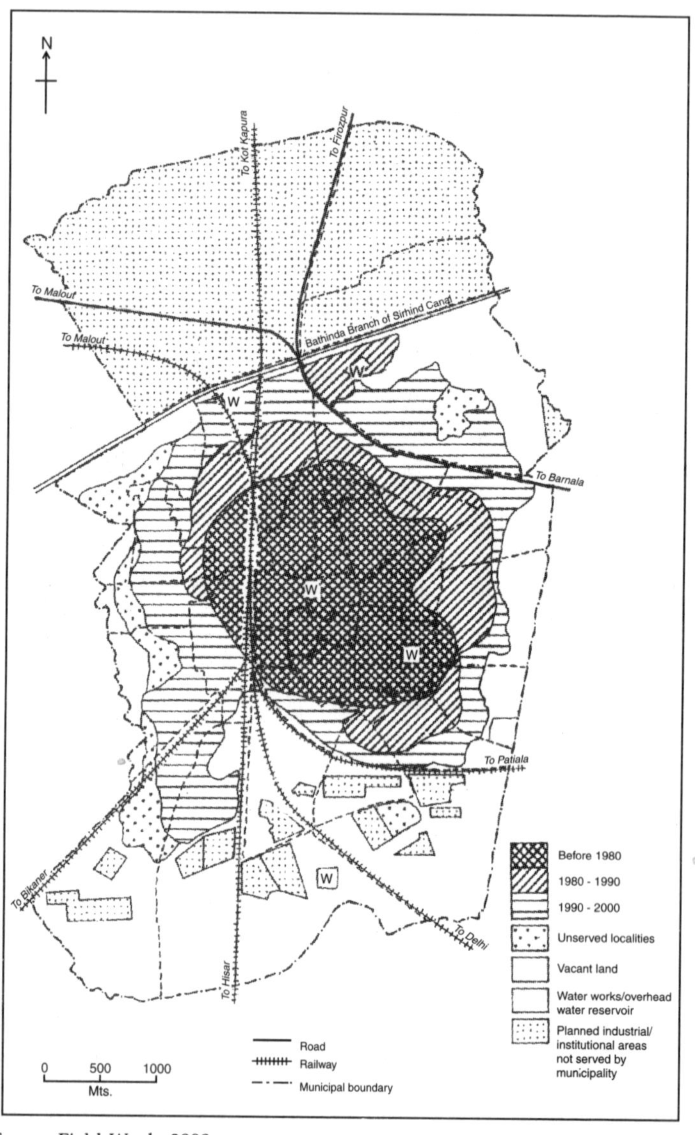

Source: Field Work, 2000.

Map 4.2

Rampura Phul Municipality
Water Supply Spatial Expansion and Coverage

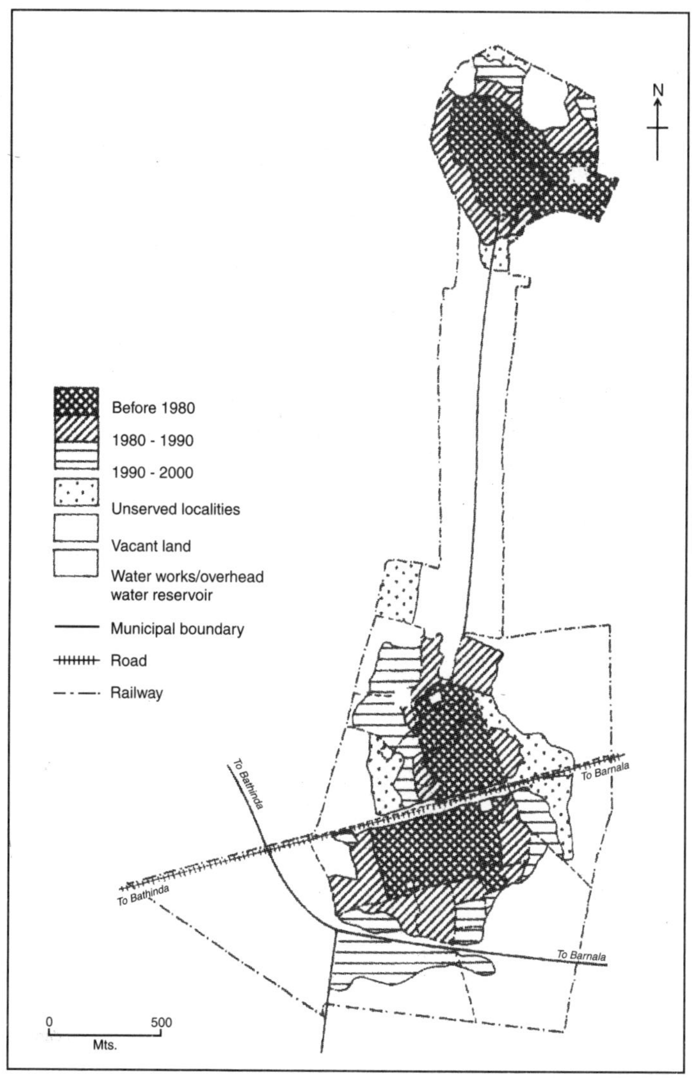

Source: Field Work, 2000.

Map 4.3

Maur Mandi Municipality

Water Supply: Spatial Expansion and Coverage

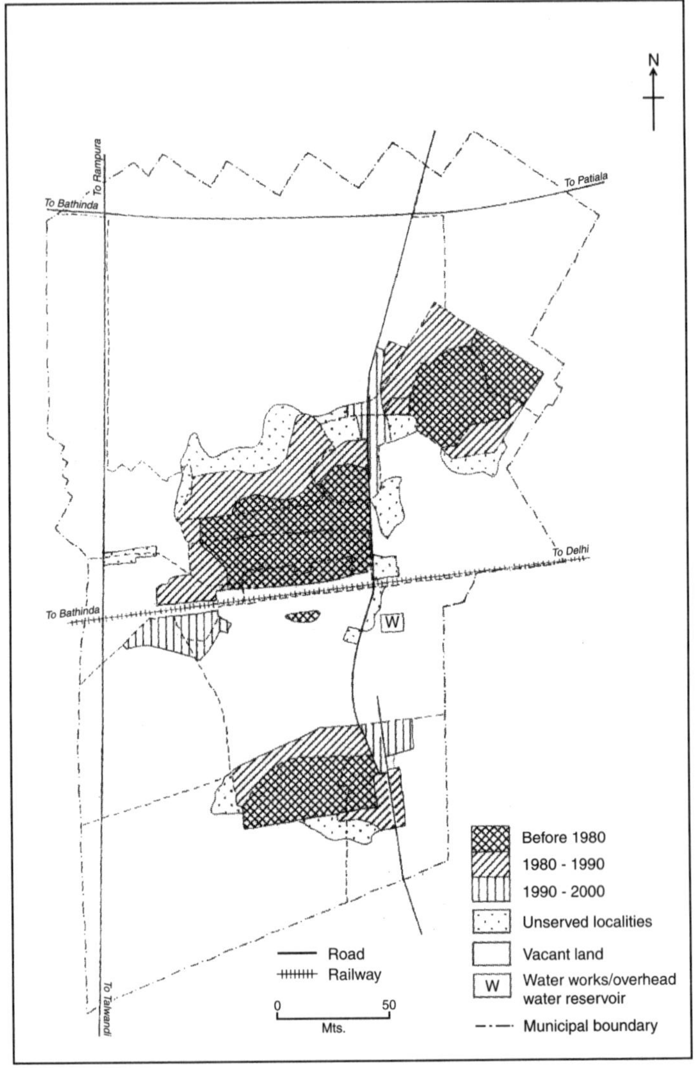

Source: Field Work, 2000.

Map 4.4

Raman Mandi Municipality

Water Supply: Spatial Expansion and Coverage

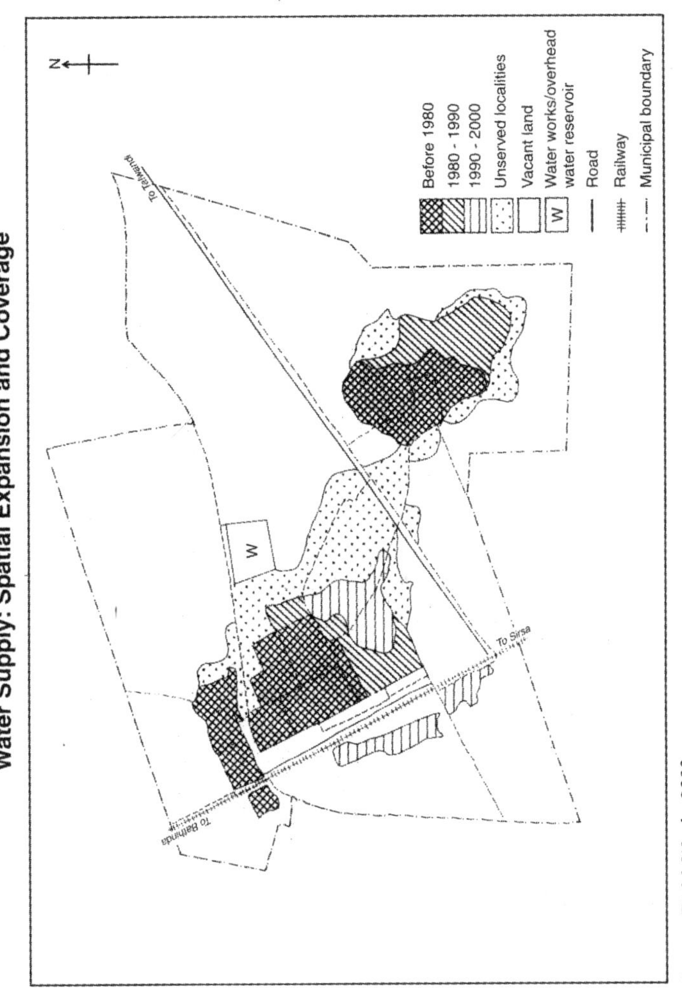

Source: Field Work, 2000.

Map 4.5

Goniana Mandi Municipality

Water Supply: Spatial Expansion and Coverage

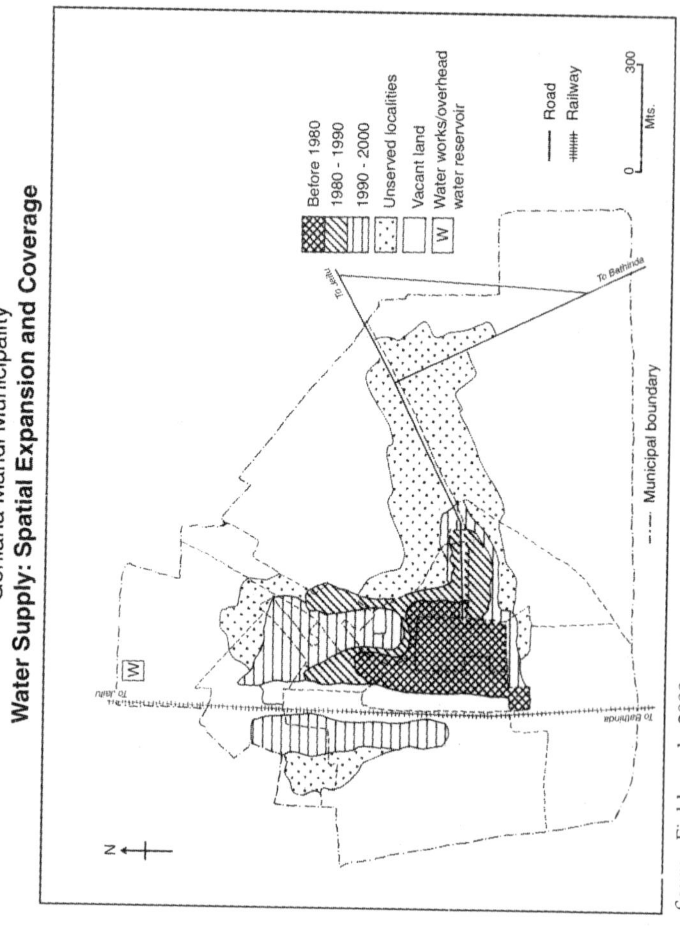

Source: Field work, 2000.

Map 4.6

Bhucho Mandi Municipality
Water Supply: Spatial Expansion and Coverage

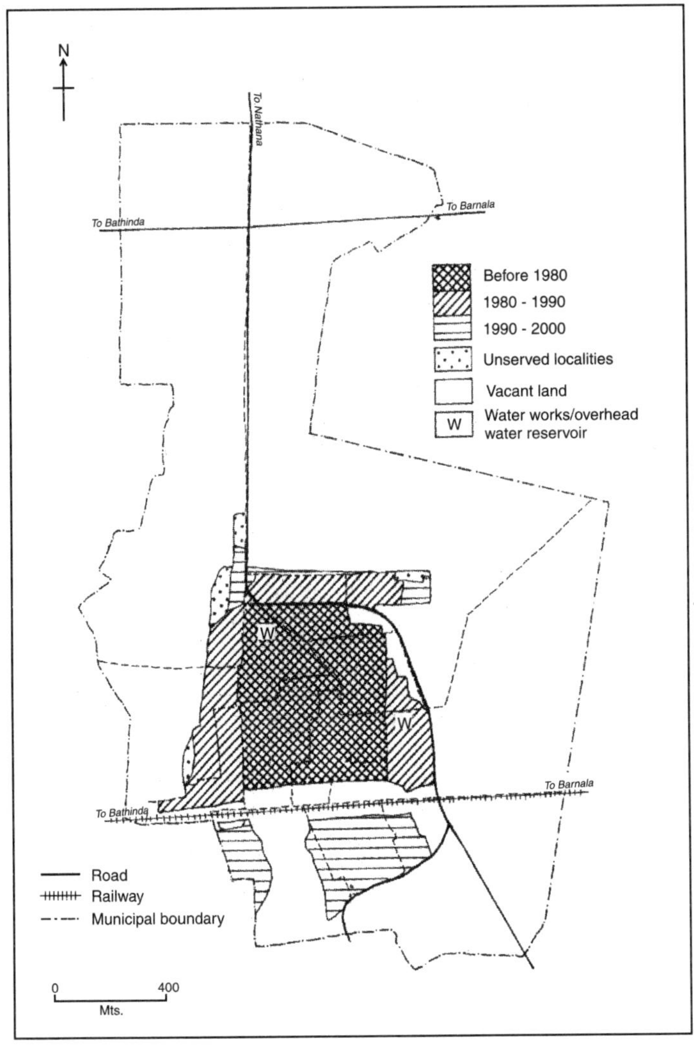

Map 4.7

Kot Fatta Municipality

Water Supply: Spatial Expansion and Coverage

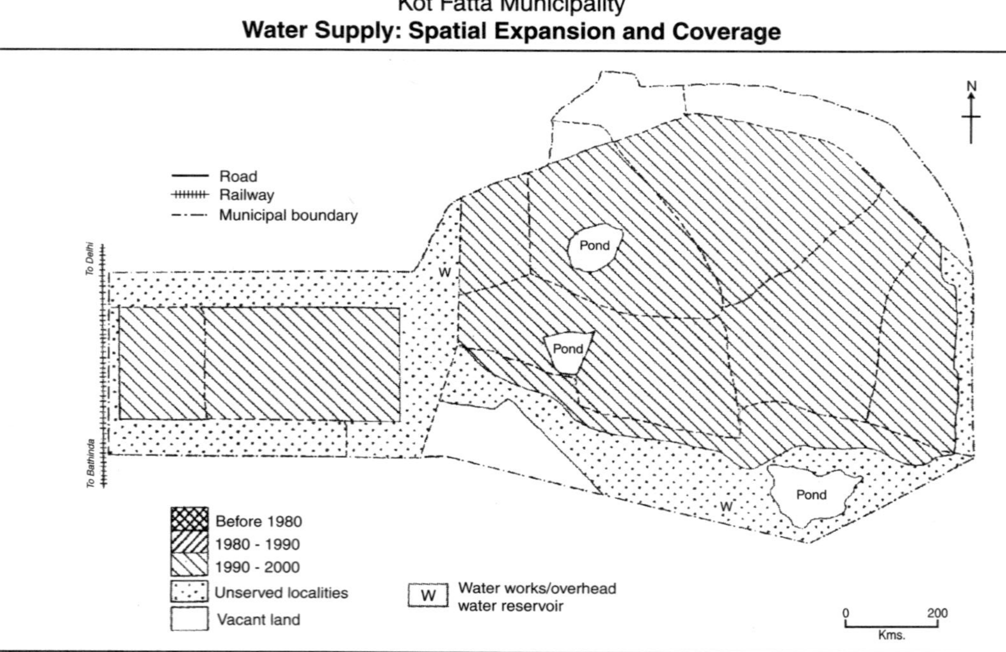

Source: Field Work, 2000.

Map 4.8

Sangat Mandi Municipality

Water Supply: Spatial Expansion and Coverage

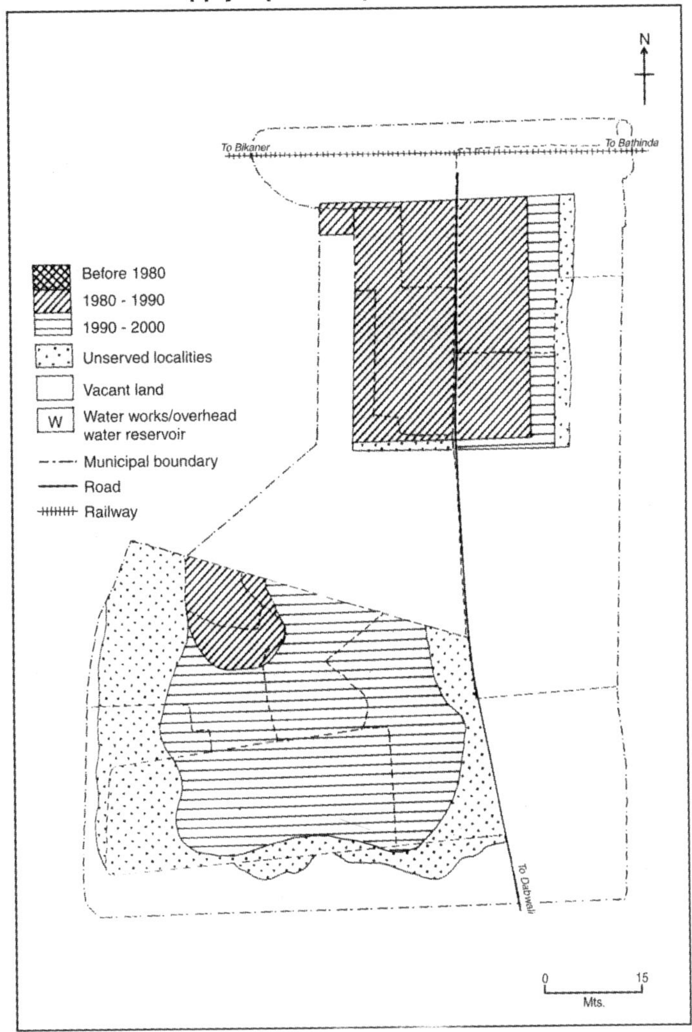

Source: Field Work, 2000.

EXPENDITURE PATTERN AND TRENDS

A. Aggregate Expenditure on Water Supply

On an average, municipalities in Bathinda district incurred an expenditure of more than Rs. 71 lakh per annum on water supply during the years 1980-98. It comes to about Rs. 9 lakh per municipality per annum. However, there were wide inter-municipal variations in this regard. It varied from a high of Rs. 43.31 lakh in Bathinda town to a low of Rs. 75 thousand in Sangat Mandi town. The amount spent on water supply by Bathinda municipal town makes up 61 per cent of total municipal expenditure in the district. Coincidently its population comprised 60 per cent of total urban population in the district in 1991 enumerating the expenditure share of Bathinda municipality as little higher than its population share.

In 1982-83, aggregate annual expenditure for all municipalities was about Rs. 25 lakh (Table 4.2) averaging to about Rs. 4 lakh per municipality. The range was from a high of about Rs. 13 lakh in Bathinda town to a low of little over Rs. 1 lakh in Goniana Mandi. It must be mentioned, however, that two of the eight municipalities in the district were not providing this facility to their residents. These municipalities were Kot Fatta and Sangat Mandi.

In 1987-88, when aggregate annual expenditure for all the municipalities was about Rs. 41 lakh or Rs. 6 lakh per municipality, it varied from a high of Rs. 17 lakh in Bathinda town to a low of only Rs. 0.62 lakh in Sangat Mandi—a new entrant in the field of water supply service. Inter-municipal variations in expenditure on water supply declined marginally as compared to 1982-83. This is supported in a marginal decline in co-efficient of variability index to 0.89 in 1987-88 from 0.94 in 1982-83.

In 1992-93, total municipal expenditure on water supply rose to more than Rs. 94 lakh from Rs. 41 lakh in 1987-88. It varied from a maximum of more than Rs. 63 lakh in Bathinda town to a minimum of more than one lakh rupees in Sangat Mandi. The share of Bathinda municipality in total municipal expenditure on water supply in the district was about 67 per cent. Its population share of the total urban population in the district was about 60 per cent in 1991. Evidently, its expenditure share was much higher

TABLE 4.2

Bathinda District: Expenditure on Water Supply as Percentage of Aggregate Municipal Expenditure, 1980–98

(*Rs. in lakhs*)

Name of town	*Civic status*	*1982-83**			*1987-88**			*1992-93**			*1996-97**			*1980-98**		
		Aggregate expenditure	*Expenditure on water supply*	*Percentage. of aggregate expenditure*	*Aggregate expenditure*	*Expenditure on water supply*	*Percentage of aggregate expenditure*	*Aggregate expenditure*	*Expenditure on water supply*	*Percentage. of aggregate expenditure*	*Expenditure on water supply*	*Aggregate expenditure*	*Percentage of aggregate expenditure*	*Aggregate expenditure*	*Expenditure on water supply*	*Percentage of aggregate expenditure*
1	2	3	4	5	6	7	8	9	10	11	12	13	14	15	16	17
Bathinda	I	207.10	12.72	6.14	456.43	17.0	3.72	755.21	63.35	8.39	1135.78	104.24	9.18	583.39	43.31	7.42
Rampura Phul	III	34.62	2.11	6.09	55.62	4.40	7.91	104.96	9.12	8.69	162.77	15.53	9.54	81.35	6.94	8.53
Maur Mandi	III	14.61	2.15	14.72	31.80	2.80	8.81	52.30	4.16	7.95	77.11	8.44	10. 95	40.30	3.92	9.73
Raman Mandi	IV	12.20	2.75	22.54	28.50	2.74	9.61	53.35	5.73	10.74	85.41	11.84	13.86	40.36	5.09	12.61
Goniana Mandi	IV	14.30	1.33	9.30	28.70	9.41	32.79	41.46	3.72	8.97	54.33	7.06	12.99	32.52	5.19	15.96
Bhucho Mandi	IV	18.04	3.83	21.23	39.60	3.75	9.47	42.47	4.31	10.15	90.16	7.15	7.93	42.84	4.94	11.53
Kot Fatta	V	1.10	Nil	Nil	4.70	Nil	Nil	5.65	2.70	47.79	7.68	1.85	24.09	4.46	1.06	23.77
Sangat Mandi	VI	1.60	Nil	Nil	2.90	0.62	21.38	8.99	1.09	12.12	11.63	1.62	13.93	5.69	0.75	13.18
Aggregate Expenditure		303.57	24.89	8.20	648.25	40.72	6.28	1064.39	94.18	8.85	1624.87	157.73	9.71	830.91	71.20	8.57
Average per municipality		50.60	4.15	8.20	92.61	5.82	6.28	133.05	11.77	8.85	203.11	19.72	9.71	103.86	8.90	8.57
C.V.		1.70	0.94		1.76	0.89		1.78	1.67		1.75	1.63	1.76		1.48	

*Annual averages, calculated at t-year. First three are five years average, while fourth one is a three years average and fifth one eighteen years average.

C.V. stands for Coefficient of Variability.

Source: Data calculated from *Classified Abstracts* of different municipalities for various years.

than its share of total urban population in the district. Inter-municipal disparities in expenditure on water supply widened in 1992-93 as compared to 1987-88. Co-efficient of variability index value rose from 0.89 in 1987-88 to 1.67 in 1992-93. It was, in fact, a reversal of the earlier trends, observed between 1982-83 and 1987-88.

The municipal expenditure on water supply grew fast to reach Rs. 158 lakh in 1996-97. It varied from more than Rs. 104 lakh in Bathinda town to only about Rs. 2 lakh in Sangat Mandi. The inter-municipal disparities had marginally declined in comparison to 1992-93, but were still very wide. In fact, inter-municipal disparities in absolute expenditure on water supply expanded with higher growth in amounts after 1987-88.

In this context, proportional share of expenditure incurred by municipalities on water supply can provide a more realistic picture. The average share of municipal expenditure on water supply in the districts comes to about 9.0 per cent of total municipal expenditure during 1980-98. However, there were wide inter-municipal variations in this regard. It varied from a high of about 24 per cent in Kot Fatta to a low of about 7 per cent in Bathinda town. In this way, the minimum and maximum expenditure share differed by more than three times.

In 1992-93, when inter-municipal differentials in expenditure share on water supply were the highest, it varied from a high of about 48 per cent in Kot Fatta to a low of about 8.0 per cent in Maur Mandi. In other words, Kot Fatta municipality incurred nearly half its total municipal expenditure on water supply, while it was only about one-twelfth of the total expenditure in the case of Maur Mandi. It must be mentioned, however, that the tap water supply service was inducted in Kot Fatta as late as 1994-95 and the municipality had to incur heavy expenditure on infrastructure inputs and recruitment of staff for the purpose.

In 1982-83, water supply service was provided 8.2 per cent of total municipal expenditure in the district. Then, too, it varied from a high of about 23.0 per cent in Raman Mandi to a low of only about 6.0 per cent in Rampura Phul.

Coming to 1987-88, this proportion made up only about 6.0 per cent. In this way, the share of water supply in aggregate municipal expenditure in the district registered a decline by 2 per cent points during the period from 1982-83 to 1987-88.

However, the increase in proportional share led to increase in inter-municipal differentials during 1987-88. It varied from a high of about 33.0 per cent in Goniana Mandi to a low of only about 4.0 per cent in Bathinda municipality. Significantly, Bathinda municipality's share of about 4.0 per cent was the lowest recorded for any municipality in the district for the entire study period, 1980-98.

The proportional share of municipal expenditure on water supply has increased in recent years. It was nearly 10 per cent in 1996-97 and the highest recorded share for the period 1980 to 1998. Among municipalities, it varied from a high of 24 per cent in Kot Fatta to a low of about 8 per cent in Bhucho Mandi, in a ratio of 1:3. In general, the small municipal towns were spending relatively higher proportional share of their aggregate expenditure on water supply than the medium and large towns, while in absolute terms, big towns were spending more than the small towns on this component.

Briefly, during the last 18 years (1980 to 1998), municipalities in Bathinda district incurred annually an average amount of more than Rs. 71 lakh on water supply, making about up for 9.0 per cent of total average annual municipal expenditure in the district. In other words, nearly one-eleventh share of average annual municipal expenditure in Bathinda district was committed to the supply of water. In general, municipal expenditure on water supply in the district ranged between 6 and 10 per cent during the study period. Nevertheless, there have been wide inter-municipal variations both in absolute and proportional terms. In absolute terms, it varied from a maximum of more than Rs. 43 lakh per annum in Bathinda town to a minimum of Rs. 75 thousand in Sangat Mandi. The combined share of the two largest municipalities, Bathinda and Rampura Phul, made up Rs. 50.25 lakh or 71 per cent of total expenditure of all municipalities on water supply. Against this, share of three smallest municipalities, Sangat Mandi, Kot Fatta and Bhucho Mandi, made up for less than 10 per cent of the total. In proportional terms, it varied from a high of about 24 per cent in Kot Fatta to a low of only about 8 per cent in Bathinda. In general, the small sized municipal towns incurred higher share of their average annual expenditures on water supply in comparison to the large-sized municipal towns. On the contrary, however, in absolute terms it was the reverse as the large-sized municipalities spent higher than the small-sized municipalities. It seems that the large-sized municipalities are more efficient in spending on water supply than the smaller ones.

It must be pointed out, however, the reverse is true when it comes to spatial and social justice. In other words, the large-sized municipalities maintained economic efficiency and the small-sized municipalities took care of spatial and social justice through provision of municipal services like water supply at the cost of economic efficiency.

B. Change in Expenditure, 1980-98

Municipal expenditure on water supply in the district increased by 133 lakh on annual average basis during 1980-98. It increased from an annual average amount of about Rs. 25 lakh in 1982-83 to Rs. 158 lakh in 1996-97. This increase was unevenly distributed in time and space. In other words, there were wide temporal and inter-municipal variations in expenditure on water supply in Bathinda district.

The expenditure increased to about Rs. 41 lakh in 1987-88 from about Rs. 25 lakh in 1982-83. This amounted to an increase of about Rs. 16 lakh or about 64 per cent on average annual basis. At the municipal level, it varied from an increase of more than six times in Goniana Mandi to a decrease of one-fifth in Bhucho Mandi. On the whole, the two municipalities, namely, Rampura Phul and Goniana Mandi registered high increase against the low increase in two other municipalities viz. Bathinda and Maur Mandi. There were two municipalities, namely, Raman Mandi and Bhucho Mandi where the share of expenditure on water supply registered a decline. Of the remaining municipalities, Sangat Mandi did not supply water to its residents during 1982-83, hence study of change in expenditure is not possible and Kot Fatta municipality had not initiated this facility for its residents.

Between 1987-88 and 1992-93, when average annual municipal expenditure on water supply increased by about Rs. 53 lakh from Rs. 41 lakh in 1987-88 to Rs. 94 lakh in 1992-93, it registered an increase of about 129 per cent. At the level of individual municipality, seven out of the eight municipalities in the district registered increase in expenditure on water supply during this period. The highest increase of 273 per cent was registered in Bathinda, followed by Raman Mandi with 109 per cent and

Rampura Phul with 107 per cent. Against this, Goniana Mandi registered a decline of about 61 per cent in its annual expenditure on water supply. Sangat Mandi and Maur Mandi registered moderate increase, and Bhucho Mandi a very slight increase.

In 1996-97, average annual municipal expenditure on water supply jumped to Rs. 158 lakh from Rs. 94 lakh in 1992-93, registering an increase of Rs. 64 lakh or 68 per cent. There were wide inter-municipal variations in this regard. It ranged from an increase of 107 per cent in Raman Mandi to a decrease of 31 per cent in Kot Fatta. Three municipalities of Raman Mandi, Maur Mandi and Bhucho Mandi registered high increase. Against this, Sangat Mandi registered very low increase. Bathinda and Rampura Phul recorded moderate increase.

Change in proportional share of municipal expenditure on water supply presents another interesting facet. Four of the six municipalities, providing this service to their residents, recorded decrease in their expenditure share on water supply between 1982-83 and 1987-88. Against this, dominant majority of municipalities had recorded an increase in absolute amount of expenditure on water supply. Decrease in proportional share was as high as 13 per cent in Raman Mandi. In contrast, Goniana Mandi town recorded an increase that was as high as about 24 per cent (Table 4.3).

TABLE 4.3

Bathinda District: Change in Expenditure on Water Supply, 1980-98

(*Figures in %*)

Name of town	*Civic status*	*1982-83* over 1987-88*	*1987-88* over 1992-93*	*1992-93* over 1996-97*
Bathinda	I	–2.42	4.67	0.79
Rampura Phul	III	1.82	0.78	0.85
Maur Mandi	III	–5.91	–0.86	3.00
Raman Mandi	IV	–12.93	1.13	3.12
Goniana Mandi	IV	23.49	–23.82	4.02
Bhucho Mandi	IV	–11.76	0.68	–2.22
Kot Fatta[2]	V	—	—	–23.70
Sangat Mandi[1]	VI	—	–9.26	1.81

*Annual averages.

Notes: 1. Sangat Mandi did not supply water to its residents before 1985-86.
2. Kot Fatta started water supply in 1994-95.

Source: Data calculated from *Classified Abstracts* of different municipalities for various years.

During 1987-88–1992-93, four of the seven municipalities providing this facility, recorded increase in their respective shares. Goniana Mandi, which had earlier recorded the highest increase of 24 per cent in its share, registered a decrease of the same magnitude. Other municipalities which recorded decrease in expenditure shares include Sangat Mandi and Maur Mandi towns. Among those registering increase, Bathinda municipality witnessed the highest increase of about 5 per cent and Bhucho Mandi recorded the lowest (less than 1 per cent). Increase or decrease in proportional share cut across the municipal status. For an illustration is the case of Rampura Phul and Maur Mandi, both being class III towns. The former recorded an increase while the latter a decrease in respective expenditure shares on water supply.

Between 1992-93 and 1996-97, majority of municipalities recorded an increase in their respective shares of expenditure on water supply. It varied from a high of 4 per cent in Goniana Mandi to a low of less than 1 per cent in Bathinda and Rampura Phul. On the other side of the scale, Kot Fatta which started water supply service in 1994-95, recorded a decline of about -24 per cent.

In sum, Rampura Phul is the only municipality, which has always been recording increase in its share on water supply during the period 1980-98. There is, however, no municipality which recorded a regular decrease in its share of expenditure on water supply. Gradual increase in proportional share of expenditure on water supply of majority of municipalities in the district during 1992-93 to 1996-97 indicates a greater thrust on water supply service by the municipalities in recent years.

C. Per Capita Expenditure

Municipal expenditure on water supply if seen in per capita terms provides a more realistic picture. Hence, an effort has been made to analyse the municipal expenditure on water supply in per capita terms.

In 1982-83, municipalities in Bathinda district incurred a per capita expenditure of Rs. 13 on water supply on an average annual basis (Table 4.4). It rose to Rs. 77 per capita per annum by

TABLE 4.4

Bathinda District: Per Capita Expenditure Incurred on Water Supply by Municipalities, 1980-98

Name of town	Civic status	1982-83*		1987-88*		1992-93*		1996-97*		1980-98	
		Expenditure on water supply (Rs. in lakhs)	Per capita expenditure (in Rs.)	Expenditure on water supply (Rs. in lakhs)	Per capita expenditure (in Rs.)	Expenditure on water supply (Rs. in lakhs)	Per capita expenditure (in Rs.)	Expenditure on water supply (Rs. in lakhs)	Per capita expenditure (in Rs.)	Expenditure on water supply (Rs. in lakhs)	Per capita expenditure (in Rs.)
Bathinda	I	12.72	11	17.00	15	63.55	54	104.24	89	43.31	37
Rampura Phul	III	2.11	7	4.40	14	9.12	29	15.53	49	6.94	22
Maur Mandi	III	2.15	11	2.80	15	4.16	22	8.44	45	3.92	21
Raman Mandi	IV	2.75	19	2.74	19	5.73	40	11.84	83	5.09	36
Goniana Mandi	IV	1.33	15	9.41	109	3.72	43	7.06	82	5.19	60
Bhucho Mandi	IV	3.83	49	3.75	48	4.31	55	7.15	91	4.94	63
Kot Fatta	V	—	—	—	—	2.70	54	1.85	37	1.06	21
Sangat Mandi	VI	—	—	—	—	1.09	38	1.62	57	0.75	26
All Towns		24.89	13	40.72	20	94.18	46	157.73	77	71.20	35

* Annual averages, calculated at the mid-year. First three are five years average, while fourth one is a three years average and fifth one eighteen years average.

Note: Per capita subsidy has been calculated on the basis of 1981 Census data. In case of Bathinda population figures used for calculation of subsidies confined to areas falling under the jurisdiction of Bathinda M.C. Two public sector units, Fertilizer and Thermal Plant make their own arrangements for provision of services and hence have been excluded from the calculations/ computations.

Source: Data calculated from *Classified Abstracts* of different municipalities for various years.

1996-97, registering an increase of about six times in 18 years. It is, however, to be noted here that only six out of the eight municipalities in the district provided water supply service to their residents during the entire study period (1980-98).

In 1982-83, even though the average was Rs. 13 per capita expenditure on water supply, variations were recorded from a high of Rs. 49 in Bhucho Mandi to a low of Rs. 7 in Rampura

Phul showing a ratio of 1:7 between the low and the high expending municipalities (Fig. 4.2). In 1987-88, when this average was Rs. 20, it ranged from a high of Rs. 109 in Goniana Mandi to a low of Rs. 14 in Rampura Phul, giving a ratio of 1:8. Obviously, inter-municipal variations on water supply enlarged during this period. However, the ratio came down to 1:2.5 in 1992-93. It varied from a high of Rs. 55 per capita in Bhucho Mandi to a low of Rs. 22 in Maur Mandi. The average figure for all the municipalities during the period was Rs. 46 per capita. Notably, the per capita expenditure on water supply increased more than two-fold during 1987-88 and 1992-93.

In 1996-97, inter-municipal gap in per capita municipal expenditure on water supply declined. It varied from a high of Rs. 91 in Bhucho Mandi to a low of Rs. 37 in Kot Fatta, giving a difference of less than 3 times between the two, with the former being a Class IV and the latter a Class V town. Four of eight municipalities in the district incurred an expenditure which was higher than the average (Rs. 77). In general, Class IV towns spent higher per capita expenditure on water supply than the Class III towns in the district. It may be inferred that the large-sized municipalities were placed better than the small sized in economic efficiency, whereas the latter had an edge over the former in terms of equity.

Briefly, per capita municipal expenditure on water supply, which registered an increase of more than six times during the 18 year period, 1980-98, differed widely both in spatial and temporal terms. Notwithstanding the wide inter-municipal variations, no definite trend has been observed in this regard. The differential has been maximum in 1987-88 and minimum in 1996-97. Further, the small-sized municipalities, in general, incurred higher per capita expenditure on water supply than the large-sized municipalities in the district.

The foregoing indicates that the equity criterion in water supply provision is more operative in case of small-sized municipal towns, whereas efficiency criterion was more relevant in case of the large-sized municipal towns. Relatively faster growth in per capita municipal expenditure on water supply in the case of the large-sized municipal towns has been responsible for narrowing down the inter-municipal gaps that existed in this regard in the beginning.

Fig. 4.2

Bathinda District: Per Capita Expenditure and Subsidy on Water Supply: A Comparison

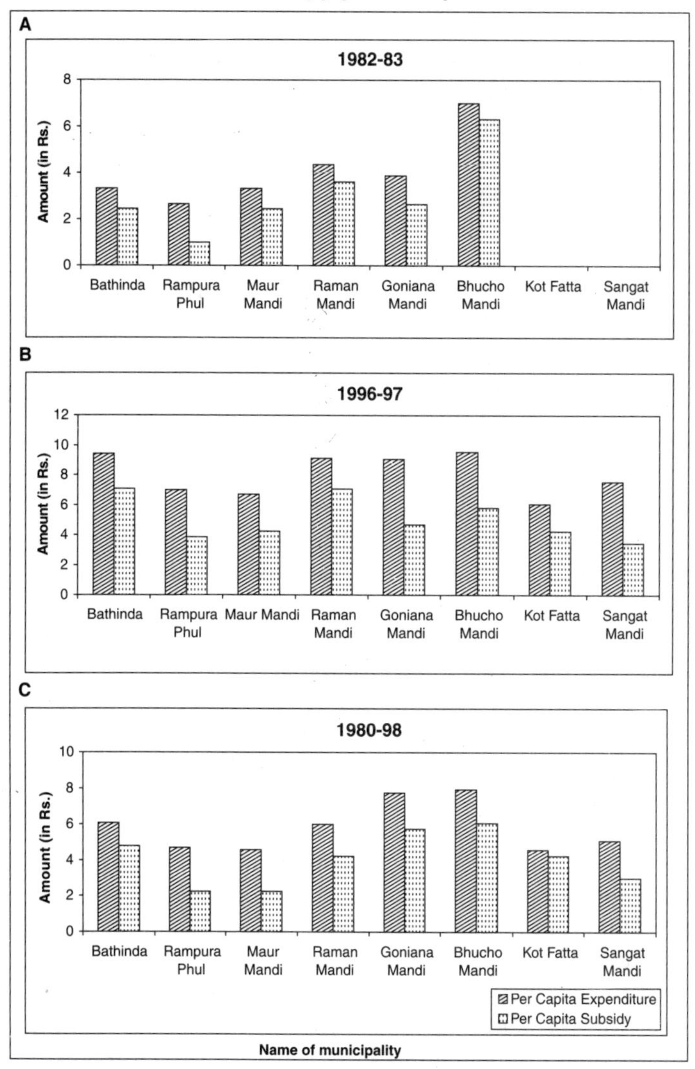

Notes: (i) In 1982-83, water supply service has not been started in Kot Fatta and Sangat Mandi towns

(ii) Towns have been listed in order of their population size and civic status

INCOME PATTERN AND TRENDS

A. Aggregate Income from Water Supply

Tap water connection is the main source of income to municipalities, supplying drinking water. There are three types of connections: domestic, institutional and industrial/commercial. Generally, industrial/commercial rates are higher than the former two.

An aggregate amount of about Rs. 586 lakh was earned from the supply of water by municipalities in Bathinda district during 1980-98. This comes to about Rs. 33 lakh per annum, and makes up about 4.0 per cent of the total income earned by the municipalities (Table 4.5). In other words, only about four in each hundred rupees earned by municipalities as an income from various urban services to their residents come through the supply of water. In 1982-83, average annual income earned by all the municipalities was about Rs. 11 lakh. It rose to about Rs. 79 lakh in 1996-97, registering an increase of more than seven times in 18 years. In the mean time, municipal expenditure on water supply had grown by six times. Evidently, there is a broad conformity between the increase in municipal expenditure on and income earned from the water supply.

There are, however, wide inter-municipality variations in this regard. During 1980-98, Bathinda municipality earned about Rs. 17 lakh from the water supply service against only Rs. 16 thousand in Kot Fatta on an annual (average) basis. Income earned by Bathinda municipality comes to more than one-half or 52 per cent of aggregate income earned by all municipalities in the district. Income earned by the four small-sized municipalities makes up only about 16 per cent in aggregate municipal income from water supply. Against this, their combined expenditure on the water supply make up about 17 per cent in aggregate municipal expenditure on urban services during 1980-98. Evidently, the small-sized municipalities in the district spent more but earned less from the water supply.

In 1982-83, municipalities in the district earned about Rs. 11 lakh from water supply when only six of the eight municipalities in the district were supplying tap water to their residents. Kot Fatta and Sangat Mandi, the two small-sized municipal towns, had not initiated tap water supply system. About 56 per cent of

TABLE 4.5

Bathinda District: Municipal Income from Water Supply as Percentage of Total Municipal Income, 1980-98

(*Rs. in lakhs*)

Name of town		*1982-83**			*1987-88**			*1992-93**			*1996-97**			*1980-98**		
	Civic status	*Aggregate income*	*Income earned from water supply*	*Percentage of aggregate income*	*Aggregate income*	*Income earned from water supply*	*Percentage of aggregate income*	*Aggregate income*	*Income earned from water supply*	*Percentage of aggregate income*	*Aggregate income*	*Income earned from water supply*	*Percentage of aggregate income*	*Aggregate income*	*Income earned from water supply*	*Percentage of aggregate income*
1	*2*	*3*	*4*	*5*	*6*	*7*	*8*	*9*	*10*	*11*	*12*	*13*	*14*	*15*	*16*	*17*
Bathinda	I	219.55	6.18	2.81	518.52	8.78	1.69	719.97	17.73	2.46	1162.29	46.35	3.99	598.73	16.81	2.81
Rampura Phul	III	32.53	1.65	5.07	51.34	3.32	6.47	101.80	7.51	7.38	164.23	10.74	6.54	78.95	5.26	6.66
Maur Mandi	III	15.31	1.03	6.73	29.94	1.99	6.65	56.29	4.00	7.11	78.51	5.12	6.52	41.29	2.76	6.68
Raman Mandi	IV	13.10	0.85	6.49	32.10	2.00	6.23	53.19	3.65	6.87	83.13	4.64	5.58	41.19	2.58	6.26
Goniana Mandi	IV	14.05	0.70	4.98	28.82	1.48	5.14	45.20	3.29	7.28	54.73	5.21	9.52	33.59	2.39	7.12
Bhucho Mandi	IV	17.31	0.68	3.93	26.21	1.42	5.42	40.89	2.72	6.65	88.50	4.47	5.05	38.20	2.08	5.45
Kot Fatta	V	1.01	Nil	Nil	4.63	Nil	Nil	3.78	Nil	Nil	7.80	0.95	12.18	3.92	0.16	4.08
Sangat Mandi	VI	1.46	Nil	Nil	3.29	0.21	6.38	7.52	0.78	10.37	11.74	1.27	10.82	5.69	0.49	8.61
Aggregate income		314.32	11.09	3.53	694.85	19.20	2.76	1028.64	39.68	3.86	1650.73	78.75	4.77	841.56	32.53	3.87
Average per municipality		52.39	1.85	3.53	99.26	2.74	2.76	146.95	5.67	3.86	206.34	9.84	4.77	105.20	4.07	3.87
C.V.		1.75	1.06		1.89	0.95		1.75	0.93	1.76	1.43			1.79	1.24	

*Annual averages, calculated at the mid-year. First three are five years average, while fourth one is a three years average and fifth one eighteen years average.

C.V. stands for Coefficient of Variability.

Source: Data calculated from *Classified Abstracts* of different municipalities for various years.

the municipal income in the district, earned from the water supply, was the share of Bathinda municipality alone. The combined income of three top-most municipalities was four-fifths or 80 per cent of total income earned by all municipalities from water supply in the district. Against this, their combined expenditure on water supply comes to about two-thirds or 68 per cent. Evidently, the large-sized municipalities displayed higher economic efficiency as compared to the small-sized municipalities in the district.

In 1996-97, when the municipal earnings from this source rose to about Rs. 79 lakh, inter-municipal variations widened further. The amount varied from a high of more than Rs. 46 lakh in Bathinda to a low of only Rs. 95 thousand in Kot Fatta. Co-efficient of variation index value rose to 1.43 in 1996-97 from 1.06 in 1982-83. Thus, inter-municipal variations enlarged after some decline in 1987-88 and 1992-93.

Income from water supply as a share in aggregate municipal income provides a different picture. The average (annual) income share on water supply for all municipalities was about 4 per cent of total municipal income in the district. Bathinda, the largest municipal town in the district, averaged only about 3 per cent being the lowest for any of the eight municipalities in the district. Against this, Maur Mandi, a Class III town, earned about 7 per cent. In proportional terms, the Class III municipal towns earned higher income from water supply in comparison to Class I, and Class IV towns in the district.

In proportional terms, municipal income from water supply varied from a high of about 9 per cent in Sangat Mandi to a low of only about 3 per cent in Bathinda town during 1980-98. In other words, income from water supply contributed less than one-tenth of Sangat Mandi's total annual (average) income from different services, while contributing only a meager share of one-fortieth in the case of Bathinda municipality. In general, water supply contributed a substantial proportion to the total income earned by the small-sized municipalities, whereas it made only a marginal share in the income of the large-sized municipalities.

B. Change in Income, 1980-98

In 1987-88, when total municipal income from water supply was more than Rs. 19 lakh or about 3 per cent of total annual (average) municipal income, it varied from a high of about Rs. 9 lakh in Bathinda town to a low of Rs. 21,000 in Sangat Mandi with Kot Fatta yet to start tap water supply. The share of Bathinda municipality in total municipal income from this source was now reduced to about 46 per cent from about 56 per cent earlier in 1982-83. This was attributed mainly to substantial rise in income of other municipalities, especially the Class IV municipal towns, from this source. For example, income of Raman Mandi from water supply grew by 135 per cent against only 42 per cent in Bathinda municipality between 1982-83 and 1987-88. It is noteworthy to mention here that domestic connections are the only source of water supply in Raman Mandi town. It is this source of water supply that provides income to municipalities. Hence, higher growth of income on water supply to Raman Mandi is on expected lines. In general, the income of small-sized municipal towns grew faster from water supply than that of the large-sized municipal town in the district during this period.

In 1992-93, the average (annual) municipal income from water supply rose to about Rs. 40 lakh from about Rs. 19 lakh in 1987-88, registering an increase of 110 per cent. During this period, income varied from a high of about Rs. 18 lakh in Bathinda municipality to a low of Rs. 0.78 lakh in Sangat Mandi. In this way, inter-municipal differentials marginally narrowed down in 1992-93 as compared to 1987-88. It is well supported in co-efficient of variability index value which declined to 0.93 in 1992-93 from 0.95 in 1987-88. Income accruing to Bathinda municipality made up only about 45 per cent in total municipal income from water supply in the district. This was attributed mainly to relatively high growth of income to other municipalities from water supply. For example, income of Sangat Mandi increased by 271 per cent and that of Goniana Mandi by 122 per cent. Against this, income earned by Bathinda municipality grew only by 102 per cent. It is also to be noted here that the expenditure share of Bathinda municipality made up more than 67 per cent of aggregate municipal expenditure on water supply against income share of 45 per cent. Evidently, Bathinda municipality, which had maintained a lead over the other municipal towns in the district in terms of economic efficiency, was gradually losing its hold in this context.

In 1996-97, municipal income from water supply rose to about Rs. 79 lakh from about Rs. 40 lakh in 1992-93, registering an increase of about 98 per cent. Evidently, the increase in municipal income from water supply registered slight decline as compared to earlier periods but inter-municipal differentials in income from water supply widened. Among municipalities, the increase in proportional terms varied from a high of 161 per cent in Bathinda municipality to a low of only 27 per cent in Raman Mandi. Three municipalities of Rampura Phul, Maur Mandi and Raman Mandi registered an increase of less than 50 per cent during the period from 1992-93 to 1996-97. The share of Bathinda municipality in aggregate income of all the municipalities from the water supply further increased to 59 per cent in 1996-97 from 45 per cent during in 1992-93. This is attributed mainly to high growth of its income from water supply. Evidently, Bathinda municipality recovered lost ground as was witnessed from the decrease during the earlier periods. However, so far as proportional share of income earned from the water supply by Bathinda town is considered, it had been the lowest share among all the municipalities in the district. Its share of about 4.0 per cent made less than one-third of the share of Kot Fatta (12.18 per cent), a new player in the field of tap water supply.

C. Per Capita Income

Municipal income from the water supply, if seen in per capita terms provides a more realistic picture of inter-municipal comparisons in absolute or proportional terms.

During 1980-98, municipalities in Bathinda district earned Rs. 16 per capita per annum from water supply. There were, however, wide inter-municipal variations in this context. It varied from a high of Rs. 28 in Goniana Mandi to a low of only Rs. 3 in Kot Fatta, giving a difference of nine times between the lowest and the highest per capita income from water supply (Table 4.6). Of the eight municipalities in the district, four recorded per capita income figure above the average, against three having this below the average. Remaining one municipality has this figure same as the average for all the municipalities in the district.

In 1982-83, when average per capita income from water supply was Rs. 6 for all the municipalities, it varied from a high of Rs. 9

TABLE 4.6

Bathinda District: Per Capita Municipal Income from Water Supply, 1980-98

Name of town	*Civic status*	*1982-83**		*1987-88**		*1992-93**		*1996-97**		*1980-98**	
		Income earned from water supply (Rs. in lakhs)	*Per capita income (in Rs.)*	*Income earned from water supply (Rs. in lakhs)*	*Per capita income (in Rs.)*	*Income earned from water supply (Rs. in lakhs)*	*Per capita income (in Rs.)*	*Income earned from water supply (Rs. in lakhs)*	*Per capita income (in Rs.)*	*Income earned from water supply (Rs. in lakhs)*	*Per capita income (in Rs.)*
Bathinda	I	6.18	5	8.78	8	17.73	15	46.35	40	16.81	14
Rampura Phul	III	1.65	5	3.32	10	7.51	24	10.74	34	5.26	16
Maur Mandi	III	1.03	5	1.99	11	4.00	21	5.12	27	2.76	15
Raman Mandi	IV	0.85	6	2.00	14	3.65	25	4.64	32	2.58	18
Goniana Mandi	IV	0.70	8	1.48	17	3.29	38	5.21	61	2.39	28
Bhucho Mandi	IV	0.68	9	1.42	18	2.72	35	4.47	57	2.08	27
Kot Fatta	V	—	—	Nil	—	Nil	—	0.95	19	0.16	3
Sangat Mandi	VI	—	—	0.21	7	0.78	27	1.27	44	0.49	17
All Towns		11.09	6	19.20	9	39.68	20	78.75	38	32.53	16

* Annual averages, calculated at the mid-year. First three are five years average, while fourth one is a three years average and fifth one eighteen years average.

Note: Per capita subsidy has been calculated on the basis of 1981 census data. In case of Bathinda population figures used for calculation of subsidies confined to areas falling under the jurisdiction of Bathinda M.C. Two public sector units—Fertilizer and Thermal Plant make their own arrangements for provision of services and hence have been excluded from the calculations/computations.

Source: Data calculated from *Classified Abstracts* of different municipalities for various years.

in Bhucho Mandi to a low of Rs. 5 in Bathinda, Rampura Phul and Maur Mandi. Two of the eight municipalities in the district were not then providing this service to their residents. In 1987-88, average per capita income rose to Rs. 9 from Rs. 6 in 1982-83, registering an increase of about 50 per cent. Against this, the increase in per capita municipal expenditure on this account was about 79 per cent during the same period. Evidently, per capita municipal income registered much lower increase than that of the expenditure on the water supply.

However, inter-municipal variations in per capita income from the water supply increased during this period. It varied from a high of Rs. 17 in Bhucho Mandi to a low of Rs. 7 in Sangat Mandi, giving a difference of more than two times between the lowest and the highest. Earlier in 1982-83, this difference was less. This indicates that with the growth in per capita income of municipalities from the water supply, inter-municipal variations in income from this source also widened.

In 1992-93, the per capita income to municipalities from the water supply in Bathinda district was Rs. 20. Among other municipalities, it varied from a high of Rs. 38 in Goniana Mandi to a low of Rs. 15 in Bathinda municipality, giving a difference of more than double quantum.

In 1996-97, this per capita income rose to Rs. 38 from Rs. 20 in 1992-93. Among the municipalities, it varied from a high of Rs. 61 in Goniana Mandi to a low of Rs. 19 in Kot Fatta, giving a difference of more than three times. Evidently, inter-municipal variations in per capita income from water supply grew further with rise in per capita income between 1992-93 and 1996-97.

Briefly, municipalities in Bathinda district earned only Rs. 16 per capita per annum from the water supply during 1980-98. Per capita income of municipalities has been growing over the period but at differential rates. The increase has been as low as 50 per cent between 1982-83 and 1987-88 and as high as 122 per cent between 1987-88 and 1992-93. The inter-municipal differentials in per capita income from the water supply have, although declined over the period, yet no set pattern has been noticed in this regard. Class IV municipal towns, in general, earned higher in per capita terms from the water supply while the earning of Class V municipalities was low.

SUBSIDY COMPONENT

A. Aggregate

As stated before, municipalities in Bathinda district incurred an annual average amount of more than Rs. 71 lakh on the water supply during 1980-98. Against this, municipalities earned an income of about Rs. 33 lakh from this service. Thus, an amount of about Rs. 39 lakh or 54 per cent of the total municipal expenditure on water supply was the subsidy in this service. In other words, municipalities in the district provided more than half of their annual average expenditures on water supply in the form of subsidy. Evidently, major share of municipal expenditure on water supply in the district went into subsidizing this service.

B. Inter-Municipal Variations

There were, nevertheless, wide inter-municipal variations in this regard. Among the municipalities, it varied from a high of about Rs. 27 lakh in Bathinda to a low of Rs. 0.26 lakh in Sangat Mandi (Table 4.7). More than two-thirds or 68 per cent of the total subsidy provided by all municipalities was the share of Bathinda municipality alone. Against this, its share in total municipal expenditure on the water supply in the district made up 61 per cent. Evidently, Bathinda municipality's share in total municipal subsidy on water supply was more than its share in total municipal expenditure on this service. This can be explained by factors such as:

- Bathinda city being the district headquarters and large in area size, there have been a large number of stand posts to cater to the need of the general public for drinking water. The water supplied through stand posts is free of cost,
- Bathinda being a large town area-wise and population-wise, the chances of pilferage in distribution of water are also higher, and
- The size of the slum population, where water supply is made free of charge, has been large in Bathinda town in comparison to other towns in the district.

Bhucho Mandi and Kot Fatta have also recorded higher shares in total municipal subsidy on water supply in comparison to their shares in aggregate municipal expenditure on this service (Table 4.7).

Rampura Phul, the second largest municipal town in the district, shared only about 4 per cent of total amount of municipal subsidy water supply in the district. Against this, its share in

TABLE 4.7
Bathinda District: Municipal Subsidy on Water Supply, 1980-98

Name of town	*Expenditure (Rs. in lakhs)*	*Income (Rs. in lakhs)*	*Subsidy (Rs. in lakhs)*	*Per capita subsidy (in Rs.)*
Bathinda	43.31*	16.81*	26.50*	23*
	(61.22)	(51.27)	(68.53)	
Rampura Phul	6.94	5.26	1.68	5
	(9.80)	(16.04)	(4.34)	
Maur Mandi	3.92	2.76	1.16	6
	(5.54)	(8.42)	(3.00)	
Raman Mandi	5.09	2.58	2.51	18
	(7.15)	(7.87)	(6.49)	
Goniana Mandi	5.19	2.39	2.80	33
	(7.19)	(7.29)	(7.24)	
Bhucho Mandi	4.94	2.08	2.86	37
	(6.35)	(6.34)	(7.40)	
Kot Fatta	1.06	0.16	0.90	18
	(1.50)	(0.49)	(2.33)	
Sangat Mandi	0.75	0.49	0.26	09
	(1.06)	(1.49)	(0.67)	
All Towns	71.20	32.53	38.67	19
	(100.0)	(100.0)	(100.0)	

*Annual averages.

Notes: 1. Per capita subsidy has been calculated on the basis of 1981 census data. In case of Bathinda population figures used for calculation of subsidy confined to areas falling under the jurisdiction of Bathinda Municipal committee. Two public sector units, Fertilizer and Thermal Plants make their own arrangement in provision of services, provided to their residents. Hence, excluded from the calculations.

2. Figures in parentheses indicate to percentage share in total.

Source: Data calculated from *Classified Abstracts* of different municipalities for various years.

total municipal income from water supply came to 16 per cent. Goniana Mandi shared more than 7 per cent of total subsidy on water supply.

The subsidy as a share in municipal expenditure on water supply by individual municipalities provides other interesting insights. Subsidy as share in total municipal expenditure on water supply varied from a high of 85 per cent in Kot Fatta, a late entrant in tap water supply service, to a low of 24 per cent in Rampura Phul. For half the municipalities in the district, the subsidy component made up more than half of their expenditure on water supply. In other words, the dominant share of expenditure on water supply in half the municipalities in the district goes as subsidy. Against this, two municipalities, Rampura Phul and Maur Mandi, provide less than one-third of their expenditure as subsidy on water supply. In relative terms, the Class III municipal towns provide low proportion of their municipal expenditure as subsidy on water supply, while Class I and Class V towns recorded a higher proportional share. Further, over the period, the share of subsidy had been increasing both at the level of individual municipalities as well as at the aggregate level.

C. Spatio-Temporal Changes

The subsidy as a share of total municipal expenditure on water supply differed widely both in time and space.

In 1982-83, it ranged from a high of 82 per cent in Bhucho Mandi to a low of only 22 per cent in Rampura Phul, giving a difference of about four times between the lowest and the highest proportions (Table 4.8). In other words, more than 82 paisa of each rupee incurred by Bhucho Mandi on water supply goes to subsidy, whereas the subsidy component made up only about 22 paisa of each rupee in Rampura Phul municipality. Coming to 1987-88, when overall situation did not change much, individual municipalities registered varied changes in their subsidy components. For example, the subsidy component which made 69 per cent in Raman Mandi in 1982-83 declined to only 27 per cent of its expenditure on water supply in 1987-88. In contrast to this, the share of subsidy in Goniana Mandi rose to 84 per cent from 47 per cent during the same time. In general, the subsidy as percentage of the total municipal expenditure on water supply decline in towns of Bathinda district between 1982-83 and 1987-88. In terms of economic efficiency, this may be considered a healthy sign.

In 1992-93, majority of municipalities recorded decline in the share of the subsidy on water supply. However, there has been an increase at the aggregate level. The overall share of subsidy was now 58 per cent as compared to 53 per cent in 1987-88. At the level of individual municipalities, there has been several contrasting pictures. For example, the subsidy component made

TABLE 4.8

Bathinda District: Subsidy as Percentage of Municipal Expenditure on Water Supply, 1980-98

Name of town	Civic status	*1982-83**		*1987-88**		*1992-93**		*1996-97**		*1980-98**	
		Subsidy (Rs. in lakhs)	*% to expenditure on water supply*	*Subsidy (Rs. in lakhs)*	*% to expenditure on water supply*	*Subsidy (Rs. in lakhs)*	*% to expenditure on water supply*	*Subsidy (Rs. in lakhs)*	*% to expenditure on water supply*	*Subsidy (Rs. in lakhs)*	*% to expenditure on water supply*
Bathinda	I	6.54	51.42	8.22	4.35	45.62	72.01	57.89	55.54	26.50	61.19
Rampura Phul	III	0.46	21.80	1.08	24.55	1.61	17.65	4.79	30.84	1.68	24.21
Maur Mandi	III	1.12	52.09	0.81	26.93	0.16	3.85	3.32	39.34	1.16	29.59
Raman Mandi	IV	1.90	69.09	0.74	27.00	2.08	36.30	7.20	60.81	2.51	49.31
Goniana Mandi	IV	0.63	47.37	7.93	84.27	0.43	11.56	1.85	26.20	2.80	53.95
Bhucho Mandi	IV	3.15	82.25	2.33	62.13	1.59	36.89	2.68	37.48	2.86	57.89
Kot Fatta	V	—	—	—	—	2.70	100.00	0.90	48.64	0.90	84.91
Sangat Mandi	VI	—	—	0.41	66.13	0.31	28.44	0.35	21.60	0.26	34.67
All Towns		13.80	55.74	21.52	52.85	54.50	57.87	78.98	50.07	38.67	54.31

*Annual averages, calculated at the mid-year. First three are five years average, while fourth one is a three years average and fifth one eighteen years average.

Source: Data calculated from *Classified Abstracts* of different municipalities for various years.

up 100 per cent of municipal expenditure in Kot Fatta, a new entrant in the field of tap water supply. While it made up only about 4 per cent in Maur Mandi. Interestingly, subsidy component declined by more than 25 per cent in the case of Maur Mandi between 1987-88 and 1992-93. Other towns, where the share of subsidy declined during this period include Rampura Phul, Goniana Mandi, Bhucho Mandi and Sangat Mandi. The aggregate share of subsidy registered an increase mainly because the share of subsidy recorded a sharp increase in towns of Kot Fatta and Bathinda. In fact, Kot Fatta was the new entrant in this regard and its total expenditure on water supply was made up from the subsidy component.

In 1996-97, the share of subsidy declined to about 50 per cent from 58 per cent in 1992-93. This share of subsidy varied from a high of 61 per cent in Raman Mandi to a low of 22 per cent in Sangat Mandi. With decline in aggregate share of subsidy in total municipal expenditure on water supply, inter-municipal differentials also declined. Bathinda and Raman Mandi were now the two municipalities where the subsidy made up for more than half the total municipal expenditure on water supply. In remaining municipalities, this share was less than a half. Maur Mandi registered the highest increase in its share of subsidy where it rose to about 39 per cent in 1996-97 from just about 4 per cent in 1992-93. Against this, Kot Fatta recorded the highest decrease where the subsidy share came down to about 49 per cent from 100 per cent during the same period.

Briefly, the water supply is a highly subsidized service in towns of Bathinda district. More than half the municipal expenditure on water supply in the district goes as a subsidy component. There were, however, wide inter-municipal and temporal variations in this regard. Subsidy component remaining more than half the total municipal expenditure on water supply in the district from 1980 to 1995 came down to just half thereafter. It has, thus, registered a decline in recent years. In comparative terms, the Class III municipalities provided the lower proportion of their expenditure on water supply as a subsidy than the other class category of towns. Bathinda, the largest municipal town in the district, provided not only more than 60 per cent of its expenditure on water supply as subsidy but also its share in total municipal subsidy on water supply was higher than its share in total municipal expenditure in the district on this service. In Kot Fatta, one of the smallest towns in the district, the subsidy component was still as high as 85 per cent.

D. Per Capita Subsidy

There were wide inter-municipal differentials in per capita subsidy on water supply in the district. During 1980-98, it varied from a high of Rs. 37 per capita per annum in Bhucho Mandi (calculated on the basis of 1981 Census population figures) to a low of Rs. 5 in Rampura Phul (Table 4.9). The former is a Class IV municipal town and the latter a Class II municipal town.

TABLE 4.9
Bathinda District: Per Capita Municipal Subsidy on Water Supply, 1980-98

Name of town	1982-83*		1987-88*		1992-93*		1996-97*		19990-98*	
	Subsidy (Rs. in lakhs)	Subsidy per capita (in Rs.)	Subsidy (Rs. in lakhs)	Subsidy per capita (in Rs.)	Subsidy (Rs. in lakhs)	Subsidy per capita (in Rs.)	Subsidy (Rs. in lakhs)	Subsidy per capita (in Rs.)	Subsidy (Rs. in lakhs)	Subsidy per capita (in Rs.)
Bathinda	6.54 (47.39)	6	8.22 (39.05)	7	45.62 (83.71)	39	57.89 (73.30)	50	26.50 (68.53)	23
Rampura Phul	0.46 (3.33)	1	1.08 (4.95)	3	1.61 (2.95)	5	4.79 (6.06)	15	1.68 (4.34)	5
Maur Mandi	1.12 (8.12)	6	0.81 (3.71)	4	0.16 (0.29)	1	3.32 (4.20)	18	1.16 (3.06)	6
Raman Mandi	1.90 (13.77)	13	0.74 (3.39)	5	2.08 (3.82)	15	7.20 (9.12)	50	2.51 (6.49)	18
Goniana Mandi	0.63 (4.57)	7	7.93 (36.34)	92	0.43 (0.79)	5	1.85 (2.34)	22	2.80 (7.24)	33
Bhucho Mandi	3.15 (22.83)	40	2.33 (10.68)	30	1.59 (2.92)	20	2.68 (3.39)	34	2.86 (7.40)	37
Kot Fatta	—		—		2.70 (4.95)	54	0.90 (1.14)	18	0.90 (2.33)	18
Sangat Mandi	—		0.41 (1.88)	14	0.31 (0.57)	11	0.35 (0.44)	12	0.26 (0.67)	9
All Towns	13.80 (100)	7	21.52 (100)	11	54.50 (100)	27	78.98 (100)	38	38.67 (100)	19
C.V.	0.91	1.06	1.05	1.35	2.16	0.93	1.85	0.53	1.71	0.60

*Annual averages, calculated at the mid-year. First three are five years average, while fourth one is a three years average and fifth one eighteen years average.

Notes: (i) Figures in parentheses indicate to percentage share in total.

(ii) Per capita subsidy has been calculated on the basis of 1981 census data. In case of Bathinda population figures used for calculation of subsidies confined to areas falling under the jurisdiction of Bathinda M.C. Two public sector units, Fertilizer and Thermal Plant make their own arrangements for provision of services and hence have been excluded from the calculations/computations.

(iii) C.V. stands for Coefficient of Variability.

Source: Data calculated from *Classified Abstracts* of different municipalities for various years.

Bathinda, a Class I municipal town in the district, also provided high per capita subsidy (Rs. 23) on water supply. Rs. 19 per capita being the average for all municipalities, five out of the eight municipalities in the district had this figure below the average and three of them including, Rampura Phul, Maur Mandi and Sangat Mandi had this figure nearly half the average.

In 1982-83, the subsidy component was Rs. 7 per head per annum. Then too, it varied from a low of Re. 1 in Rampura Phul to a high of Rs. 40 in Bhucho Mandi, giving a ratio of 1:40. Three of the six municipalities, providing tap water supply service during the period, gave less than Rs. 7 per capita (per annum) subsidy on water supply.

In 1987-88, when the per capita subsidy rose to Rs. 11 from Rs. 7 in 1982-83, inter-municipal variations were reduced. It varied from a low of only Rs. 3 in Rampura Phul to a high of Rs. 92 in Goniana Mandi, giving a ratio of 1:30. Inter-municipal variations were, although considerably reduced, yet quite large.

In 1992-93, registering a sharp increase, the subsidy component in expenditure on water supply rose to Rs. 27 from Rs. 11 in 1987-88 (Fig. 4.3). However, inter-municipal variations enlarged further to reach the ratio of 1:54. The former is represented by Maur Mandi with Rs. 1 and the latter by Kot Fatta at Rs. 54. Again, majority of municipalities had this figure below the average for all the municipalities. Evidently, inter-municipal differentials in per capita subsidy widened further to reach higher than the 1982-83 levels.

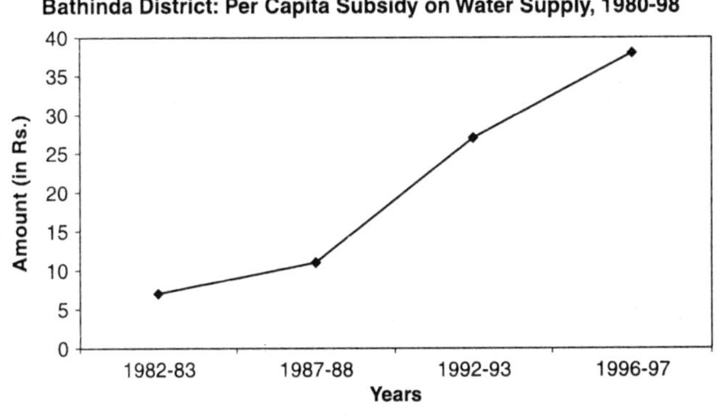

Fig. 4.3

In 1996-97, when per capita subsidy grew to Rs. 38 from Rs. 27 in 1992-93, inter-municipal variations ranged from a high of Rs. 50 in Bathinda and Raman Mandi municipalities to a low of Rs. 12 in Sangat Mandi. Majority of municipalities recorded per capita subsidy on water supply below the average for all the municipalities (Figs. 4.4 and 4.5). The inter-municipal variations in per capita subsidy were lowest for all sub-periods. The same is confirmed in the lowest value of co-efficient of variability index (0.53) this time.

Briefly, there were wide inter-municipal variations in per capita subsidy on water supply. On the whole, Rampura Phul, a Class III municipal town, provided the lowest per capita annual (average) amount of subsidy on water supply in the district during 1980-98. Against this, Bhucho Mandi, a Class IV municipal town, recorded the highest per capita amount of subsidy. In general, Class III municipal towns, as a category, provided the lowest per capita amount of subsidy on water supply. In contrast, Class IV and V category of towns provided the highest per capita amount of subsidy on water supply in the district.

Inter-municipal differentials in per capita subsidy on water supply have been changing over the period. These differentials kept on growing between 1980 and 1990 but afterwards the differentials gradually declined with the increase in subsidy amount in the case of the municipalities providing a low per capita subsidy earlier. The increase in per capita amount of subsidy was generally marked with a decline in inter-municipal differentials in subsidies, hinting at some threshold level beyond which the subsidy could not be raised.

Spatial Discrimination in Distribution of Subsidy

As it is clear from the earlier discussion, water supply service is highly subsidized in the district. The recovery rate is less than one-half of the municipal expenditure on water supply service.

But the benefit of tapped water supply is only possible if such water supply source is available in a town or part of it. In Sangat Mandi town tapped water supply was introduced in 1985-86 and in Kot Fatta only recently in 1994-95. Before that the residents, there used to depend on hand-pumps, installed mostly from their own financial resources. The water supply targets also differ

Fig. 4.4

Bathinda District: Trends in Per Capita Subsidy on Water Supply

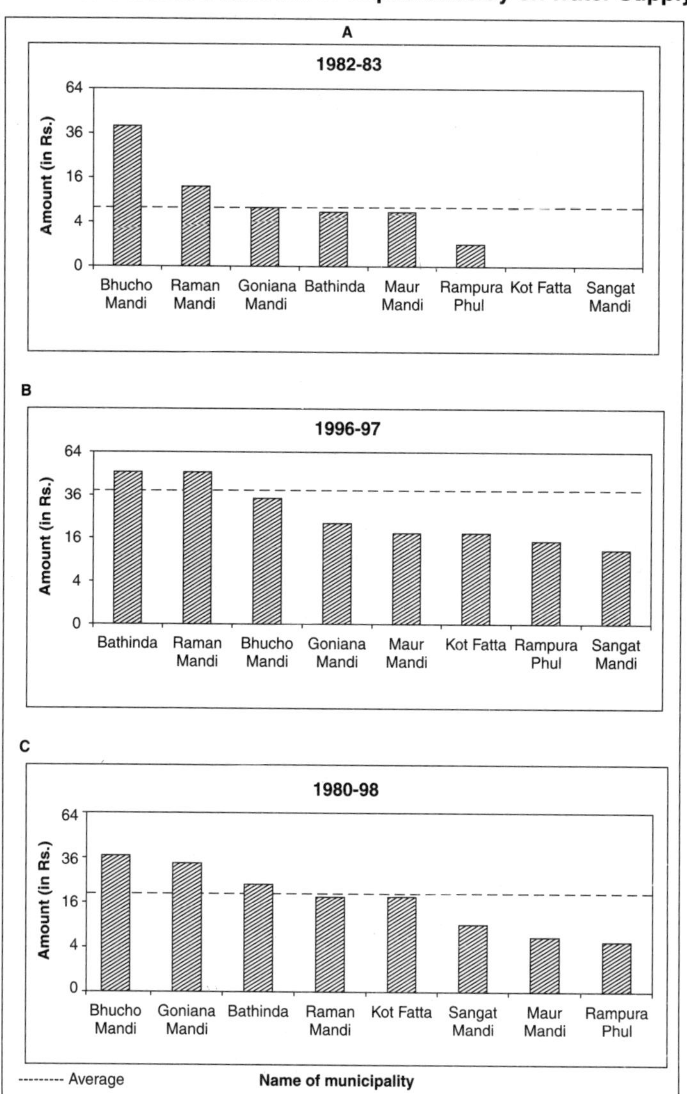

Note: In 1982-83, water supply service was not available in Kot Fatta and Sangat Mandi towns.

Fig. 4.5

Bathinda District: Inter-municipal Disparities in Per Capita Subsidy on Water Supply

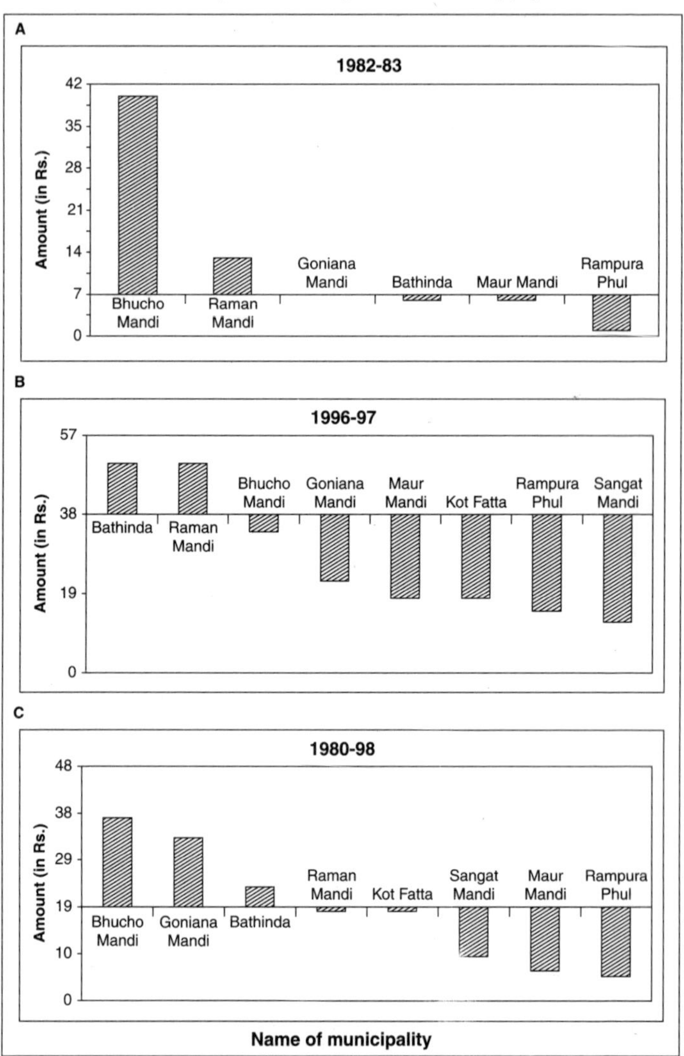

Note: In 1982-83, water supply service was not available in Kot Fatta and Sangat Mandi towns.

widely among towns in the district. It ranged from 38 gallons per day per capita in Bhucho Mandi town to only 20 gallons in Rampura Phul and Maur Mandi towns (Table 4.10).

TABLE 4.10
Bathinda District: Per Day Per Capita Water Supply Targets in Different Towns

Town	*Water supply (in gallons)*	*Town*	*Water supply (in gallons)*
1. Bhucho Mandi	38	5. Goniana	28
2. Bathinda	35	6. Sangat Mandi	22
3. Raman Mandi	30	7. Rampura Phul	20
4. Kot Fatta	30	8. Maur Mandi	20

Source: Collected from different municipal committees offices through fieldwork.

It is quite interesting to note that water supply targets of Class III towns of Rampura Phul and Maur Mandi are quite low in comparison to towns in Class IV and V. Further, in summer months from April to July every year, most of the towns in the district find it difficult to maintain the specified targets of water supply. Peripheral areas and slum localities do suffer the most due to the gap in actual and targeted water supply norms.

Canal water, as a source of water supply, in big towns especially in Bathinda City is used mostly in central parts of the town. In peripheral and slum areas it is mainly the hand-pumps. Canal water is generally sweet.

Another source of discrimination lies in water supply hours and availability of water supply pressure. Supply hours are not only irregular but also water pressure remains low in peripheral areas, areas resided by low income groups and slum localities. Moreover, in rich localities, households with higher affordability have installed booster pumps to increase water pressure. Moreover, in several cases such households have installed their own water pumps. In the process, hardest lit are the slum localities and peripheral areas resided in by the lower income group households.

Main Highlights

The following conclusions emerged strongly out of the preceding discussions:

- In line with other parts of India, water supply is one of the statuary functions of municipal bodies in Bathinda district.

Nevertheless, the total urban population has not yet been covered in the district under safe drinking water facility.

- Owing to the peculiar geographical conditions and the poor ground water quality in Bathinda district, the supply of safe drinking water is almost essential requirement on the part of local bodies in their respective jurisdictions. Since, the ground water quality is poor, the surface water, mainly the canal water, is the main source of water supply in the towns of Bathinda, using both the piped and non-piped modes for this purpose. The domestic connections and stand posts are covered under the piped water supply sources and the hand-pumps under the non-piped water supply sources.
- The expansion and intensification of water supply network in the district took place mainly after 1980. Before that the number of tap water connections had not only been limited but also confined to six out of the eight municipal towns in the district. Moreover, nearly three-fifths of total such connections were in a single town of Bathinda. Over the period, spread of tap water connections in towns of Bathinda has become spatially more justified, yet more than half of such connections are still confined to a single town of Bathinda.
- About Rs. 71 lakh making up 9 per cent of total municipal expenditure in the district was annually incurred on water supply during 1980-98. In other words, water supply received nearly Rs. 9 out of every Rs. 100 spent by municipalities in Bathinda on various services. However, there were wide inter-municipal and temporal variations in this regard.
- As per the expectations, the larger municipal towns incurred much higher amounts, in absolute terms, on water supply than the small-sized towns in the district. The average annual expenditure of Bathinda municipality, on water supply during 1980-98 was about 58 times higher than that of Sangat Mandi, the smallest town in the district. However, in proportional terms Bathinda incurred only about 7 per cent and Kot Fatta, another small-sized municipality, about 24 per cent of its total annual expenditure on this account.

Obviously, the large towns were guided by the principle of economic efficiency in spending on the water supply in comparison to small municipalities, where the concept of equity prevails over the efficiency criterion.

- Per capita expenditure, a more realistic measure of municipal expenditure on water supply, reveals that the small-sized municipalities spent more in per capita terms than the large-sized municipalities. However, there were not only wide inter-municipal disparities in this regard, which kept on widening between 1980 and 1990, there had been a tendency towards narrowing these down in recent years. Higher growth in per capita expenditure of municipalities spending less earlier was largely responsible for this. On the whole, the small-sized municipalities incurred higher per capita expenditure on water supply than the large-sized municipalities in the district during the study period.
- Nearly an amount of 33 lakh per annum, making nearly 4 per cent in average annual municipal income in the district from different sources, was the income from the water supply during 1980-98. In other words, Rs. 4 out of every hundred rupees earned by municipalities came from water supply.
- There were wide inter-municipal and temporal differentials in municipal income earned from water supply. Municipal income from water supply grew more than seven times between 1982-83 and 1996-97, from Rs. 11 lakh to Rs. 79 lakh. More than half the total municipal income from water supply in the district was earned by a single municipality of Bathinda. Against this, four municipalities, in combination, earned less than one-sixth of this income. This income contributed more than one-tenth in the total annual income of Sangat Mandi municipality. Against this, water supply contributed only one-fortieth of the income of Bathinda town. Over the period, three municipalities of Bathinda, Goniana Mandi and Sangat Mandi have registered a decline in shares of their income from the water supply, while the remaining five recorded an increase on this count.
- Per capita municipal income from the water supply differs widely both in spatial and temporal terms. During 1980-98, municipalities in Bathinda district earned an average annual

amount of Rs. 16 per capita from the water supply. While the per capita income in absolute terms maintained an incremental trend during 1980-98, the growth in per capita income kept on declining to the extent of becoming marginal towards the end of the study period. Broadly, a correspondence was noticed between the per capita expenditure and the per capita earnings of municipalities from the water supply in the district. In other words, municipalities spending higher on water supply also earned higher, in per capita terms, from this source. Inter-municipal disparities in per capita income from water supply have been fluctuating over the period.

- The major share of municipal expenditure on water supply in the district goes as subsidy. On an average, municipalities in the district provided an amount of about Rs. 39 lakh or more than 54 per cent of their aggregate expenditure annually as subsidy on water supply during 1980-98. There were wide inter-municipal differentials in this regard. More than two-thirds of the total municipal subsidy on water supply was the share of Bathinda municipality. On the other side of the scale, the combined share of the four municipalities made up only about one-tenth of the total amount of subsidy on water supply service. Rampura Phul, the second largest municipal town in the district, shared only about 4 per cent of the total municipal subsidy on water supply in the district. Class IV, V and VI towns provided higher proportion of their expenditure as subsidy on water supply than the Class III municipal towns in the district. Kot Fatta, a Class V category of town in the district provided as high as 85 per cent of its expenditure on water supply as subsidy on this service.
- On an average, municipalities in Bathinda district provided Rs. 19 as per capita subsidy on water supply annually during 1980-98. It varied from a low of Rs. 5 in Rampura Phul to a high of Rs. 37 in Bhucho Mandi. Per capita amount of subsidy on water supply kept on growing over the period but its growth has been the highest between 1987-88 and 1992-93 when per capita amount of subsidy increased by more than twice. Thereafter, per capita subsidy amount increased by only 40 per cent during 1992-93 – 1996-97.

- Inter-municipal variations in per capita amount of subsidy on water supply find a negative relationship with rise in amount of per capita subsidy. In 1996-97, when per capita subsidy on water supply rose to its peak level of Rs. 38, inter-municipal variations were the least. It seems that there is a threshold point beyond which the growth of subsidy is to be limited. This may be the reason for decline in inter-municipal disparities in per capita amount of subsidy on water supply in the district after it attained a reasonably high level in 1992-93.
- There has been wide inter-town and intra-town spatial discrimination in distribution of subsidy component in water supply. Tap water supply, as a source of water supply, was introduced as late as in 1994-95 in Kot Fatta, whereas it was introduced long back in Bathinda City. Further, canal water which is sweet to drink is supplied in central parts of the city, while peripheral areas have to depend on hand-pumps as the main source of water supply.

SEWERAGE AND DRAINAGE

Both sewerage and drainage services are complimentary to each other. The former is a method of carrying away drainage and waste material through the underground drains or pipelines, while the later is for carrying out the same through surface drains. Further, drainage system is a pre-requisite for sewer system, hence areas/localities having sewer systems in the towns should have drainage systems also. In almost all the towns in Punjab or even in other states also, drainage system came first and the sewerage system later. The latter is not only a relatively new method of draining the waste material and water but also requires heavy investment.

Notwithstanding the complementary nature of both the services, it is interesting to note that municipalities maintain separate expenditure heads for each of them. Probably the former is a fully subsidized municipal service, while the latter is a partially subsidized urban service.

In the following, sewerage and drainage services are discussed in sequential order to answer the questions:

— How have these services evolved over time and space in towns of Bathinda district?
— How much of the area and population are still uncovered by these services and where they are located in different towns in the district?
— What is spatio-temporal pattern of expenditure on and income from these services?
— What is the absolute and per capita amount of subsidy on these services?
— What are the spatio-temporal variations in subsidy element on these services?
— Is there any spatial discrimination in the distribution of subsidy on these services?

I

SEWERAGE

Sewerage, a method of carrying away drainage and waste material through underground drains or pipelines, is one of the obligatory functions of municipalities in Punjab. The human excrete, in particular, is carried from its source toilet to pits or drainage wells, or dry stream brads where it may be treated, or it may soak into the ground or made to flow into a water body or agricultural fields. This method is replacing the earlier non-piped methods, open and covered drains, for its superiority over the non-piped methods in keeping a town free from filth, dirt and diseases. Its importance is growing with increased magnitude and complexity of urban environmental problems. Moreover, in non-piped methods night soil was carried away from individual households by scavengers who carried it on, their heads and it was considered very indignified. However, the paucity of funds with the municipal bodies combined with an inability to develop easy, simple and cost-effective sewerage system, have been major hindrances in the way of making piped sewerage system a universal phenomenon even in metropolitan centres, such as Delhi and Mumbai.

In municipal towns of Bathinda district, the underground sewerage system is not only a recent addition, but it also has limited coverage. This system is yet to touch Kot Fatta and Sangat Mandi towns. Besides none of the towns in the district, including Bathinda city, can boast of total coverage (Table 4.11). Paucity of funds with the municipal government coupled with a lack of desired attention to the issue are largely responsible for this. Nevertheless, the growing significance of a well developed sewerage system to conserve and preserve the urban environment can hardly be minimized. Today, the availability and quality of the piped sewer system in a town or any of its parts is a buzzword. The cost of land and of already constructed houses in urban localities shoot up with the introduction of a sewer system therein. In fact, the quality of life in a town or part of it depends considerably on the availability or non-availability of an efficient sewer system.

SEWERAGE SYSTEM: EVOLUTION AND EXPANSION

In 1963 the sewer system was introduced for the first time in Bathinda and Bhucho Mandi towns of the district (Table 4.11). After a gap of 10 years it was introduced in Maur Mandi in 1973 and a year later in Rampura Phul. By 1980, Raman Mandi and Goniana Mandi were also added to this list. In this way, in 1980 this facility was available in six of the eight towns in the district. The process has been slow and incomplete. Municipalities of Kot Fatta and Sangat Mandi are yet to be covered under the sewer system and in six towns, where it is available, the entire population has not yet been covered.

The population covered varies from a maximum of three-fifths in Goniana and Bhucho Mandi to a minimum of less than one-third in Maur Mandi. By 2000, it was estimated that more than half the total urban population in the district was yet to be covered under the system. This included among others the entire population of Kot Fatta and Sangat Mandi towns.

In all, there were 19,530 sewer connections in towns of Bathinda district in the year 2000. Bathinda, a Class I town, alone had three-fourth of them. In 1991, population of Bathinda town made up only about three-fifths or 60 per cent of the total urban population of the district. The Class III[2] towns of Rampura Phul and Maur

2. In 1991, there was no Class II town in the district.

TABLE 4.11

Bathinda District: Availability of Sewerage System and Population Covered under it by Various Municipalities

Name of town	*Civic status*	*Year of start*	*Estimated population covered in percentage*	*Total number of connections in 2000*	*Percentage to toal connections*
Bathinda	I	1963	56	15026	77.0
Rampura Phul	III	1974	41	1487	7.6
Maur Mandi	III	1973	30	472	2.4
Raman Mandi	IV	1980	35	620	3.2
Goniana Mandi	IV	1980	60	855	4.3
Bhucho Mandi	IV	1963	60	1070	5.5
Kot Fatta*	V	—	—	—	—
Sangat Mandi*	VI	—	—	—	—
All Towns			49	19530	100.0

* Facility not available.

Source: Data calculated from *The Sewerage Register* of various municipalities.

Mandi, together, had another 10 per cent of the total sewer connections in the district. Against this, their combined population made up 23 per cent of the total urban population of the district. Raman Mandi, Goniana Mandi and Bhucho Mandi, having the remaining 13 per cent of the sewer connections, had 14 per cent of the total urban population in the district[3].

Briefly, the process of coverage under the sewer system in urban Bathinda has not only been slow but also incomplete. None of the six towns having sewer systems in the district was fully covered and two towns were unserviced. This is not a happy situation especially in view of growing significance of the sewerage system in maintaining good quality of urban environment and life.

The sewer as well as drainage system have been evolved in a phased manner in towns of the district. In all the towns, it started with city centres and later on moved to outer areas. Peripheral areas in almost all the towns are still lacking in both the services. In contrast, central parts in all the towns, except Kot Fatta and Sangat Mandi towns, are enjoying both the services of sewerage

3. Remaining 4 per cent of the total urban population in the district was in Kot Fatta and Sangat Mandi towns which were not having underground sewer system.

and drainage. Of the six towns, where sewerage system is available, Bhucho Mandi town had the largest percentage share of its area and population covered under both sewerage and drainage before 1980 (see Maps 4.9 to 4.16). Bhucho Mandi is a Class IV town and ranks sixth among eight towns in the district with respect to population size. Bathinda, a Class I town with largest population size among all the eight towns in the district, was next (Map 4.9). Bhucho Mandi is considered a rich municipal town in the district because of its income sources. This municipality has prime land and sells parts of it whenever the need arises.

Rampura Phul, which had the third largest area and population covered under both sewerage and drainage before 1980, is the second largest town in the district. However, the notable fact about the availability of sewerage and drainage in this twin town before 1980 is that sewerage facility was available only in Rampura and not in Phul. In 2000, when the field survey was conducted by the present researcher, Phul town did not have the sewerage system (Map 4.10). Further, all the peripheral areas of Phul township did not have either of the two facilities. Phul seems to be discriminated against in favour of Rampura town probably because Rampura has the market or 'Mandi'.

Raman Mandi, which had the smallest area and population was covered under both sewerage and drainage before 1980. However, extensive parts of the municipal area are still unserved by either of the two facilities (Map 4.12). Almost the same is true of Maur Mandi town (Map 4.11) though it is quite surprising because Maur Mandi town is the third largest with respect to population. This town is largely served by the drainage facility.

Spatial expansion in sewerage network happened in different phases. While it was almost equally spread over 1980-90 and 1990-2000 phases in Bathinda town, almost the entire expansion in Raman Mandi town took place during 1980-90 phase (Map 4.12). In Maur Mandi town, the progress in this context has been quite slow after 1980. In almost all towns, the spatial expansion in sewerage and drainage has been contiguous but in Bathinda town a pocket falling west of the railway line is far away from the mainstream. In fact, more than 90 per cent of the sewerage service in the town lies East of the railway line.

Map 4.9

Bhathinda Municipality
Sewerage and Drainage
Spatial Expansion and Coverage

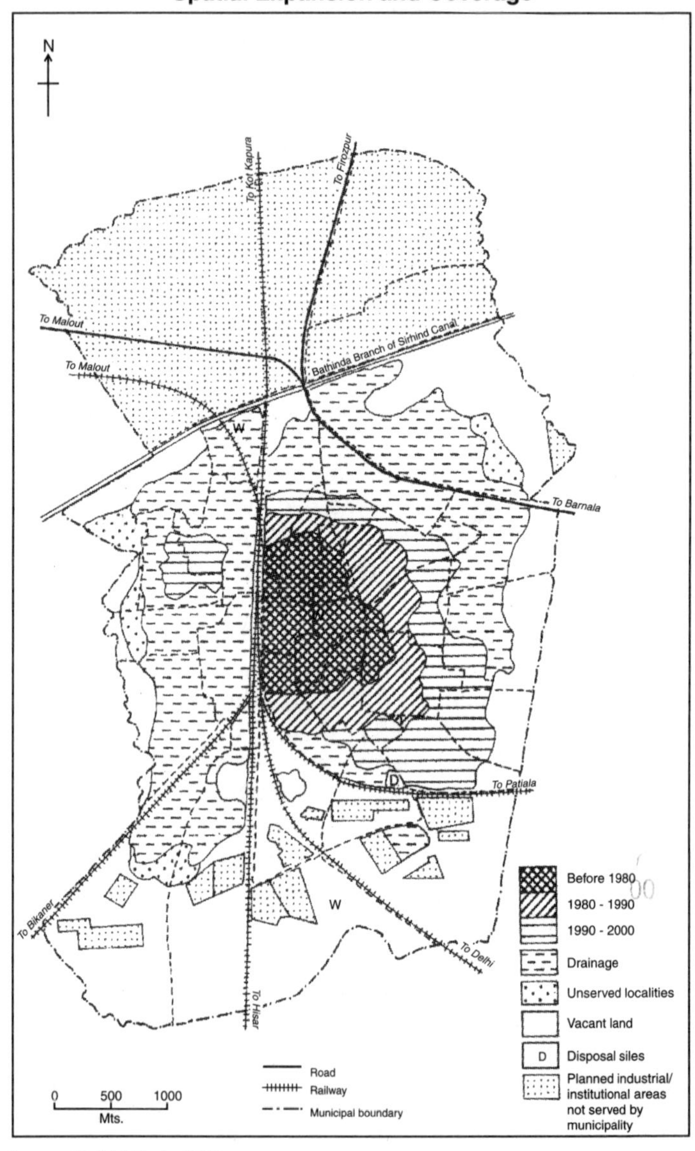

Source: Field Work, 2000.

Map 4.10

Rampura Phul Municipality
Sewerage and Drainage
Spatial Expansion and Coverage

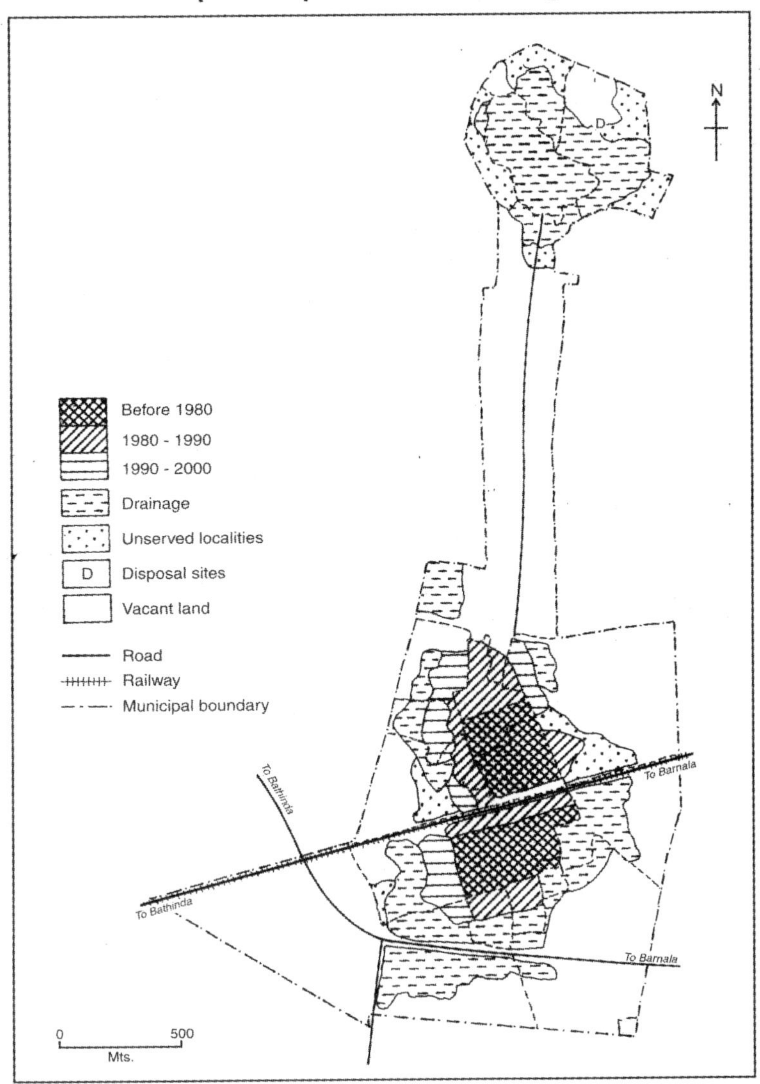

Source: Field Work, 2000.

Map 4.11

Maur Mandi Municipality
Sewerage and Drainage
Spatial Expansion and Coverage

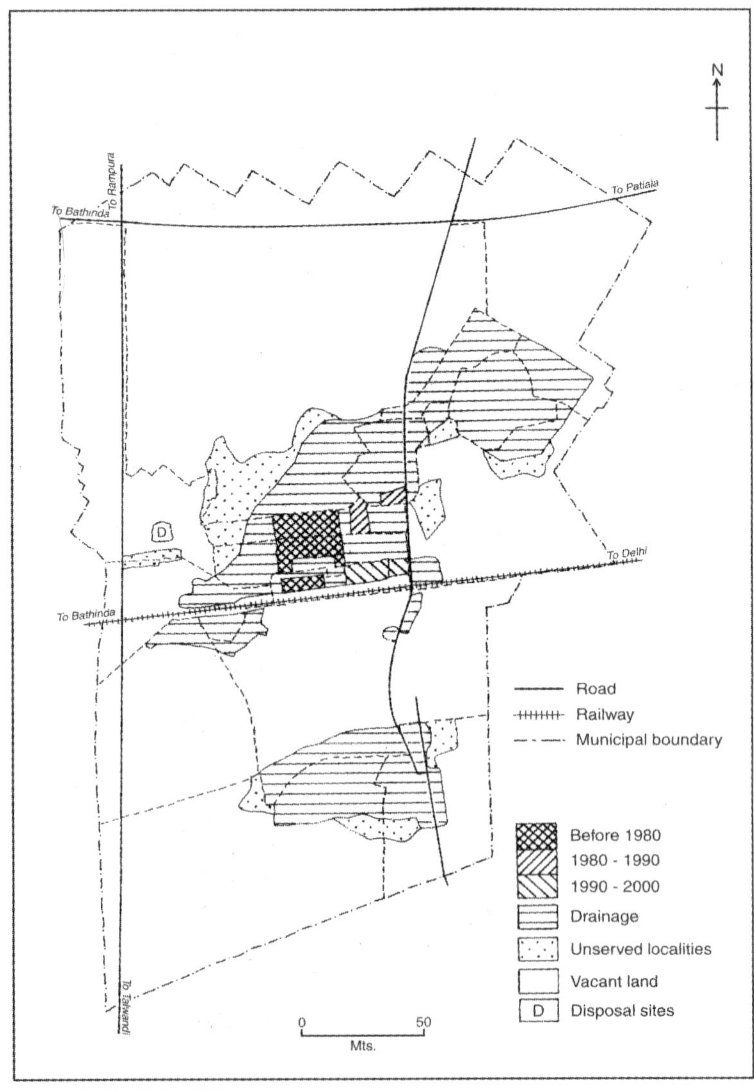

Source: Field Work, 2000.

Map 4.12

Raman Mandi Municipality

Sewerage and Drainage Spatial Expansion and Coverage

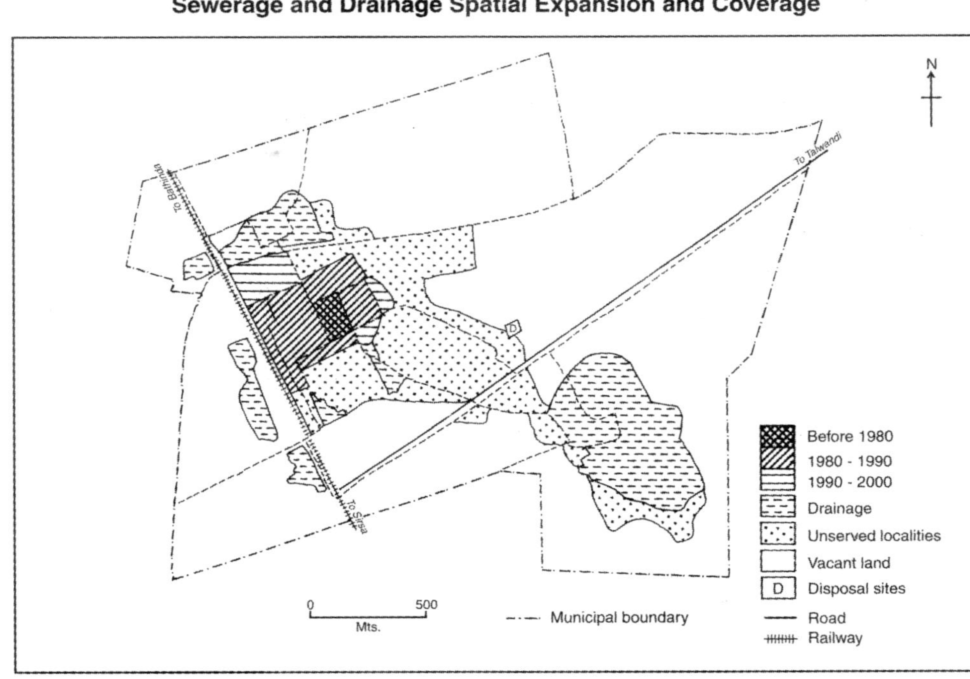

Source: Field Work, 2000.

Map 4.13

Goniana Mandi Municipality

Sewerage and Drainage Spatial Expansion and Coverage

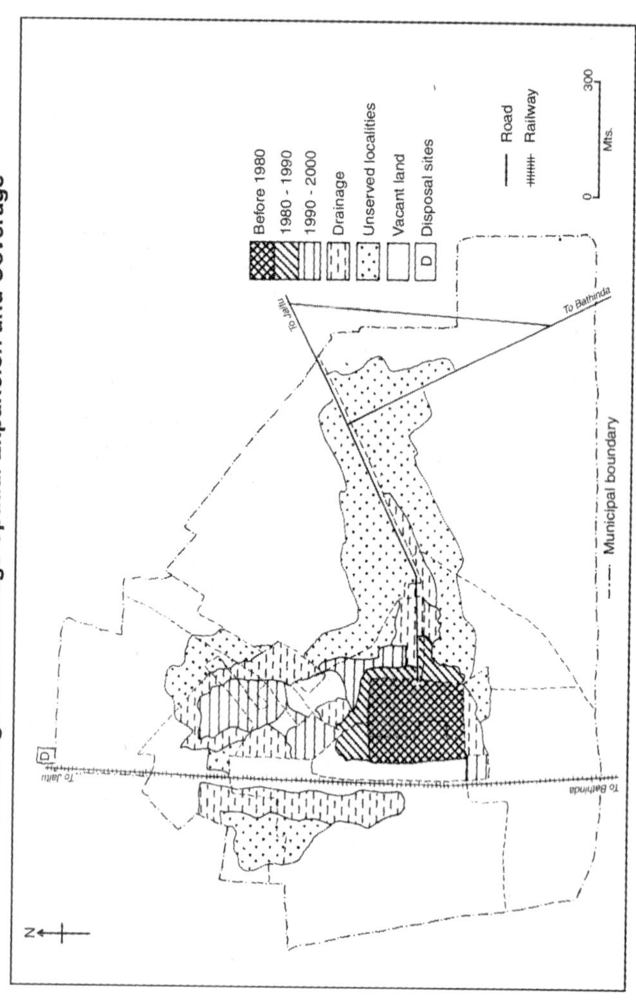

Source: Field Work, 2000.

Map 4.14

Bhucho Mandi Municipality
Sewerage and Drainage
Spatial Expansion and Coverage

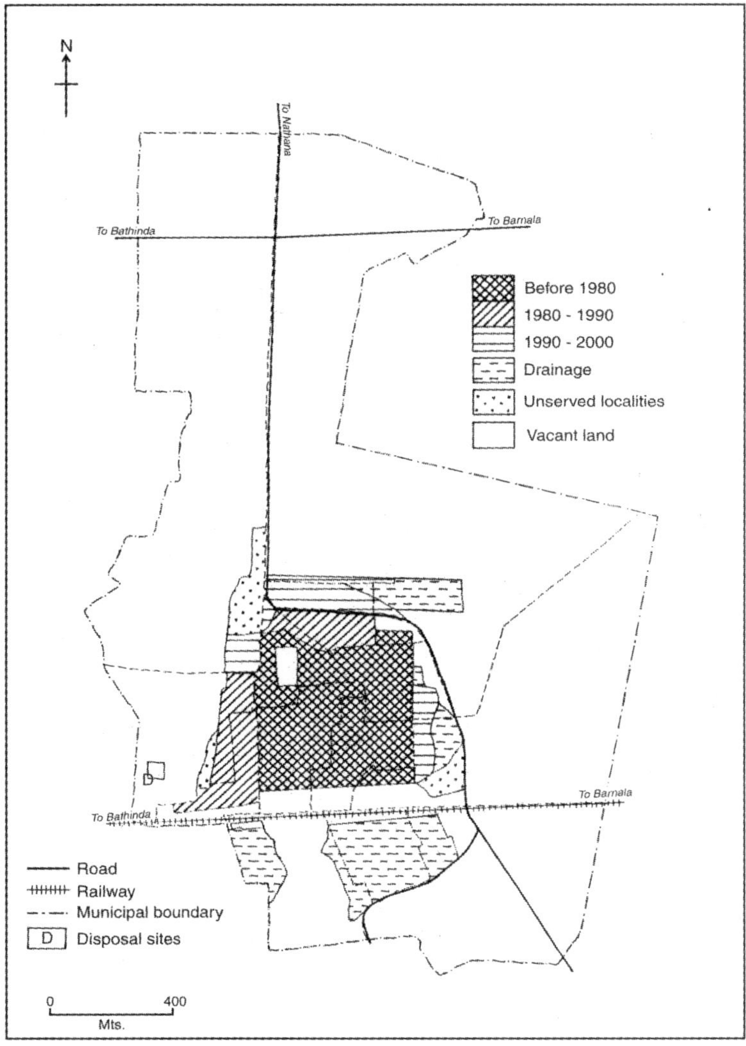

Source: Field Work, 2000.

Map 4.15

Kot Fatta Municipality

Drainage: Spatial Expansion and Coverage

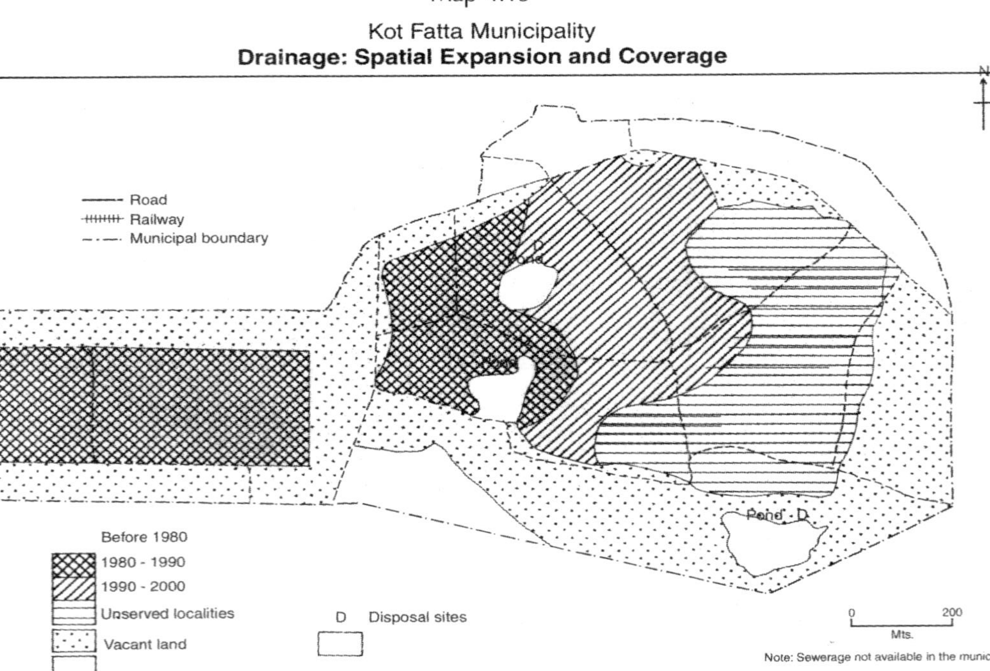

Source: Field Work, 2000.

Map 4.16

Sangat Mandi Municipality
Drainage: Spatial Expansion and Coverage

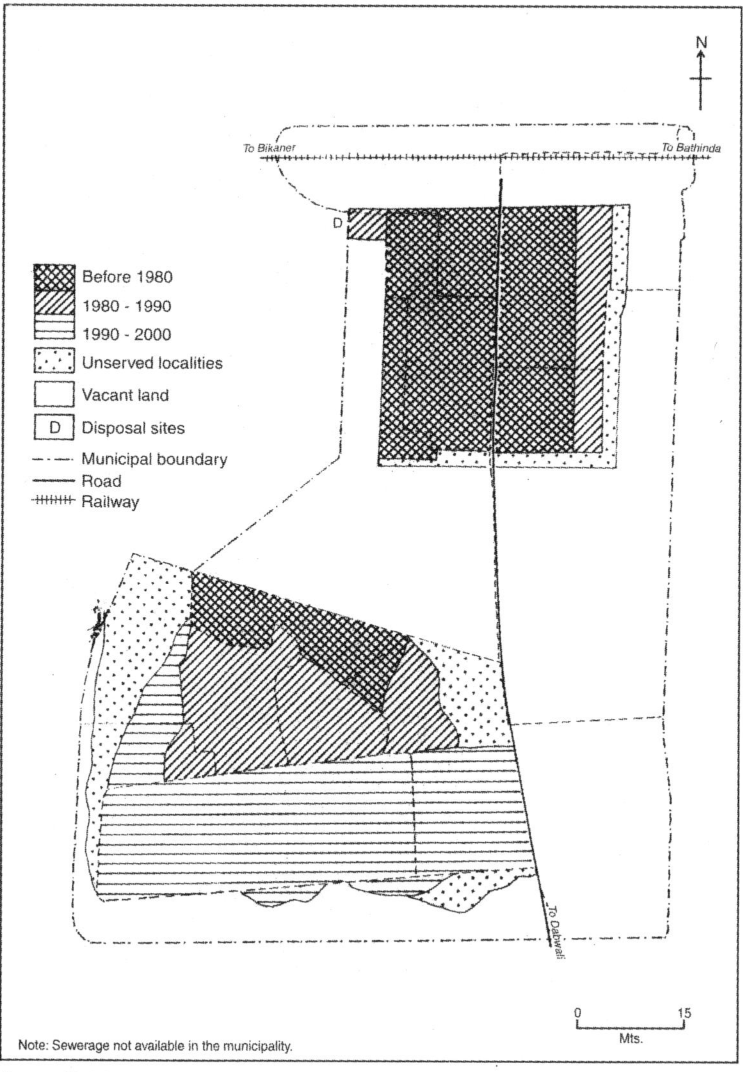

Source: Field Work, 2000.

Subsidy on Sewerage: Pattern and Change

In Bathinda district, the sewer system is one of the highly subsidized municipal services. On annual average basis, municipalities in the district incurred an amount of Rs. 124 lakh on this account during 1980-98 (Table 4.12). Against this, municipalities earned only Rs. 10 lakh as income, which was the fee on sewer connections. Thus, Rs. 114 lakh, making up about 92 per cent in average annual expenditure on sewerage, was the subsidy component. In other words, Rs. 92 out of every Rs. 100 spent by the municipalities on the sewerage system in Bathinda district was the subsidy element.

There were, however, wide inter-municipal variations in this context. Of the total annual subsidy amount of Rs. 114 lakh, provided by all the municipalities in the district on sewerage, Rs.105 lakh or 92 per cent was contributed by the Bathinda municipality. Against this, its share in total municipal expenditure on sewerage had been 90 per cent and its income share in total municipal income from sewer connections was 66 per cent (Table 4.12).

On the other hand, the share of Rampura Phul, the second largest municipality in the district, was about 4 per cent in total subsidy against its share of more than 6 per cent in total municipal income from sewer connections. Similarly, the shares of Maur Mandi and Raman Mandi were lower than their respective shares in the aggregate municipal income from sewer connections. Their combined subsidy share was 1.3 per cent against their income share of about 9 per cent. The sewerage being a highly subsidized service in the district, it is directly proportional to the number of sewer connections in a town.

In this regard, Goniana Mandi[4] needs special mention. It earned more than 14 per cent of the aggregate annual income of all municipalities from sewer connections against its share of less than half of a per cent in total municipal subsidy on this count. Bhucho Mandi is another town where the income share was nearly double of its share in subsidy. In fact, Bathinda is the only municipality in the district which earns lower share of income

4. Goniana Mandi municipality charges Rs. 12 per toitet seat from the service consumers. Against this, all the other municipalities in the district charge Rs. 10 or less per seat.

TABLE 4.12

Bathinda District: Municipal Expenditure on Sewerage as Percentage of Total Municipal Expenditure, 1980-98

(*Rs. in lakhs*)

Name of town	*Civic status*	*1982-83**			*1987-88**			*1992-93**			*1996-97**			*1980-98**		
		Aggregate expenditure	*Expenditure on sewerage*	*Percentage. of aggregate expenditure*	*Aggregate expenditure*	*Expenditure on sewerage*	*Percentage of aggregate expenditure*	*Aggregate expenditure*	*Expenditure on sewerage*	*Percentage. of aggregate expenditure*	*Aggregate expenditure*	*Expenditure on sewerage*	*Percentage of aggregate expenditure*	*Aggregate expenditure*	*Expenditure on sewerage*	*Percentage of aggregate expenditure*
1	*2*	*3*	*4*	*5*	*6*	*7*	*8*	*9*	*10*	*11*	*12*	*13*	*14*	*15*	*16*	*17*
Bathinda	I	207.10	43.20	20.86	456.43	75.91	16.63	755.21	171.90	22.76	1135.78	185.86	16.36	583.39	111.81	19.17
Rampura Phul	III	34.62	1.54	4.49	55.62	2.76	4.96	104.96	6.32	6.02	162.77	10.63	6.53	81.35	4.72	5.80
Maur Mandi	III	14.61	0.53	3.63	31.80	0.97	3.05	52.30	1.21	2.31	77.11	1.77	2.30	40.27	1.05	2.61
Raman Mandi	IV	12.20	0.56	4.59	28.50	0.78	2.74	53.35	01.39	2.61	85.41	3.68	4.31	40.36	1.37	3.40
Goniana Mandi	IV	14.30	1.31	9.16	28.70	1.17	4.08	41.46	2.03	4.90	54.33	4.44	8.17	32.52	1.99	6.12
Bhucho Mandi	IV	18.04	2.38	13.19	39.60	3.48	8.79	42.47	2.75	6.48	90.16	5.04	5.59	42.84	3.23	7.54
Kot Fatta	V	1.10	—	—	4.70	—	—	5.65	—	—	7.68	—	—	4.46	Nil	Nil
Sangat Mandi	VI	1.60	—	—	2.90	—	—	8.99	—	—	11.63	—	—	5.69	Nil	Nil
Aggregate Expenditure		303.57	49.52	16.31	648.25	85:07	13.12	1064.39	185.60	17.44	1624.87	211.42	13.01	830.91	124.17	14.94
Average per Municipality		50.60	8.25	16.31	108.04	14.18	13.12	177.40	30.93	17.44	270.81	35.24	13.01	138.49	20.70	14.94
C.V.	1.70	1.90		1.76	1.95		1.78	2.04		1.75	1.91				1.76	1.97

* Annual averages calculated at the mid-year. First three are the five year average, fourth one is three year average and fifth and last is 18 year average.

C.V. stands for Coefficient of Variability.

Source: Data calculated from *Classified Abstracts* of different municipalities for various years.

than its share of subsidy on this count. It is, however, worth mentioning that the total number of sewer connections in municipalities other than Bathinda is quite small. Hence, their combined share in the total municipal subsidy on sewerage makes for less than 8 per cent. At the same time, they earn, in combination, about 34 per cent of the total municipal income from this source in the district. Naturally, the subsidy element is relatively less in the small municipal towns in comparison to the large sized municipal towns in the district.

The subsidy as a percentage of municipal expenditure on sewerage is also highly revealing. The average for all the municipalities was 92 per cent during 1980-98. It varied from a high of about 94 per cent in Bathinda municipality to a low of only 27 per cent in Goniana Mandi (Table 4.13). As stated earlier, Goniana Mandi is one such municipality that charges relatively higher amount per toilet seat in comparison to other municipalities. The second lowest share (60 per cent) but distinctively higher than Goniana Mandi, was given by Maur Mandi. Against this, Bhucho Mandi, though a small-sized municipal town gave 85 per cent of its total expenditure on sewerage as subsidy on this count. It ranked third after Bathinda and Rampura Phul. A variety of factors including the differential rates charged by municipalities on per toilet seat basis, the number of total sewer connections in a town, per meter cost of developing underground sewerage system, and administrative and civic status of a town were responsible for these variations in the share of municipal subsidy on sewerage.

The change in share of subsidy as a proportion to municipal expenditure on sewerage is highly revealing. It increased to about 94 per cent in 1996-97 from about 85 per cent in 1982-83 (Table 4.13). In the mean time, subsidy as percentage to total municipal expenditure has declined to about 12 per cent from about 14 per cent (Table 4.14). It can be inferred that the expenditure on sewerage service was gradually receiving a low priority in overall municipal expenditure in the district, whereas the subsidy component is growing due to low and slow growing income from this service. Secondly, for popularistic reasons almost all the municipalities keep the rates of toilet seats low. Hence, subsidy element keeps on rising. In almost all the towns, even the initial investment and maintenance costs were not realised.

TABLE 4.13

Bathinda District: Subsidy as Percentage to Total Municipal Expenditure on Sewerage, 1980-98

Name of town	Civic status	1982-83*		1987-88*		1992-93*		1996-97*		1980-98*	
		Subsidy	% of amount spent upon sewerage	Subsidy	% of amount spent upon sewerage	Subsidy	% of amount spent upon sewerage	Subsidy	% of amount spent upon sewerage	Subsidy	% of amount spent upon sewerage
Bathinda	I	37.02	85.69	69.22	91.19	164.96	95.96	178.09	95.82	105.01	93.92
Rampura Phul	III	1.46	94.81	2.41	87.32	5.46	86.39	8.87	83.44	4.30	91.10
Maur Mandi	III	0.37	69.81	0.60	61.86	0.66	54.55	1.03	58.19	0.63	60.00
Raman Mandi	IV	0.39	69.64	0.45	57.69	0.68	48.92	2.84	77.17	0.89	64.96
Goniana Mandi	IV	0.81	61.83	0.26	22.22	.03	1.48	1.60	36.04	0.53	26.63
Bhucho Mandi	IV	2.22	93.28	3.18	91.38	2.03	73.82	4.14	82.14	2.75	85.14
Kot Fatta	V	—	—	—	—	—	—	—	—	—	—
Sangat Mandi	VI	—	—	—	—	—	—	—	—	—	—
All Towns		42.27	85.36	76.12	89.48	173.82	93.65	196.57	92.98	113.88	91.71
C.V.		1.90	0.16	1.99	0.36	2.10	0.51	1.99	0.27	2.03	0.33

* Annual averages calculated at the mid-year. First three are the five year averages, fourth one is three year average and fifth and last is 18 year average.

Note: C.V. stands for Coefficient of Variability.

Source: Data calculated from *Classified Abstracts* of different municipalities for various years.

There were, however, inter-municipal variations in the context. While, the share of subsidy recorded an increasing trend in Bathinda municipality, no set trend has been observed in the case of other municipalities in the district. Frequent ups and downs in subsidy share have been the marked feature in the case of Raman Mandi and Goniana Mandi towns. For example, subsidy component made up about 49 per cent in Raman Mandi's expenditure on sewerage in 1992-93, which rose to more than 77 per cent in 1996-97. Similarly, the subsidy component was less than 2 per cent in Goniana Mandi in 1992-93, which rose to as high as 62 per cent in 1982-83 (Table 4.13).

TABLE 4.14

Bathinda District: Subsidy on Sewerage as Percentage to Aggregate Municipal Expenditure, 1980-98

Name of town	*Civic status*	*1982-83**		*1987-88**		*1992-93**		*1996-97**		*1980-98**	
		Subsidy	*%age of aggregate expenditure*	*Subsidy*	*%age of aggregate expenditure*	*Subsidy*	*%age of aggregate expenditure*	*Subsidy*	*%age of aggregate expenditure*	*Subsidy*	*%age of aggregate expenditure*
Bathinda	I	37.02	17.88	69.22	15.17	164.96	21.84	178.09	15.68	105.01	18.00
Rampura Phul	III	1.46	4.22	2.41	4.33	5.46	5.20	8.87	5.45	4.30	5.29
Maur Mandi	III	0.37	2.53	0.60	1.89	0.66	1.26	1.03	1.34	0.63	1.56
Raman Mandi	IV	0.39	3.20	0.45	1.58	0.68	1.27	2.84	3.33	0.89	2.21
Goniana Mandi	IV	0.81	5.66	0.26	0.91	.03	0.072	1.60	2.94	0.53	1.63
Bhucho Mandi	IV	2.22	12.31	3.18	8.03	2.03	4.78	4.14	4.59	2.75	6.42
Kot Fatta	V	—	—	—	—	—	—	—	—	—	—
Sangat Mandi	VI	—	—	—	—	—	—	—	—	—	—
All Towns		42.27	13.92	76.12	11.74	173.82	16.33	196.57	12.10	113.88	13.71

* Annual averages calculated at the mid-year. First three are the five year averages, fourth one is three year average and fifth and last is 18 year average.

Source: Data calculated from *Classified Abstracts* of different municipalities for various years.

Per Capita Subsidy

On an average, municipalities in Bathinda district provided for Rs. 58 per capita per annum as subsidy on sewerage during 1980-98 (Fig. 4.6). There were, however, wide inter-municipal disparities in this regard. It varied from a high of Rs. 91 in Bathinda municipality to a low of Rs. 3 in Maur Mandi (Table 4.15). In other words, Bathinda municipality provided 30 times higher per capita amount of subsidy on sewerage in comparison to Maur Mandi town. Other municipalities providing the low per capita subsidy on this account included Raman Mandi, Goniana Mandi and Rampura Phul. Per capita subsidy amount was lower than the average in five of the six municipalities having

Fig. 4.6

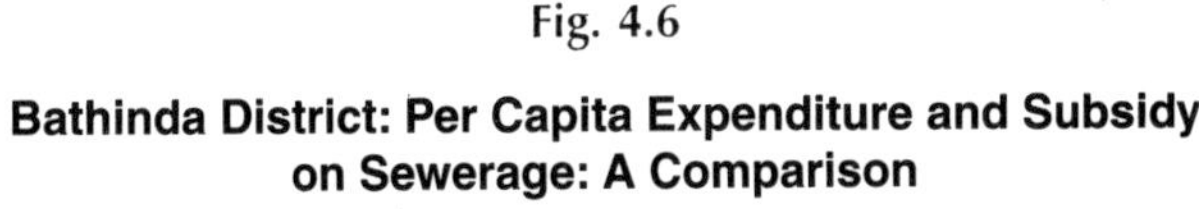

Bathinda District: Per Capita Expenditure and Subsidy on Sewerage: A Comparison

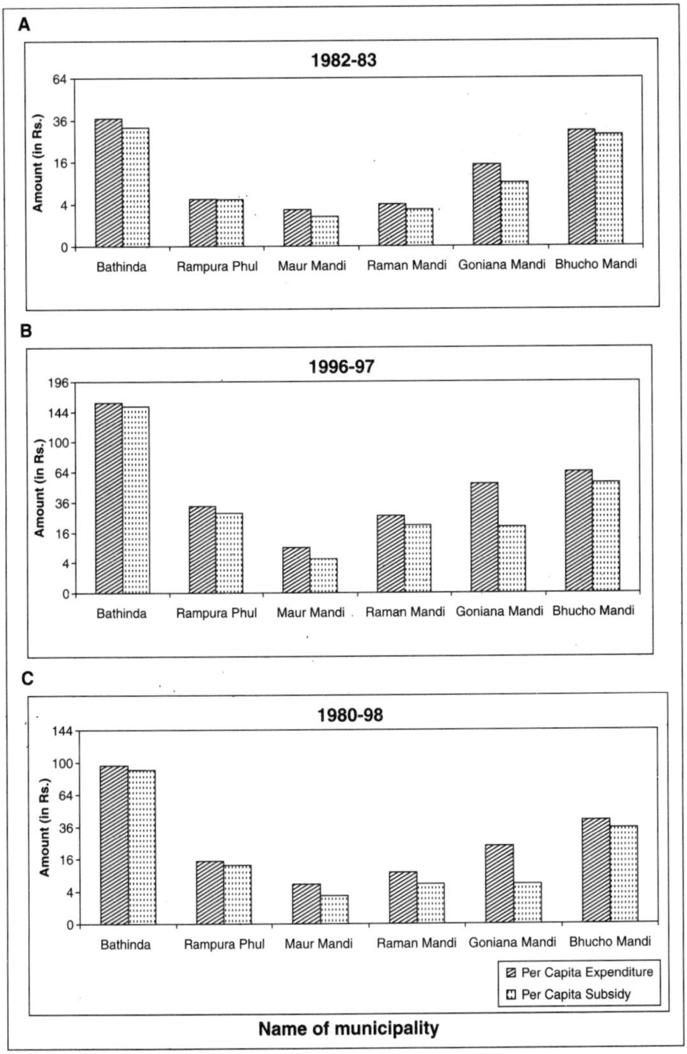

A

1982-83

Amount (in Rs.)

64
36
16
4
0

Bathinda Rampura Phul Maur Mandi Raman Mandi Goniana Mandi Bhucho Mandi

B

1996-97

Amount (in Rs.)

196
144
100
64
36
16
4
0

Bathinda Rampura Phul Maur Mandi Raman Mandi Goniana Mandi Bhucho Mandi

C

1980-98

Amount (in Rs.)

144
100
64
36
16
4
0

Bathinda Rampura Phul Maur Mandi Raman Mandi Goniana Mandi Bhucho Mandi

Per Capita Expenditure
Per Capita Subsidy

Name of municipality

Notes: (i) Sewerage service is not available in Kot Fatta and Sangat Mandi towns.
(ii) Towns have been listed in order of their population size and civic status.

underground sewerage system in the district. Bathinda and Bhucho Mandi towns, which provided this amount higher than the average for all municipalities, in fact, could do so because of their higher capacity to generate income from their revenue sources.

TABLE 4.15

Bathinda District: A Comparison of Municipal Subsidy on Sewerage, 1980-98

Name of town	*Expenditure (Rs. in lakh)*	*Income (Rs. in lakh)*	*Subsidy (Rs. in lakh)*	*Subsidy per capita (in Rs.)*
Bathinda	111.81*	6.80*	105.01*	91*
	(90.05)	(66.08)	(92.21)	
Rampura Phul	4.72	0.65	4.07	13
	(3.80)	(6.32)	(3.57)	
Maur Mandi	1.05	0.42	0.63	3
	(0.85)	(4.08)	(0.55)	
Raman Mandi	1.37	0.48	0.89	6
	(1.10)	(4.66)	(0.78)	
Goniana Mandi	1.99	1.46	0.53	6
	(1.60)	(14.19)	(0.47)	
Bhucho Mandi	3.23	0.48	2.75	35
	(2.60)	(4.66)	(2.41)	
Kot Fatta	—	—	—	—
Sangat Mandi	—	—	—	—
All Towns	124.17	10.29	113.88	58
	(100.0)	(100.0)	(100.0)	

* Annual averages.

Notes: 1. Per capita subsidy has been calculated on the basis of 1981 Census data. In case of Bathinda city population figures used for calculation of subsidy confined to areas falling under the jurisdiction of Bathinda Municipal committee. Two public sector units, Fertilizer and Thermal Plant make their own arrangements for provision of services, to their residents. Hence they are excluded from calculations.

2. Figures in parentheses indicate percentage share in total.

Source: Data calculated from classified abstract of different municipalities for various years.

Bathinda municipality, which provided the highest per capita subsidy on sewerage, has the largest area and population size among all the municipalities in the district. Its population was 4.5 times more and area was six times more than the second ranking municipal town (Rampura Phul) in the district. District headquarters are located here and it is the fastest growing town in the district. Evolving and maintaining a large network of sewerage system requires large capital investment. At the same time, low rates charged on per sewer seat basis, low recovery of arrears from defaulters and lack of heavy fines on delayed payments, etc. have contributed to this situation. Municipal incomes from sewerage service are not only low but also slow both in absolute and per capita terms. For example, income earned from sewerage service by Bathinda municipality made only about 1 per cent in its total municipal income earned from various services. Against this, expenditure incurred on this service made for more than 19 per cent in total municipal expenditure during 1980-98. During the same period, while municipal income from this service grew only by about 26 per cent, the expenditure has increased by more than 330 per cent. This has resulted in rapid growth of municipal subsidy in Bathinda town on this count, both in absolute and per capita terms. Per capita amount of subsidy has grown from Rs. 32 in 1982-83 to Rs. 153 in 1996-97, registering an increase of 378 per cent (Table 4.16).

Over the period, there have been frequent ups and downs in the per capita amount of subsidy on sewerage. In 1982-83, it was Rs. 21, for all the municipalities, which rose to Rs. 39 in 1987-88 and then to Rs. 88 in 1992-93. Thereafter, it increased to Rs. 99 in 1996-97. This shows that though the absolute amount of subsidy on sewerage has been growing but its rate of increase has been coming down in recent years. While the subsidy amount increased by about 126 per cent during 1987-88–1992-93, it has grown only by about 13 per cent during 1992-93–1996-97. It seems that macro-economic reforms of 1991, wherein reduction in government subsidies on various goods and services was one of the main objectives, have shown their impact even at the level of micro-level institutions.

The change in per capita amount of subsidy on sewerage differed widely among the municipalities. Between 1982-83 and 1996-97, it ranged from an increase of more than six times in Raman Mandi to less than one time in Bhucho Mandi. Three municipalities, namely, Maur Mandi, Goniana Mandi and Bhucho Mandi registered an increase of less than three times. Against this, Raman Mandi and Rampura Phul recorded an increase of more than five times. Bathinda municipality, the largest municipal town in the district, recorded an increase of about five times.

TABLE 4.16

Bathinda District: Per Capita Municipal Subsidy on Sewerage, 1980-98

Name of town	*1982-83**		*1987-88**		*1992-93**		*1996-97**		*1980-98**	
	Subsidy (Rs. in lakhs)	*Subsidy per capita (in Rs.)*	*Subsidy (Rs. in lakhs)*	*Subsidy per capita (in Rs.)*	*Subsidy (Rs. in lakhs)*	*Subsidy per capita (in Rs.)*	*Subsidy (Rs. in lakhs)*	*Subsidy per capita (in Rs.)*	*Subsidy (Rs. in lakhs)*	*Subsidy per capita (in Rs.)*
Bathinda	37.02 (87.58)	32	69.22 (90.94)	60	164.96 (94.90)	142	178.09 (90.60)	153	105.01 (92.21)	91
Rampura Phul	1.46 (3.45)	5	2.41 (3.17)	8	5.46 (3.14)	17	8.87 (4.51)	28	4.07 (3.57)	13
Maur Mandi	0.37 (.88)	2	0.60 (0.79)	3	0.66 (0.38)	4	1.03 (0.53)	5	0.63 (0.55)	3
Raman Mandi	0.39 (0.92)	3	0.45 (0.59)	3	0.68 (0.39)	5	2.84 (1.44)	20	0.89 (0.78)	6
Goniana Mandi	0.81 (1.92)	9	0.26 (0.34)	3	.03 (0.02)	0.35	1.60 (0.81)	19	0.53 (0.47)	6
Bhucho Mandi	2.22 (5.25)	28	3.18 (4.18)	41	2.03 (1.17)	26	4.14 (2.11)	53	2.75 (2.41)	35
Kot Fatta	—		—		—		—	—	—	
Sangat Mandi	—		—		—		—	—	—	
All Towns	42.27 (100)	21	76.12 (100)	39	173.82 (100)	88	196.57 (100)	99	113.88 (100)	58
C.V.	1.90	0.92	1.99	1.15	2.10	1.54	1.99	1.08	2.03	1.21

* Annual averages calculated at the mid-year. First three are the five year averages, fourth one is three year average and fifth and last is 18 year average.

Notes: (i) Figures in parentheses indicate percentage share in total.

(ii) Per capita subsidy has been calculated on the basis of 1981 census data. In case of Bathinda population figures used for calculation of subsidies confined to areas falling under the jurisdiction of Bathinda M.C. Two public sector units, Fertilizer and Thermal Plant make their own arrangements for provision of services and hence have been excluded from the calculations/computations.

(iii) C.V. stand for Coefficient of Variability.

Source: Data calculated from *Classified Abstracts* of different municipalities for various years.

On the whole, municipalities which provided high amount of per capita subsidy on sewerage recorded relatively low increase in this amount and *vice-versa*. This has been responsible for marginal decline in inter-municipal disparities in per capita amount of municipal subsidy on sewerage during 1980-98.

A comparison of per capita municipal expenditure, income and subsidy on sewerage in the district is highly revealing. While per capita municipal expenditure on sewerage finds a weak or even negative association with per capita income of municipalities from this service, per capita municipal expenditure recorded strong positive association with per capita municipal subsidy on this service. In other words, municipal subsidy on sewerage is highly guided by the municipal expenditure on this service. But the municipal expenditure on this service makes no barometer to gauge the per capita amount of municipal subsidy on this service. For example, Goniana Mandi, a Class IV municipal town, incurred a per capita expenditure of Rs. 23 on sewerage to earn Rs. 17 per capita during 1980-98. Against this, Bhucho Mandi, also a Class IV town, spent Rs. 41 per capita to earn only Rs. 6 per capita for sewerage during the same period.

Another interesting feature, which also emerged out of such an examination, is the association between per capita municipal income from sewerage which is not only weak but also bent towards negative over the period. It shows that no efforts were made on the part of municipalities in the district to rationalize the component of subsidy on urban services.

Spatial Discrimination in Distribution of Subsidy Component

It is evidently clear from the above discussion that sewerage is one of the highly subsidized urban services in the district. Nearly 92 per cent of the aggregate expenditure on sewerage system in the district goes in the form of subsidy. On per capita basis, it comes to Rs. 58 per annum during 1980-98. Its complementary service of drainage is fully subsidized, on which an amount of Rs. 19 per capita is additional. In all, Rs. 77 per capita was a combined per capita annual average subsidy on sewerage and drainage services. Nevertheless, benefits of the facility were enjoyed neither in all towns, nor by all citizens in individual towns.

Firstly, in towns of the Kot Fatta and Sangat Mandi where the facility of sewerage was not at all available, the entire population and area therein has been deprived of the benefits of this facility. Secondly, while the residents of Bathinda city are enjoying this facility, of course in limited areas, since 1963, the facility came in recently (in 1980) in towns of Raman Mandi and Goniana Mandi towns. Thirdly, more than three out of every four sewer connections in all towns in the district were confined to Bathinda City wherein resided only less than two of every three urban dwellers in Bathinda district. Fourthly, while about 60 per cent of the total in towns of Goniana Mandi and Bhucho Mandi were covered under this facility, it has been just 30 per cent in the case of Maur Mandi town. In this way, there is wide inter and intra-town discrimination in distribution of subsidy on sewerage facility.

In the following an attempt will be made to examine the nature and intensity of spatial discrimination in distribution of subsidy element in sewerage with the help of a case study of Bathinda City, Rampura Phul, Bhucho Mandi and Sangat Mandi towns.

As per the information from the Bathinda municipal committee office, localities namely, Civil Lines, Ganesha Basti, Birla Mills colony and old parts of the city received the priority in sewerage system which was started in 1963. Before 1980, nearly one-tenth of the area and less than one-third of the total population in the city were fully or partially covered under sewerage and drainage. During 1980-98, another one-tenth of the area and more than one-tenths of the city's population were covered. By 1990, following ten localities were covered. These include Civil Lines, Ganesha Basti, Birla Colony, old part of the city, Model Town, Town Planning Scheme 3-I and 3-II, Shant Nagar, Nai Basti and Chandsar Basti. This whole area had been contiguous falling East of the railway line, passing in a North-South direction in the city. By 1990, six wards were fully covered, nine partially covered and one more was marginally covered. This made one-fifth of the area and more than two-fifths of the total population of the city.

During 1990-2000, coverage under sewerage further extended to new areas, notable feature of coverage during 1990-2000 has been that some localities lying west of the railway line were for the first time covered under the sewerage system. Otherwise, whatever little coverage was available in localities lying west of the railway line, it has been under the drainage only. Areas thus covered under sewerage, outside the previously covered localities included Gopal Nagar, Paras Ram Nagar, and Railway Colony. By the end of 2000, more than two-fifths (41 per cent) of the area and nearly three-fifths (56 per cent) of the population were covered under the sewerage system (Table 4.17). The areas localities having sewerage, also have drainage. In all, there were more than 15,000 sewer connections in different parts of the city.

TABLE 4.17

Bathinda District: Area and Population Covered under the Sewerage Drainage in Sampled Towns by 2000

Name of town	*Civic status*	*Area covered (in acres) under*				*Population covered (in numbers) under*			
		Sewerage & drainage	*Drainage only*	*Uncovered area*	*Total*	*Sewerage & drainage*	*Drainage only*	*Uncovered area*	*Total*
Bathinda	I	1884.6	2524.3	210.0	4618.9	80982	54207	8957	144146
		(40.8)	(54.6)	(4.6)	(100.0)	(56.2)	(37.6)	(6.2)	(100.0)
Rampura	III	165.5	200.1	37.0	402.6	14449	18764	2134	35347
Phul		(41.1)	(49.7)	(9.2)	(100.0)	(40.9)	(53.1)	(6.0)	(100.0)
Bhucho	IV	96.3	34.6	7.4	138.3	6581	2738	589	9908
Mandi		(69.6)	(25.0)	(5.4)	(100.0)	(66.4)	(27.6)	(6.0)	(100.0)
Sangat	V	—	79.0	2.5	81.5	—	2494	188	2682
Mandi			(96.9)	(3.1)	(100.0)	(7.0)	(93.0)	7.0	(100.0)

Notes: (i) Area and population figures are estimates. Area has been estimated using square method.
(ii) Area figures relates to 2000 and population figures 1991 census.
(iii) Figures in parentheses indicate share in total.

In this way, about three-fifths of the area and more than two-fifths of the population in the city was without sewerage facility. Of this area and population, dominant share had only the drainage system. There has been still about 5 per cent of the total area and more than 6 per cent of the population that were covered neither by sewerage nor drainage. During the fieldwork, it was found that such areas were partially located in five wards numbering 4, 29, 30, 31 and 33 and resided in by population having low socio-economic status. Some of the localities that have not yet been covered by sewerage and/or drainage are quite populous (Table 4.18).

On the other side of the scale, sewerage system is working satisfactorily only in selected localities, such as Civil Lines, parts of the old city, Shant Nagar and Model Town. In rest of the localities, maintenance of the system is poor, making a clear cut case of discrimination. The localities inhabitated by government officials, professionals and rich business are looked after well at

TABLE 4.18

Bathinda District: Coverage under Sewerage/Drainage by Municipal Wards

Name of town	*Wards covered under*		
	Sewerage & drainage	*Drainage*	
		Fully	*Partially/Marginally*
Bathinda City	6, 7, 9, 11, 12, 15, 16, 17, 18, 19, 20, 21, 22, 23, 24, 25, 35	5, 8, 10, 13, 14, 22, 26, 27 28, 32, 34	4, 29, 30, 31, 33
Rampura Phul	5, 11, 12, 13, 14, 15, 16,	2, 4, 6, 7, 8, 9, 15, 17	1, 3, 5, 10, 13
Bhucho Mandi	2, 3, 4, 9, 10, 13	1, 5, 6, 7,	8, 11, 12
Sangat Mandi	—	1, 2, 3, 6, 8, 9	4, 5, 7

Note: Ward numbers 1-3 of Bathinda city are not served by Bathinda Municipal Committee. These planned institutional/industrial areas are served by independent authorities.

the cost of other localities. In case of some localities, the choked sewer overflows the drain and finally enters into the streets. It stinks all around.

Water logging is the main cause of the failure of sewerage system. Besides, there are some engineering defects, as land gradient was not given due respect in laying the underground pipes. Wherever, the pipes are not replaced or their alignment is improper, sewerage system failed. It is more typical of low income localities. This is more or less true of other towns in the district.

In the twin towns of Rampura and Phul, where only about two-thirds of the population is covered under sewerage facility, the sewerage system is confined only to Rampura Mandi township. Any locality in Phul town is yet to be covered under sewerage system. Not only that, in Phul town the whole population has not yet been covered under the drainage system (Map 4.10). Within Rampura township also, it was mainly the central part that is covered under sewerage system, peripheral areas are covered only under the drainage system. Of the total geographical area of the town, 41 per cent is covered under sewerage, and drainage, about 50 per cent under drainage only and the remaining about 9 per cent is totally uncovered. Interestingly more than 60 per cent coverage under the sewerage system had been completed before 1980. Of the remaining 40 per cent, one-half took place during 1980-90 and the remaining half during 1990-2000. Areas covered after 1980 are contiguous to areas covered before 1980. The areas covered under the sewerage system make a somewhat elongated shape in the North-South direction, mostly covering government offices, localities resided in by high income households and the market area. Areas falling in their surroundings, which are resided in by low income households, are covered under the drainage system only, which at several places does not work well especially during the rainy season.

Bhucho Mandi town, where coverage under both, sewerage and drainage is about 70 per cent and another 25 per cent is covered under drainage, has the least spatial discrimination among the towns in the district (Map 4.14). Not only the coverage is large but also quality of sewerage is good. It is only in the areas where industrial labour live near industrial units such as Gurmeet & Co. Cotton Mills and Ice Factory, neither sewer nor drains are available. During fieldwork it was observed that both the sewerage and drainage in almost all parts of the town has been well maintained. Even during the rainy season, it caused little problem.

Sangat Mandi, a Class V town, does not have the sewerage system. It is only the drainage system with a coverage of 97 per cent area and 93 per cent population. Ward numbers 4, 5 and 7 are still partially or marginally covered under drainage. The quality and maintenance were, however, not good. Nevertheless, there was little discrimination notice in this regard. This indicates that spatial discrimination was more a phenomenon of big urban centres than the small towns in the district.

Main Highlights

The following conclusions emerge strongly from the preceding discussions:

- Evolved in a phased manner, underground sewerage system is yet to reach all towns and entire urban population in Bathinda district. Sangat Mandi and Kot Fatta, two of the smallest towns in the district, are yet to introduce this facility in their respective territorial jurisdictions and more than half the urban population in the district was deprived of this facility in 2000. In some parts of each town the open drainage system was prevalent. Peripheral and slum localities suffered the most in this regard.

- Nevertheless, sewerage is among the most important function of municipalities in Bathinda district. An average amount of Rs. 114 lakh per annum, making about 92 per cent in total expenditure on sewerage and 14 per cent in aggregate municipal expenditure in the district, was the subsidy component on this service during 1980-98. In other words, Rs. 14 out of every Rs. 100 annually incurred by municipalities on various services and Rs. 92 out of every Rs. 100 spent on sewerage system was the subsidy component on sewerage in the district.
- There are wide spatial and temporal variations in distribution of subsidies on sewerage. During 1980-98, it varied from a high of 18 per cent of total expenditure in Bathinda town to a low of less than 2 per cent in Maur Mandi. During the same period, subsidy component was maximum, about 94 per cent of total expenditure on sewerage, in Bathinda town and minimum, at 27 per cent, in Goniana Mandi.
- In relative terms, the small-sized municipalities in the district earn higher shares of income from sewerage services than do the large sized towns. The combined income share of the five small-sized municipal towns becomes quite high in total municipal income from sewerage service than the combined share in total municipal subsidy on sewerage service in the district. On an average, the combined share of five small municipal towns made up 34 per cent in total municipal income in the district from sewerage service. Against this, their combined share in subsidy on this count made only 18 per cent during 1980-98. Notably, Goniana Mandi, one of the small-sized municipalities, earned 14.2 per cent of the aggregate municipal income from sewer connections, in comparison to its share of less than one per cent in total amount of subsidy provided by all municipalities on this service. Against this, Bathinda, the largest municipality in the district, earned only 66 per cent of total municipal income from this source in comparison to imparting subsidy to the tune of 92 per cent in aggregate amount of subsidy by municipalities. Evidently, the small-sized municipalities earn more than they spend on this facility.

- Per capita amount of subsidies differed widely among municipalities. Against the average per capita subsidy of Rs. 58 during 1980-98, it varied from a high of Rs. 91 in Bathinda municipality to a low of Rs. 3 in Maur Mandi. Majority of the small-sized municipalities provided low per capita subsidy in comparison to the large sized municipal towns in the district. Differential rates charged by municipalities on per toilet seat basis at the time of sewer connections was one of the important factors in wide inter-municipal variations in subsidy on and income from sewerage service.
- Per capita amount of municipal subsidy on sewerage has been growing in the district during 1980-98. However, the growth rate has slowed down in recent years. Increase in proportional terms has declined to about 13 per cent between 1992-93 and 1996-97, from about 126 per cent during 1987-88–1992-93. It seems that macro-economic reforms of 1991, wherein reduction in government subsidies was one of the major objectives, have shown their impact even at the micro-level institutions. However, factors such as low and stagnating rates charged on sewer connections for popularistic reasons, and lack of any practice of imposing heavy fines on delayed payments cannot be ignored totally.
- There has been wide spatial discrimination in availability and quality of sewerage and drainage facilities in different towns of the district. While, more than one-half of the total urban population in the district was yet to avail themselves of the facility of sewerage, peripheral localities in all the towns were yet to get any of the two facilities of sewerage and drainage. In Bathinda town, the largest urban centre in the district, 90 per cent of the sewerage system was confined to localities falling East of the railway line. Whereas in Rampura Phul, twin towns, Phul township was completely devoid of sewerage facility. Hence, the subsidy given on sewerage facility by Rampura Phul municipality was completely enjoyed by the residents of Rampura township alone.

II

DRAINAGE

While the sewerage system is an underground phenomenon, the drainage system is on the surface. The drainage, one of the statutory functions of the municipals bodies, is imperative especially for those localities where underground sewer systems do not exist. For the slum areas, it is considered as the most important service. In the absence of drainage, dirty water stays on the site and causes unhygienic conditions and is conducive to the spread of diseases.

Before we proceed to analyse the subsidy component in drainage service provided by municipalities in Bathinda district, a brief discussion is necessary on condition and working of drainage system in different Class category of towns in the district. Beginning with Bathinda municipal town, which is Class I town and also the district headquarters. The Bathinda municipality maintains a fairly well spread network of drains. Although the major parts of the city are covered by sewerage system, yet drains are necessary especially to carry the rainwater. The need for a well-maintained drainage system in the city has become all the more important now that the sewer system is collapsing in many localities.

Most parts of Bathinda Municipal town have been covered under this service. The localities, where the sewerage system is damaged, are served by open drains. Roughly, only 5 per cent of the total municipal area has neither drainage nor sewerage systems. Ward numbers 4, 29, 30, 31 and 33 find mainly lower castes and low income households residing in the area (Table 4.18).

The quality of the drainage system in the city varies from one part to another. It is good in localities where the sewer system is in proper order. Against this, in localities where the sewerage system has gone out of order, the drainage system is also poor. In such localities, the garbage enters the drain and blocks it. Generally, things become more problematic during the rainy season i.e., from the months July to September. The localities which are more prone to such a situation include Mall Road, Power House Road, Court Road, Dhobiana Road, Nai Basti, Ajit

Road, Ganesha Basti and parts of old Bathinda town. Naturally, such a locality requires special attention of the municipal authorities to save the residents from hardship and ugly sanitation conditions during the rainy season.

Rampura Phul, a Class III and the second largest in the district, has only about two-fifths of its localities covered under the sewer system. Another half has only the drainage system and one-tenth is covered neither under sewerage nor drainage. Drains are a necessity for those localities, which are without the sewer system[5] and also for carrying out the rain water. All the drains are open, but in some parts of the town especially in the market areas drains, in front of shops, have been covered by shopkeepers on their own.

There are two main drains in the town. The first one starts from Shaheed Smark College to the Factory Road and passes through the backside of the Geeta Bhawan, covering a distance of 600 meters. The second drain starts from the Patiala Mandi Bus Stand and goes upto the Gandhi Basti, covering a distance of about one kilometer. The former drain passes through both the high and low income areas, while the latter passes mainly from the areas inhabited by the low income households in the town. During the rainy season, the entire area gets flooded with water because the drains get choked at several places with polythene bags.

Bhucho Mandi, a Class IV town and 6th in terms of population size, in the district, has nearly 95 per cent of its municipal area covered under either sewerage or drainage system. Seventy per cent is under both sewerage and drainage and about 25 per cent under drainage only. The drainage system is mainly open, except in the main market area where shopkeepers have covered the drain in front of their shops. The main drain starts from Ram Bilas Basti and terminates at the disposal works, installed by the municipality, covering a distance of about 600 meters.

It was observed during field visits to the town that the drainage system functions well in Bhucho Mandi town.

Sangat Mandi, a Class VI town and the smallest in the district, does not have the sewer system, linking individual houses. Hence,

5. Rampura Phul, composed of Rampura and Phul twin towns. Phul is more or less a semi-urban area where residents are cultivating households in large number. Phul does not have the sewer system. It is entirely covered by drains.

the water from the individual houses enters into the covered sullage drain through the open drains. There is no separate provision for covered drains except the sewerage line made of stone pipe, starting from the bus stand and going up to the railway crossing. The waste water from the individual houses falls into manholes joining the sewerage stone pipe measuring 6 inches through the open drains, ending near the railway crossing. The covered stone pipe functions very well and the area remains clean and fresh. While the open drains have adverse environmental effect.

In 2000 about 97 per cent of area and 93 per cent of population in Sangat Mandi town was covered under the drainage system. However, about 3 per cent of area and 7 per cent of population in the town were yet to be covered under any kind of drainage or sewerage system. During the field survey, it was noticed that the quality of drainage system does not differ much from one part of the town to the other. The drainage system works reasonably well except during the rainy season.

Expenditure on Drainage

During the 1980-98 period municipalities in Bathinda district incurred an amount of about Rs. 719 lakh on drainage, accounting for the total municipal expenditure in the district. On an average, it came to about 40 lakh per annum for all municipalities. The expenditure incurred by the municipalities on the drainage system under their jurisdictions also makes up the subsidy component as this facility is provided by municipalities free of charge to their residents. In this way, expenditure and subsidy on drainage are one and the same thing.

In the following, inter-municipal and temporal changes in municipal expenditure or subsidy on drainage system in the district has been examined. In 1996-97 an average amount of about Rs. 74 lakh, making 4.53 per cent of total municipal expenditure, was spent by municipalities on drainage, per annum. Earlier in 1982-83, this amount was about Rs. 24 lakh, making about 8 per cent in total municipal expenditure on urban services. In this way, while the absolute amount has grown by about 68 per cent, this amount as a share in total municipal expenditure declined by half (Table 4.19).

TABLE 4.19

Bathinda District: Municipal Expenditure on Drainage as Percentage to Total Municipal Expenditure, 1980-98

(*Rs. in lakhs*)

Name of town	*Civic status*	*1982-83**			*1987-88**			*1992-93**			*1996-97**			*1980-98**		
		Aggregate expenditure	*Expenditure on drainage*	*Percentage in aggregate expenditure*	*Aggregate expenditure*	*Expenditure on drainage*	*Percentage in aggregate expenditure*	*Aggregate expenditure*	*Expenditure on drainage*	*Percentage in aggregate expenditure*	*Aggregate expenditure*	*Expenditure on drainage*	*Percentage in aggregate expenditure*	*Aggregate expenditure*	*Expenditure on drainage*	*Percentage in aggregate expenditure*
Bathinda	I	207.10	18.64	9.0	456.43	31.37	6.87	755.21	26.75	3.54	1135.78	56.25	4.95	583.39	30.70	5.26
Rampura Phul	III	34.62	2.78	8.03	55.62	0.81	1.46	104.96	4.42	4.21	162.77	4.59	2.82	81.35	2.99	3.68
Maur Mandi	III	14.61	0.73	5.0	31.80	1.08	3.40	52.30	1.52	2.91	77.11	3.89	5.04	40.30	1.57	3.90
Raman Mandi	IV	12.20	0.38	3.11	28.50	0.65	2.28	53.35	1.40	2.62	85.41	3.04	3.56	40.36	1.18	2.92
Goniana Mandi	IV	14.30	0.40	2.80	28.70	0.23	0.80	41.46	1.74	4.20	54.33	1.20	2.21	32.52	0.82	2.52
Bhucho Mandi	IV	18.04	0.74	4.10	39.60	0.60	1.52	42.47	1.77	4.17	90.16	3.18	3.53	42.84	1.39	324
Kot Fatta	V	1.10	0.09	8.18	4.70	0.50	10.64	5.65	1.52	26.90	77.68	1.39	18.10	4.46	0.82	18.39
Sangat Mandi	VI	1.60	—	—	2.90	0.61	21.03	8.99	1.00	11.12	11.63	—	—	5.69	0.45	7.91
Aggregate Expenditure		303.57	23.76	7.83	639.25	35.85	5.61	1064.39	40.12	3.77	1624.87	73.54	4.53	830.91	39.92	4.80
Average per municipality		43.37	3.39	7.83	79.91	4.48	5.61	133.05	5.02	3.77	232.12	10.51	4.53	103.86	4.99	4.80
C.V.		1.70	1.85		1.76	2.27		1.78	1.65		1.75	1.78		1.76	195	

*Annual averages.

Notes: (i) Since no income is earned by municipalities on this service, the expenditure and subsidy is one and the same thing.

(ii) C.V. stands for Coefficient of Variability.

Source: Data calculated from *Classified Abstracts* of different municipalities for various years.

This speaks of the reduced importance of drainage system in the context of overall municipal expenditure in the district. However, it is also true that the focus is now shifting to the development of a sewerage system, needing high capital investment but which is environmentally more viable.

In 1987-88, when the total expenditure on drainage increased to about Rs. 36 lakh from about Rs. 24 lakh in 1982-83, it made 5.61 per cent of total municipal expenditure on various urban service. Evidently, it increased in absolute terms but declined in proportional terms. At the level of municipalities, it varied both in absolute as well as proportional terms. It ranged from a high of Rs. 31.4 lakh in Bathinda municipal town to a low of only Rs. 23 thousand in Goniana Mandi. Infact, the expenditure on drainage incurred by Bathinda municipal town is so high that it made nearly 88 per cent of total municipal expenditure on this service in the district. While the population of Bathinda is about 60 per cent of total urban population in the district.

However, in proportional terms, things were quite different. Sangat Mandi town, a Class VI town, incurred more than 21 per cent of total municipal expenditure on drainage. Against this, Goniana Mandi, a Class IV town, spent only about 1.0 per cent of its total expenditure on this count. Bathinda municipal town, a Class I town, incurred about 7 per cent on drainage. Rampura Phul, a Class III town and the second largest municipality in the district, incurred only about 1.5 per cent. Thus it seems that the civic status of a town and expenditure incurred by it on drainage find no association with each other.

Coming to 1992-93, when the average share for all the municipalities came down to less than 4.0 per cent from about 6.0 per cent in 1987-88, it ranged from a high of about 27 per cent in Kot Fatta to a low of 2.6 per cent in Raman Mandi. Sangat Mandi, a Class VI town and the smallest urban centre in the district, spent the second highest share of more than 11 per cent. Earlier in 1987-88, its expenditure on drainage was more than 21 per cent. In general, it has been observed that municipalities with lower civic status were spending higher shares of their total municipal expenditures on drainage than the higher status municipal towns in the district. A close examination of municipal expenditures on sewerage and drainage reveal that, in general, higher civic status municipal towns in the district were spending much higher on sewerage than on drainage and *vice-versa*. In fact, Kot Fatta and Sangat Mandi towns, two of the smallest towns in the district, were dependent only on the drainage system and were yet to start with sewerage system. Hence, they incurred expenditure only on drainage system.

It is interesting to note that the inter-municipal disparities in absolute amount of expenditure on drainage declined considerably in 1992-93, as compared to 1987-88. As is evident from the fall in co-efficient of variability index value which came down to 1.65 in 1992-93 from 2.27 in 1987-88. Inter-municipal disparities in expenditure on drainage were considerably reduced. Nevertheless, inter-municipal disparities in this regard were still quite high.

In 1996-97, when average share of expenditure on drainage for all the municipalities rose to 4.5 per cent from 3.8 per cent in 1992-93, it varied from a high of more than 18 per cent in Kot Fatta to a low of 2.2 per cent in Goniana Mandi town. Bathinda, a Class I town and the largest urban centre in the district, incurred about 5 per cent and Rampura Phul, the second largest town in the district, only about 3 per cent. However, in terms of absolute amount their combined share made up about 83 per cent of total expenditure on drainage. Bathinda alone shared more than 76 per cent of the total. Notably, Sangat Mandi town which incurred more than 11 per cent of its municipal expenditure on drainage in 1992-93, did not spend a single penny in 1996-97 on this account. Earlier in 1982-83, Sangat Mandi town did not spend any amount on drainage. Both of these are small municipal towns, in terms of area and population. Their income sources are also meagre. Obviously, small municipal towns with low income are not regular in spending on drainage. Another interesting fact about the municipal expenditure on drainage in 1996-97 is that inter-municipal disparities in absolute amount of expenditure widened in comparison to 1992-93. Co-efficient of variability index value increased further to 1.78 from 1.65 in 1992-93.

It emerges from the above analysis of municipal expenditure in the district on drainage that there have been frequent changes in proportional share of expenditure incurred by different municipalities on this count. However, the proportional share of subsidy provided by the municipality of Bathinda on drainage has remained relatively stable as compared to other municipalities in the district. In comparative terms, fluctuations in expenditure share have been minimum in Bathinda town and maximum in Sangat Mandi town during 1980-98. Further, no association has been found between the civic status of a town and its expenditure share on drainage. However, the absolute amount of expenditure on drainage by municipalities finds a close association with their civic status.

Bathinda, a Class I category town, recorded a dominant share in total municipal expenditure/subsidy on drainage in Bathinda district. The share of Bathinda municipality in total municipal expenditure/subsidy on drainage has never been less than two-thirds, and it was as high as about nine-tenths (88 per cent) in 1987-88. Bathinda town enjoys the status of district headquarters, hence for its higher administrative and civic status along with large area and population size it invests more for provision of drainage facility. The administrative and civic status of a town is given due consideration in distribution of grants from the state. Moreover, the large towns earn higher income from their own sources.

Change in Expenditure Share

The change in share of municipal expenditure on drainage provides a mixed picture. Barring Kot Fatta, no other municipality recorded increase in municipal expenditure share on drainage between 1982-83 and 1987-88. In fact, all other municipalities registered a decrease in their respective shares. The highest decrease was recorded in Rampura Phul (–6.57 per cent) and the lowest (–0.83 per cent) in Raman Mandi town (Table 4.20). It is interesting to note that during the corresponding period their respective shares on sewerage also recorded a decline. One can infer that in the latter half of the 1980s both sewerage and drainage figured as a low priority in the overall context of municipal expenditure on various services. Against this, the period between 1987-88 and 1992-93 recorded a reversal in the trend. During this period, six out of eight municipalities recorded an increase in their shares of expenditure on drainage. Further, the decline in expenditure share of Maur Mandi town was not very significant (–0.49 per cent). Besides, Kot Fatta town recorded the highest increase of more than 16 per cent and Raman Mandi registered the lowest increase of 0.34 per cent. On the whole, municipal towns with lower civic and administrative status recorded higher increase in their respective shares in comparison to higher civic and administrative status towns. Quite interestingly, Bathinda, the largest and the highest administrative status town in the district, recorded the highest decrease (–3.33 per cent).

TABLE 4.20
Bathinda District: Change in Expenditure/Subsidy on Drainage by Municipalities, 1980-98

(*Share in percentage*)

Name of town	*1982-83* over 1987-88*	*1987-88* over 1992-93*	*1992-93* over 1996-97*
Bathinda	–2.13	–3.33	1.41
Rampura Phul	–6.57	2.75	–1.39
Maur Mandi	–1.60	–0.49	2.13
Raman Mandi	–0.83	0.34	0.94
Goniana Mandi	–2.0	3.4	–1.99
Bhucho Mandi	–2.58	2.65	–0.64
Kot Fatta	2.46	16.26	–8.80
Sangat Mandi	**	9.91	**

* Annual averages.

** Since no expenditure was made on drainage by Sangat Mandi town in 1982-83 and 1996-97, it is not possible to show the picture of change between 1982-83 and 1987-88; and 1992-93 and 1996-97.

Source: Data calculated from *Classified Abstracts* of different municipalities for various years.

In between 1992-93 and 1996-97, the picture of change in shares of municipal expenditure on drainage became mixed. Three of the eight municipal towns in the district recorded decrease and four registered increase in their respective shares. Since the eight municipalities of Sangat Mandi town did not spend any amount in drainage in 1996-97, it is not possible to calculate change in its case. Kot Fatta, the second lowest municipal town in the district, recorded the highest decline (–8.8 per cent). Against this, Maur Mandi town, a Class III town in the district, registered the highest increase (2.13 per cent).

Briefly, none of the eight municipalities in the district recorded either a continuous increase or decrease in its share of expenditure on drainage during 1980-98. While the dominate majority recorded decrease in their shares of expenditure on drainage between 1982-83 and 1987-88, the reverse was true of the period between

1987-88 and 1992-93. The period between 1992-93 and 1996-97 recorded a mixed pattern. With some exceptions, municipalities with lower civic and administrative status recorded higher increase and lower decrease in their shares respectively of expenditure/subsidy on drainage than higher civic and administrative status towns. This was mainly because of the fact that the latter towns were shifting their priorities towards expansion in sewerage facility, which demand much higher capital investment. Against this, the latter were depending heavily on drainage system due to lower investment capacity. The lower civic and administrative towns were not even spending regularly on the expansion and maintenance of the drainage system.

Per Capita Subsidy

On an average, municipalities in Bathinda district provided an amount of Rs. 19 per capita per annum on drainage during 1980-98. Among municipalities, it varied from a high of Rs. 26 in Bathinda to a low of Rs. 8 in Maur Mandi and Raman Mandi. Over the period, this amount increased by over 200 per cent: from Rs. 12 in 1982-83 to Rs. 37 in 1996-97. Between 1992-93 and 1996-97, the increase was the highest for the entire sub-period during 1980-98 (Fig. 4.7). In relative terms, small population sized municipalities provided higher per capita subsidy on drainage than medium-sized municipalities in the district. It can be inferred that the municipalities, which have been spending low to no investment in sewer system due to low investment capacity, have only the alternative of investing in the drainage system. Earlier, in discussions on municipal expenditure on sewerage it was noticed that the lower civic and administrative status towns invest very little, both in absolute and per capita terms, on sewerage system. Nevertheless, in absolute terms, about 77 per cent of total average annual subsidy amount was provided by Bathinda municipality alone (Table 4.21).

There were, however, wide inter-municipal and temporal variations in this regard. In 1982-83, it varied from a high Rs. 16 in Bathinda town to a low of only Rs. 2 in Kot Fatta town, with average for all the municipalities being Rs. 12. During this period, Sangat Mandi town did not make any investment on this account. As is evident from co-efficient of variability index (0.66) inter-municipal disparities in per capita expenditure/subsidy were quite high (Table 4.22).

Fig. 4.7

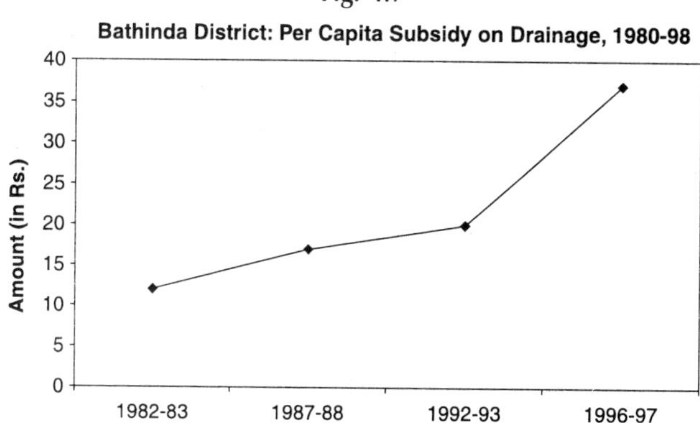

TABLE 4.21

Bathinda District: A Comparison of Subsidy on Drainage by Municipalities, 1980-98

Name of town	*Subsidy (Rs. in lakh)*	*Subsidy per capita (in Rs.)*
Bathinda	30.70* (76.90)	26*
Rampura Phul	2.99 (7.49)	9
Maur Mandi	1.57 (3.93)	8
Raman Mandi	1.18 (2.96)	8
Goniana Mandi	0.82 (2.05)	10
Bhucho Mandi	1.39 (3.48)	18
Kot Fatta	0.82 (2.05)	16
Sangat Mandi	0.45 (1.13)	16
All Towns	39.92 (100.0)	19

* Annual averages.

Notes: 1. Per capita subsidy has been calculated on the basis of 1981 census data. In case of Bathinda population figures used for calculation of subsidy confined to areas falling under the jurisdiction of Bathinda Municipal committee. Two public sector units, Fertilizer and Thermal Plant make their own arrangement for provision of services to their residents. Hence excluded from the calculations.

2. Figures in parentheses indicate percentage share in total.

Source: Data calculated from *Classified Abstracts* of different municipalities for various years.

TABLE 4.22

Bathinda District: Trends in Municipal Subsidy on Drainage, 1980-98

Name of town	*Subsidy per capita (in Rs.)*				
	*1982-83**	*1987-88**	*1992-93**	*1996-97**	*1980-98**
Bathinda	16	27	23	48	26
Rampura Phul	9	3	14	14	9
Maur Mandi	4	6	8	21	8
Raman Mandi	3	5	10	21	8
Goniana Mandi	5	3	20	14	10
Bhucho Mandi	9	8	23	41	18
Kot Fatta	2	10	31	28	16
Sangat Mandi	—	21	35	—	16
All Towns	12	17	20	37	19
C.V.	0.66	0.80	0.44	0.46	0.43

*Annual averages.

Note: Per capita subsidy has been calculated on the basis of 1981 census data. In case of Bathinda population figures used for calculation of subsidy confined to areas falling under the jurisdiction of Bathinda Municipal committee. Two public sector units, Fertilizer and Thermal Plant make their own arrangement in provision of services to their residents. Hence excluded from the calculations.

Source: Data calculated from *Classified Abstracts* of different municipalities for various years.

Coming to 1987-88, when per capita municipal expenditure/subsidy varied from a high of Rs. 27 in Bathinda town to a low of Rs. 3 in Rampura Phul and Raman Mandi towns, and average for all the municipalities rose to Rs. 17 from Rs. 12 in 1982-83. High increase in per capita amount in the case of Bathinda and Kot Fatta municipal towns and the joining of Sangat Mandi in the list of municipalities spending on this account was mainly responsible for this rise in per capita expenditure/subsidy. Otherwise, there has been a sharp decline in the case of Rampura Phul. Inter-municipal disparities in this regard widened in 1987-88, as compared to 1982-83. This is evidently clear in the increase of co-efficient of variability index value to 0.80 in 1987-88 from 0.66 in 1982-83.

Coming to 1992-93, scenario of per capita expenditure/subsidy on this count changed radically. Not only was there a sharp rise in per capita amount of subsidy given by lower civic and administrative status towns but also Sangat Mandi town, the smallest municipal town in the district recorded the high per capita amount of Rs. 35. The second highest amount (Rs. 31) was recorded by the second smallest municipal town, Kot Fatta. Bathinda municipal town, the largest town in the district, which remained at the top earlier both in 1982-83 and 1987-88, was relegated to third position which was shared by Bhucho Mandi, a Class IV town. Further, it is interesting to note that inter-municipal disparities in per capita expenditure/subsidy reduced considerably with a sharp increase in expenditure/subsidy amount on drainage in the case of lower civic and administrative status towns in the district. The index value of co-efficient of variability was now reduced to 0.44 from 0.88 in 1987-88.

Coming to 1996-97, when average per capita amount of subsidy on drainage rose to Rs. 37 from Rs. 20 in 1992-93, per capita amount ranged from a high of Rs. 48 in Bathinda town to a low of Rs. 14 in Rampura Phul and Goniana Mandi town. This time inter-municipal disparities in per capita subsidy increased marginally as co-efficient of variability index value moved to 0.46 from 0.44 in 1992-93. Sangat Mandi town, which had incurred highest per capita amount of expenditure/subsidy in 1992-93, did not spend a single penny on this account in 1996-97. Recovering from the third rank, in 1992-93, it regained top position in 1996-97. On the whole, inter-municipal disparities in per capita amount of subsidy on drainage were the highest in 1987-88 and the lowest in 1992-93 (Fig. 4.8). In general, Class I, Class IV and Class V towns in the district provided high per capita amount of subsidy, against this Class III towns provided the low per capita subsidy on drainage. Further, since subsidy and expenditure were one and the same thing, subsidy on drainage found direct association with per capita municipal expenditure on this service. In other words, higher the per capita expenditure of a municipality on an urban service, higher was the per capita subsidy amount given by the municipality on that service. Further, the expenditure of a municipality on various services found a strong association with its income sources. In that sense, subsidy on urban services finds a positive association with income of the respective municipality. In this regard, Bhucho Mandi town, though a Class IV town which ranks sixth in terms of population size, ranked next only to Bathinda town which was at the top. Rampura Phul, the second largest town in the district, provided a per capita amount of subsidy on drainage during 1980-98 that was just half of Bhucho Mandi town. Further, over the period the former registered decrease, while the latter experienced increase in its

Fig. 4.8

Bathinda District: Inter-municipal disparities in per capita subsidy on drainage

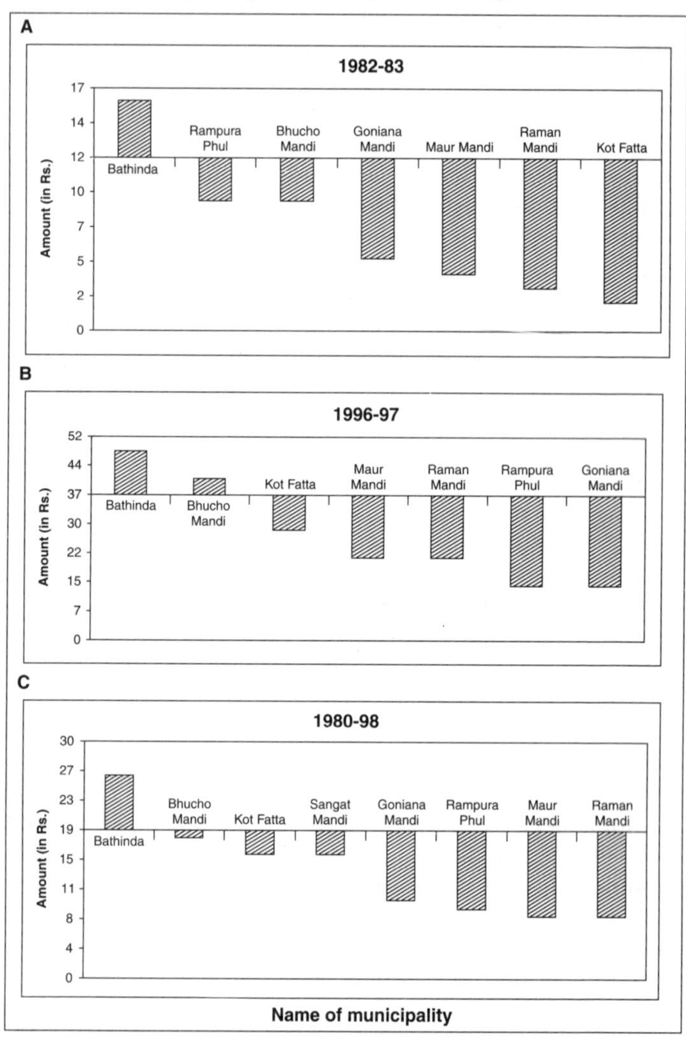

Note: In Sangat Mandi town no expenditure was incurred on drainage in 1982-83 and 1996-97.

per capita amount of subsidy on drainage (Fig. 4.9). It is mainly because Bhucho Mandi town had higher income sources as compared to Rampura Phul.

As stated earlier, Bhucho Mandi town has a large chunk of urban land under its possession which the municipality auctions from time to time to generate additional revenue income. During the fieldwork it was noted that Bhucho Mandi township had relatively better quality of drainage and sewerage system in comparison to all other towns in the district.

Spatial Discrimination in Subsidy on Sewerage and Drainage

A study of internal distribution of drainage facilities in Bathinda, Rampura Phul, Bhucho Mandi and Sangat Mandi towns, representing different class category of towns in the district, reveal that there are wide spatial variations in this regard. There are localities which are served by both sewerage and drainage systems while there are also localities which have none.

For instance, in Bathinda a Class I town and the largest in the district, more than two-fifths (41 per cent) of the total municipal area and about three-fifths (or 56 per cent) of its population was enjoying both the facilities of drainage and sewerage. Against this, nearly 5 per cent of its area and more than 6 per cent of population was not served by either.

Remaining about 55 per cent of its area and 40 per cent of the population was served by drainage only. It is to be noted here that unserved localities were peripherally located and resided in by the lower economic status and lower caste people. Their literacy level was also low, indicating low level of awareness among such people. On the other side of the scale, localities in the Central part of the town and dominated by high economic status and upper castes were enjoying both the facilities of sewerage and drainage (Table 4.18 and Map 4.9).

Rampura Phul, Class III and the second largest town in the district, reveals another interesting picture. In this twin township, made of Rampura and Phul about 91 per cent of the area and 94 per cent population were served by either the drainage or sewerage or both. But the localities served both by drainage and sewerage were confined completely to Rampura Mandi area, in contrast more than two-thirds of the unserved localities were in Phul (Table 4.18 and Map 4.10). Definitely, Phul is discriminated

Fig. 4.9

Bathinda District: Trends in Per Capita Subsidy on Drainage

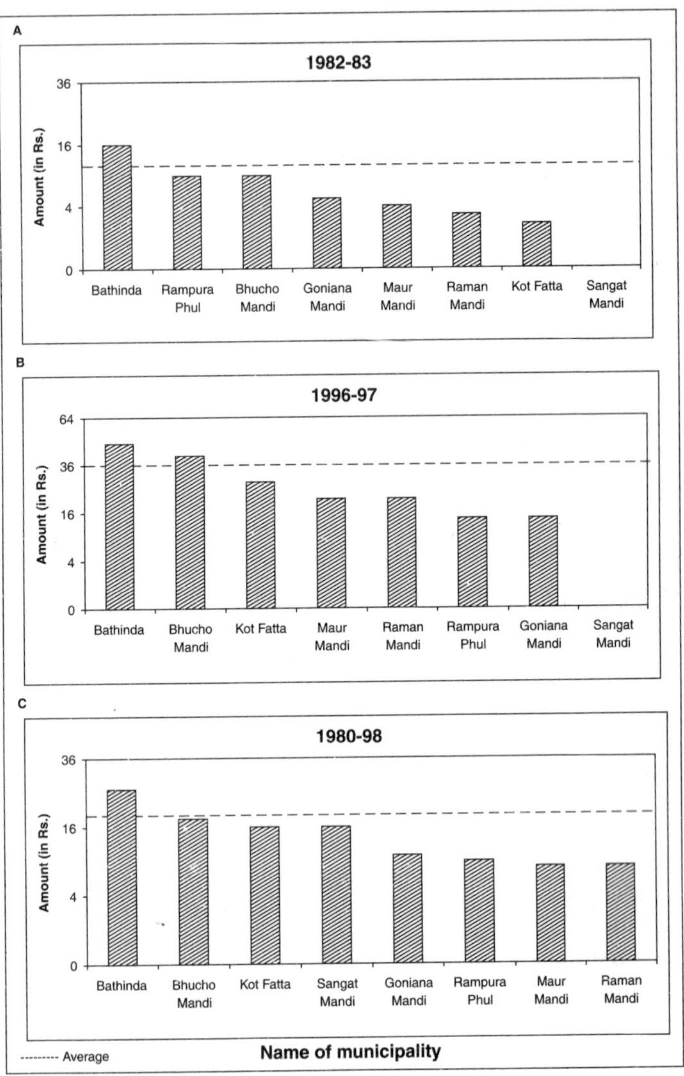

Note: In 1982-83 and 1996-97 drainage service was not available in Sangat Mandi town.

against in favour of Rampura in terms of area and population served by the facility of sewerage and drainage. More than 9 per cent of its area and about 6 per cent population, which are unserved by any of the two facilities, were peripherally located in both parts of Rampura Phul town.

Localities served by sewerage and drainage both were resided in mainly by high economic status people but there was no such clear-cut demarcation in terms of caste or social status of the people. Thus, even though discrimination is certainly there, it is less well marked in comparison to Bathinda township.

Bhucho Mandi, a Class IV town in the district, where nearly 70 per cent of area and 66 per cent of population was served by sewerage and drainage both, showed (Table 4.18) that there was the highest area and population coverage under the sewerage and drainage both among all the towns in the district and there is very little discrimination in provision of these facilities (Map 4.14). The entire area falling under the market mandi is fully covered under both the facilities and only the newly emerged localities are unserved.

Nevertheless there is no clear cut demarcation between the localities served by sewerage and drainage both or by drainage only on the basis of economic status and/or caste hierarchy. It was less significant that there was spatial discrimination in relatively small towns in comparison to big towns in provision of urban services such as sewerage and drainage. However, high per capita expenditure or subsidy on drainage and sewerage, as incurred in the case of Bhucho Mandi town, indicated relatively low level of economic efficiency.

Sangat Mandi town, a Class VI and the smallest urban centre in the district, had only the provision of drainage facility. It was yet to introduce the sewer system. By 2000, its 97 per cent of area and 93 per cent population were covered under drainage system. Before 1980, only about one-third of the municipal area was covered under the drainage system. Another one-fifth was added during 1980-91, while the largest expansion (of 40 per cent) took place recently between 1991 and 2000 (Map 4.16). Except few patches on the margins, the northern parts of the townscape show full coverage under the drainage system. The southern areas were covered with drainage after 1980 while peripheral areas are still uncovered.

Having a low capacity for generating income for investment in development of urban infrastructure, small towns, in general, fail to provide adequate good quality infrastructure to their residents. This is evidently clear from the case of Sangat Mandi and Kot Fatta towns which are unable to provide the facility of sewerage to their residents. Further, other small towns such as Maur Mandi, Goniana Mandi and Raman Mandi which have been able to provide the facility of sewerage have done so only in a limited area. No doubt, there is relatively less spatial discrimination within such towns in availability of urban services but quality and adequacy of services remains the biggest causality in such towns.

Main Highlights

- On an average, municipalities in Bathinda district incurred nearly Rs. 40 lakh per annum on construction and maintenance of drainage during 1980-98. Since, the municipalities in the district provided this service free of any charges the entire amount automatically became the subsidy element of this service. Hence, on an average Rs. 40 lakh were transferred as subsidy on drainage to their residents by the municipalities in Bathinda, annually.
- There were wide inter-municipal variations in this regard. Bathinda municipality, which has only about 60 per cent of total urban population in the district, provided nearly 77 per cent of subsidy the amount rendered by the all municipalities on annual basis.
- Notwithstanding an increase of more than 200 per cent in absolute amount of subsidy on drainage in the district, its share in aggregate municipal expenditure declined by about half, from about 8 per cent in 1982-83 to less than 5 per cent in 1996-97. Further, there were wide inter-municipal variations in proportional share of municipal expenditure on drainage which were widening over the period. The ratio between the highest and the lowest shares which was 3:1 in 1982-83 rose to 26:1 in 1987-88. After this it came down gradually but remained much higher than the 1982-83 level. Notably, however, this ratio was of much higher order in the case of absolute amount of subsidy on drainage.
- No definite trend has been noticed in municipal expenditure/subsidy on drainage in the district. It has been changing frequently in time and space. In relative terms,

fluctuations have been the minimum in the case of Bathinda municipality and the maximum in Rampura Phul. In temporal context, it has been the minimum in 1996-97 and the maximum in 1987-88. Further, no association has been found between the civic status of a town and its expenditure/subsidy on drainage. In general, Class III towns in the district provided lower amount as well as proportional subsidy on drainage, the Class I and Classes IV and V towns were providing more.

- On an average, the municipalities in Bathinda district provided an annual amount of Rs. 19 as subsidy on drainage during 1980-98. This amount increased by more than 200 per cent between 1982-83 and 1996-97, recording the sharpest increase between 1992-93 and 1996-97. There were, however, wide inter-municipal disparities in this context. During 1980-98, it varied from a high of Rs. 26 per capita in Bathinda municipality to a low of Rs. 8 in Raman Mandi and Maur Mandi towns. The disparities in per capita amount of subsidy were the highest in 1987-88 and the lowest in 1992-93.
- Per capita municipal subsidy on drainage finds no association with either the civic status or population size of a town. Towns with lower civic status and population were also providing high per capita subsidy alongwith high civic status and population size. Bhucho Mandi, a Class IV town with second lowest population size town in the district, recorded the second highest per capita subsidy after Bathinda town on drainage. Against this, Rampura Phul, a Class III and second largest town in the district, provided the lowest amount of subsidy on drainage. In fact, per capita municipal subsidy finds a strong positive association with per capita municipal expenditure, on drainage, which in turn was positively associated with per capita municipal income. In a way, per capita municipal subsidy finds a strong positive association with per capita municipal income and expenditure on drainage.

PUBLIC HEALTH AND SANITATION

Ever since the municipal administration was introduced in British India in the late 19th century, sanitation or garbage disposal has been one of the most important obligatory functions of municipal bodies. After Independence, the medical services, which were earlier under the administrative control of municipal bodies, were transferred to the Directorate of Health Services, Government of Punjab. However, the public health along with sanitation has stayed with the municipal bodies.

After Independence, concomitant with administrative and development activities, the urban population and the number of towns both have increased rapidly in India. Urban population has grown by four times and the urban centers nearly doubled during 1951-2001. The same has been true of Punjab also. Urban population in the state has increased by more than four times from 1.99 million to 8.25 million during 1951-2001. In Bathinda district, urban population has grown to 352 thousand in 2001 from only 126 thousand in 1951. Along with rapid growth of urban population, towns are expanding physically, requiring both intensification as well as expansion in public health and sanitation service. Moreover, booming consumerism in recent years has been responsible for further complicating the sanitation scenario in urban India.

This chapter examines the context of subsidy in public health and sanitation in terms of its size, proportion, per capita amount and trends during 1980-98. Further an attempt will be made to correlate the subsidy element with the size, administrative status and functions of municipalities of towns in Bathinda district. But before that inter-municipal variations in sanitary staff and sanitary infrastructure have been examined in brief.

Sanitary Staff in Municipal Towns of Bathinda

In 1997-98, there were in all 907 sanitary workers in municipalities of Bathinda district (Table 4.23). Of them, 622 or about 69 per cent were employed in Bathinda municipality alone. It is to be noted here that norms for sweeping are set by municipalities to divide sweeping work among the sweepers (See Box 1). In 2001, population of Bathinda city made up 62 per cent of the total urban population in the district. Earlier in 1981, when Bathinda city employed 60 per cent of total sanitary staff, it had 58 per cent of the total urban population in the district. The share of Bathinda municipality in total sanitary staff in the district has been not only high in comparison to its share in urban population but also growing over the period.

TABLE 4.23
Bathinda District: Sanitary Staff/Population Ratio, 1997-98

Name of town	*Civic status*	*Sanitary supervisors*	*Tractor trolley drivers*	*Sewer men*	*Sweeper*	*Total*	*Sanitation staff population ratio*
Bathinda	I	6	7	14	595	622	256
Rampura Phul	III	2	4	5	103	114	312
Maur Mandi	III	1	2	3	61	67	376
Raman Mandi	IV	1	2	2	30	35	494
Goniana Mandi	IV	1	1	3	27	32	325
Bhucho Mandi	IV	1	1	3	27	32	313
Kot Fatta	V	Nil	Nil	Nil	01	01	5611
Sangat Mandi	VI	Nil	1	Nil	3	04	683
All Towns		12	18	30	847	907	1046

Source: Data Calculated from *Sanitation Register* of different municipalities.

Rampura Phul and Maur Mandi, both Class III category towns, have another 181 or one-fifth of the total sanitary workers. Their combined population makes for more than one-fifth of the total urban population in the district. Raman Mandi, Goniana Mandi and Bhucho Mandi, all Class IV category towns, employed about 11 per cent sanitary workers, against their combined population making up 14 per cent of total urban population in the district. Remaining five sanitary workers, which make up less than one per cent of the total sanitary workers in urban Bathinda, were employed in Kot Fatta and Sangat Mandi municipal towns, having 3 per cent of the total urban population in the district. Interestingly, there was only one sweeper in Kot Fatta municipal town and he too was employed to sweep the municipal office rather than to sweep the town roads/clean drains/collect or dispose-off garbage in the town. Clearly, Class category of towns finds a positive association with proportional share in total sanitary staff in the district.

Bathinda, the largest municipal town in the district, has on a proportional bases one sanitary worker for every cluster of 256 persons or 51 households. Against this Kot Fatta, one of the smallest municipal towns in the district, has one worker for 5611 persons or 1122 households. The average for Rampura Phul, the second largest town in the district, was one worker for 312 persons. The average for all the municipalities was one worker for 1046 persons or 206 households (Table 4.23).

In brief, municipal status and strength of sanitary staff find a close association with each other in Bathinda District. The sanitary worker-population ratio was highly in favour of the large-sized than the small-sized municipal towns of the district.

Infrastructure for Sanitation

Due to higher spending capacity, the big municipal towns in the district have larger and technically superior infrastructure than the smaller ones. Bathinda, the largest municipal town and the district headquarters, had about two-third or 65 per cent of the total *'Khonchas'*, a basic tool used to collect garbage, available with all the municipalities in the district (Table 4.24). Its share in total urban population of the district was 62 per cent in 2001. Another 26 per cent of the total of such tools has been with Class III municipalities, namely, Rampura Phul and Maur Mandi. Their combined population made up about 23 per cent of total urban population in the district. Against this, Kot Fatta and Sangat Mandi towns, Class V and VI towns, together share less than one per cent of total *'Khonchas'*. Their combined population made up 3 per cent of total urban population in the district. One-half of the 16 tractor trolleys available with all the towns were in Bathinda town. Another three were with Rampura Phul, the second largest town in the district. There has been none with Kot Fatta town. Municipal status and sanitary infrastructure, on the whole, find a positive association with each other. In other words, higher the municipal status of a town, higher is the quality and technological superiority of the sanitary infrastructure it may have.

Composition of sanitary infrastructure is highly revealing. While, the large area and population sized municipalities are opting for modern equipments for collection and disposal of

TABLE 4.24
Bathinda District: Sanitation Infrastructure, 1997-98

Name of town	*Civic status*	*Tractor Trolley*		*Sprinkler*		*Hand barrows/ Rehri*		*Khoncha*	
		Number	*Percentage*	*Number*	*Percentage*	*Number*	*Percentage*	*Number*	*Percentage*
Bathinda	I	8	50	4	44.45	175	56.27	201	65.26
Rampura Phul	III	3	18.75	1	11.11	50	16.08	50	16.23
Maur Mandi	III	1	6.25	1	11.11	25	8.04	30	9.74
Raman Mandi	IV	1	6.25	1	11.11	10	3.21	10	3.25
Goniana Mandi	IV	1	6.25	1	11.11	25	8.04	8	2.60
Bhucho Mandi	IV	1	6.25	1	11.11	23	7.40	7	2.28
Kot Fatta	V	—	—	—	—	1	0.32	1	0.32
Sangat Mandi	VI	1	6.25	—	—	2	0.64	1	0.32
All Towns		16	100.00	9	100.00	311	100.00	308	100.00

*In addition, Bathinda has one dump placer, ten containers and one uni fog machine.

Source: Data Calculated from *The Sanitation Register* of different municipalities.

garbage, the lower-status municipalities continue to employ the traditional methods. For example, Bathinda Municipality had 8 out of the total 16 tractor-trollies available with all the municipalities in the district in 1997-98, while there was only one tractor-trolley each with Maur Mandi, Raman Mandi, Goniana Mandi and Bhucho Mandi. Kot Fatta, the second smallest municipal town in the district, had no other sanitation equipment except one hand driven *rehri* and one *khoncha*. The need for larger territorial coverage and greater quantity of garbage, that is to be collected and disposed off, compelled the big municipal towns to acquire modern sanitary collection and disposal equipments. This was necessary to increase efficiency of the garbage collection and disposal work. In addition, there are some other factors that contribute directly or indirectly to sanitation conditions and cost involved in garbage collection and disposal. Some of these are as follows:

1. Aware of the financial and administrative constraints which such municipal towns face for efficient management of urban services, the residents habitually sweep and clean the space in and around their residences as a community effort.
2. Incidence of spatial discrimination in availability of sanitary facilities happens to be greater in bigger municipal towns than the smaller ones. In big cities, larger proportion of sanitary staff and technically superior equipments are deployed in so called VIP wards or habitation in comparison to wards occupied by the hoi polloi or general masses. During the course of the fieldwork, the researcher learnt from reliable sources and also observed personally that some of the sweepers in Bathinda town were permanently posted, though unofficially, at residences of important district level officials like the Deputy Commissioner (DC), the Superintendent of Police (SP), the District and Sessions Judge and Executive Officer of the Municipality as well as other important public figures like the President, Vice-President and Secretary of the municipal body. In the process, the peripheral and slum areas suffered heavily.
3. In small towns, the negligence of duty on the part of sanitary staff can easily be noticed by the supervisory staff as well as the general public. However, such an identification exercise becomes quite difficult in big towns. Similarly, preferential treatment to select persons is also limited as the number of higher officials is few and also they prefer to live in big towns. Hence, the chances of discrimination in sanitation services gets minimized both in spatial and social terms.
4. Above all, the vital role of the executive officers/chief councillors/mayor of municipal bodies in towns to manage and organise the municipal functions can hardly be over looked. Dynamic and committed officials took full interest in all matters of municipal functioning including the sanitation work. Hence, whenever and wherever such individuals were posted or elected, the sanitation work was

maintained well irrespective of the strength of staff and availability of equipment.

Box I

Sanitation Norms Applied by Bathinda Municipality

1. Male sweepers are assigned the work of cleaning drains and women sweepers are given the task of sweeping the roads.
2. Each sweeper is assigned the sweeping of an area one kilometer long and 16 feet wide on the roads per day. The distance is reduced by one-half or 500 metres per day if there is a drain on both sides of such a road.
3. Bus stands, railway station, jails and hospitals have their own independent arrangements for the purpose. However, the collection and disposal of garbage from these places to the landfills is the responsibility of the municipal staff.

Source: Fieldwork, 2000.

Subsidy on Public Health and Sanitation Service

A. Aggregate Picture

Municipalities in Punjab provide public health and sanitation services free of cost to their residents. Hence, the entire expenditure incurred by the municipalities on this service turns into subsidy.

During 1997-98, municipal bodies in Bathinda district incurred nearly one-fourth or 24 per cent of their total expenditure on public health and sanitation. The average for the municipalities in Punjab was 12.2 per cent. Obviously, municipalities in Bathinda incur much higher expenditure on public health and sanitation than their counterparts in the state as a whole. As the total expenditure incurred by the municipalities on this service ultimately becomes the subsidy component, it is very clear that the municipalities in Bathinda provide much higher share of subsidy on this service than their counterparts in Punjab.

In the period 1980-98, municipalities in Bathinda district incurred an average amount of Rs. 153 lakh per annum on public health and sanitation, which made up 18.4 per cent of average annual expenditure of all municipalities in the district (Table 4.25).

There are, however, wide inter-municipal variations in this regard. Bathinda municipality alone shared Rs. 102.45 lakh or about 67 per cent (Table 4.25). Against this, Kot Fatta municipality provided only Rs. 24 thousand or less than 0.2 per cent of total amount of subsidy by all municipalities. Wide inter-municipal variations are also confirmed in high value (1.67) of co-efficient of variability (C.V.). Rampura Phul and Maur Mandi, both Class III category towns, incurred Rs. 30.5 lakh or about 20 per cent of total municipalities on this count in the district. In this way, 87 per cent of total subsidy on public health and sanitation was provided by the three largest municipal towns in the district. Their combined population made 81 per cent of total urban population in Bathinda district in 1991. Obviously, the big municipal towns in the district share higher proportion of subsidy on public health and sanitation as compared to their share in total urban population in the district. It is also to be noted that Bathinda is the district headquarters and the largest service centre in the district, while Rampura Phul and Maur Mandi are townships.

On the other side of the scale, the five small sized municipal towns, whose combined population was about one-fifth of the total urban population of the district, provided only about Rs. 20 lakh or 13 per cent of total municipal subsidy on this count. Kot Fatta, a Class V category town, incurred the lowest expenditure of Rs. 24 thousand on annual average basis. This made for a small fraction of combined expenditure of all the municipalities in the district.

In line with its civic and administrative status, Bathinda municipality has been providing the dominant share in total municipal subsidy on this count during the study period. In 1996-97, it shared 68 per cent or 234.34 lakh of Rs. 344.55 lakh spent by all the municipalities in the district on sanitation. In other words, about seven out of every Rs. 10 provided by municipalities in Bathinda district as subsidy on sanitation went to the residents of Bathinda municipality. The population of Bathinda town made up about 60 per cent of total urban population of the district in 1991. However, its area made up about 71 per cent of the total

TABLE 4.25

Bathinda District: Municipal Expenditure on Public Health and Sanitation, 1980-98

(Rs. in lakhs)

Name of town	Civic status	1982-83*			1987-88*			1992-93*			1996-97*			1980-98*		
		Aggregate expenditure	Expenditure on sanitation	Percentage share of aggregate expenditure	Aggregate expenditure	Expenditure on sanitation	Percentage share of aggregate expenditure	Aggregate expenditure	Expenditure on sanitation	Percentage share of aggregate expenditure	Aggregate expenditure	Expenditure on sanitation	Percentage share of aggregate expenditure	Aggregate expenditure	Expenditure on sanitation	Percentage share of aggregate expenditure
1	2	3	4	5	6	7	8	9	10	11	12	13	14	15	16	17
Bathinda	I	207.10	28.75	13.88	456.43	65.30	14.31	755.21	134.16	17.76	1135.78	234.34	20.63	583.39	102.45	17.56
Rampura Phul	III	34.62	3.95	11.41	55.62	9.0	16.18	104.96	30.74	29.29	162.77	47.06	28.91	81.35	19.96	24.54
Maur Mandi	III	14.61	2.94	20.12	31.80	7.06	22.20	52.30	15.28	29.22	77.11	21.11	27.38	40.30	10.54	26.15
Raman Mandi	IV	12.20	2.62	21.48	28.50	5.28	18.53	53.35	9.11	17.08	85.41	14.31	16.75	40.36	7.11	17.62
Goniana Mandi	IV	14.30	2.34	16.36	28.70	4.60	16.03	41.46	8.22	19.83	54.33	13.38	24.63	32.52	6.44	19.80
Bhucho Mandi	IV	18.04	1.83	10.14	39.60	3.68	9.29	42.47	7.48	17.61	90.16	12.92	14.33	42.84	5.76	13.45
Kot Fatta	V	1.10	0.12	10.91	4.70	0.24	5.11	5.65	0.24	4.25	7.68	0.46	5.99	4.46	0.24	5.38
Sangat Mandi	VI	1.60	0.22	13.75	2.90	0.28	9.66	8.99	0.73	8.12	11.63	0.97	8.34	5.69	0.50	8.79

(Contd.)

TABLE 4.25 (*Contd.*)

Name of town	*Civic status*	*1982-83**			*1987-88**			*1992-93**			*1996-97**			*1980-98**		
		Aggregate expenditure	*Expenditure on sanitation*	*Percentage share of aggregate expenditure*	*Aggregate expenditure*	*Expenditure on sanitation*	*Percentage share of aggregate expenditure*	*Aggregate expenditure*	*Expenditure on sanitation*	*Percentage share of aggregate expenditure*	*Aggregate expenditure*	*Expenditure on sanitation*	*Percentage share of aggregate expenditure*	*Aggregate expenditure*	*Expenditure on sanitation*	*Percentage share of aggregate expenditure*
1	*2*	*3*	*4*	*5*	*6*	*7*	*8*	*9*	*10*	*11*	*12*	*13*	*14*	*15*	*16*	*17*
Aggregate Expenditure		303.57	42.77	14.09	648.25	95.44	14.72	1064.39	205.96	19.35	1624.87	344.55	21.20	830.91	153.00	18.41
Average per municipality		37.95	5.35	14.09	81.03	11.93	14.72	133.05	25.75	19.35	203.11	43.07	21.20	103.86	19.13	18.41
C. V.		1.70	1.67		1.76	1.71		1.78	1.63		1.75	1.71		1.76	1.67	

* Annual averages calculated at the mid-year. First three are the five year averages, fourth one is three year average and fifth and last is 18 year average.

Notes: (i) C.V. stands for Coefficient of Variability.

(ii) Since no income is earned by municipalities on account of this service, hence expenditure and subsidy are the same.

Source: Data calculated from *Classified Abstracts* of different municipalities for various years.

urban area in the district. It means that the share of Bathinda municipality in total municipal subsidy on sanitation finds a close association with its share in area rather than the population share in total of all municipalities. Rampura Phul, which shares 14 per cent portion in total subsidy, has almost the same share in total urban population in the district. The combined share of these two towns makes more than four-fifths in aggregate amount of subsidy on this service. Remaining about 18 per cent is shared by the remaining six municipalities, having together about 27 per cent of urban population and about 18 per cent of total municipal area in the district. In this way, while the proportional share of subsidy on sanitation and geographical area almost match with each other, the share in subsidy and population of towns differ widely. Further, as evident from co-efficient of variability index value of 1.71, there were very wide inter-municipal variations in the expenditure subsidy on public health and sanitation.

Earlier in 1982-83, the share of Bathinda municipality in aggregate amount of municipal subsidy on sanitation in district was 67 per cent or more than two-thirds. Then, the combined share of Bathinda and Rampura Phul, two of the largest municipal towns in the district, made up about 76 per cent. The rest of the municipalities in the district claimed only about one-fourth of the total. As is evident from the C.V. index, inter-municipal variations in expenditure/subsidy, though quite high, were relatively lower than those of 1996-97.

Coming to 1987-88, the share of Bathinda municipality rose to more than 68 per cent in total amount of municipal subsidy on sanitation. Rampura Phul had a 9 per cent share in the total. In this way, the combined share of both the municipalities increased further to 78 per cent in 1987-88. Maur Mandi, the third largest municipal town in the district, shared more than 7 per cent. Thus, the combined share of three of the largest municipalities in the district made up more than 85 per cent of total municipal expenditure. Remaining about 15 per cent was shared by five municipalities, having about 23 per cent of the total urban population in the district. Obviously, the combined share of bigger sized municipalities further increased, resulting in widening of inter-municipal variations in expenditure or subsidy on public health and sanitation. The same is clear from increased value of co-efficient of variability which rose from 1.67 in 1982-83 to 1.71 in 1987-88.

In 1992-93, when the total amount of municipal expenditure/ subsidy on public health and sanitation rose to about Rs. 206 lakh, on annual average basis, the combined share of three top-most municipal towns increased to more than 87 per cent. It was mainly due to sharp rise in share of Rampura Phul which rose to about 15 per cent from about 9 per cent in 1987-88. Otherwise, the share of Bathinda municipal town, individually, declined to about 65 per cent from more than 68 per cent in 1987-88. The share of Maur Mandi town has been almost the same as in 1987-88. Inter-municipal variations, though large, were yet low in comparison to those of 1987-88. Co-efficient of variability index value was now 1.63 in place of 1.71 in 1987-88. In brief, large population and area sized towns have been expending higher amount on public health and sanitation as compared to small-sized towns in the district. As the entire expenditure, incurred by the municipalities on this service obtained nothing in return, the expenditure and subsidy on this service came to be one and the same thing. In this way, the overwhelming share of the total municipal subsidy on this service was provided by large sized municipal towns in the district. Further, there have been wide inter-municipal variations in this regard. Even though there was no set pattern in this regard.

In case of the large towns, the quantum of garbage as well as distance covered to collect and dispose-off the collected garbage have been increasing with time. In addition, the public awareness about cleanliness has grown over the period. To cope up with the changing scenario, the municipalities in large towns are now opting for more mechanized methods of garbage collection and disposal. Modern mechanized equipment being costly, the municipalities have to make heavy capital investment to acquire them. Consequently, the amount of subsidy has also gone up in such towns.

B. Subsidy as Proportion of Municipal Expenditure and Change in it

Subsidy on sanitation as share in expenditure of individual municipalities differs widely in the district. In 1996-97, it varied from a high of about 29 per cent in Rampura Phul to a low of 6 per cent in Kot Fatta, giving a difference of about five times (Table 4.25). Three municipalities of Rampura Phul, Maur Mandi and Goniana Mandi had this share higher than the average (21.2 per cent) for all the municipalities. In contrast, Kot Fatta and Sangat Mandi, which spent less than half the average for all the municipalities, seem to leave the residents on their own, as very little expenditure is incurred on public health and sanitation. The modern sanitation equipment, such as air lifters, tractor trolleys, dumpers and other equipment required for the purpose, are almost non-existence in these municipalities. All this, in turn, reflects upon the availability and quality of sanitation services in these towns. In contrast, municipal towns of Bathinda, Rampura Phul and Maur Mandi have made large investments in modern equipment, required for handling sanitation work efficiently. All three comprise the largest municipal towns in the district and earn higher income from various sources including market fee as 'mandi' towns.

TABLE 4.26

Bathinda District: Change in Proportional Share of Municipal Expenditure on Public Health and Sanitation, 1980-98

(Figures in percentage)

Name of town	*Civic status*	*1982-83* over 1987-88*	*1987-88* over 1992-93*	*1992-93* over 1996-97*
Bathinda	I	0.43	3.45	2.87
Rampura Phul	III	4.77	13.11	-0.38
Maur Mandi	III	2.08	7.02	-1.84
Raman Mandi	IV	–2.95	–1.45	–0.33
Goniana Mandi	IV	–0.33	3.80	4.80
Bhucho Mandi	IV	–0.84	8.31	–3.28
Kot Fatta	V	–5.80	–0.86	1.74
Sangat Mandi	VI	–4.09	–1.54	–0.22
All Towns		0.67	4.63	1.85

*Annual averages.

Source: Data calculated from *Classified Abstracts* of different municipalities for various years.

Earlier, in 1982-83, average annual share of subsidy was about 14 per cent, which increased to about 21 per cent in 1996-97. An increase of 7 per cent points is impressive and indicates the growing importance of this function in the overall context of municipal expenditure on services. It is, however, to be noted here that the major change took place in 1987-88 and 1992-93 when proportional share of subsidy rose to more than 19 per cent in 1992-93 from less than 15 per cent in 1987-88, registering a change of more than 4 per cent points (Table 4.25). At the level of individual towns, Rampura Phul recorded the highest increase of more than 13 per cent points as its expenditure share rose to about 29 per cent from about 16 per cent during this period. This was followed by Bhucho Mandi, registering an increase of more than 8 per cent points. In contrast Kot Fatta, Sangat Mandi and Raman Mandi recorded a decrease in their shares of expenditure/subsidy on sanitation.

Bathinda town, which is one of the eight towns in the state that were first to be covered under the Integrated Development of Small and Medium Towns (IDSMT) programme, introduced during the 6th Plan (1980-85) with sanitation improvement as one of its main components, recorded an increase of more than 3 per cent in its share during this period.

In between 1992-93 and 1996-97 when average share for all the municipalities increased by about 2 per cent, from 19.4 per cent to 21.2 per cent, three municipalities, namely, Rampura Phul, Maur Mandi, and Raman Mandi recorded decline in their respective shares. Rest of the municipalities recorded an increase.

On the whole, proportional share of subsidy on sanitation has been consistently growing in Bathinda municipality during 1980-98 (Table 4.26). In Rampura Phul and Maur Mandi towns it has been increasing during all sub-periods, identified to study change in subsidy share. The reverse was true of Raman Mandi, Kot Fatta and Sangat Mandi. In case of remaining municipalities, the proportional share of subsidy on sanitation has been fluctuating during the period 1980-98.

In fact, the quantum jump in subsidy share noticed in the case of Rampura Phul was largely attributed to increase in salary bill of the sanitation staff. This was confirmed during the discussions with municipal staff of Rampura Phul, held at the time of fieldwork in July 2000 by the researcher during the course of data collection.

Evidently, proportional share of subsidy on sanitation and changes therein varied widely among the municipalities in the district. While proportional share was invariably higher in the case of relatively large sized municipalities, no set pattern has been noticed regarding the change in proportional share of subsidy.

C. Composition of Expenditure/Subsidy

Municipal expenditure on sanitation is classified in two broad categories: (i) salaries, and (ii) contingencies. The former refers to salary paid to the sanitary staff and the latter to expenditure on maintenance and purchase of equipment, required for collection and disposal of garbage and environmental cleaning. Tractor trolley, dumper, broom, hand-driven garbage disposal, sprinkler, etc. are the equipments used for the purpose.

Interestingly, the dominant share of expenditure on sanitation goes towards the salary of the sanitary staff. Moreover, the share of salary bill in total expenditure has grown rapidly over the period (Table 4.27). The share of salaries was as high as more than 95 per cent in the total expenditure on sanitation in 1996-97 as against 83 per cent in 1982-83. Rapid increase in the share of the salaries component occurred between the mid-eighties and the early nineties. This coincides with the implementation of the Fourth Pay Commission[6] recommendations pertaining to the revision of pay-scales of the government and semi-government employees by the State government. Following this, the share of salaries in total expenditure on sanitation has remained above 90 per cent in total municipal expenditure on this head. In this way, very little amount is left with municipalities to spend on actual sanitation work.

There are wide inter-municipal variations in this regard. In 1982-83, when salary accounted for 100 per cent of total municipal expenditure on sanitation of Kot Fatta and Sangat Mandi towns, it made up only 82 per cent in Rampura Phul. In this way, Kot Fatta and Sangat Mandi towns did not spend a single penny on building sanitary infrastructure, while Rampura Phul spent about Rs. 18 per hundred on this account. The average for all the municipalities was less than Rs. 17.

On the whole, in six out of eight municipalities in the district more than 85 per cent of the total municipal expenditure/subsidy on public health and sanitation was in the form of salary bill of the sanitary staff. Bathinda and Rampura Phul were the two towns where salary bill made up about 82 per cent in total municipal

6. The Fourth Pay Commission gave its recommendation to the Union Government in 1998 and the Punjab Government implemented Commission's Recommendation in 1999.

TABLE 4.27

Bathinda District: Composition of Municipal Expenditure/Subsidy on Public Health and Sanitation, 1980-98

(*Rs. in lakhs*)

Name of town	*Civic status*	*1982-83**			*1987-88**			*1992-93**			*1996-97**			*1980-98**		
		Salary	*Contingency*	*Total*	*Salary*	*Contingency*	*Total*	*Salary*	*Contingency*	*Total*	*Salary*	*Contingency*	*Total*	*Salary*	*Contingency*	*Total*
1	*2*	*3*	*4*	*5*	*6*	*7*	*8*	*9*	*10*	*11*	*12*	*13*	*14*	*15*	*16*	*17*
Bathinda	I	23.46 (81.60)	5.29 (18.4)	28.75 (100)	56.22 (86.90)	9.08 (13.91)	65.30 (100.0)	125.68 (93.68)	8.48 (6.32)	134.16 (100.0)	224.50 (95.83)	9.78 (4.17)	234.28 (100)	94.47 (92.2)	7.98 (7.8)	102.45 (100)
Rampura Phul	III	3.20 (81.01)	0.75 (18.99)	3.95 (100)	6.24 (69.33)	2.76 (30.67)	9.00 (100)	28.82 (93.75)	1.92 (6.25)	30.74 (100)	44.50 (94.76)	2.46 (5.24)	46.96 (100)	18.04 (90.4)	1.92 (9.6)	19.96 (100)
Maur Mandi	III	2.59 (88.1)	0.35 (11.9)	2.94 (100)	6.43 (91.08)	0.63 (8.92)	7.06 (100)	14.11 (92.34)	1.17 (7.66)	15.28 (100)	19.53 (92.52)	1.58 (7.48)	21.11 (100)	9.68 (91.8)	0.86 (8.2)	10.54 (100)
Raman Mandi	IV	2.44 (93.13)	0.18 (6.87)	2.62 (100)	5.00 (94.70)	0.28 (5.30)	5.28 (100)	8.70 (95.49)	0.41 (4.51)	9.11 (100)	13.44 (93.92)	0.87 (6.08)	14.31 (100)	6.72 (94.5)	0.39 (5.5)	7.11 (100)
Goniana Mandi	IV	2.00 (85.47)	0.34 (14.53)	2.34 (100)	3.94 (85.65)	0.66 (14.35)	4.60 (100)	7.61 (92.58)	0.61 (7.42)	8.22 (100)	12.80 (95.67)	0.58 (4.33)	13.38 (100)	5.90 (91.6)	0.54 (8.4)	6.44 (100)
Bhucho Mandi	IV	1.65 (90.16)	0.18 (9.84)	1.83 (100)	3.34 (90.76)	0.34 (9.24)	3.68 (100)	6.82 (91.18)	0.66 (8.82)	7.48 (100)	12.16 (94.19)	0.75 (5.81)	12.91 (100)	5.31 (92.2)	0.45 (7.8)	5.76 (100)
Kot Fatta	V	0.12 (100)	No	0.12 (100)	0.24 (100)	No	0.24 (100)	0.24 (100)	No	0.24 (100)	0.46 (100)	No	0.46 (100)	0.24 (100)	—	0.24 (100)
Sangat Mandi	VI	0.22 (100)	No	0.22 (100)	0.28 (100)	No	0.28 (100)	0.70 (95.89)	0.03 (4.11)	0.73 (100)	0.94 (96.91)	0.03 (3.09)	0.97 (100)	0.49 (98.0)	0.01 (2.0)	0.50 (100)

(*Contd.*)

TABLE 4.27 (*Contd.*)

Name of town	*Civic status*	*1982-83**			*1987-88**			*1992-93**			*1996-97**			*1980-98**		
		Salary	*Contingency*	*Total*	*Salary*	*Contingency*	*Total*	*Salary*	*Contingency*	*Total*	*Salary*	*Contingency*	*Total*	*Salary*	*Contingency*	*Total*
1	2	3	4	5	6	7	8	9	10	11	12	13	14	15	16	17
Aggregate Expenditure		35.68 (83.4)	7.09 (16.6)	42.77 (100)	81.69 (85.6)	13.75 (14.4)	95.44 (100)	192.68 (93.6)	13.28 (6.4)	205.96 (100)	328.33 (95.3)	16.05 (4.7)	344.38 (100)	140.85 (92.0)	12.15 (8.0)	153.00 (100)
Average per municipality		4.46	0.89	5.35	10.21	1.72	11.93	24.09	1.66	25.75	41.04	2.00	43.04	17.61	1.52	19.13

*Annual averages calculated at the mid-year. First three are the five year averages, fourth one is three year average and fifth and last is 18 year average.

Note: Figures in parentheses indicate percentage share in total.

Source: Data calculated from *Classified Abstracts* of different municipalities for various years.

expenditure on public health and sanitation. Notably, the small-sized municipal towns incur very little on building infrastructure for sanitation work.

In 1987-88, when salary bill for all towns made up about 86 per cent in total municipal expenditure on public health and sanitation, it varied from a high of 100 per cent in Kot Fatta and Sangat Mandi towns to a low of about 69 per cent in Rampura Phul. A majority of municipal towns had this proportion higher than the average for all the municipalities. Except Rampura Phul, which recorded sharp decline in the share of salary bill in the total municipal expenditure on public health and sanitation, all the other municipalities recorded an increase in the share of salary component in their municipal expenditure on this service.

In 1992-93, when municipal expenditure on public health and sanitation increased by about 116 per cent, from Rs. 95.44 lakh in 1987-88 to Rs. 205.96 lakh in 1992-93, the salary component increased by 136 per cent. Against this, the contingency component recorded a marginal decline of about 3 per cent. In fact, contingency amount recorded an absolute decline of Rs. 47,000 during this period: from Rs. 13.75 lakh in 1987-88 to Rs. 13.28 lakh in 1992-93. It is really a matter of serious concern that the mounting salary bills were leaving very little with municipalities to spend on developmental work. It is interesting to note that the share of salary component increased in case of all the municipalities between 1987-88 and 1992-93, except in the case of those where it was already too high. Among municipalities, it varied from a high of 100 per cent in Kot Fatta to a low of about 92 per cent in Maur Mandi in 1992-93 (Table 4.27).

In 1996-97, when average share of salary component for all the municipalities in the district made up more than 95 per cent, it varied from a high of 100 per cent in Kot Fatta town to a low of 93 per cent in Maur Mandi town. Between 1992-93 and 1996-97, the salary component increased by more than 70 per cent. Against this, the contingency increased by only 20 per cent. Obviously, the component of salary in municipal expenditure on public health and sanitation has been growing fast over the period. Against this, the contingency component was either stagnating or growing marginally. Under the circumstances, very little was left with municipalities in the district after payment of salaries to staff for actual work relating to sanitation and consequently public health and sanitation conditions were bound to suffer badly in the process. Moreover, slum localities and peripheral area were worst hit.

D. Per Capita Expenditure/Subsidy on Sanitation

Subsidy on sanitation in per capita terms provides a more realistic picture than in terms of absolute or proportional share. Hence, in the following per capita subsidy levied on sanitation has been examined in spatio-temporal context.

During 1980-98, municipal towns in Bathinda incurred an amount of Rs. 75 per capita per annum on sanitation. The entire per capita amount was in the form of subsidy as municipalities in the district did not earn revenue against this service. There were, however, wide inter-municipal variations in this regard. Per capita amount varied from a high of Rs. 88 in Bathinda municipality to a low of Rs. 5 in Kot Fatta (Table 4.28 and Fig. 4.10). In the three municipalities of Raman Mandi, Sangat Mandi and Kot Fatta it was Rs. 50 or lower. While in the three municipalities of Bathinda, Goniana Mandi and Bhucho Mandi it was more than Rs. 70. On the whole, higher civic and administrative municipal towns alongwith those having large 'mandis' were spending more on sanitation than those having lower civic and administrative status. The higher expenditure was directly associated with higher subsidy. It is, however, interesting to note that disparities in per capita subsidy were of much lower order than that in absolute amount of subsidy. This is supported by much lower value of co-efficient of variability (0.51) in case of per capita amount than in the absolute amount (1.67) of subsidy on sanitation.

Per capita amount of subsidy on sanitation has been increasing over the period (Fig. 4.11). This was Rs. 21 for all the municipalities in 1982-83 which rose to Rs. 167 in 1996-97, registering an increase of about eight times in 18 years. In 1982-83, when the annual average for all the municipalities was Rs. 21, per capita subsidy amount varied from a high of Rs. 27 in Goniana Mandi to a low of Rs. 2 in Kot Fatta. Three municipalities of Bathinda, Bhucho Mandi and Goniana Mandi showed higher than the average. On the other end of the scale, Sangat Mandi and Kot Fatta had less than half the average for all the municipalities. Nevertheless, inter-municipal disparities in per capita expenditure/subsidy, though

TABLE 4.28

Bathinda District: Per Capita Municipal Expenditure/Subsidy on Public Health & Sanitation, 1980-98

Name of town		1982-83*		1987-88*		1992-93*		1996-97*		1980-98*	
	Civic status	Average expenditure (Rs. in lakhs)	Expenditure per Capita (Rupees)	Average expenditure (Rs. in lakhs)	Expenditure per Capita (Rupees)	Average expenditure (Rs. in lakhs)	Expenditure per Capita (Rupees)	Average expenditure (Rs. in lakhs)	Expenditure per Capita (Rupees)	Average expenditure (Rs. in lakhs)	Expenditure per Capita (Rupees)
Bathinda	I	28.75	25	65.30	56	134.16	116	234.34	201	102.45	88
Rampura Phul	III	3.95	12	9.00	28	30.74	96	47.06	148	19.96	63
Maur Mandi	III	2.94	16	7.06	37	15.28	81	21.11	112	10.54	56
Raman Mandi	IV	2.62	18	5.28	37	9.11	64	14.31	100	7.11	50
Goniana Mandi	IV	2.34	27	4.60	54	8.22	96	13.38	156	6.44	75
Bhucho Mandi	IV	1.83	23	3.68	47	7.48	96	12.92	165	5.76	74
Kot Fatta	V	0.12	2	0.24	5	0.24	5	0.46	9	0.24	5
Sangat Mandi	VI	0.22	8	0.28	10	0.73	26	0.97	34	0.50	17
All Towns		42.77	21	95.44	46	205.96	100	344.55	167	153.00	75
C.V.		1.67	0.50	1.71	0.52	1.63	0.50	1.71	0.54	1.67	0.51

* Annual averages calculated at the mid-year. First three are the five year averages, fourth one is three year average and fifth and last is 18 year average.

Notes: (i) Per capita subsidy has been calculated on the basis of 1981 Census data. In case of Bathinda population figures for calculating subsidies were confined to areas falling under the Bathinda M.C. jurisdiction. Two public sector units, Fertilizer and Thermal Plant make their own arrangements and have been excluded from the calculations/computations.

(ii) C.V. stands for Coefficient of Variability.

Source: Data calculated from *Classified Abstracts* of different municipalities for various years.

Fig. 4.10

Bathinda District: Trends in Per Capita Subsidy on Public Health and Sanitation

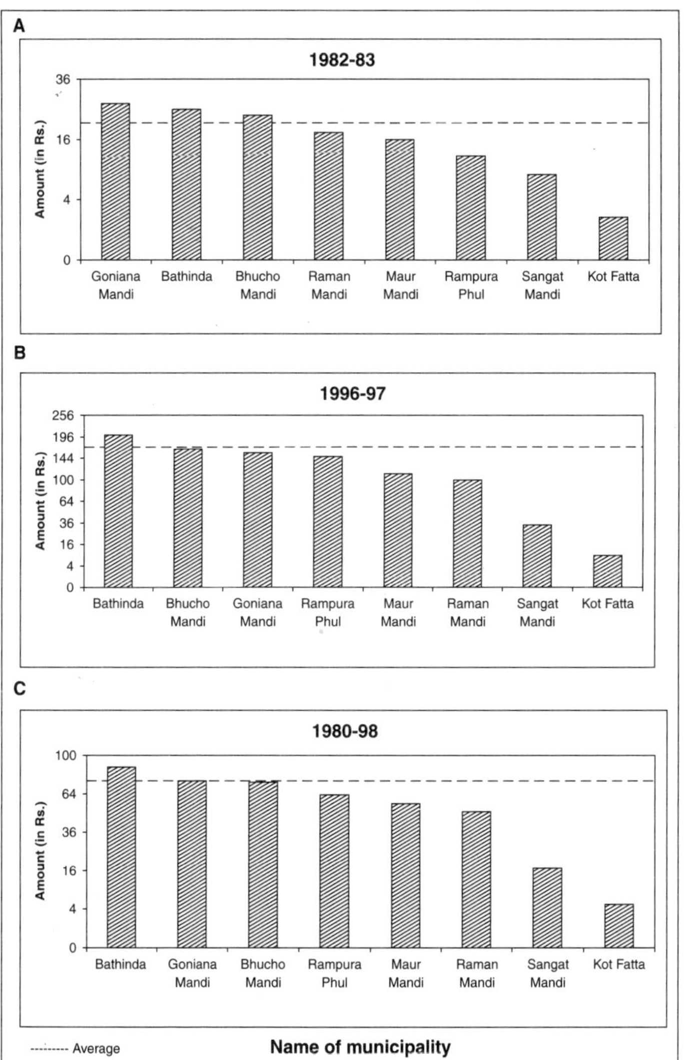

quite high, were the lowest recorded during the period 1980-98. This is supported by relatively low value on co-efficient of variability index (0.50).

Fig. 4.11

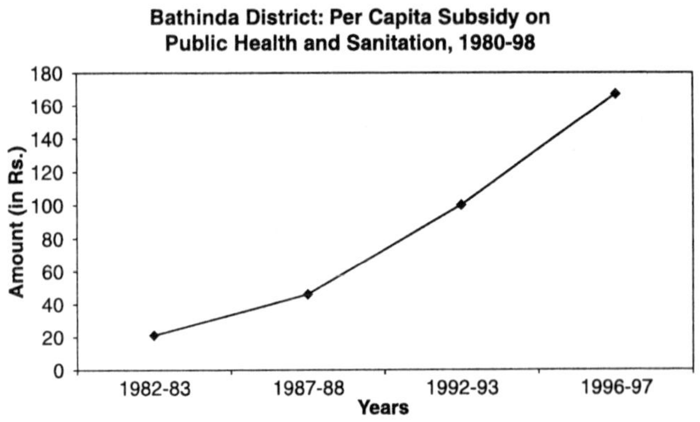

Bathinda District: Per Capita Subsidy on Public Health and Sanitation, 1980-98

In 1987-88, average amount of per capita subsidy increased to Rs. 46 from Rs. 21 in 1982-83. With this increase in per capita amount, inter-municipal disparities widened. It varied from a high of Rs. 56 in Bathinda municipality to a low of Rs. 5 in Kot Fatta. Co-efficient of variability index value moved to 0.52 from 0.50 in 1982-83. Five of the eight municipalities in the district had lower per capita amount of subsidy than the average for all the municipalities.

In 1992-93 when average per capita amount of subsidy rose to Rs. 100 from Rs. 46 in 1987-88, inter-municipal disparities registered marginal decline. The value of co-efficient of variability index came down again to 0.50 from 0.52 in 1987-88. It is interesting to note that rapid growth of subsidy amount was marked with reduction in inter-municipal disparities in per capita subsidy. It varied from a high of Rs. 116 in Bathinda town to a low of Rs. 5 in Kot Fatta. All municipalities recorded rapid increase in per capita amount of subsidy on sanitation between 1987-88 and 1992-93. However, the increase was highest in the case of Rampura Phul, second largest municipal town in the district while no change took place in per capita amount of subsidy in Kot Fatta, the second smallest municipal town in the district.

After narrowing down in 1992-93, inter-municipal disparities in per capita amount of subsidy on sanitation widened again in 1996-97 (Fig. 4.12). Per capita amount of subsidy on sanitation in 1996-97 ranged from a high of Rs. 201 in Bathinda municipality to a low of Rs. 9 in Kot Fatta, showing a ratio of 22:1. Increase in disparities was also supported in higher value of co-efficient of variability index (0.54) in 1996-97 as compared to 1992-93 (0.50). Once again, Bathinda was at the top and Kot Fatta municipality at the bottom. Municipalities providing per capita amount of subsidy higher than Rs. 150 included Bathinda, Goniana Mandi and Bhucho Mandi municipal towns. However, in Kot Fatta and Sangat Mandi towns, it was less then Rs. 50. Bathinda is a Class I town, Goniana Mandi and Bhucho Mandi Class IV towns, and Kot Fatta and Sangat Mandi Class V and Class VI towns, respectively. On the whole, class category of a town combined with administrative status and revenue income play a significant role in the inter-municipal disparities in distribution of subsidy on sanitation in the district.

Spatial Discrimination

Public health and sanitation is one of the fully subsidized urban services in Bathinda district. There is, however, wide inter-town and intra-town discrimination in maintaining sanitation conditions. While sanitation staff population ratio is quite low in almost all the eight towns in the district, the ratio is particularly very low in Kot Fatta, Sangat Mandi, and Raman Mandi towns. It is notable that in the town of Kot Fatta there was only one sweeper, taking care of only the Municipal Committee Office. Rest of the households in the town sweep their surroundings and streets on their own. In Sangat Mandi, where there were only three sweepers employed for sanitation, swept the streets and drains after a gap of three to four days.

In Bathinda City, localities inhabited by high income/ government officials and main markets were looked after much better than others. It was complained by several residents of peripheral localities and those resided in by low income group households that sweepers swept streets in their localities quite irregularly and none of the officials heeded their repeated requests as the sweepers took special care of the residences of high officials

Fig. 4.12

Bathinda District: Inter-municipal Disparities in Per Capita Subsidy on Public Health and Sanitation

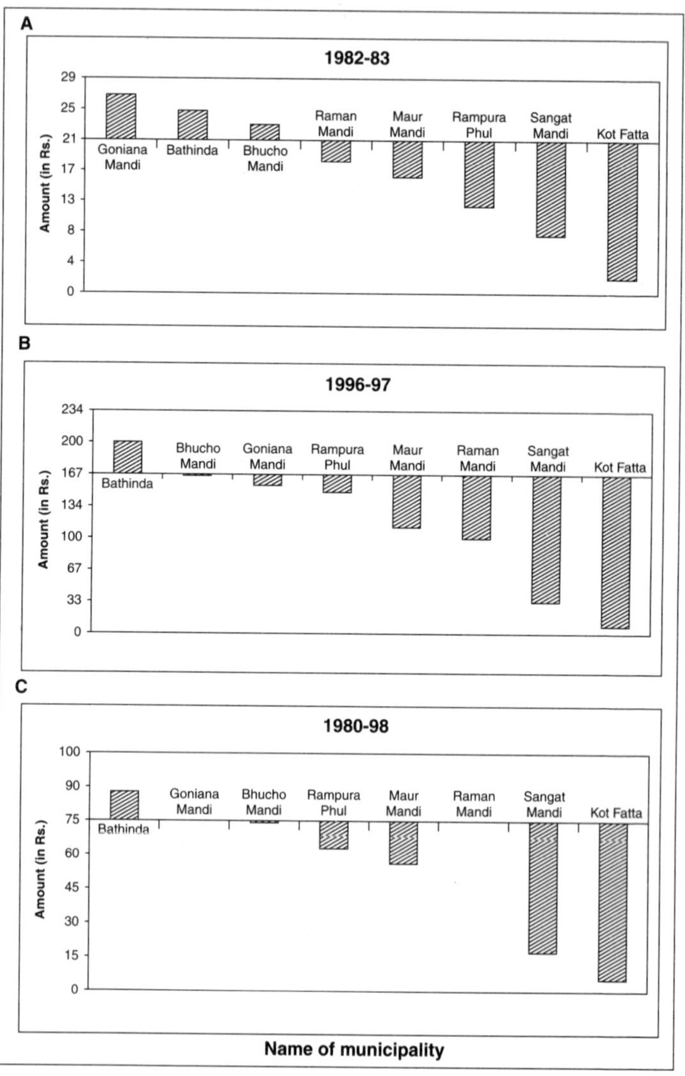

of the municipal committee, officers in state bureaucracy and the influencial councillors.

Main Highlights

The following points emerge strongly from the preceding discussions:

- Public health and sanitation, which has been one of the most important obligatory functions of municipal administration in India, has assumed added significance and complexicity due to rapid growth and physical expansion of urban centres. The emerging scenario demands high investment by municipalities both in human capital as well as modern equipment.
- There are wide inter-municipal variations in availability of sanitary workers and equipment in Bathinda district. Bathinda, the largest municipal town in the district, has one sanitary worker after each 256 persons or 51 households. Against this, the average for Kot Fatta, the second smallest town in the district, has only one sweeper and he, too, merely sweeps the municipal office rather than sweeping roads, cleaning drains, collecting or disposing-off garbage, etc. Further, eleven of the sixteen tractor trolleys in municipal towns of the district are in the two largest towns (Bathinda and Rampura Phul). There is no tractor trolley in Kot Fatta town. In fact, Kot Fatta municipal town does not have any equipment for sanitation work except a hand driven *rehri* and a *khoncha*. Civic and administrative status of a town along with its capacity to generate revenue and to spend on urban services find association with sanitary staff-population ratio and availability of modern equipment for sanitation work therein.
- During the period 1980-98, municipalities in Bathinda district incurred an annual average expenditure of Rs. 153 lakh on public health and sanitation, making up more than 18 per cent of the total municipal expenditure of the district on different services. There are, however, wide inter-municipal variations. It varied from a high of 26 per cent in Maur Mandi, a Class III town, to a low of 5 per cent in Kot Fatta

town. Relatively large population-sized 'Mandi' towns along with Bathinda, which functions as the district headquarters and the only Class I town in the district, incurred higher proportionate shares of their aggregate expenditure on sanitation.

- The entire municipal expenditure on public health and sanitation in the district was actually the subsidy element on this service, as the municipalities provide this facility to their residents free of charge.
- There were wide spatio-temporal variations in the distribution of subsidy on sanitation. In aggregate terms, three of the largest municipalities viz., Bathinda, Rampura Phul and Maur Mandi, shared 87 per cent of total municipal expenditure on sanitation in the district during 1980-98. Their combined population made up 81 per cent of the total urban population in the district in 1991. Against this, five small-sized municipal towns shared only 13 per cent of municipal subsidy but had about 20 per cent of total urban population in the district. Bathinda municipal town alone has more than two-thirds of total municipal subsidy on this service, against its share of about three-fifths in the total urban population in the district. In contrast, Kot Fatta shares less than 0.2 per cent of the total urban population in the district. In 1982-83, Bathinda municipality provided 14 per cent of total average annual expenditure on different services as subsidy on sanitation, which increased to about 21 per cent in 1996-97. In contrast, Kot Fatta, the second smallest municipal town, recorded a decrease of about 6 per cent in 1996-97 from about 11 per cent in 1982-83. Inter-municipal disparities, in absolute terms as well as proportion of subsidy on sanitation, were very wide but showed a mixed trend. Disparities widened between 1982-83 and 1987-88, but declined somewhat between 1987-88 and 1992-93. The disparities, however, increased again between 1992-93 and 1996-97.
- Composition of expenditure/subsidy on sanitation has been highly revealing. During 1980-98, more than nine-tenths of total municipal expenditure in the district on sanitation went into paying salary to sanitary staff, leaving only less than

one-tenth for purchase and maintenance of equipment, etc. for the purpose. The share rose to more than 95 per cent of total municipal expenditure on sanitation in 1997-98 from 83 per cent in 1982-83. Implementation of Fifth Pay Commission's recommendations by the Panjab Government in 1988 resulted in hefty increase in the salaries of government and semi-government employees. As a result, the share of salary component in municipal expenditure rose from 85.6 per cent in 1987-88 to 95.3 per cent in 1996-97. This left very little with municipalities to invest in building and maintaining infrastructure for public health and sanitation work. Small sized, low income municipalities were the hardest hit in this regard. The whole municipal expenditure on sanitation work in Kot Fatta, the second smallest municipal town in the district, was consumed in paying the salary of sanitary staff; leaving nothing for the purchase of even a broom. This had serious implications for public health and sanitation conditions in some towns of Bathinda district.

- Per capita municipal subsidy on sanitation provided another interesting insight. During 1980-98, municipalities in Bathinda provided Rs. 75 per capita per annum as subsidy on sanitation. The subsidy amount ranged from a high of Rs. 88 in Bathinda municipality to a low of only Rs. 5 in Kot Fatta. Higher civic and administrative status coupled with higher capacity to mobilize financial resources were largely responsible for wide inter-municipal variations.
- Per capita municipal subsidy on sanitation has been growing over the period in the district. However, the fastest growth in per capita subsidy amount was recorded between 1987-88 and 1992-93. Notably, this growth in subsidy amount was marked with reduction in inter-municipal disparities in per capita subsidy on sanitation. Hence, it may be called a period of growth with spatial justice. After 1992-93, the growth of per capita subsidy amount on sanitation slowed down, but inter-municipal disparities in per capita amount of subsidy on sanitation marginally widened. Nevertheless, the trend in disparities has been undulated during the period 1980-98.

- There has been inter and intra-town discrimination distribution of subsidy on public health and sanitati While, there was not a single sweeper to sweep the roa and the drains of Kot Fatta town, there was one sweep after each about 256 persons in Bathinda City and wit Bathinda City localities inhabited by the high income gro people and/or the government officials and special *baz* were given greater attention at the cost of low inco localities.

FIRE BRIGADE SERVICE

The 'fire service' in India is deemed as the fourth line of defen the others being the three wings of the defence forces, the arm navy and the air force. This service is crucial not only during t War but also in normal peace times. The need for fire servic has grown with the expansion in area under human habitati especially the urban settlements, development of industri intensity of land use and size of population. Its availability almost indispensable under conditions characterized by mul storeyed buildings, *Jhuggi-Jhoparies*, use of wood in constructi and location of buildings containing vast official records.

The role and importance of the fire service goes beyond savi of life and property of the people from fire. The fire personn rescue the people from sewers and wells and those accidenta entrapped in lifts or other such hazards. Clearly, the importan of fire service is growing with the increase in number of high ri buildings, proliferation of slums and intensification of land u in urban areas, especially in cities and metros. However, the fi service requires big capital investment difficult to afford for t small and medium sized towns. That is the reason for this servi remaining confined, in general, to large sized municipal town Small-sized municipal towns generally depend upon the big on for this service. In Punjab, only 31 out of total 132 municip towns have fire brigade service. In Bathinda district, two out the eight municipal towns have the fire service. These inclu Bathinda and Rampura Phul. However, the fire service maintain by these towns is made available not only to the other municip towns in the district but also to those located in adjoining distric

Bathinda bears all the expenditure required to run and maintain e fire service available with this municipal town. However, the penditure on fire service in Rampura Phul is borne jointly nong Rampura Phul, Maur Mandi and Raman Mandi in the tio of 2:1:1, respectively.

The fire service is charged at the rate of Rs. 250 per hour per hicle[7]. These rates are fixed by the Directorate of Local overnment Bodies, Punjab, headquartered at Chandigarh and e applicable to all the municipal towns in the state. Earlier, ese charges were Rs. 100 per hour. Then, the operational cost of e fire tender was coming to Rs. 210 per hour for petrol vehicle d Rs. 140 per hour for diesel vehicle. In this way, the charges d always been quite low as compared to the direct cost involved. otably, however, the above stated charges are claimed only om the insured buildings. These could be residential, commercial industrial in nature. Strangely no charges are claimed if the ilding is not insured with any of the Insurance agencies but lls within the municipal limits. Evidently, the houses and ildings not insured under any insurance scheme enjoy 100 per nt subsidy on the fire services. Also, the service is provided e of cost to the important public properties, fairs and festivals, d at the time of accident, gas leakage, floods or canal tragedy d other hazards of similar nature. If the affected building is cated outside the municipal limits, then the charges are @ . 250 per hour per vehicle, irrespective of its insurance status. ll 2000, there was hardly any income earned against the ovision of fire brigade service in any town in the district.

re Services: Infrastructure and Staff

In Bathinda town, the fire service was started as early as in 59. In comparison the fire service came as late as 1985 in mpura Phul. Thus, before 1985 the fire service was available ith only one municipal town in the entire district .

Currently, there are, in all, five fire tenders in the district, ree in Bathinda and two in Rampura Phul. In addition, Bathinda wn has one jeep for lifting water to extinguish fires in multi-

During fieldwork, it came to the notice that Rampura Phul municipality was charging Rs. 200 per hour per vehicle in place of Rs. 250 fixed by the Directorate of Local Bodies, Punjab.

storeyed buildings. This facility of a jeep is not available w Rampura Phul municipality (Table 4.29-A). Further, the trai and portable pumps, available with Bathinda municipal tov have not been yet acquired by the Rampura Phul municipali Hence, Bathinda municipality has a considerable edge ov Rampura Phul in the availability of infrastructure and facilit associated with the fire service.

TABLE 4.29 A

Bathinda District: The Fire Service Infrastructure with Municipalities, 1997-98

Name of town	*Civic status*	*Installation year*	*Fire tender*	*Jeep to lift the water*	*Trailer pump*	*Portable pump*	*To*
Bathinda	I	1959	03	01	01	01	0
Rampura Phul	III	1985	02	Nil	Nil	Nil	0
All Towns			05	01	01	01	0

Note: Municipal towns of Maur Mandi, Raman Mandi, Goniana Mandi, Bhu Mandi, Kot Fatta and Sangat Mandi do not own fire services independen

Source: Data calculated from *The Fire Brigade Service Registers* of differ municipalities.

Likewise, the strength of the fire service staff is also mu larger in Bathinda town than in Rampura Phul. In all, there we 32 fire services personnel in Bathinda town in comparison to in Rampura Phul. However, in fire service staff-population ra Rampura Phul enjoys a considerable edge over Bathinda ci While there was only one fire service personnel for every fi thousand population cluster in Bathinda town, this ratio was o to sixteen hundred persons in Rampura Phul (Table 4.29-B).

The number of fire calls attended by the fire brigade va from year to year and month to month. In the year 1989-90, in there were 87 fire calls, attended by the fire brigade in Bathin city. April, May, June, October and November are the months maximum fire calls. The April, May and June fires are associat with the dry season and stormy winds as any fire spreads quickl October and November are noted for fires in cotton factori Hence, majority of fire calls during these two months are fro the cotton factories. This is a cotton growing area of Punjab.

TABLE 4.29 B

Bathinda District: Strength of the Fire Services Staff with Municipalities, 1997-98

Name of town	*Civic status*	*Assistant divisional fire*	*Fire station officer*	*Sub-fire officer*	*Leading fire man*	*Drainers*	*Mechanics*	*Fireman*	*Total*	*Fire services staff-population ratio*
Bathinda	I	01	01	02	02	03	01	22	32	1:4970
Rampura Phul	III	No	No	02	02	04	No	14	22	1:1615
Total		01	01	04	04	07	01	36	54	

Note: Municipal towns of Maur Mandi, Raman Mandi, Goniana Mandi, Bhucho Mandi, Kot Fatta and Sangat Mandi do not own fire services independently.

Source: Data calculated from *The Fire Brigade Service Registers* of different municipalities.

Expenditure: Pattern and Change

During 1980-98, municipalities in Bathinda district incurred an average annual amount of Rs. 14.61 lakh on fire brigade service (Table 4.30). This amount made up about 2.0 per cent in total municipal expenditure on different services during this period. There were wide inter-municipal variations in this regard. Bathinda municipality alone incurred an amount of Rs. 9.65 lakh or more than 66 per cent of total annual municipal expenditure on fire brigade service in the district. Against this, Bathinda city shares nearly 60 per cent of the total urban population in the district. However, Bathinda city contains a number of localities, markets, buildings, factories such as oil mills, cotton ginning factories which are highly prone to fire. The remaining amount of Rs. 4.96 lakh or 34 per cent of total such expenditure in the district is shared among Rampura Phul, Maur Mandi and Raman Mandi towns in the ratio of 2:1:1.

The expenditure on fire brigade service has been growing over the period in the district. In 1982-83, average annual municipal expenditure on fire brigade service had been Rs. 2.72 lakh. The total expenditure was done by Bathinda municipality as no other municipal town in the district was maintaining fire service in

TABLE 4.30

Bathinda District: Municipal Expenditure/Subsidy on Fire Services as a Share in Total Municipal Expenditure 1980-98

(Rs. in lakhs)

Name of town	Civic status	1982-83*			1987-88*			1992-93*			1996-97*			1980-98*		
		Aggregate expenditure	Expenditure on fire service	Percentage of aggregate expenditure	Aggregate expenditure	Expenditure on fire service	Percentage of aggregate expenditure	Aggregate expenditure	Expenditure on fire service	Percentage of aggregate expenditure	Aggregate expenditure	Expenditure on fire service	Percentage of aggregate expenditure	Aggregate expenditure	Expenditure on fire service	Percentage of aggregate expenditure
1	2	3	4	5	6	7	8	9	10	11	12	13	14	15	16	17
Bathinda	I	207.10	2.72	1.31	456.43	7.02	1.54	755.21	12.77	1.69	1135.78	20.37	1.79	583.39	9.65	1.65
Rampura Phul	III	34.62	—	—	55.62	1.83	3.29	104.96	3.89	3.71	162.77	5.32	3.27	81.35	2.48	3.05
Maur Mandi	III	14.61	—	—	31.80	0.91	2.86	52.30	1.94	3.71	77.11	2.66	3.45	40.30	1.24	3.08
Raman Mandi	IV	12.20	—	—	28.50	0.91	3.19	53.35	1.94	s3.64	85.41	2.66	3.11	40.36	1.24	3.07
Aggregate Expenditure		268.53	2.72	1.01	572.35	10.67	1.86	965.82	20.54	2.13	1461.07	31.01	2.12	745.40	14.61	1.96

*Annual averages.

Note: Since no income is earned by municipalities in the district on account of this service, hence expenditure and subsidy is one and the same thing.

Source: Data calculated from *Classified Abstracts* of different municipalities for various years.

those days. Coming to 1987-88, when Rampura Phul in association with Maur Mandi and Raman Mandi towns established fire brigade services at Rampura Phul town, the expenditure on fire brigade service jumped to Rs. 10.67 lakh. In this way, the expenditure on fire brigade services in the district increased by nearly four times. About 66 per cent of this amount was shared by Bathinda city and remaining by Rampura Phul, Maur Mandi and Raman Mandi towns in the ratio of 2:1:1. Registering an increase of 158 per cent, expenditure of Bathinda municipal town rose to Rs. 7.02 lakh in 1987-88 from Rs. 2.72 lakh in 1982-83. It was during this period, the fire brigade service in Bathinda city added one more fire tender to its fleet.

TABLE 4.31

Bathinda District: Change in Municipal Expenditure on Fire Services, 1980-98

(*Figure in percentage*)

Name of town	*Civic status*	*1982-83* over 1987-88**	*1987-88* over 1992-93**	*1992-93* over 1996-97**
Bathinda	I	0.23	0.15	0.10
Rampura Phul	III	3.29	0.42	-0.44
Maur Mandi	III	2.86	0.85	-0.26
Raman Mandi	IV	3.19	0.45	-0.53

*Annual averages.

Source: Data calculated from *Classified Abstract* of different municipalities for various years.

Coming to 1992-93, municipal expenditure on fire brigade service in the district rose to Rs. 20.54 lakh. In this way, it registered an increase of 93 per cent between 1987-88 and 1992-93. Earlier between 1982-83 and 1987-88, this increase was about 300 per cent. New addition of fire brigade service in Rampura Phul was mainly responsible for such a high increase in the expenditure amount on fire services in the district. In 1992-93, Bathinda, a Class I town in the district, shared 62 per cent of total such expenditure in the district. Earlier in 1987-88, it shared 66 per cent of total such expenditure in the district. The decline in its share was mainly due to the higher growth in expenditure done by other municipalities on fire service. The expenditure done by Bathinda municipality grew by 82 per cent against an increase of 113 per cent in combined expenditure done by Rampura Phul, Maur Mandi and Raman Mandi towns.

In 1996-97, when municipal expenditure on fire service in the district rose to Rs. 31.01 lakh from Rs. 20.54 lakh in 1992-93, the expenditure on fire service increased by 51 per cent. It is to be noted here that the growth of expenditure on fire brigade service in the district had been declining over the period. In the initial years of the establishment of fire brigade service, the purchase of fire tenders and the recruitment of crews required large investment. After the infrastructure was developed, it was mainly the maintenance of infrastructure and payment of salaries to the staff on which the municipalities had to incur expenditure. Against the average growth of expenditure on fire brigade by 51 per cent, 37 per cent in the case of remaining municipalities, spending in combination, the share of Bathinda municipality in total expenditure on fire service made up 66 per cent in 1996-97. Earlier in 1992-93, this share had been 62 per cent.

Briefly, municipal expenditure on fire service has been growing over the period in the district. However, its growth rate has been slowing down gradually. While it increased by about 300 per cent between 1982-83 and 1987-88, the growth rate came down to only 51 per cent during 1992-93–1996-97 (Table 4.31). In the initial years, building of infrastructure for fire service and recruitment of crew needed huge capital investment, later on main expenditure had been on maintenance and payment of salaries to staff. Of this total expenditure on fire services in the district, Bathinda city shared about two-thirds of the total such expenditure in the district. Mainly because of its status as district headquarters and large size, Bathinda city has more localities, buildings, markets and factories that pose greater vulnerability to fire.

Main Highlights

- The Bathinda municipality was the first to acquire the fire brigade service among all the towns in the district. It acquired the fire brigade in 1959. Rampura Phul, the only other town to have a fire fighting service acquired it as late as in 1985. Thus, Bathinda and Rampura Phul are the only municipalities that run and maintain fire services in the district. The fire services available in these two towns are shared not only with other towns in the district but also with towns and places in adjoining districts.

TABLE 4.32

Bathinda District: Per Capita Municipal Expenditure on Fire Service, 1980–98

(Rs. in lakhs)

Name of town	*Civic status*	*1982-83**		*1987-88**		*1992-93**		*1996-97**		*1980-98**	
		Expenditure on fire brigade service	*Expenditure per capita (in Rs.)*	*Expenditure on fire brigade service*	*Expenditure per capita (in Rs.)*	*Expenditure on fire brigade service*	*Expenditure per capita (in Rs.)*	*Expenditure on fire brigade service*	*Expenditure per capita (in Rs.)*	*Expenditure on fire brigade service*	*Expenditure per capita (in Rs.)*
Bathinda	I	2.72	2	7.02	6	12.77	11	20.37	17	9.65	8
Rampura Phul	III	Nil	Nil	1.83	6	3.89	12	5.32	17	2.48	8
Maur Mandi	III	Nil	Nil	0.91	5	1.94	10	2.66	14	1.24	7
Raman Mandi	IV	Nil	Nil	0.91	6	1.94	14	2.66	19	1.24	9
Aggregate expenditure		2.72	2	10.67	6	20.54	11	31.01	17	14.61	8
C.V.				0.95	0.08	0.87	0.13	0.95	11	0.96	0.09

*Annual averages.

Notes: (i) Since no income is earned by municipalities on account of this service, hence expenditure and subsidy is one and the same thing.

(ii) Per capita expenditure/subsidy has been calculated on the basis of 1981 Census data. In case of Bathinda population figures used for calculation of subsidies confined to areas falling under the jurisdiction of Bathinda M.C. Two public sector units Fertilizer and thermal plant make their own arrangement for provision of services. Hence excluded from the calculation.

(iii) C.V. Co-efficient of Variability Index.

Source: Data calculated from *Classified Abstracts* of different municipalities for various years.

- Rampura Phul shares its expenditure on fire brigade service with Maur Mandi and Raman Mandi municipality in the ratio of 2.1:1, respectively.
- The fire service is charged for only in the case of insured buildings or buildings/establishments located outside the municipal limits. All others get this service free of charge. Public buildings, fairs and religious congregations, irrespective of their location, are provided this service totally free.
- On average annual basis, municipalities in Bathinda district spent Rs. 14.61 lakh on fire brigade service during 1980-98. Bathinda municipality shared two-third of this expenditure and remaining one-third was shared by Rampura Phul alongwith Maur Mandi and Raman Mandi towns.
- Municipal expenditure on fire brigade service has been growing over the period. It has increased to Rs. 31.01 lakh in 1996-97 from Rs. 2.72 lakh in 1982-83, on an average annual basis. However, the growth rate of expenditure on fire service has been slowing down over the period. It came down to 51 per cent between 1992-93 and 1996-97 from about 300 per cent during 1982-83 and 1987-88.
- While the expenditure on fire brigade service has been mounting regularly, there is hardly any regular income to municipalities from this service. Evidently, a very large component of subsidy is involved.

SECTION II

5

Infrastructure Services

ROADS

An efficient and well laid roads network needs little emphasize for its significant contribution in the movement of goods, services and people within a town and its linkages with its surrounding region. The different functional zones (residential, work and recreational areas) in a city get linked through the transport network. It works like the circulatory system of blood in our bodies. It is for this functional significance that the municipalities construct and maintain roads in areas falling under their territorial jurisdiction. This facility is provided free of charge. Hence, the entire expenditure incurred by the municipalities in Bathinda district on the construction and maintenance of roads becomes the subsidy component on this service.

During 1980-98, nearly Rs. 197 million was incurred by the municipalities in the district on construction and maintenance of municipal roads. It is, however, to be noted that a substantial proportion of this amount goes in payment of salary of the staff and to acquire equipment used to construct and maintain roads. This amount made up about 13 per cent of the total municipal expenditure during the period and on an average annual basis it comes to about 109 lakh for all the municipalities (Table 5.1).

In the following, an examination is attempted of the spatio-temporal pattern of expenditure/subsidy* on road construction and maintenance by municipalities in Bathinda district. It is to be noted that municipalities construct and maintain roads which

*Since the municipalities do not earn any revenue from the provision of roads, expenditure and subsidy on roads become one and the same thing. Hence, the terms expenditure and subsidy have been used inter-changeably.

TABLE 5.1

Bathinda District: Expenditure/Subsidy on Municipal Roads as Percentage to Total Municipal Expenditure, 1980–98

(Rs. in lakhs)

Name of town	Civic status	1982–83*			1987–88*			1992–93*			1996–97*			1980–98*		
		Aggregate expenditure	Expenditure on roads	Percentage of aggregate	Aggregate expenditure	Expenditure on roads	Percentage of aggregate expenditure	Aggregate expenditure	Expenditure on roads	Percentage of aggregate expenditure	Aggregate expenditure	Expenditure on roads	Percentage of aggregate expenditure	Aggregate expenditure	Expenditure on roads	Percentage of aggregate expenditure
1	2	3	4	5	6	7	8	9	10	11	12	13	14	15	16	17
Bathinda	I	207.10	22.91 (57.4)	11.06	456.43	55.38 (71.6)	12.13	755.21	98.30 (72.9)	13.02	1135.78	182.95 (77.56)	16.11	583.39	79.54 (72.7)	13.63
Rampura Phul	III	34.62	5.80 (14.5)	16.75	55.62	3.74 (14.8)	6.72	104.96	13.89 (10.3)	13.23	162.77	16.03 (6.80)	9.85	81.35	9.18 (8.4)	11.28
Maur Mandi	III	14.61	2.81 (7.0)	19.23	31.80	5.28 (6.8)	16.60	52.30	3.84 (2.9)	7.34	77.11	5.81 (2.46)	7.53	40.30	4.28 (3.9)	10.62
Raman Mandi	IV	12.20	1.82 (4.6)	14.92	28.50	4.58 (5.9)	16.07	53.35	3.53 (2.6)	6.62	85.41	7.57 (3.21)	8.86	40.36	4.02 (3.7)	9.96
Goniana Mandi	IV	14.30	2.65 (6.6)	18.53	28.70	3.98 (5.1)	13.87	41.46	4.87 (3.6)	11.75	54.33	4.90 (2.08)	9.02	32.52	4.01 (3.6)	12.33
Bhucho Mandi	IV	18.04	3.70 (9.2)	20.51	39.60	3.70 (4.8)	9.34	42.47	8.88 (6.6)	20.91	90.16	18.28 (7.75)	20.78	42.84	7.57 (6.9)	17.67
Kot Fatta	V	1.10	0.20 (1.5)	18.18	4.70	0.24 (0.3)	5.11	5.65	0.41 (0.3)	7.26	7.68	—	—	4.46	0.24 (0.3)	5.38

(Contd.)

TABLE 5.1 *(Contd.)*

Name of town	*Civic status*	*1982–83**			*1987–88**			*1992–93**			*1996–97**			*1980–98**		
		Aggregate expenditure	*Expenditure on roads*	*Percentage of aggregate*	*Aggregate expenditure*	*Expenditure on roads*	*Percentage of aggregate expenditure*	*Aggregate expenditure*	*Expenditure on roads*	*Percentage of aggregate expenditure*	*Aggregate expenditure*	*Expenditure on roads*	*Percentage of aggregate expenditure*	*Aggregate expenditure*	*Expenditure on roads*	*Percentage of aggregate expenditure*
1	2	3	4	5	6	7	8	9	10	11	12	13	14	15	16	17
Sangat Mandi	VI	1.60	Nil	Nil	2.90	0.40 (0.5)	13.79	8.99	1.20 (0.9)	13.35	11.63	0.35 (0.15)	3.00	5.69	0.50 (0.5)	8.79
Aggregate Expenditure		303.57	39.89 (100.0)	13.14	639.25	77.30 (100.0)	12.09	1064.39	134.92 (100.0)	12.68	1624.87	235.89 (100)	14.52	830.91	109.34 (100.0)	13.16
C.V.		1.70	1.26		1.76	1.80		1.78	1.84		1.75	1.82		1.76	1.83	

*Annual averages.

Notes: (i) Figures in parentheses indicate percentage share in total.

(ii) Since no income is earned by municipalities on account of this service, hence expenditure and subsidy is one and the same thing.

(iii) C.V. stands for Coefficient of Variability.

Source: Data calculated from Classified Abstracts of different municipalities for various years.

fall within the municipal limits, the other roads are constructed and maintained either by the State or the national governments.

Municipal Roads: Spatial Expansion and Coverage

Municipal roads in the district have been developed in a phased manner. For example, only about 46 per cent areas of Bathinda municipal town were covered with roads before 1980. This proportion was less than one-third in the case of Rampura Phul, the second largest town in the district (Table 5.2).

Construction of roads in different municipal towns of the district took place in different periods. While in Sangat Mandi town, almost similar area sizes were covered in all the three phases, area coverage differed widely in different phases in case of Bathinda and Bhucho Mandi towns. In Bhucho Mandi town where 45 per cent of the area was covered in the first phase only 20 per cent was covered in the third phase (1990-2000).

None of the towns in the district can boast of total coverage under roads. In all the towns, peripheral areas are still without roads. By 2000, only about 92 per cent of the municipal area and 95 per cent of the total population under municipal limits in towns of Bathinda district were covered under municipal roads (see Maps 5.1 to 5.8). In other words, more than 8 per cent of the areas and 5 per cent of the total population were still uncovered by municipal roads. There are wide internal disparities in this regard. While most of the localities falling East of the railway line in Bathinda town had been covered under the municipal roads before 1980, the coverage has been scanty for localities West of the railway line (Map 5.1). In areas located East of the railway line, major expansion in road network took place after 1980 and peripheral areas were yet to be covered. Another notable feature is the quality of roads. While in areas falling East of the railway line, majority of the roads are metalled, those in areas located West of the railway line are mostly un-metalled.

Raman Mandi town makes a typical case where most of the areas falling South-East of Talwandi road are still without roads (Map 5.4). In these new localities, no municipal road existed before 1990 and more than half of this area was still unserved by roads.

Bhucho Mandi town is another interesting case. Here the major parts of the settled area within the municipal limits was covered

TABLE 5.2

Bathinda District: Area and Population Covered under Municipal Roads in Sampled Towns

Name of town	*Civic status*	*Area covered in acres*						*Population covered in numbers*					
		Before 1980	*1980-90*	*1990-2000*	*Total*	*Uncovered area*	*Grand total*	*Before 1980*	*1980-90*	*1990-2000*	*Total*	*Uncovered Population*	*Grand total*
Bathinda	I	852.2	373.0	476.7	1701.9	155.6	1857.7	69451	29636	37426	136513	7107	143620
		(46)	(20)	(26)	(92)	(8)	(100)	(48)	(21)	(26)	(95)	(5)	(100)
Rampura Phul	III	153.1	140.8	170.4	464.3	24.7	489.0	9912	12947	10595	33454	1894	35348
		(31)	(29)	(35)	(95)	(5)	(100)	(28)	(37)	(30)	(95)	(5)	(100)
Bhucho Mandi	IV	61.8	44.5	27.2	133.5	4.9	138.4	3996	2893	2609	9498	489	9987
		(45)	(32)	(20)	(97)	(3)	(100)	(40)	(29)	(26)	(95)	(5)	(100)
Sangat Mandi	V	29.6	29.6	27.2	86.4	2.5	88.9	1600	739	313	2652	70	2722
		(33)	(33)	(31)	(97)	(3)	(100)	(59)	(27)	(11)	(97)	(3)	(100)

Notes: (i) Area and population figures are estimates. Area has been estimated using square method.
(ii) Area figures relates to 2000 and population figures 1991 Census.
(iii) Figures in parentheses indicate percentage share in total.

Map 5.1

Bathinda Municipality
Roads : Spatial Expansion and Coverage

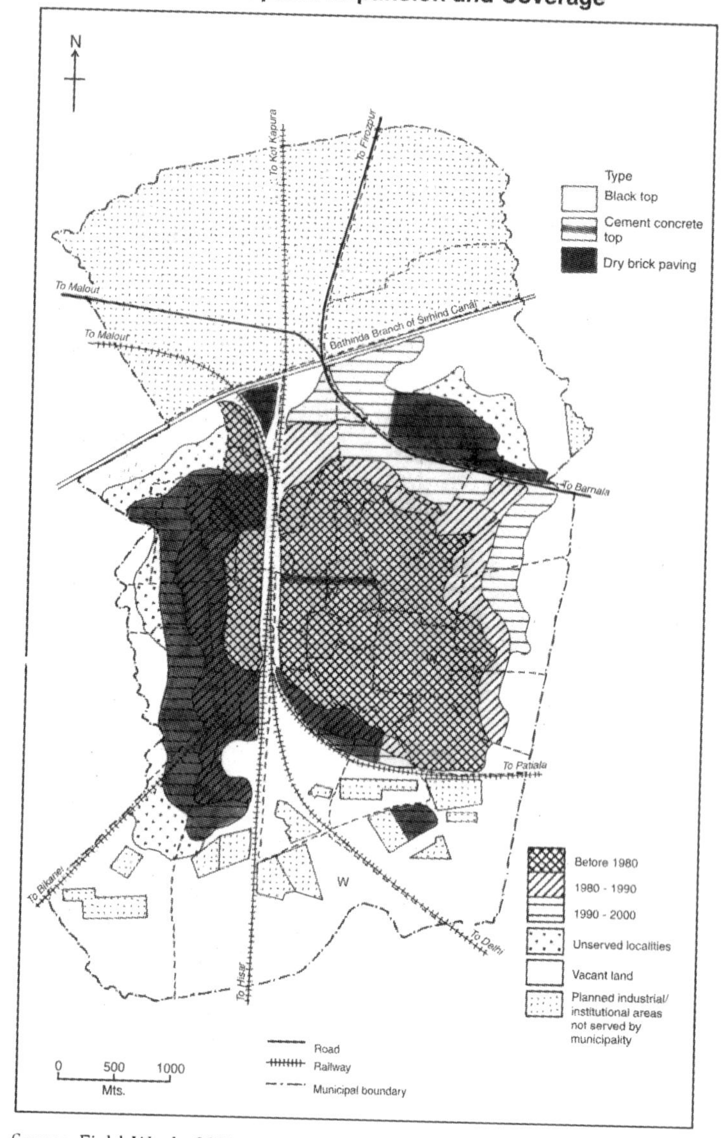

Source: Field Work, 2000.

Map 5.2

Rampura Phul Municipality
Roads Spatial Expansion and Coverage

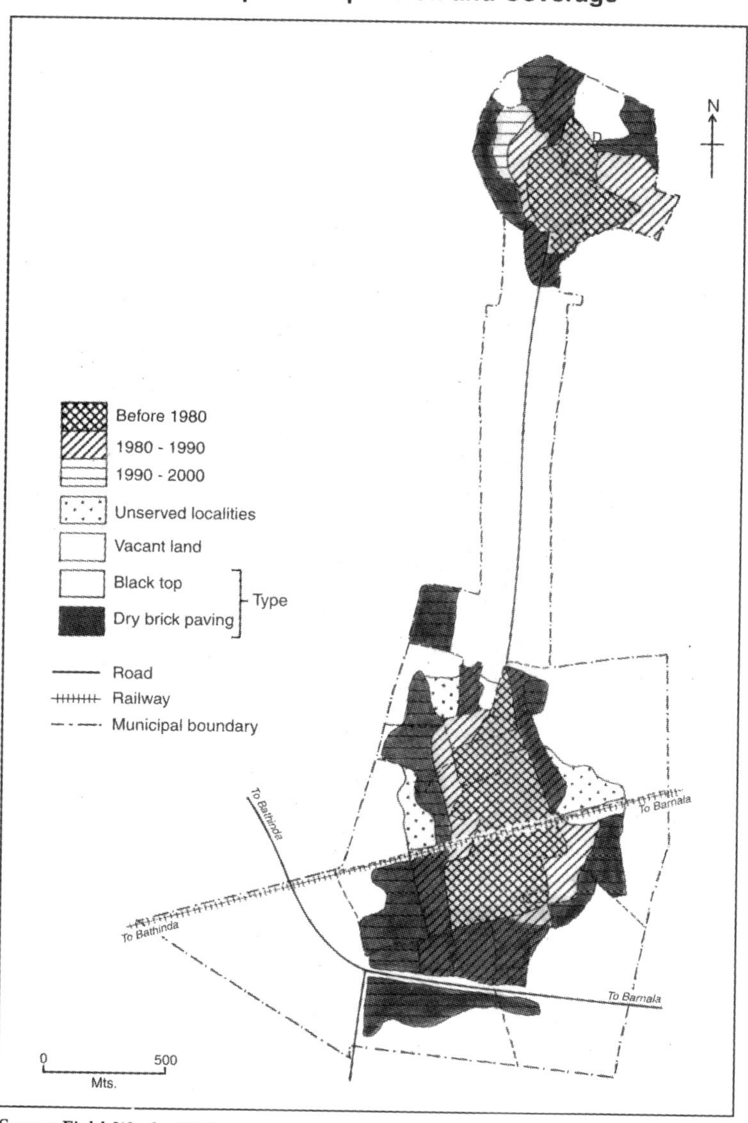

Source: Field Work, 2000.

Map 5.3

Maur Mandi Municipality

Roads: Spatial Expansion and Coverage

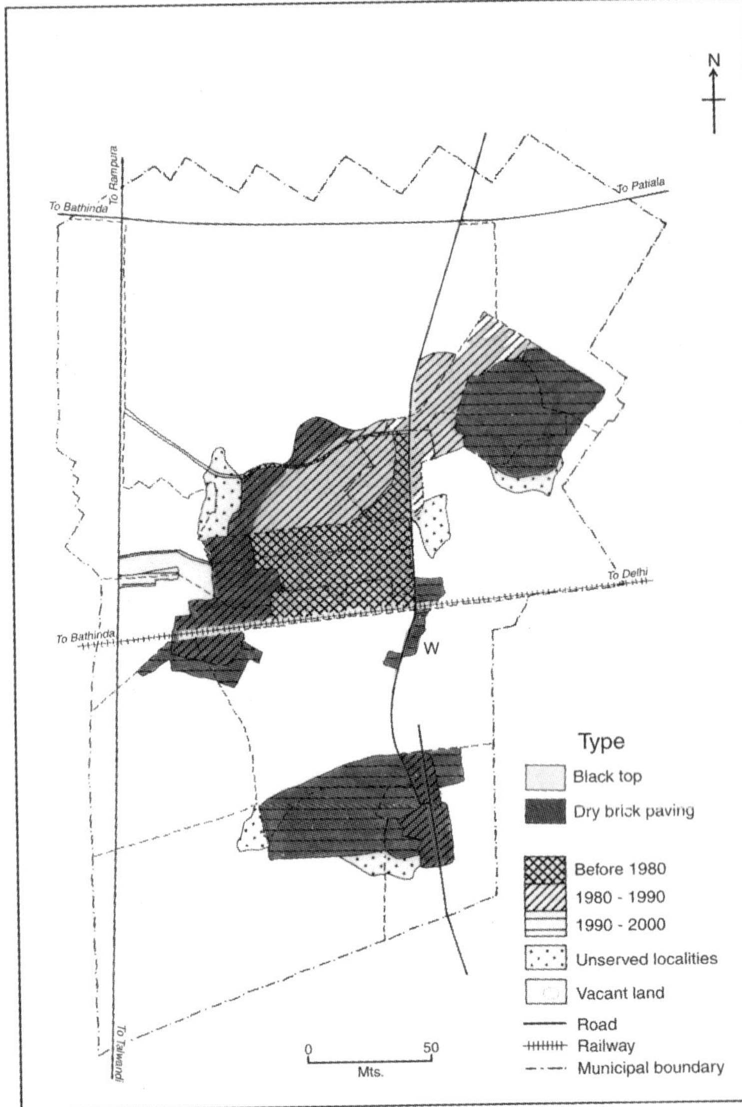

Source: Field Work, 2000.

Map 5.4

Raman Mandi Municipality

Roads: Spatial Expansion and Coverage

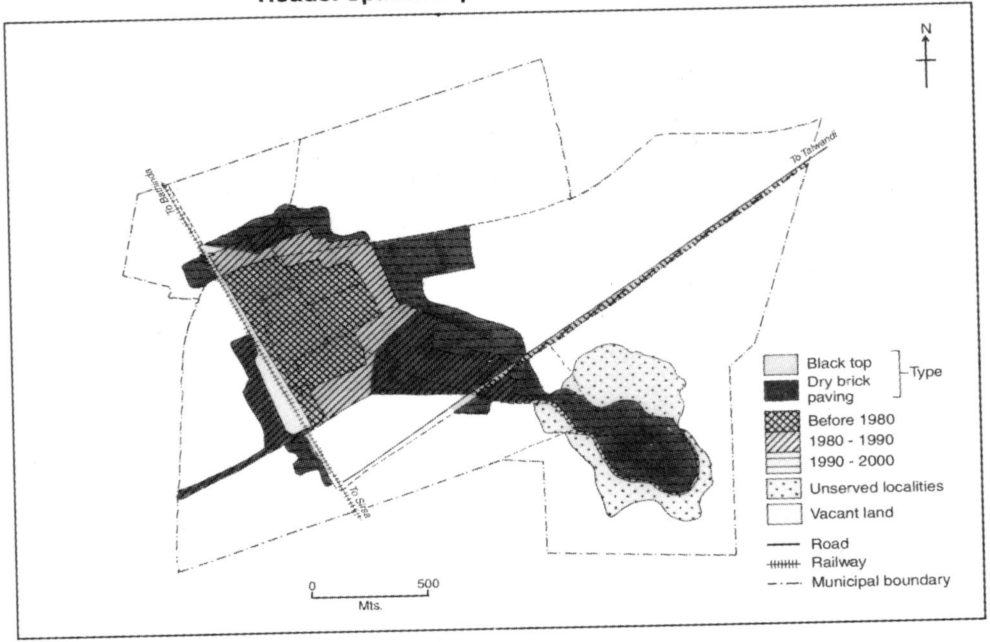

Source: Field Work, 2000.

Map 5.5

Goniana Mandi Municipality

Roads: Spatial Expansion and Coverage

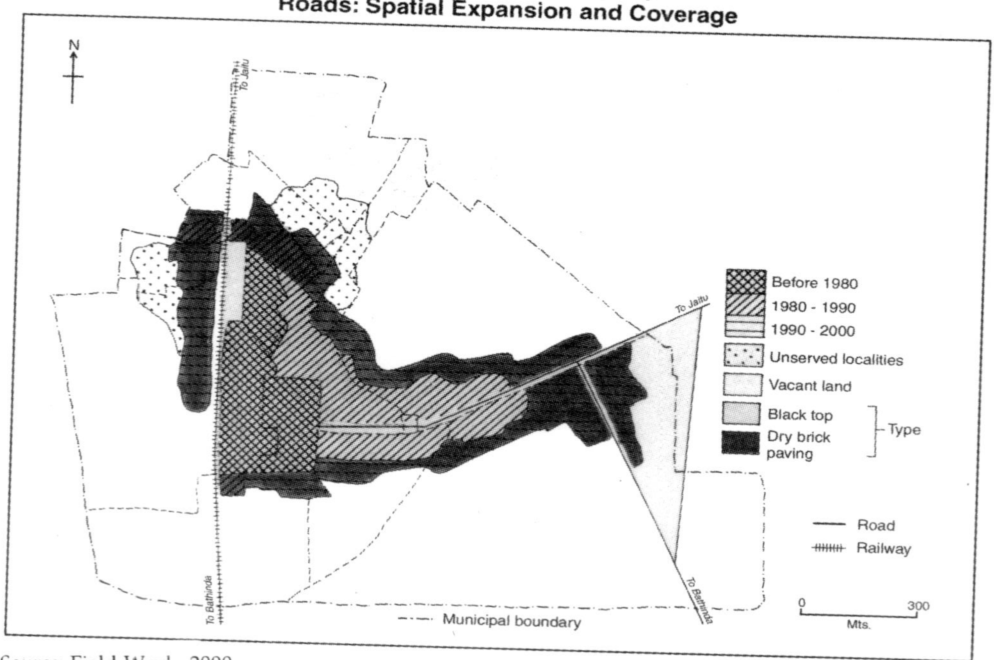

Source: Field Work, 2000.

Map 5.6

Bhucho Mandi Municipality

Roads: Spatial Expansion and Coverage

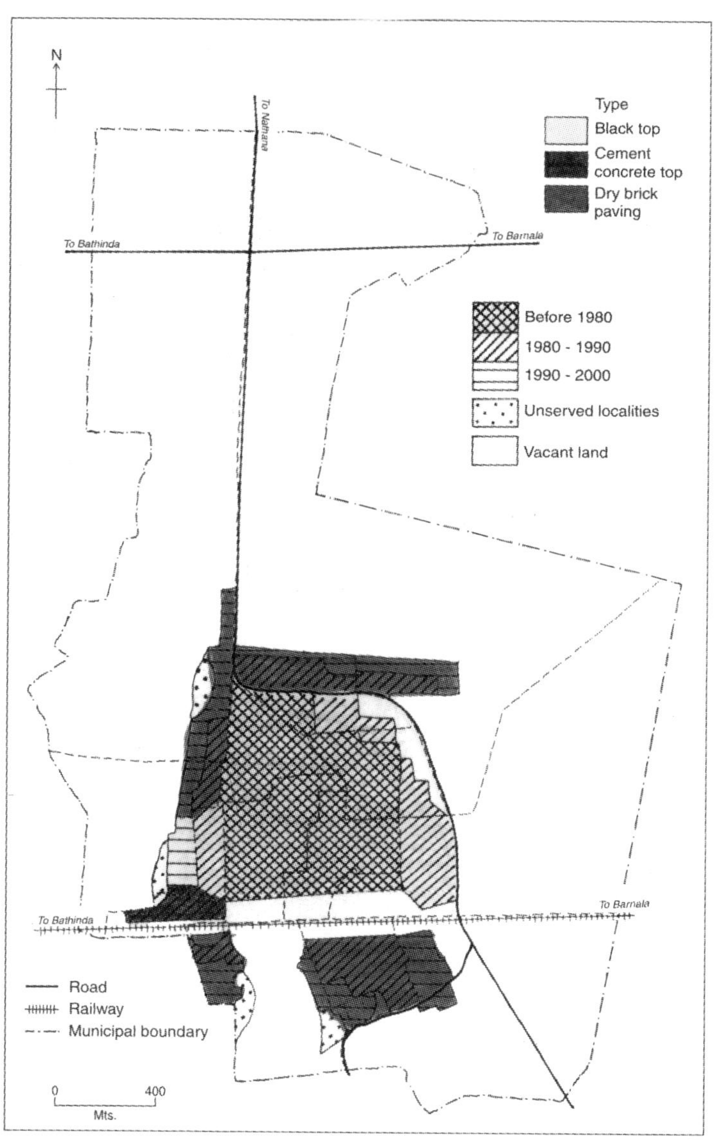

Source: Field Work, 2000.

Map 5.7

Kot Fatta Municipality

Roads: Spatial Expansion and Coverage

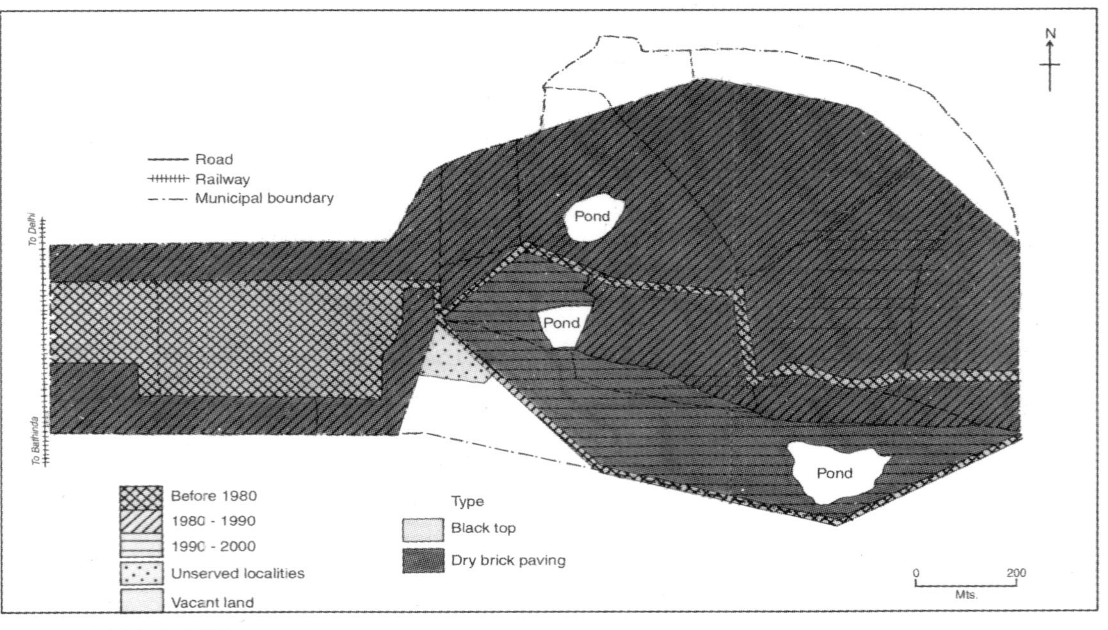

Source: Field Work, 2000.

Map 5.8

Sangat Mandi Municipality

Roads: Spatial Expansion and Coverage

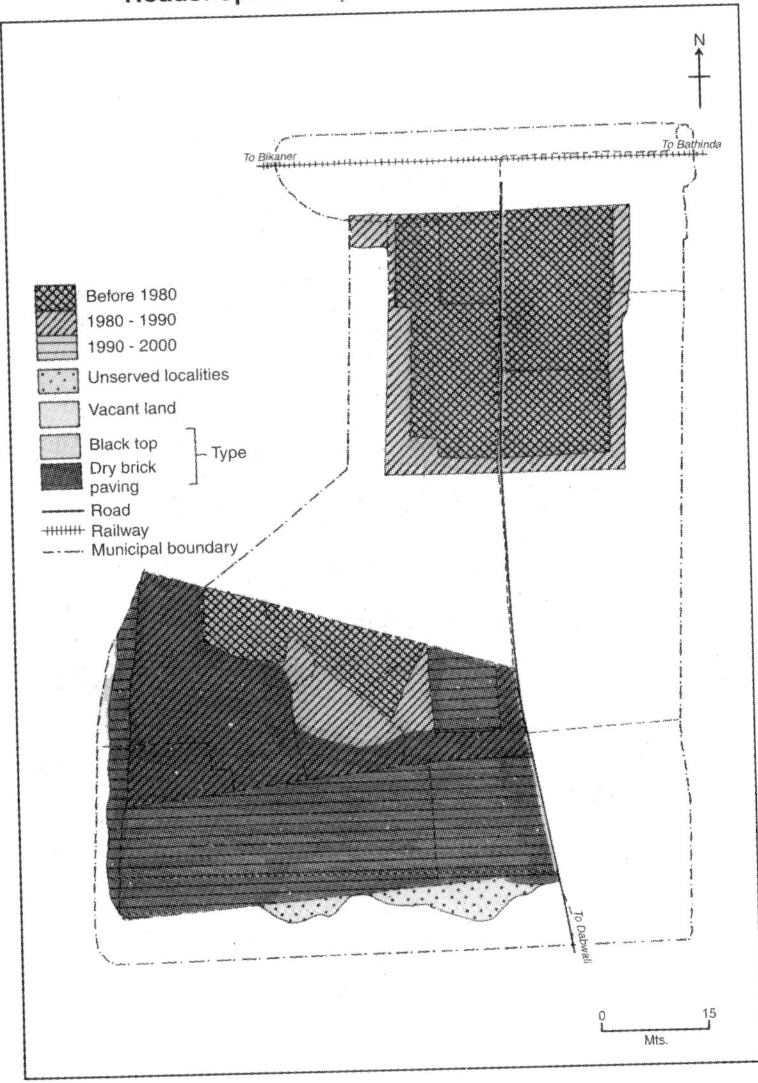

Source: Field Work, 2000.

by municipal roads even before 1980. It is only a few localities in peripheral areas where municipal roads are not in existence, otherwise the entire settled part has good quality roads (Map 5.6).

Sangat Mandi town, the smallest urban centre in the district, had one-third of its settled areas connected under the municipal roads before 1980. Another one-third area was provided municipal roads between 1980-90. By 2000, more than 97 per cent of the area and population was covered under the municipal roads. Only a small patch, located on the southern margin of localities falling West of Dabwali road, is without municipal roads. Most municipal roads are, however, of poor quality. The length of good quality metalled road is very limited and that too is confined to northern parts of the town (Map 5.8).

In brief, municipal roads in Bathinda district have been developed in a phased manner. Coverage under municipal roads before 1980 varied from a high of 46 per cent area in Bathinda town to a low of 31 per cent of Rampura Phul. Expansion in road coverage took place in different phases in different towns of the district. While in Sangat Mandi town, construction of municipal roads was almost equally spread over three phases (before 1980, 1980-90 and 1991-2000), in Bathinda and Rampura Phul towns, major expansion in roads network took place during 1991-2000. No town in the district can, however, boast of total coverage under the municipal roads, yet the coverage was higher in small towns rather than the large towns. However, the quality of roads in small towns was not that good. Majority of road length in Sangat Mandi town, the small urban centre in the district, was unmettaled. There were wide intra-town variations in terms of availability of municipal roads and peripheral areas in all towns were still without the facility of municipal roads. In Bathinda town, the largest town in the district, areas falling West of the railway line have quite low coverage in comparison to localities falling East of the railway line. The same was true of other towns also.

Subsidy: Pattern and Change

Against the annual average share of 13 per cent for all the municipalities during 1980-98, the proportion of share in expenditure on roads varied from a high of about 15 per cent in 1996-97 a low of about 13 per cent in 1992-93. Obviously, there were not wide temporal variations in proportional share of municipal expenditure on roads in the district. However, in absolute terms, the amount of expenditure has grown by about 500 per cent between 1982-83 and 1996-97: from about Rs. 40 lakh in 1982-83 to Rs. 236 lakh in 1996-97. The highest jump took place between 1992-93 and 1996-97 when the total amount rose to about Rs. 236 lakh in 1996-97 from Rs. 135 lakh in 1992-93, registering an increase of above 75 per cent. Obviously, expenditure on construction and maintenance of municipal roads has increased rapidly in recent years. Three main factors are responsible for this:

- — rise in cost of construction and maintenance of roads,
- — increased inflation rate, and
- — expansion of roads network in towns.

There are wide inter-municipalities variations in proportional share of subsidy on roads. In 1996-97, it ranged from a high of about 21 per cent in Bhucho Mandi town, a Class IV category town, to a low of 3 per cent in Sangat Mandi, a Class VI category town[9] in the district. The average share for all the municipalities was about 15 per cent. Bathinda, the Class I and largest town had a share of about 16 per cent which was the second highest share after Bhucho Mandi.

In 1982-83 when average share of municipal expenditure on roads in the district was 13 per cent, inter-municipal variations ranged from a high of about 21 per cent in Bhucho Mandi municipality to a low of 11 per cent in Bathinda city (Table 5.1) giving a ratio of about 1:2 between the highest and the lowest shares. Sangat Mandi, a Class VI town and the smallest in the district, did not spend a single penny on this account during this period. It is interesting to note that Bathinda, the largest town in the district, spent a small share (11 per cent) on roads, yet its share was more than 57 per cent of total municipal expenditure on roads in the district, in absolute terms.

9. Two of the eight municipalities in the district, in the year 2000 were not regularly incurring expenditure on construction and maintenance of roads. These include Kot Fatta and Sangat Mandi municipalities.

Coming to 1987-88, when average annual expenditure share for all the municipalities came down to 12 per cent, it varied from a low of 5 per cent in Kot Fatta, a Class V town, to a high of about 17 per cent in Maur Mandi, a Class III town. Sangat Mandi, which did not spend a single penny during 1982-83, incurred a share of about 14 per cent in 1987-88. Bhucho Mandi town, which had the highest share earlier in 1982-83, ranked third in 1987-88. Bathinda town, whose proportional share increased only by about one per cent in comparison to 1982-83, recorded about 72 per cent in total municipal expenditure on roads in the district in 1987-88.

In 1992-93, when the average annual share of municipal expenditure on roads rose to about 13 per cent from 12 per cent in 1987-88, it ranged from a low of less than 7 per cent in Maur Mandi town to a high of about 21 per cent in Bhucho Mandi town. It is interesting to note that towns which incurred low proportional share of their total expenditures on roads earlier in 1987-88 registered high increase in their shares between 1987-88 and 1992-93 and *vice versa*. Bhucho Mandi and Raman Mandi towns represent the typical cases of this kind. Bhucho Mandi, whose share of expenditure made up 9.34 per cent in 1987-88, had gone up to 20.91 per cent in 1992-93. Against this, the proportional share of Raman Mandi town dropped to 6.62 per cent in 1992-93 from 16.07 per cent in 1987-88.

Another notable feature of municipal expenditure on construction and maintenance of roads has been the significant increase in absolute amount of expenditure on roads on the one hand, and further rise in share of Bathinda municipal town in total amount of municipal expenditure on roads in the district, on the other. Absolute expenditure increased by more than 74 per cent, from Rs. 77.30 lakh to Rs. 134.92 lakh, on average annual basis. This shows that maintenance of roads was paid due attention between 1987-88 and 1992-93. The share of Bathinda municipal town, which was about 72 per cent in 1987-88 rose to about 73 per cent in 1992-93. Against this, Bathinda town's share was 60 per cent of the total urban population in the district. Following the same path, the share of Bhucho Mandi town rose to about 7 per cent from about 5 per cent during the same period. In combination, their share made up about 80 per cent of total municipal expenditure on roads in the district in 1992-93. Bathinda town maintains a large network of municipal roads including the Mall Road, overlaid with cement concrete. This road has a dual carriage way with a well maintained central grass verge. Bhucho Mandi town has well maintained roads.

There has been a further increase in share of municipal expenditure on roads in the district. It rose to about 15 per cent in 1996-97 from about 13 per cent in 1992-93. Among these eight municipalities, three recorded an increase, four a decrease and the remaining one (Kot Fatta town) did not spend a single penny on this account. Bathinda town recorded the highest increase in its share, while Rampura Phul registered the highest decrease. It is to be noted here that two of the largest municipal towns in the district have registered opposite tendencies.

In absolute terms, municipal expenditure on roads in the district grew by 75 per cent: from Rs. 134.92 lakh in 1992-93 to Rs. 235.89 lakh, annually. It shows that the increase in expenditure on roads has maintained its previous trend. However, Bathinda town further consolidated its position by sharing about 78 per cent of the total municipal expenditure on roads in the district. Earlier in 1992-93, its share in total municipal expenditure was 73 per cent. In absolute terms, its expenditure grew by 86 per cent against a general growth of 75 per cent for all the municipalities in the district. Bhucho Mandi is another town which registered increase not only in its share of total municipal expenditure on roads from 7 per cent in 1992-93 to 8 per cent in 1996-97, but also shared more than 85 per cent of total such expenditure in the district in 1996-97. Earlier in 1992-93 they shared, in combination, 80 per cent of total such expenditure in the district. Against this, their combined shares in total urban population and area in the district in 1991 made 64 per cent and 72 per cent, respectively. Both these towns have constructed and maintain not only a relatively large network of roads but also keep them in good condition.

On the whole, Bathinda town has the dominant share in total municipal expenditure on roads in the district. Its share in total municipal subsidy on roads has never been below 57 per cent and it was as high as 78 per cent in 1996-97 (Table 5.1). During 1980-98, its average share was about 73 per cent of total municipal expenditure in the district. Rampura Phul, the second largest municipal town in the district, ranked next to Bathinda with more than 8.0 per cent. Among the eight towns Bathinda town enjoys the status of district headquarters and Rampura Phul of sub-divisional headquarters.

Bhucho Mandi, a Class IV town in the district and ranking at sixth place in population size, was placed third with about 7 per cent of total municipal expenditure on roads during the same period. As far as the share of expenditure on road in total municipal expenditure of individual towns is considered, Bhucho Mandi recorded the highest share of about 18 per cent during 1980-98. Even Bathinda town was placed far behind Bhucho Mandi with about 14 per cent share. In contrast, Sangat Mandi and Kot Fatta, two of the smallest towns in the district, were not only irregular in spending on construction and maintenance of roads but also incurred only a marginal share of less than one per cent of total municipal expenditure on roads in the district. In this way, despite Bhucho Mandi town being an exception, administrative and civic status of a town in the district found a positive association with expenditure on roads.

The change in proportional share of subsidy on municipal roads has been both negative and positive. While the change in proportional share has been positive all through 1980-98 in the case of Bathinda town, the reverse was true of Goniana Mandi. Among the remaining municipalities, none recorded an increase or decrease in two consecutive sub-periods during 1980-98 (Table 5.3). It reveals that there is no consistency in municipal expenditure on roads in the district. Secondly, it seems that expenditure on municipal roads is loosing its importance in overall context of municipal expenditures in the district. This is well reflected in worsening conditions of municipal roads in almost all towns in the district.

Per Capita Subsidy

During 1980-98, municipalities in Bathinda district incurred a per capita amount of Rs. 53, on average annual basis, on construction and maintenance of roads. Since municipalities earn no income from this service, the entire amount turns into subsidy. In other words, Rs. 53 has been provided as subsidy for provision of roads by municipalities in Bathinda district, on an annual average basis.

TABLE 5.3
Bathinda District: Change in Expenditure/Subsidy on Roads by Municipalities, 1980-98

(*Figures in percentage*)

Name of town	*Civic status*	*1982-83* over 1987-88**	*1987-88* over 1992-93**	*1992-93* over 1996-97**
Bathinda	I	1.07	0.89	3.09
Rampura Phul	III	–10.03	6.51	–3.38
Maur Mandi	III	–2.63	–9.26	0.19
Raman Mandi	IV	1.15	–9.45	2.24
Goniana Mandi	IV	–4.66	–2.12	–2.73
Bhucho Mandi	IV	–11.17	11.57	–0.63
Kot Fatta	V	–13.07	2.15	**
Sangat Mandi	VI	**	–0.44	–10.35

*Annual averages.
**Calculation of change in expenditure share could not be possible, since municipalities were not regularly spending on construction and maintenance of roads.
Source: Data calculated from Classified Abstracts of different municipalities for various years.

There were, however, wide inter-municipal variations in this regard. It varied from a low of Rs. 5 in Kot Fatta to a high of Rs. 97 in Bhucho Mandi town. Kot Fatta has not been regular in spending on the provision of roads, while Bhucho Mandi has not only been regular in spending that also has been at the top, except during 1987-88, in terms of per capita spending on the provision of roads during 1980-98 (Table 5.4). Bhucho Mandi was followed by Bathinda, the largest town in the district, spent only Rs. 69 on this count. On the whole it was not the civic or administrative prowess but the capacity to generate financial resources and then to make expenditure on the provision of roads that has played the most important role in inter-municipal disparities in per capita municipal subsidy on the provision of roads in the district.

Per capita expenditure on roads rose by more than five times during 1980-98: from Rs. 20 in 1982-83 to Rs. 117 in 1996-97 (Fig. 5.1). During this period, the highest growth took place between 1982-83 and 1987-88 when it increased by 90 per cent. It grew by more than 77 per cent from 1992-93 to 1996-97 and by 74 per cent between 1987-88 and 1992-93.

There have been wide inter-municipal differentials in growth of per capita expenditure/subsidy on the provision of roads.

TABLE 5.4

Bathinda District: Per Capita Expenditure/Subsidy on Municipal Roads, 1980-98

Name of town	Civic status	1982-83*		1987-88*		1992-93*		1996-97*		1980-98*	
		Expenditure on roads (Rs. in lakhs)	Expenditure per capita (in Rs.)	Expenditure on roads (Rs. in lakhs)	Expenditure per capita (in Rs.)	Expenditure on roads (Rs. in lakhs)	Expenditure per capita (in Rs.)	Expenditure on roads (Rs. in lakhs)	Expenditure per capita (in Rs.)	Expenditure on roads (Rs. in lakhs)	Expenditure per capita (in Rs.)
Bathinda	I	22.91	20	55.38	48	98.30	85	182.95	157	79.54	69
Rampura Phul	III	5.80	18	3.74	12	13.89	44	16.03	50	9.18	29
Maur Mandi	III	2.81	15	5.28	28	3.84	20	5.81	31	4.28	23
Raman Mandi	IV	1.82	13	4.58	32	3.53	25	7.57	53	4.02	28
Goniana Mandi	IV	2.65	31	3.98	46	4.87	57	4.90	57	4.01	47
Bhucho Mandi	IV	3.70	47	3.70	47	8.88	114	18.28	234	7.57	97
Kot Fatta	V	0.20	4	0.24	5	0.41	8	—	—	0.24	5
Sangat Mandi	VI	Nil	Nil	0.4	14	1.20	42	0.35	12	0.50	17
All Towns		39.89	20	77.30	38	134.92	66	235.89	117	109.34	53
C.V.		1.26	0.61	1.80	0.56	1.84	0.67	1.82	0.88	1.83	0.72

*Annual averages.

Notes: (i) Since no income is earned by municipalities on account of this service, hence expenditure and subsidy is one and the same thing.

(ii) Per capita expenditure has been calculated on the basis of 1981 Census data. In case of Bathinda population figures for calculating subsidies confined to areas falling under the Bathinda M.C. jurisdiction. Two public sector units, Fertilizer and Thermal Plant make their own arrangements and have been excluded from the calculations/computations.

(iii) C.V. stands for Coefficient of Variability.

Source: Data calculated from *Classified Abstracts* of different municipalities for various years.

Fig. 5.1

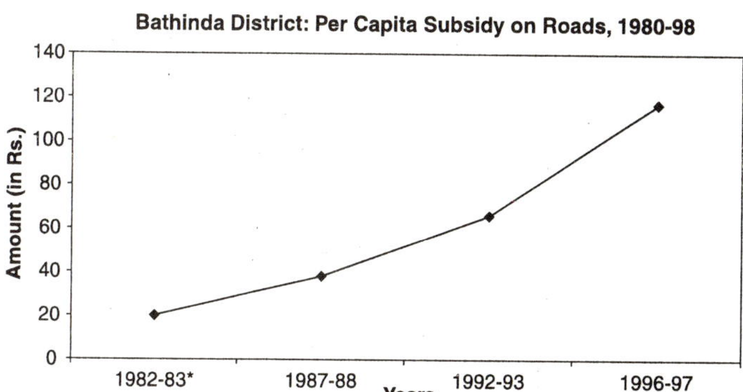

*Annual averages, calculated at the mid-year. For example, subsidy among from 1980 to 1985 has been used to calculate per capita subsidy in 1982-83 and so on.

Between 1982-83 and 1987-88, when average increase was 90 per cent, it ranged from a high of 146 per cent in Raman Mandi, a Class IV town, to a low of 25 per cent in Kot Fatta, a Class V town in the district. There was no change in Bhucho Mandi while Sangat Mandi town did not spend on the provision of roads in 1982-83. Bathinda, the largest town in the district, registered the second highest increase of 140 per cent followed by 86 per cent in Maur Mandi. It is intriguing to note that Rampura Phul, the second largest town in the district, registered a decrease of 33 per cent. In fact, there has been an absolute decline of Rs. 2.06 lakh.

Between 1987-88 and 1992-93, when average per capita expenditure on the provision of roads increased by 74 per cent, it showed a high of 266 per cent in Rampura Phul while Raman Mandi town recorded a marked deceleration in growth of per capita expenditure on the provision of roads.

It is interesting to note that Rampura Phul, which recorded the deceleration of 33 per cent between 1982-83 and 1987-88 registered the highest increase of 266 per cent during this period and Raman Mandi, recording highest increase during the pervious period, registered the second highest deceleration (–22 per cent) after Maur Mandi (–29 per cent) during this period. Bhucho Mandi makes another interesting case. It recorded not only the third highest increase after Rampura Phul and Sangat Mandi towns in its per capita expenditure on the provision of roads but also has the highest per capita expenditure on this provision in 1992-93. Sangat Mandi had a relatively low per capita expenditure on the provision of roads yet it recorded the second highest increase of 200 per cent during 1987-88–1992-93.

Between 1992-93 and 1996-97, when average growth in per capita expenditure on provision of roads was 77 per cent, it presented a contrast in Raman Mandi, a Class IV town, which recorded the highest decrease of 112 per cent in its per capita expenditure on the provision of roads during this period. It had experienced deceleration in growth earlier also during 1987-88–1992-93. Against this, Goniana Mandi, another Class IV town in the district, recorded no change in its per capita expenditure, while earlier it had recorded 24 per cent increase. Bhucho Mandi, yet another Class IV town, consistently following its earlier track record, had not only the highest per capita expenditure (Rs. 234) on the provision of roads but also registered the second highest growth (105 per cent) recorded by spending about 106 per cent of its expenditure on the provision of roads.

There were wide temporal variations with regard to inter-municipal differentials in per capita expenditure on the provision of roads. In 1982-83, it ranged from a high of Rs. 47 in Bhucho Mandi to a low of Rs. 4 in Kot Fatta (Fig. 5.2). Two municipal towns, Bhucho Mandi and Goniana Mandi, having this amount higher than the average (Rs. 20) on the other hand Rampura Phul, Maur Mandi and Raman Mandi were below average, while Bathinda stood equal to average. Sangat Mandi did not spend a single penny on this account. The C.V. index being 0.61, there were wide inter-municipal inequalities in this regard.

In 1987-88, average being Rs. 38, it ranged from Rs. 48 in Bathinda town to a low of Rs. 5 in Kot Fatta. Goniana Mandi and Bhucho Mandi towns alongwith Bathinda had this amount higher than the average, while remaining five ranked below this. On the whole, Class IV municipal towns, as a group, incurred the highest per capita expenditure on this account. Nevertheless, it may be derived that the civic status of a town finds positive association with its per capita expenditure amount on the provision of roads. Notably, inter-municipal inequalities in this regard declined the 1987-88, as C.V. index came down marginally to 0.56 from 0.61 in 1982-83.

Coming to 1992-93, when per capita municipal expenditure on this count ranged from a high of Rs. 114 in Bhucho Mandi to a

Fig. 5.2

Bathinda District: Trends in Per Capita Subsidy on Roads

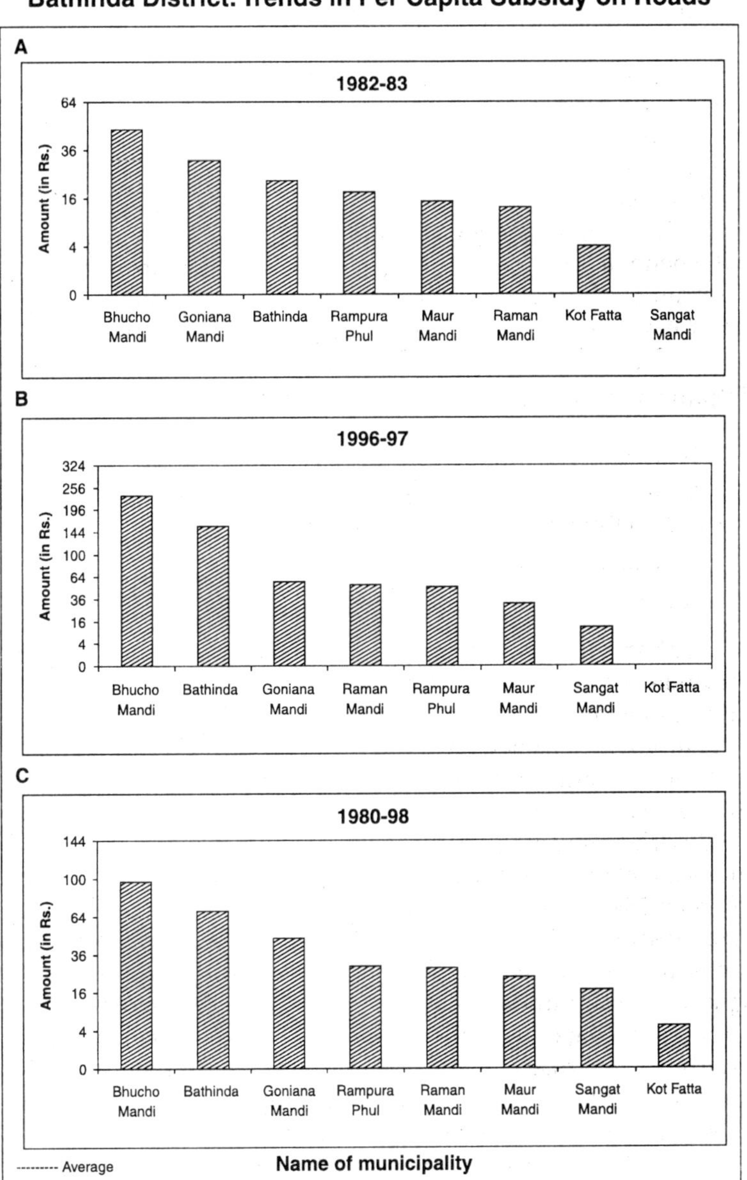

Note: In 1982-83 and 1996-97 road service was not available in Sangat Mandi and Kot Fatta towns respectively.

low of Rs. 8 in Kot Fatta, inter-municipal inequalities enlarged in this regard. C.V. index moved to 0.67 from 0.56 in 1987-88. Two municipal towns, Bhucho Mandi and Bathinda, had this amount higher than the average (Rs. 66) and the remaining six towns ranked below this.

Inter-municipal inequalities further enlarged in 1996-97, when it ranged from a high of Rs. 234 in Bhucho Mandi to a low of only Rs. 12 in Sangat Mandi. Bathinda, a Class I town, along with Bhucho Mandi town, had this amount higher than the average (Rs. 117) for all the municipalities. Kot Fatta, a Class V town, did not spend a single penny on this account. Inter-municipal inequalities widened to the highest level, as C.V. index of 0.88 was the highest of all the sub-periods during 1980-98 (see Fig. 5.3)

Spatial Discrimination

There has been a marked spatial discrimination in the provision of municipal roads in all the towns of Bathinda district. The discrimination is reflected at two levels:

— availability of roads; and
— quality and maintenance of roads.

Neither the availability of roads has been a universal phenomenon, nor the quality and maintenance of roads was uniform in all parts of the eight towns in the district.

Four towns, namely, Bathinda, Rampura Phul, Bhucho Mandi and Sangat Mandi, representative of all Class categories of towns in the district, which have been studied in details through fieldwork, revealed interesting facts and figures. Bathinda municipal town, the largest in the district, maintains a road length of about 254 kms. This spreads over an area of 110 km^2 giving a road density of 2.31 kms per km^2. It serves a population of 137 thousand as per 1991 Census figures. Accordingly, nearly 156 square kms. or more than 8 per cent of area and more than 7100 population, making about 5 per cent of the total, were still unserved by roads (Table 5.5). Locationally, all the unserved localities were in the newly developed peripheral areas (Map 5.1). Such areas were mostly inhabited by low socio-economic status groups. Literacy rates were also low (less than 40 per cent) in such areas.

Fig. 5.3

Bathinda District: Inter-municipal Disparities in Per Capita Subsidy on Roads

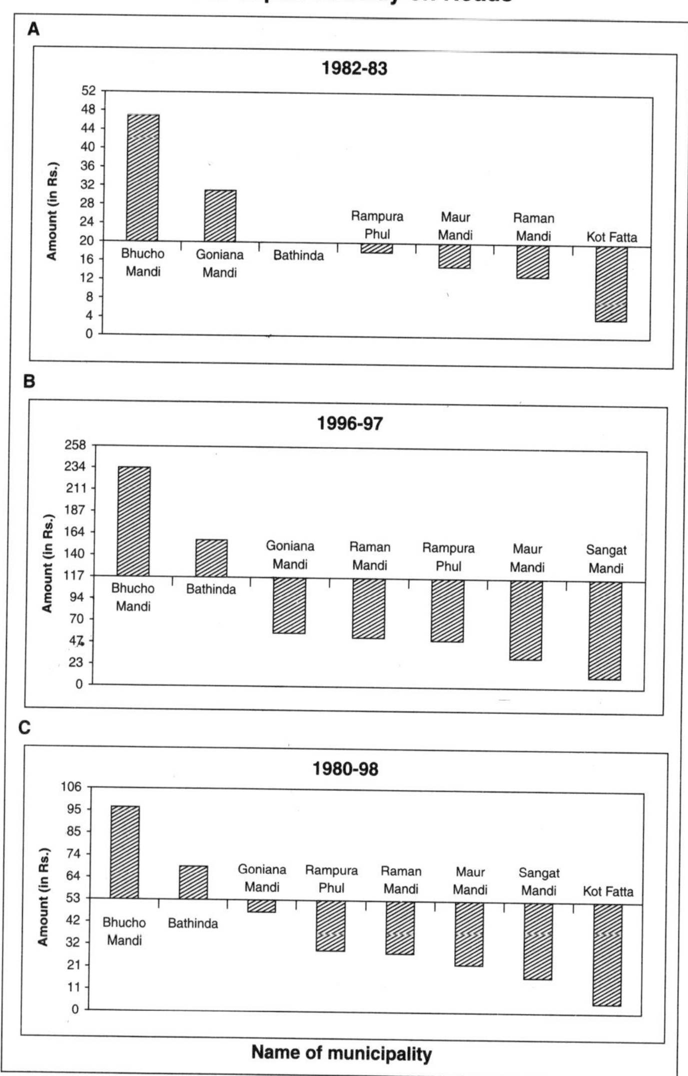

Note: In Sangat Mandi and Fatta towns, no expenditure was incurred on roads in 1982-83 and 1996-97, respectively.

According to the surface material used in construction, the roads in Bathinda town can be divided in three classes: black top, cement concrete, and unsurfaced. In the beginning, black top roads were laid in the Dhobi Bazar, Hospital Bazar, Sirki Bazar and Bank Bazar localities. Other parts of the city did not have metalled roads at the time. All such areas were markedly areas in central parts of the town. The Mall Road, which is the main road in the heart of city was completed in 1971-72. It joins the old bus stand with the railway station. This road has a dual carriage way with a well maintained central grass verge. Now it is being overlaid with cement concrete.

The main town, falling East of the railway line, was largely connected by roads before 1980. There has been, however, a small part of the habitation falling West of the railway line. It was during 1980-90 that most of the expansion in the roads network took place in localities falling west of the railway line. Even today, the quality and maintenance of roads has been far ahead in the civil lines, officers colony and other high income localities, all falling East of the railway line. In contrast roads in the middle income localities, mostly falling in wards from 29 to 35, were indifferently tracked. Once broken, these are repaired only after persistent complaints. Mostly the roads in such localities were of the unsurfaced type. The slum localities, often on the periphery of the city, were the hardest hit both in availability and maintenance of roads.

Rampura Phul, a Class III town and the second largest in the district, had more than 95 per cent of its area and population both served by roads in 2000 (Table 5.2). By 2002, total road length had reached to about 58 kms, spreading over 18 km^2 of areas (Table 5.5). This comes to a road density of 3.22 kms per km^2. In terms of total area coverage it was higher in Rampura Phul in comparison to Bathinda city. However, more than 5 per cent of the area and population of Rampura Phul were still without the facility of roads. All such areas were located on the periphery of Rampura Mandi town. It is quite interesting to note that all the unserved areas fall in Rampura township which is otherwise better served by well maintained roads in comparison to the Phul township (Map 5.2). In this twin town of Rampura Phul, most of the commercial activities are confined to Rampura township and Phul is more or a less an overgrown village.

Surprisingly sub-divisional and block headquarters are located in Phul township. More than two-thirds of the total road length, available in Rampura Phul town before 1980, was in Rampura. In this twin town, most of the road length having black top falls in Rampura, whereas un-surfaced roads dominate Phul township. Within the township, better quality and well maintained roads are in wards which have sub-divisional offices and the market mandi. Against this, the peripherally located wards, especially 4, 5, 10 and 13 suffered greatly both in terms of availability as well as maintenance of roads. In comparative terms, Rampura township was better placed both in terms of availability and maintenance of roads as compared to Phul township. During the fieldwork, residents of Phul township complained that, if broken, roads in their localities are repaired only after persistent complaints which would take a couple of months at the least.

TABLE 5.5

Bathinda District: Road Density of Four Municipalities, 2002

Name of town	*Civic status*	*Municipal area in km²*	*Length of roads in kms.*	*Density of roads in per km²*
Bathinda	I	110	253.70	2.31
Rampura Phul	III	18	57.90	3.22
Bhucho Mandi	IV	2.20	16.49	7.50
Sangat Mandi	VI	1.28	6.80	5.30

Source: Data calculated from roads register of different municipalities.

Bhucho Mandi, a Class IV town, where about 97 per cent of the area and 95 per cent of the population are served by municipal roads, has the least spatial discrimination in this regard (Table 5.2). It is a compact settlement, located at right angles made due to the crossing of railway line and a road on the South side of territorial extent of the municipal limit (Map 5.6). In 2002, it had a road length of 16.5 kms, spreading over 2.2 km^2 of area. This gives a road density of 7.5 kms per km^2, which is the highest average for any of the four towns taken for detailed analysis. Nearly half the area and more than two-fifths of the population were served by roads before 1980. Areas which were covered before 1980 have high socio-economic status. Against this, areas covered in later phases have low to medium income status. However, there has been little discrimination in quality and maintenance of roads. As already examined, per capita expenditure on construction and maintenance of roads in Bhucho Mandi has been the highest of all the towns in the district. One can, thus, infer that the spatial discrimination in provision of municipal services gets minimized in the case of small towns but per head cost of services goes up in comparison to big towns.

In Sangat Mandi, a Class VI town, more than 97 per cent of area and population were served by roads (Table 5.2). In other words, only a small segment of population and area, in newly developed localities, were unserved by roads (Map 5.8). In 2002, it had a road length of 6.8 kms over an area of 1.28 km^2, giving road density of 5.3 kms per km^2. This is the second highest average. It has been observed during the fieldwork that the quality and maintenance of roads was not very good but there was little spatial discrimination in this regard. As already stated, not only the per capita expenditure on roads was low but also municipality was not regular in spending on this count. Since no income was directly accruing to the municipalities against the construction and maintenance of roads, small-sized municipal towns, found it quite difficult to spend regularly from their limited resources.

Briefly, there is a distinct difference in the maintenance and construction of roads between the high and low income localities in all the towns of the district. Low income localities along with slum bastis, having peripheral locations, suffered the most in the process. There is glaring spatial discrimination in this regard. However, spatial discrimination was less sharp in case of small towns as compared to big towns. The discrimination was the sharpest in case of Bathinda city and the least in Sangat Mandi town.

Secondly, construction and maintenance of roads is a costly affair for any Municipal Committee. It does not yield any income and is subsidized entirely. (Some income could be earned by all towns in the district by allowing advertisement boards/holdings along the main roads).

Main Highlights

The following conclusions emerge strongly from the foregoing discussions:

- The road network, which facilitates the circulation within the city and links different functional zones for efficient working of towns as a system, has been one of the important municipal functions in Bathinda district and other towns of Punjab.

- Municipalities in Bathinda district incurred an amount of Rs. 197 million on construction and maintenance of municipal roads during 1980-98, giving an average amount of Rs. 109 lakh per annum by all the municipalities in the district. In proportional terms, it made 13 per cent of total municipal expenditure in the district during 1980-98.
- The municipalities did not earn a single penny on the provision of road construction and maintenance under their jurisdictions. Hence, the entire municipal expenditure on this account ultimately turns into the subsidy component. In this way, municipalities in Bathinda district provide 13 per cent of their total expenditure as subsidy on municipal roads.
- There are, however, wide inter-municipal and temporal variations in distribution of subsidies on this count. Of the average amount of more than Rs. 109 lakh, per annum expenditure or subsidy on this count, Bathinda municipality shared nearly 73 per cent of total municipal expenditure in the district. Bathinda, along with Rampura Phul and Bhucho Mandi towns incurred 88 per cent of total such municipal expenditure in the district. Against this, remaining five municipal towns of Maur Mandi, Raman Mandi, Goniana Mandi, Sangat Mandi and Kot Fatta, in combination, shared only 12 per cent of total municipal expenditure on this service.
- Municipal expenditure/subsidy on the provision of roads as a share in their total expenditure has been changing over the period. However, the proportional share has been ranging between 12 and 15 per cent. 1996-97 being the peak year and 1987-88 as the sluggish year.
- In general, the change in the share of municipal expenditure on the provision of roads has been negative. Nevertheless, Bathinda and Goniana Mandi towns present a contrasting picture. The former recording increase and the latter registering decrease in its share during different sub-periods.

Of late, negative change in proportional share of subsidy for all the municipal towns in the district indicates the reduced priority accorded to construction and maintenance of roads in overall context of municipal expenditure.

- Per capita expenditure on roads presents an interesting picture. One of the Class IV category of towns, Bhucho Mandi, provided the highest per capita amount of Rs. 97 during 1980-98. Bathinda, the largest and only Class I town in the district, ranked distantly second to it with Rs. 69 per capita. On the other extreme, Kot Fatta provided only Rs. 5 per capita on this count. Trends in per capita expenditure indicate that it continued to grow over the period. The growth rate has been the highest between 1982-83 and 1987-88 and the lowest between 1987-88 and 1992-93. At the level of individual municipal towns the trend differed widely. It was only in the case of Bathinda municipal town where per capita amount of expenditure on the provision of road construction and maintenance has consistently been growing, though at different rates, but no consistent trend is observed in case of other towns. Kot Fatta and Sangat Mandi were, in fact, not consistent even in spending on this provision.
- There has been wide spatial discrimination in distribution of municipal expenditure/subsidy on the provision of road construction and maintenance within the different towns in the district. The localities which were peripherally located and or resided in by low income and social status castes suffered the most, both in terms of availability and quality of roads. While the roads in the inner parts of each town were not only black top roads but also maintained well, it was mostly the poorly maintained un-surfaced roads that were the lot of the peripheral and low socio-economic status and caste localities. This was, however, more a distinctive feature of large towns such as Bathinda. In small towns like Kot Fatta and Sangat Mandi, it was apparently not so.

STREET LIGHTING

Lighting public streets is one of the obligatory functions of the municipal bodies. Hence, all the municipal bodies in Bathinda district are expected to maintain the necessary street light system on all the streets within their territorial limits. Lighting poles are expected to be spaced at intervals of 30 metres or one hundred feet. Sodium vapour lamps, mercury vapour lamps, tube-lights and bulbs of different size and capacity are put in service by the municipal bodies for street lighting within their territorial jurisdictions.

Seven out of the eight municipal bodies in Bathinda district maintain the street lighting system. Kot Fatta, a Class V municipal town of the district, does not maintain a street light system.

Sodium vapour lamps, though costlier but energy saving, are now on the increase and ordinary bulbs are decreasing in all the towns in the district, as a source of lighting in public street ways. For example, the number of sodium vapour lamps (250 watt), which was only six in 1987-88 in Bathinda city increased to 49 by 1988-89. Against this, the number of bulbs (100 W) came down to 41 from 72 during the same time (Singh, 1990, p. 43).

During 1980-98, nearly Rs. 480 lakh or more than 3 per cent of total municipal expenditure on different urban services was spent on street lighting by the municipalities in Bathinda district. On annual average basis, it comes to Rs. 26.69 lakh for all the municipalities in the district (Table 5.6). It is, however, to be noted here that Kot Fatta municipality does not provide this facility to its residents. Municipalities do not get any income from street lighting. In other words, this service is entirely subsidized.

Municipal Expenditure on Street Lighting

There are wide inter-municipal differentials in expenditure on street lighting. A variety of factors including area size of a town, total road length in a town, installation of new points, income level of a municipality and civic and administrative status of a municipal town come into play while determining this expenditure. As expected, Bathinda municipality provided the dominant share of total municipal expenditure on this count. Its share made 65 per cent or about two-thirds in total municipal expenditure on street lighting in the district, annually. Against this, the share of Sangat Mandi comes to about one per cent, the lowest for any municipality in the district. Rampura Phul, the second largest municipal town in the district, spent about 12 per cent of the total expenditure, while Maur Mandi spent about 7 per cent.

TABLE 5.6

Bathinda District: Expenditure on Street Lighting as Percentage of Total Municipal Expenditure, 1980-98

(*Rs. in lakhs*)

Name of town	Civic status	1982-83*			1987-88*			1992-93*			1996-97*			1980-98*		
		Aggregate expenditure	Expenditure on street lighting	Percentage of aggregate expenditure	Aggregate expenditure	Expenditure on street lighting	Percentage of aggregate expenditure	Aggregate expenditure	Expenditure on street lighting	Percentage of aggregate expenditure	Aggregate expenditure	Expenditure on street lighting	Percentage of aggregate expenditure	Aggregate expenditure	Expenditure on street lighting	Percentage of aggregate expenditure
1	2	3	4	5	6	7	8	9	10	11	12	13	14	15	16	17
Bathinda	I	207.10	7.45	3.60	456.43	16.82	3.69	755.21	42.40	5.61	1135.78	56.25	4.95	583.39	17.29	2.96
Rampura Phul	III	34.62	1.28	3.70	55.62	2.20	3.96	104.96	4.53	4.32	162.77	5.89	3.62	81.35	3.21	3.95
Maur Mandi	III	14.61	0.58	3.97	31.80	1.50	4.72	52.30	2.14	4.09	77.11	3.74	4.85	40.30	1.80	4.47
Raman Mandi	IV	12.20	0.55	4.51	28.50	0.84	2.95	53.35	1.89	3.54	85.41	3.76	4.40	40.36	1.54	3.82
Goniana Mandi	IV	14.30	0.68	4.76	28.70	0.95	3.31	41.46	1.27	3.06	54.33	2.21	4.07	32.52	1.17	3.60
Bhucho Mandi	IV	18.04	0.57	3.16	39.60	0.68	1.72	42.47	2.43	5.72	90.16	2.78	3.08	42.84	1.50	3.50
Kot Fatta	V	1.10	Nil	Nil	4.70	Nil	Nil	5.65	Nil	Nil	7.68	-	-	4.46	Nil	Nil
Sangat Mandi	VI	1.60	0.12	7.5	2.90	0.16	5.52	8.99	0.26	2.89	11.63	0.20	1.72	5.69	0.18	3.16
Aggregate Expenditure		303.57	11.23	3.70	639.25	23.15	3.62	1064.39	54.92	5.16	1624.87	74.83	4.61	830.91	26.69	3.21
C.V.		1.70	1.50		1.76	1.68		1.78	1.80		1.75	1.75		1.76	1.46	

*Annual averages.

Notes: (i) Since no income is earned by municipalities on account of this service, hence expenditure and subsidy are considered one and the same thing.

(ii) C.V. stands for Coefficient of Variability.

Source: Data calculated from *Classified Abstracts* of different municipalities for various years.

In 1982-83, when total municipal expenditure on street lighting in the district was 11.23 lakh, Bathinda city shared Rs. 7.45 lakh or more than 66 per cent of the total expenditure. Rampura Phul, the second largest town in the district, shared more than 11 per cent. Third largest share of another 6 per cent was incurred by Goniana Mandi town. These three municipalities, in combination, shared more than four-fifths of the total municipal expenditure on street lighting in the district.

Coming to 1987-88, when municipal expenditure on street lighting rose to Rs. 23.15 lakh, Bathinda city shared about 73 per cent of such expenditure in the district. Earlier in 1982-83, Bathinda city shared only 66 per cent of total expenditure on street lighting in the district. In fact, during 1982-83 and 1987-88 Bathinda municipality installed new lighting points in a big way. As a result, its expenditure on street lighting registered a high increase. For example, its expenditure on installation of new points increased by more than double in one financial year. From Rs. 3.50 lakh in 1986-87 to Rs. 7.05 lakh in 1987-88 (Singh, 1990, p. 44). Rampura Phul, a Class III town and the second largest in the district, spent over 9 per cent. The third position again went to Goniana Mandi which spent 4 per cent of total of such expenditure in the district.

In 1992-93, when total municipal expenditure on street lighting in the district rose to Rs. 54.92 lakh, Bathinda city shared Rs. 42.40 lakh or more than 77 per cent in total expenditure. Earlier in 1987-88, Bathinda shared only 73 per cent of total expenditure on street lighting. It is notable that the expenditure share of Bathinda city on street lighting has been growing over the period. It is mainly because of continuous increase in new points, with expansion of city limits and emergence of new localities, replacement of ordinary bulbs with either tube lights or sodium vapour lamps and intensification of street lighting system to the extent of making it superior to the prescribed norms for the purpose. Following the earlier pattern, Rampura Phul was placed second with more than 8 per cent of the total expenditure on this service. However, this time the third rank went to Bhucho Mandi which spent more than 4 per cent of the total expenditure.

Goniana Mandi town, which had remained at the third position both in 1982-83 and 1987-88, has been relegated to sixth position among the seven municipal towns, providing this service. Only Sangat Mandi, a Class VI town, was behind Goniana Mandi. Inter-municipal disparities in expenditure on street lighting also increased, as revealed in the increased value of C.V. index to 1.80 in 1992-93 from 1.68 in 1987-88 (Table 5.6).

Coming to 1996-97, when the municipal expenditure on street lighting in the district rose to Rs. 74.83 lakh from Rs. 54.92 lakh in 1992-93, the expenditure share of Bathinda city moved down slightly to 75 per cent from 77 per cent in 1992-93. The proportional share of second ranking Rampura Phul also marginally declined to less than 8 per cent from more than 8 per cent earlier in 1992-93. Against this, the respective shares of Raman Mandi and Maur Mandi towns rose to five per cent from less than four per cent during the same period. Defying the trend, Sangat Mandi town recorded an absolute decline in expenditure share which came down to only Rs. 20 thousand in 1996-97 from Rs. 26 thousand earlier in 1992-93.

However, municipal expenditure on street lighting has been growing over the period. On an average annual basis, it has grown to Rs. 74.83 lakh in 1996-97 from only Rs. 11.23 lakh in 1982-83. It has, thus, grown by more than six times during this period. Among municipalities, the growth in municipal expenditure on street lighting ranged from a high of about seven times (655 per cent) in the case of Bathinda city to a low of less than one time (67 per cent) in Sangat Mandi town. The former is the largest and the latter, the smallest, town in the district. Maur Mandi and Raman Mandi towns, both Class III towns, recorded an increase of more than five times, Rampura Phul and Bhucho Mandi, Class III and Class IV towns, respectively, recorded an increase of more than three times while Goniana Mandi recorded more than two times.

During 1982-83–1987-88, when the municipal expenditure on street lighting increased by 106 per cent (from Rs. 11.23 lakh to Rs. 23.15 lakh), Maur Mandi town recorded the highest increase of 159 per cent and Bhucho Mandi the lowest of only 19 per cent in their respective shares. Second highest increase of 126 per cent was recorded in Bathinda city. Rampura Phul, the second largest town in the district, was placed third with 72 per cent increase in its expenditure on street lighting. Installation of new light points or replacement of the old ones and payment of electricity bills against street lighting were the major items of expenditure on street lighting.

The expenditure on street lighting grew by 137 per cent, from Rs. 23.15 lakh in 1987-88 to Rs. 54.92 lakh in 1992-93. Earlier, it increased by 106 per cent between 1982-83 and 1987-88. Among municipalities, growth of expenditure on street lighting during this period varied from a high of 257 per cent in Bhucho Mandi to a low of only 34 per cent in Goniana Mandi. Bathinda, the Class I town of the district, was placed next to Bhucho Mandi with 152 per cent increase, Raman Mandi, a Class IV town, was placed third after Bathinda with an increase of 125 per cent in its expenditure on street lighting.

Expenditure on street lighting rose to Rs. 74.83 lakh in 1996-97, registering an increase of only 36 per cent between 1992-93 and 1996-97. This has been the lowest growth in expenditure on street lighting during the entire period of study (1980-98), indicating a sharp decline in expenditure on street lighting in recent years. This is quite surprising and needs further explanation that such a sharp decline occurred soon after a peak increase in expenditure earlier during 1987-88–1992-93.

Bhucho Mandi town, which recorded the highest increase of 236 per cent in the preceding sub-period, registered the lowest increase of 14 per cent between 1992-93 and 1996-97. Bathinda, the largest municipal town in the district, saw an increase of only 25 per cent during this period. Raman Mandi, a Class IV town in the district, recorded the highest increase (99 per cent) this time. Against this, Sangat Mandi, a Class VI town and the smallest town in the district, saw a negative change (–23 per cent) in its expenditure on street lighting. Class I, Class V and VI towns, recorded low to negative increase in this regard. It was observed during the fieldwork that maintenance of street lighting network was not only poor in small towns but also peripheral areas suffered the most in all the towns. Even persistent complaints failed to make an impact on the employees of the electricity department. It was observed that greasing palms is quite an essential feature to get maintenance work done by employees of the electricity wing in the Municipal Committee offices in different towns of the district.

Per Capita Expenditure/Subsidy

In per capita terms an average annual amount of Rs. 13 was the expenditure made by municipalities in the district on street lighting during 1980-98 (Table 5.7). Since, municipalities provided this facility free of cost to their residents, the whole amount has been the subsidy on this count. There were, however, wide inter municipal disparities in this regard. It varied from a high of Rs. 19 in Bhucho Mandi to a low Rs. 6 in Sangat Mandi town. Rest of the municipalities fall between the two limits. It is to be noted that Kot Fatta municipality was not providing this service to its residents.

TABLE 5.7

Bathinda District: A Comparison of Subsidy on Street Lighting by Municipalities, 1980-98

Name of town	*Subsidy (Rs. in lakh)*	*Subsidy per capita (in Rs.)*
Bathinda	17.29* (64.78)	15*
Rampura Phul	3.21 (12.03)	10
Maur Mandi	1.80 (6.74)	10
Raman Mandi	1.54 (5.77)	11
Goniana Mandi	1.17 (4.38)	14
Bhucho Mandi	1.50 (5.62)	19
Kot Fatta	— —	— —
Sangat Mandi	0.18 (0.67)	6
All Towns	26.69 100.0	13

* Annual averages.

Notes: 1. Per capita subsidy has been calculated on the basis of 1981 Census data. In case of Bathinda population figures used for calculation of subsidy confined to areas falling under the jurisdiction of Bathinda Municipal committee. Two public sector units, Fertilizer and Thermal Plant make their own arrangement for provision of services, and have been excluded from the calculations.

2. Figures in parentheses indicate percentage share in total.

Source: Data calculated from *Classified Abstracts* of different municipalities for various years.

Per capita expenditure of municipalities has been growing over the period on street lighting. It increased to Rs. 37 per capita in 1996-97 from Rs. 6 in 1982-83, registering an increase of more than six times. Among municipalities, this increase has been ranging from a high of eight times in Bathinda city to a low of less than two times in Sangat Mandi town. The former is the largest and the latter the smallest town in the district. However, Class category of a town and its per capita expenditure on street lighting does not find a strong association. For example, Rampura Phul, a Class III town and the second largest in the district, registered an increase of four and half time. Against this Raman Mandi and Bhucho Mandi, both Class IV towns, registered an increase of six and half times and more than five times, respectively.

In 1982-83, when per capita expenditure for all the municipalities was Rs. 6, it ranged from a high of Rs. 8 in Goniana Mandi to a low of Rs. 3 in Maur Mandi town. Bathinda city incurred per capita expenditure of Rs. 6 which was the third highest after Goniana Mandi and Bhucho Mandi towns. Rampura Phul, the second largest town, incurred Rs. 4 on per capita basis. Notably, inter-municipal disparities, as revealed by C.V. value of 0.34, were relatively low in its period (Table 5.8).

Coming to 1987-88, when per capita municipal expenditure on this facility increased to Rs. 12 from Rs. 6 in 1982-83, it ranged from a high of Rs. 15 in Bathinda city to a low of Rs. 6 in Raman Mandi, a Class IV town, and Sangat Mandi, a Class VI town. Goniana Mandi town, which ranked first earlier in 1982-83, was relegated to second position by Bathinda city. Bathinda city acquired the topmost rank mainly because of high growth in its per capita expenditure on street lighting between 1982-83 and 1987-88. Its expenditure grew by one and a half times against average growth of one time for all the municipalities. Maur Mandi, a Class III town, recorded the highest growth of 167 per cent, but its per capita had been quite low both in 1982-83 and 1987-88 periods. Bhucho Mandi, a Class IV town ranked second in 1982-83 and registered an increase of 29 per cent in its expenditure on street lighting during 1982-83 and 1987-88. This made it slip down to third rank from the second in 1982-83. It seems that expenditure on street lighting was governed more by the income or grants available with different municipal towns rather than their civic status.

TABLE 5.8
Bathinda District: Trends in Per Capita Subsidy on Street Lighting by Municipalities, 1980-98

(*Figures in Rs.*)

Name of town	*Civic status*	*1982-83** *Expenditure per capita*	*1987-88** *Expenditure per capita*	*1992-93** *Expenditure per capita*	*1996-97** *Expenditure per capita*	*1980-98** *Expenditure per capita*
Bathinda	I	6	15	37	48	15
Rampura Phul	III	4	7	14	18	10
Maur Mandi	III	3	8	11	20	10
Raman Mandi	IV	4	6	13	26	11
Goniana Mandi	IV	8	11	15	26	14
Bhucho Mandi	IV	7	9	31	36	19
Kot Fatta	V	Nil	Nil	Nil	—	Nil
Sangat Mandi	VI	4	6	9	7	6
Aggregate expenditure		6	12	27	37	13
C.V.		0.34	0.34	0.54	0.47	0.23

*Annual averages.

Notes: (i) Since no income is earned by municipalities on account of this service, hence expenditure and subsidy is one and the same thing.

(ii) Per capita expenditure/subsidy has been calculated on the basis of 1981 Census data. In case of Bathinda population figures used for calculation of subsidies confined to areas falling under the jurisdiction of Bathinda M.C. Two public sector units Fertilizer and Thermal plant make their own arrangement for provision of services. Hence, excluded from the calculation. Further population figures for Kot Fatta municipal town have been excluded for calculation of per capita subsidy amount as this facility is not provided in this town.

(iii) C.V. stands for Coefficient of Variability.

Source: Data calculated from *Classified Abstracts* of different municipalities for various years.

In 1992-93, municipal expenditure on street lighting further increased to Rs. 27 per capita per annum. It recorded an increase of 125 per cent between 1987-88 and 1992-93. Earlier, this increase was of 100 per cent. Obviously, per capita expenditure on street lighting grew faster in this sub-period in comparison to the preceding one.

There have been wide inter-municipal disparities both in distribution of per capita expenditure on street lighting and its growth. In fact, inter-municipal disparities in this regard enlarged this time as compared to the preceding period. C.V. index value rose to 0.54 in 1992-93 from 0.34 in 1987-88. Per capita expenditure varied from a high of Rs. 37 in Bathinda city to a low of Rs. 9 in Sangat Mandi town. In general, Class IV towns in the district had this amount higher than the Class III towns. For example, Bhucho Mandi, a Class IV town, had this amount more than twice that of Rampura Phul, a Class III town. In fact, Bhucho Mandi was placed next only to Bathinda city, figuring at the top. In dominant majority of municipal towns, per capita expenditure on street lighting was much lower than the average for all the municipalities.

In terms of growth of expenditure on street lighting during 1987-88 and 1992-93, Bhucho Mandi was at the top with 244 per cent and Goniana Mandi at the bottom with only 36 per cent increase. Both are Class IV towns. It is to be noted that Bhucho Mandi town recorded the lowest growth in this regard during the preceding period. The case of Maur Mandi was just reverse of Bhucho Mandi. In case of other municipalities, growth rate has been almost of the same level as during the preceding period.

Coming to 1996-97, when per capita amount of municipal expenditure on street lighting had gone to the highest level of Rs. 37 per annum, its growth rate came down sharply to only 37 per cent. Against this, growth rate in this regard had been 125 per cent. Interestingly, with decline in growth rate of expenditure on street lighting inter-municipal disparities also narrowed down, as indicated by a decline in the value to C.V. index to 0.47 from 0.54 earlier in 1992-93. Now, per capita amount of expenditure on this facility ranged from a high of Rs. 48 in Bathinda city to a low of Rs. 7 in Sangat Mandi town. It is quite surprising to note that per capita expenditure in case of Sangat Mandi declined to Rs. 9 in 1992-93. It is just opposite to the general trend, where all other municipal towns registered an increase in per capita expenditure on this facility. The fact is that there has been an absolute decline, from Rs. 26 thousand in 1992-93 to Rs. 20 thousand in 1996-97, in expenditure of Sangat Mandi, which this municipality incurred on street lighting. Conforming to the earlier situation, Bhucho Mandi recorded the second highest per capita expenditure on this facility and Class IV towns, in general, had incurred higher per capita expenditure on this account in comparison to Class III towns in the district.

The growth of expenditure on street lighting varied from a high of 100 per cent in Raman Mandi to a low of 16 per cent in Bhucho Mandi, having the second highest per capita on street lighting. Bathinda city, ranking at the top in terms of per capita expenditure on this count, registered an increase of 30 per cent. However, high per capita expenditure on street lighting and its low growth rate did not find strong positive association with each other.

Spatial Discrimination

There has been wide inter-municipal differentials in availability and quality of street lighting in all the towns of the district. It was observed during the fieldwork that the quality of street lighting had not been the same in different localities of different towns (see Maps 5.9 to 5.15). These differentials were, however, a more marked feature of big towns than small towns. For instance, the higher income localities in Bathinda city, such as Civil Lines and Model Town, the important roads, such as the Mall, Hospital Road, Goniana Road and institutional areas are fitted with better quality of street lighting through sodium vapour lamps, mercury vapour lamps and double tubelights. Against this, the frequency of bulbs and tubelights is higher in the low income localities (Map 5.9). Further, the low income localities and peripheral areas are given step-motherly treatment in replacement of fused bulbs and tubelights. Even persistent complaints failed to yield results, as the employees of the electricity wing of the municipal administration do not much care for the complaints coming from politically and economically less powerful localities.

In small towns such as Sangat Mandi, though there are spatial discriminations they are less distinctive in comparison to Bathinda city. Firstly, the overall quality as well as maintenance of the street lighting was poor (Map 5.15). It is mainly because the per capita expenditure on this count is not only very low but also declining in recent years. The growth of per capita expenditure has been tardy over the period. Politically and administratively powerful people do not like to reside in such towns. Hence, if there is any spatial discrimination in availability and quality of street lighting it is mainly in favour of municipal wards where resided the President/Vice-President and few influential councillors of the Municipal Committee.

Map 5.9

Bathinda Municipality

Street Lighting: Spatial Expansion and Coverage

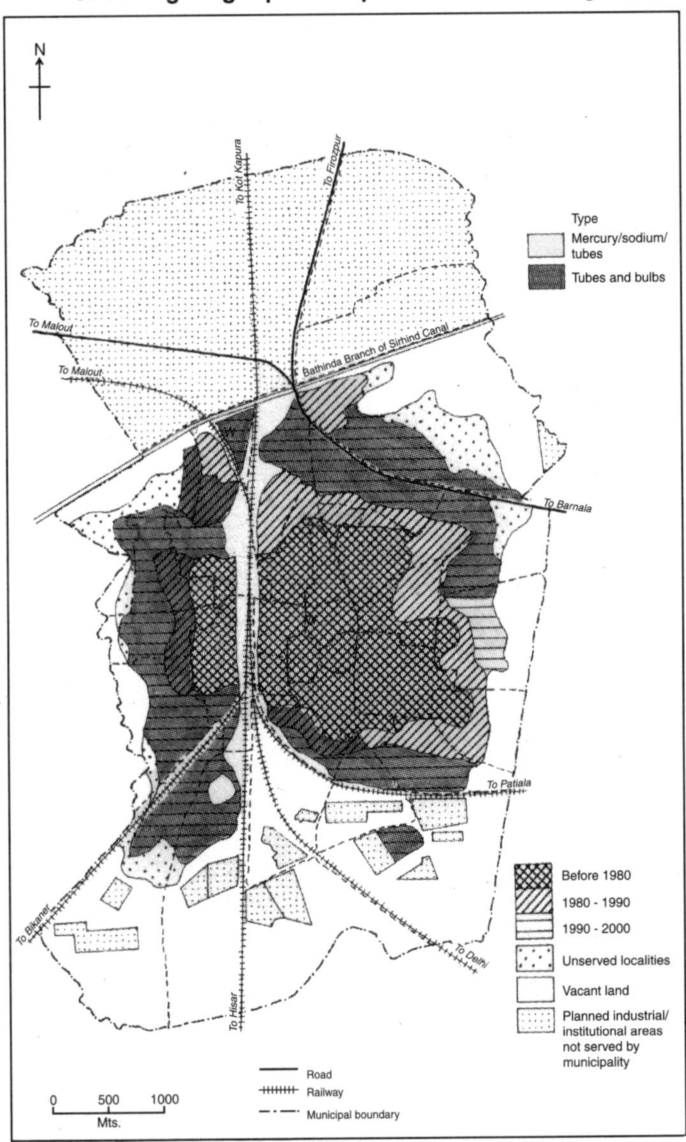

Source: Field Work, 2000.

Map 5.10

Rampura Phul Municipality

Street Lighting Spatial Expansion and Coverage

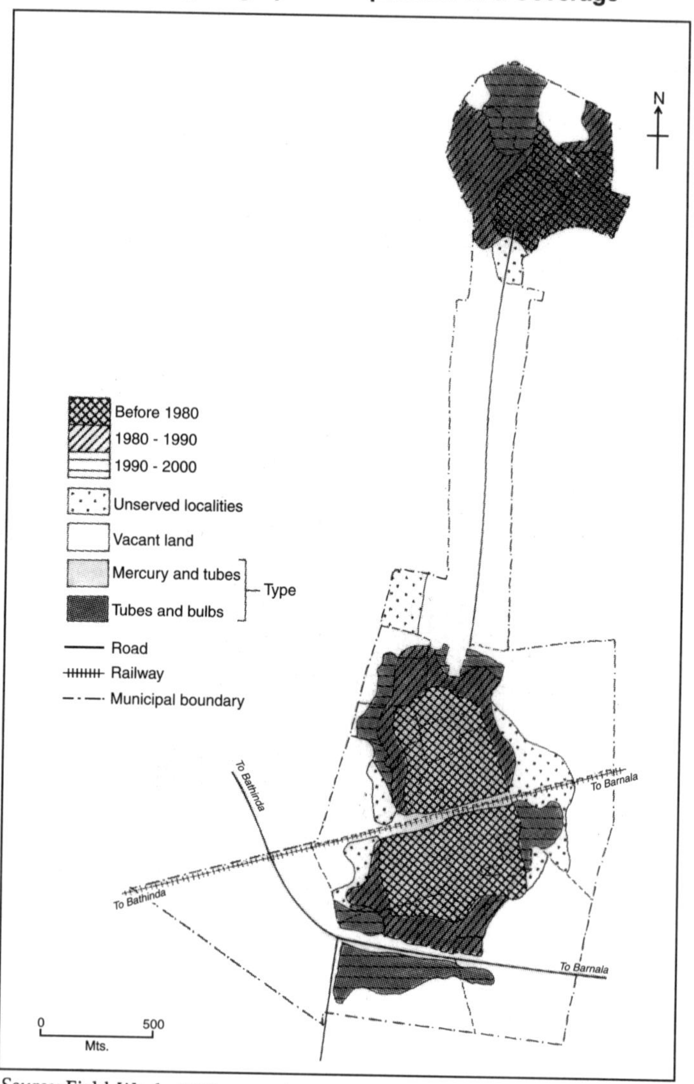

Source: Field Work, 2000.

Map 5.11

Maur Mandi Municipality

Street Lighting: Spatial Expansion and Coverage

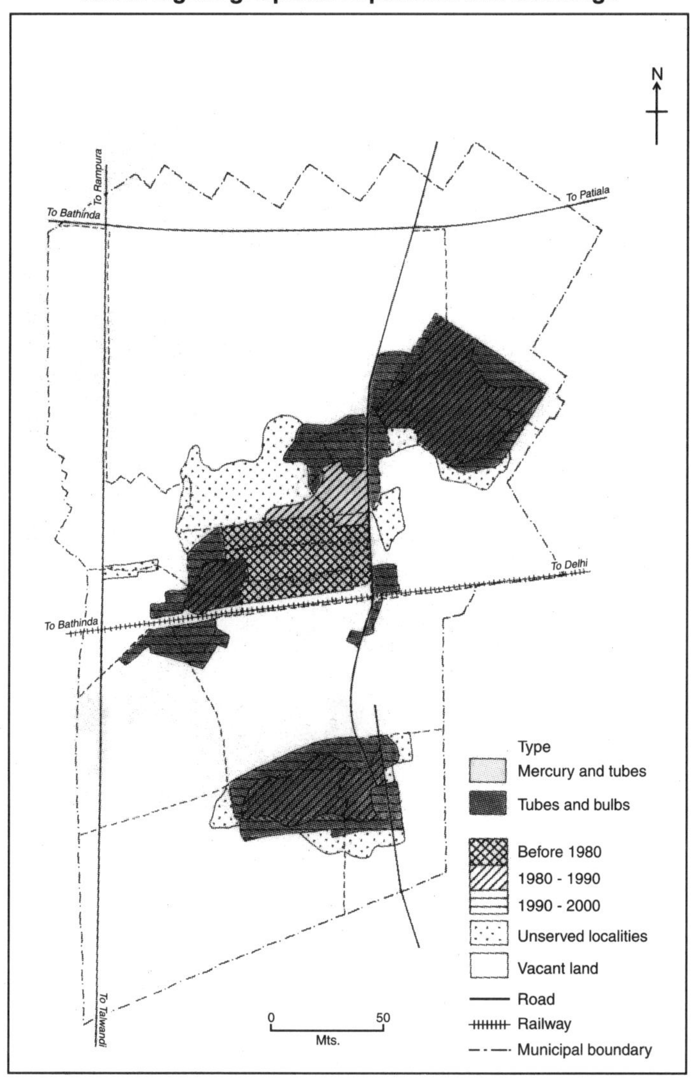

Source: Field Work, 2000.

Map 5.12

Raman Mandi Municipality

Street Lighting Spatial Expansion and Coverage

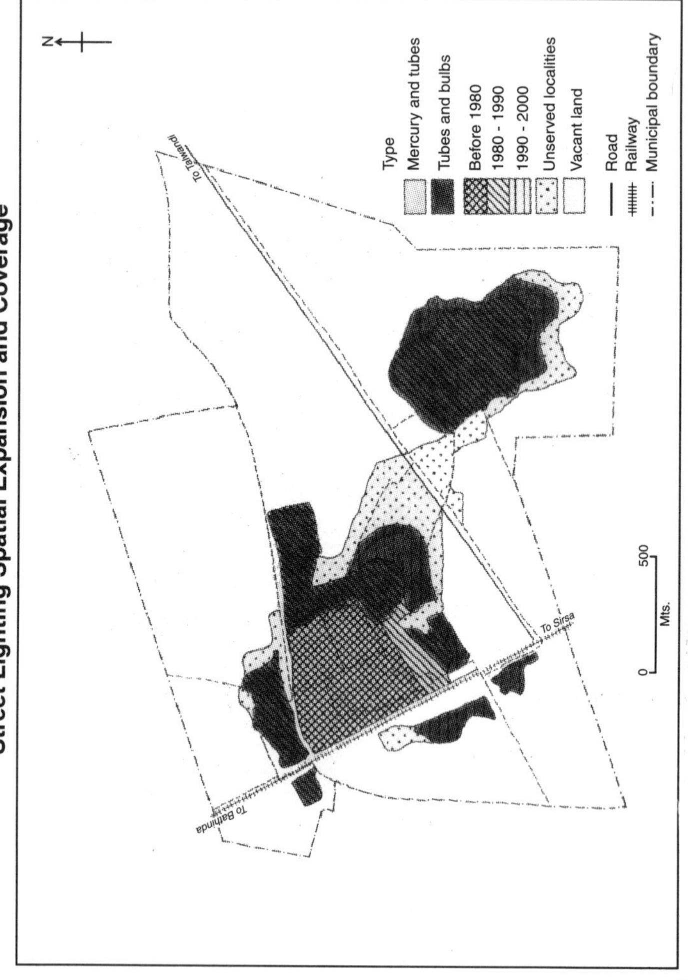

Source: Field Work, 2000.

Map 5.13

Goniana Mandi Municipality

Street Lighting: Spatial Expansion and Coverage

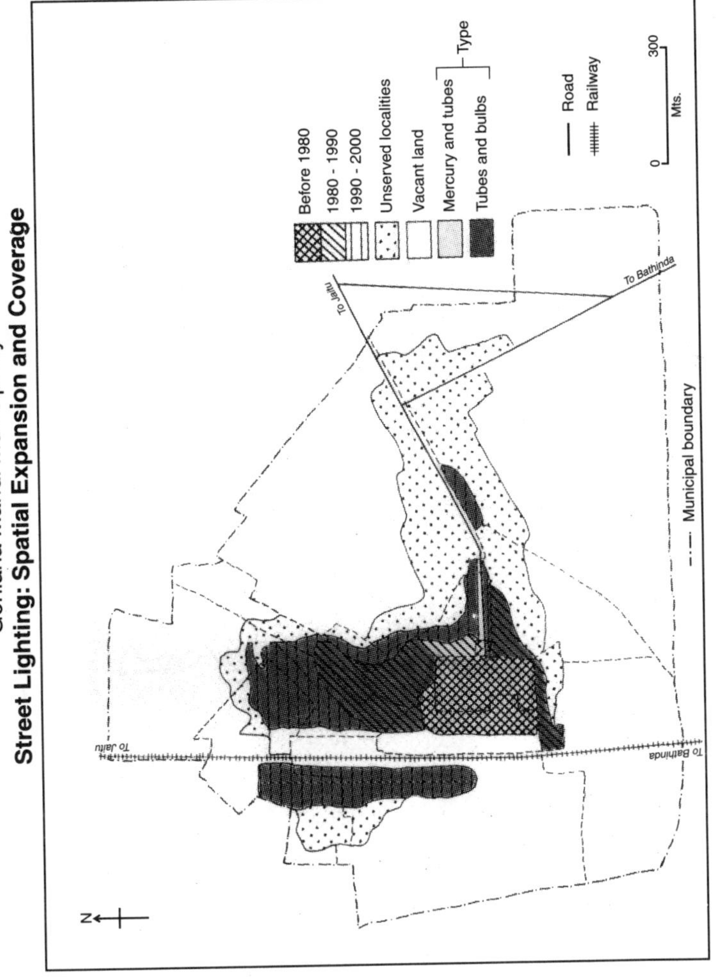

Source: Field Work, 2000.

Map 5.14

Bhucho Mandi Municipality
Street Lights: Spatial Expansion and Coverage

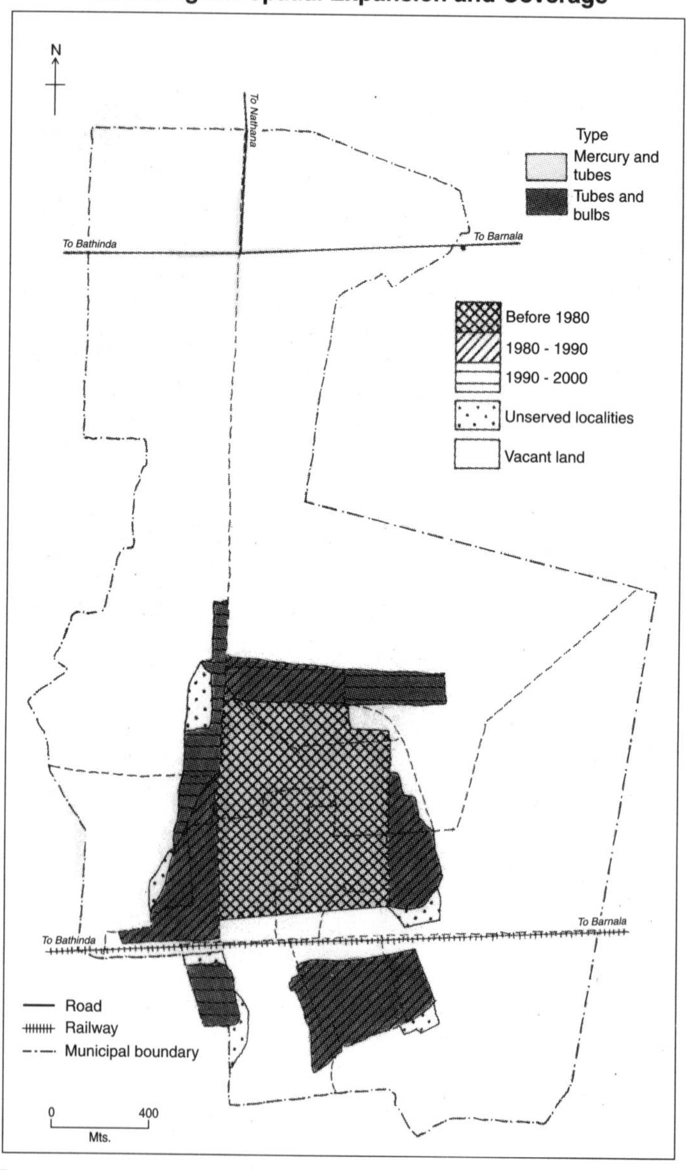

Source: Field Work, 2000.

Map 5.15

Sangat Mandi Municipality

Street Lighting: Spatial Expansion and Coverage

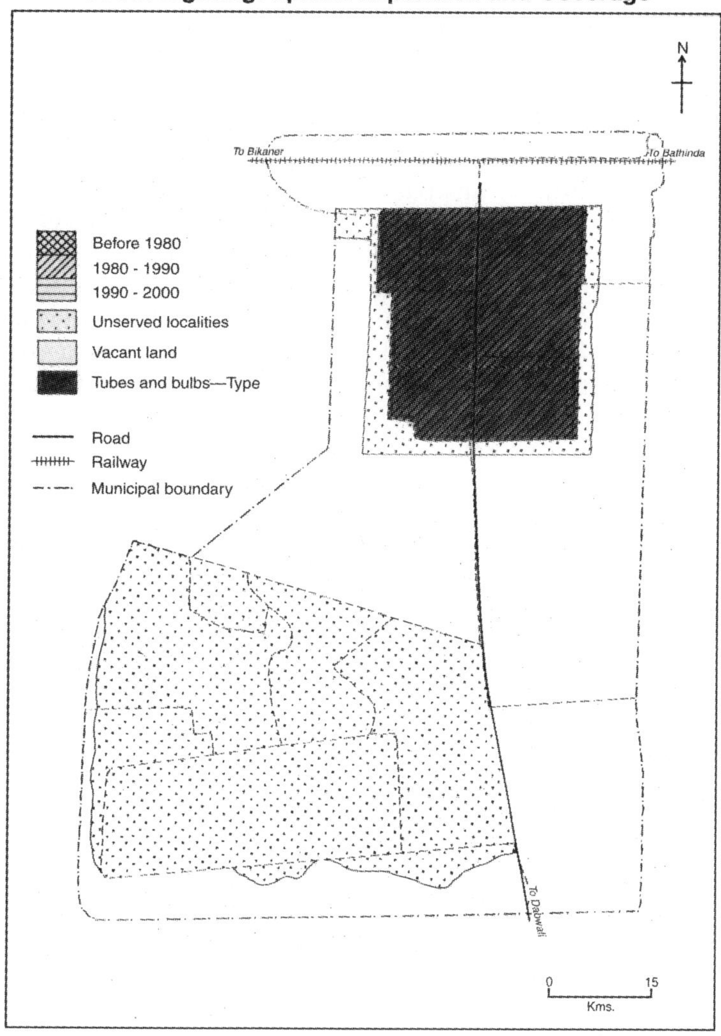

Source: Field Work, 2000.

Bhucho Mandi, a Class IV town, makes a typical case in terms of quality and maintenance of street lighting among the small towns in the district. Here, not only the quality but also maintenance of street lighting is very good. It is well comparable with Bathinda city, a Class I and district headquarters town. Bhucho Mandi, the second richest municipal town after Bathinda city, incurred relatively high expenditure on street lighting (Map 5.14). In per capita terms, its expenditure was not only the highest of all the towns but also nearly twice that of Rampura Phul, the second largest and Class III town in the district. On the other side of the scale, in the twin town of Rampura and Phul not only the quality and maintenance of street lighting differ widely between Rampura and Phul but also within Rampura also. Rampura Market Mandi and Sub-Divisional Office areas have better quality of street lighting through sodium vapour lamps, mercury vapour lamps and tubelights in comparison to peripheral and low income localities where frequency of bulbs and four single tubelights dominate. Such differentials are well marked even between Rampura and Phul townships (Map 5.10).

Briefly, there is well marked intra-municipal town discrimination in terms of the quality and maintenance of street lighting in towns of Bathinda districts. Nevertheless, spatial discrimination in this regard was a more well marked feature of the largest towns in comparison to small towns.

Main Highlights

- Municipal towns in Bathinda district incurred nearly Rs. 480 lakh or more than 3 per cent of aggregate municipal expenditure on street lighting during 1980-98. On an average, this comes to about Rs. 27 lakh per annum.
- Municipalities provide the street lighting facility to their residents free of cost. Hence, the facility of street lighting is provided and maintained for their residents by the municipalities in Bathinda entirely on a subsidized basis. A considerable share of municipal expenditure on this count goes on installation of new light points or replacement of the old ones and on payment of electricity bills against street lighting.

- There have been wide inter-municipal and temporal variations in distribution of expenditure on street lighting. Nearly two-thirds or 65 per cent of the total municipal expenditure on this facility, on average annual basis, was incurred in Bathinda city during 1980-98. Rampura Phul, the second largest town after Bathinda, incurred another 12 per cent of such expenditure. In combination, these two topmost towns in the district were spending more than three-fourths of the total of such expenditure in the district. Expenditure share of Bathinda municipality has been as high as 77 per cent in 1992-93. Also, it was during this period that three top spending municipalities, Bathinda, Rampura Phul and Bhucho Mandi, together incurred nearly nine-tenths or 90 per cent of total municipal expenditure on street lighting in the district. This took the inter-municipal disparities in expenditure on street lighting to the highest level in 1992-93. Against this, inter-municipal disparities in expenditure on this count were the lowest, though still very high, during 1982-83.
- Municipal expenditure on street lighting has been growing fast over the period. On an annual average, it increased from Rs. 11.23 lakh in 1982-83 to Rs. 74.83 lakh in 1996-97, registering an increase of nearly six times. This increase has been as high as about seven times in Bathinda city and as low as less than one time in Sangat Mandi town. The former is the biggest and the latter the smallest town in the district there has been no strong association between civic status and growth of expenditure of a town on street lighting. In general, Class IV municipal towns made much higher expenditure on street lighting than Class III towns in the district. Municipal expenditure on street lighting recorded the fastest growth between 1987-88 and 1992-93 and the lowest during 1992-93 and 1996-97. In other words, municipal expenditure on street lighting has been growing quite slowly in recent years. In general, Bhucho Mandi and Bathinda towns recorded fast and Sangat Mandi, Goniana Mandi and Rampura Phul recorded slow growth in expenditure on street lighting.
- On per capita basis, municipalities in the district incurred an amount of Rs. 13 on street lighting per annum during

1980-98. There were wide inter-municipal and temporal variations in this regard. Bhucho Mandi, a Class IV town, incurred a per capita amount (Rs. 19) more than three times the expenditure (Rs. 6) made by Sangat Mandi, a Class VI town. Per capita expenditure on street lighting followed, in general, the same pattern as in case of total expenditure on this count. However, inter-municipal variations were quite low in per capita expenditure in comparison to total municipal expenditure on street lighting. Interestingly, however, inter-municipal disparities in per capita expenditure on this count were the highest in 1992-93 when it reached Rs. 27 for all the municipalities after recording the highest growth rate of 125 per cent between 1987-88 and 1992-93. Per capita expenditure of Bathinda city on street lighting has been not only quite high but also grew the fastest during 1980-98. Sangat Mandi town represents the reverse case. In general, Class IV municipal towns in the district incurred much higher per capita expenditure on street lighting in comparison to Class III towns.

- There have been wide spatial discriminations both at inter-municipal and intra-municipal levels in distribution of subsidy on street lighting. The residents of Bhucho Mandi town enjoyed the per capita subsidy on street lighting which was more than three times that of the residents of Sangat Mandi town. Even the residents of Kot Fatta towns were not getting the facility of street lighting. Further in all towns, the quality and maintenance of street lighting differed widely between the high income localities and low income and peripherally located ones. However, the spatial discrimination was more a marked feature in big towns such as Bathinda city than in small towns, such as Sangat Mandi.

6

Environmental Improvement Services

SLUM IMPROVEMENT

In recent years, slums have emerged as one of the major negative byproducts of urbanization. While no city in India is free from slums, the problem is more acute in big ones. Different towns and cities suffer from this problem in varying degrees.

Due to a lack of an agreed uniform definition, various countries have been following varied criteria to define the slum. In India, slums have been defined under Section 3 of the Slum Areas (Improvement and Clearance) Act of 1956, wherein slums are defined as areas which are:

(i) Unfit for human habitation; and
(ii) Detrimental to human safety, health and morale due to poor design of and decay in building, over-crowding, and lack of basic amenities and facilities.

Besides this central legislation, the state governments have the freedom to have an independent Act to define slums.

Slums are localities, comprising generally a cluster of huts, with sub-normal living and environmental conditions. These could be deemed unfit for human health and morale. Slums are merely dwellings bereft of the basic minimal facilities required for human existence. What is the basic minimum is difficult to define because views on the concept of basic minimum differ in time-space continuum. Basic minimum will differ in time and space as well as with the level of socio-economic development besides a number of natural and man-made factors. Further, ideologically and politically, the basic minimum needs are perceived differently by the socialist system and the Capitalistic system. One has to bear all these paradoxes in mind, while studying the problems of slums and attempting any solution.

Since the beginning of the Sixth Five Year Plan (1980-85), the municipal bodies in all parts of India have been asked to take-up the programme of "environmental improvement of slums" in addition to their traditional obligations. This programme was evolved at the national level and the state governments were asked to implement it with the grant coming from the central government. The programme envisages the construction of drains, pavement of streets, layout of roads, provision of water supply, street lighting, community latrines and sewerage disposal facilities in slum localities.

Slums in Towns of Bathinda

The programme of slum up-gradation in Bathinda district was initiated in different years in different towns. Starting in 1980, it was first introduced in Bathinda town and it took one whole decade to reach the last municipal town of Sangat Mandi in 1989. In 1991, 52,334 persons living in 43 localities, differing in area and population sizes, were slum-dwellers. They made up about one-fifth or 20 per cent of the total urban population of the district. In other words, every fifth person in urban Bathinda was a slum dweller in 1991. This ratio comes to one-fourth for Punjab as a whole (Dyal, 1992, p. 38).

In their distribution, nine of these 43 slum localities were in Sangat Mandi town (Table 6.1). Sangat Mandi, though the smallest town in the district has the largest number of urban slums among all the towns (Map 6.2). In fact, the entire township of Sangat Mandi has been declared as a slum settlement by the state government in 1989 under the Slum Act.

Next to Sangat Mandi is Maur Mandi town where another seven such localities existed. Here, one-third or 30 per cent of the total population was the slum population. The number of such localities has been six each in Bathinda, Rampura Phul and Goniana Mandi towns (see Maps 6.1 & 6.2). The remaining towns of Raman Mandi, Bhucho Mandi and Kot Fatta, have three each.

Map 6.1

Bathinda DIstrict: **Location of Slums**

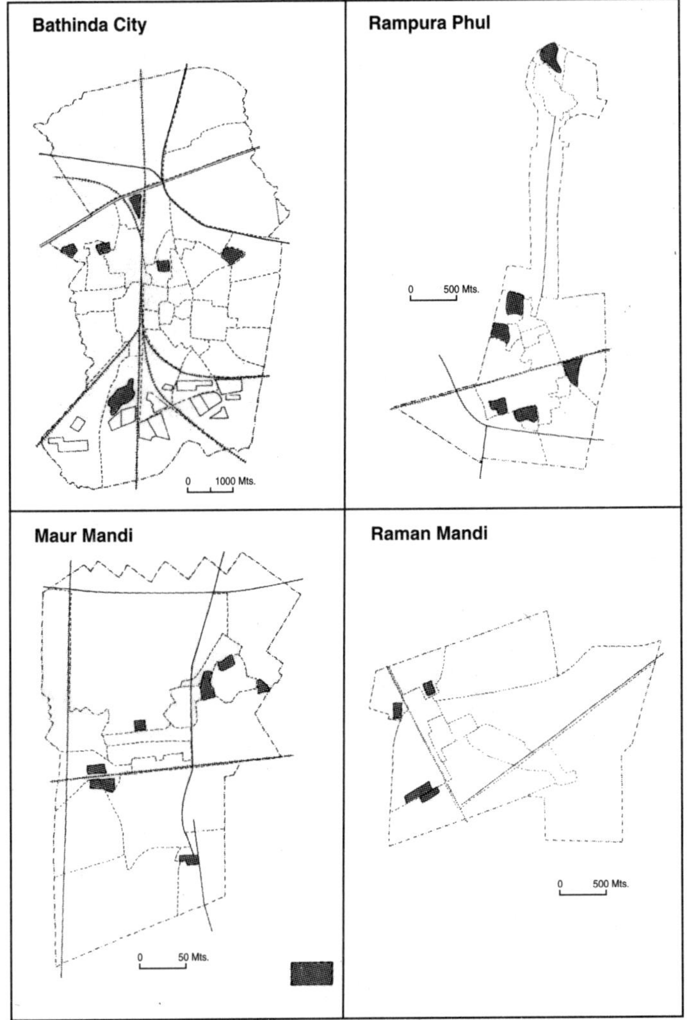

Source: Field Work, 2000.

Map 6.2

Bathinda District: **Location of Slums**

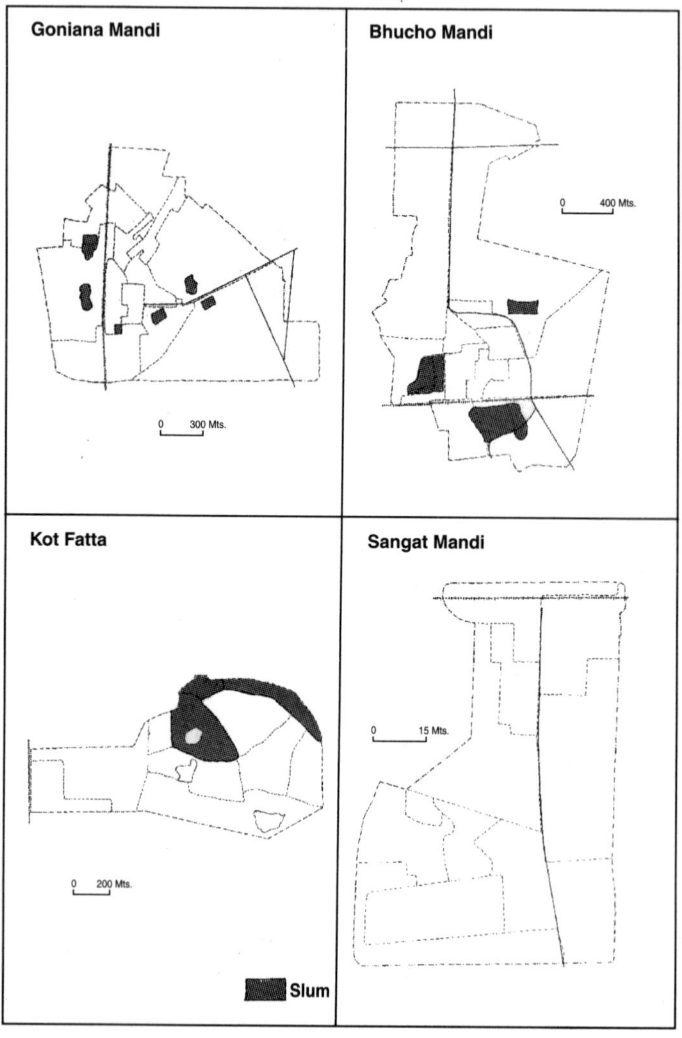

Source: Field Work, 2000.

TABLE 6.1

Bathinda District: Slum Data and Municipal Expenditure on Improvement

Name of town	*Year of programme initiation*	*Number of identified slums 1991*	*Slum population 1991*	*Percentage to total town population (%)*	*Total amount spent till 1997-98 (Rs. in Lakh)*	*Expenditure (Annual Average) (Rs. in lakh)*	*Per capita (Slum population) Annual Expenditure (in Rs.)*
Bathinda	1980	6	17745	11.16	125.44	6.97	39
Rampura Phul	1982	6	11708	32.95	38.13	2.38	20
Maur Mandi	1982	7	7500	29.79	10.57	0.66	9
Raman Mandi	1980	3	3000	17.37	7.79	0.43	14
Goniana Mandi	1982	6	2200	21.12	22.91	1.43	65
Bhucho Mandi	1980	3	5000	49.97	50.09	2.78	56
Kot Fatta	1985	3	2450	43.66	3.64	0.28	11
Sangat Mandi	1989	9	2731	100.00	7.56	0.84	31
All towns		43	52334	19.69	266.13	1.87	30

Source: Data calculated from *Classified Abstracts and Environmental Improvement of Slums Register* of different municipalities for various years.

Slum population, as a proportion of the total population, differs widely. It varied from a high of 100 per cent in Sangat Mandi town to a low of about 11 per cent in Bathinda town. In majority of municipalities, it ranged from one-third to half the total population.

Expenditure on Slum Improvement

In all, an amount of Rs. 266.13 lakh was incurred by the municipalities in Bathinda district on the slum improvement programme till 1997-98. More than 50 thousand population, identified in different years in different towns, benefited from the slum improvement programme. Roughly, the expenditure on slum improvement came to about Rs. 509 per head of slum population in the district. It is, however, to be noted here that neither the identification of slum population nor the initiation of the slum improvement programme took place simultaneously in all the towns. Therefore, a statistical figure about the expenditure on slum population may seem somewhat deceptive. Hence, one has to bear this fact in mind while looking into the following discussion on municipal expenditure for slum population.

Further, the municipalities do not earn anything in return against the expenditure on slum improvement. Thus, it could also be deemed as a total subsidy. Notably, however, since such an expenditure is targeted for specific locations and populations within a town, it is a special kind of subsidy or a case of targeted subsidy. Pavement of streets, construction of drains and metalled roads, sewerage disposal and street lighting are the main slum improvement works on which the municipalities make this expenditure. According to an estimate, about three-fifths of total expenditure under the environmental improvement of slums is incurred on pavement of streets and another one-fifth on construction of drains.

Bathinda municipality, where more than 11 per cent of total population in 1991 was made up of slum dwellers, incurred an amount of more than Rs. 125 lakh on slum improvement programmes. This amount made up more than 47 per cent of the total municipal expenditure in the district on this count. Against this, slum population of Bathinda municipal town was 34 per cent of the total of such population in towns of the district.

Evidently, its share in total municipal expenditure on slum improvement was much higher than its share in total slum population in the district. Nevertheless, Bathinda is the first town in the district to start a slum improvement programme.

Rampura Phul, the second largest town in the district, had one-third of its population identified as slum-dwellers. This population made up about 22 per cent of the entire population in the district. Rampura Phul incurred more than Rs. 38 lakh on its slum improvement programme during 1982-98. This amount made up only about 14 per cent of the total municipal expenditure on this count in the district. Evidently, there has been a mismatch between its population share and expenditure on slum population in the district. The situation was, however, just the reverse in the case of Bathinda city where the expenditure share was much higher than the population share. Even, on the basis of average annual expenditure on slums, Bathinda has a distinctive edge over Rampura Phul town. The former incurred an average annual expenditure three times higher than the expenditure incurred by the latter.

Bhucho Mandi, where nearly half the total population was declared as slum-dwellers, incurred an amount of Rs. 50 lakh on slum improvement programmes during 1980-98. It was the second highest amount incurred on slum improvement in the district. This amount made up nearly 19 per cent of the total municipal expenditure on slum improvement in the district, whereas its share in total slum population in the district has been less than 10 per cent. Obviously, like Bathinda City, Bhucho Mandi municipality also incurred much higher share of expenditure on slum improvement than its share of slum population in the district.

Kot Fatta, having 44 per cent of total population as slum-dwellers, spent less than Rs. 4 lakh on slum improvement during 1985-98. It comes to about Rs. 28,000 per annum, which is the lowest average for any municipality in the district. The share of Kot Fatta in total slum population of the district made about 5 per cent, while its share in total expenditure on slum improvement has been only about 1 per cent. Clearly, there is a huge mismatch between its share in slum population and its expenditure on such population.

The entire population of Sangat Mandi, the smallest municipal town in the district, has been declared as slum population. This population comprised of more than 5 per cent of the total slum population in the district. Against this, Sangat Mandi's share in expenditure on slum improvement in the district comes to about 3 per cent. Certainly, Sangat Mandi was better placed than Kot Fatta in this context, yet there has been a mismatch between its expenditure share on slum improvement and its share in total slum population in the district.

Goniana Mandi, where more than one-fifth of the total population comprised of slum-dwellers, incurred an amount of about Rs. 23 lakh on slum improvement. This amount made up about 9 per cent of the total expenditure on slum improvement in the district. Against this, Goniana Mandi town shared only about 4 per cent in total slum population in the district.

On the whole, three municipal towns, namely, Bathinda, Bhucho Mandi and Goniana, together, shared about three-fourth or 75 per cent of the total municipal expenditure on slum improvement against only 48 per cent of total urban slum population in the district. In contrast, three municipal towns, namely Maur Mandi, Raman Mandi and Kot Fatta, which shared about 25 per cent of the total urban slum population incurred only about 8 per cent of the total expenditure on slum improvement in the district.

Per Capita Expenditure/Subsidy on Slums

Per capita expenditure on slum population, calculated on annual average basis, provides a more realistic picture of municipal expenditure on the slums than expenditure in proportional terms.

Goniana Mandi, a Class IV category town where more than one-fifth of the total population was identified as the slum population, spent the highest per capita amount of Rs. 65 per annum during 1982-98. Against this, Maur Mandi, a Class III category town where 30 per cent of the population was identified as slum dwelling, spent the lowest per capita amount of Rs. 9 during the same period.

Bhucho Mandi, another Class IV category town where half the total population was composed of slum-dwellers, spent the second highest per capita amount of Rs. 56 per annum on slum population during 1980-1998. Sangat Mandi, the smallest municipal town in the district where entire population has been identified as slum-dwellers, incurred Rs. 31 per capita on this count during 1989-98. Against this, Bathinda, the largest and the only Class I category town in the district, spent Rs. 39 per capita on slum population.

Maur Mandi, Raman Mandi and Kot Fatta municipal towns fared quite low in this context. Their per capita expenditure on slum population ranged between Rs. 9 and Rs. 14. Their expenditure on slum population was low both in proportional as well as per capita terms. It is to be noted here that municipalities do not spend regularly on slum population. The expenditure on slum improvement by municipalities depended mainly on grants received from the government.

Main Highlights

- Environmental improvement of slums, which was initiated during the Sixth Five Year Plan (1980-85) under the Minimum Needs Programme has been a centrally sponsored programme for improving living conditions in urban slums.
- In Bathinda district, environmental improvement of urban slums was implemented in a phased manner. Towns of Bathinda, Raman Mandi and Bhucho Mandi were first to initiate this programme in 1980. On the other hand, Sangat Mandi town was the last to initiate this programme in 1989. In this way, it took nearly a decade to cover all the towns under the programme of slum improvement in the district.
- As per 1991 Census, there were 43 duly recognized slum localities of varying area and population sizes in the eight municipal towns of the district. More than 52 thousand persons or every fifth urbanite in Bathinda district is a slum-dweller.
- The number of slums and slum population differed widely among the towns of Bathinda district. While Sangat Mandi, the smallest town in the district, had the maximum number of nine slums, the towns of Raman Mandi, Bhucho Mandi and Kot Fatta had the minimum number of three slums each. Bathinda, the largest town in the district, had six slums.
- Of more than 52 thousand urban slum-dwellers in the district, about 37 thousand or 71 per cent were located in the three large towns of Bathinda, Rampura Phul and Maur

Mandi. Broadly speaking, larger the population size of a town, larger the number of slum dwellers in it. At the level of individual town, while the entire population of Sangat Mandi town is made up of slum-dwellers, it comprised only about 11 per cent in case of Bathinda. Half the population of Bhucho Mandi and two-fifths of Kot Fatta also comprised slum-dwellers. However, no association was found between the class category of a town and the share of slum population in it. Hence, urbanisation in Bathinda district contradicts the validity of the nationally proven hypothesis that class category of a town and the proportional share of slum population have a strong positive association.

- Municipalities in Bathinda district did not spend regularly on slum improvement. It depended mostly on the grants received by the municipalities from different sources. Nevertheless, an aggregate amount of Rs. 266.13 lakh, making for less than 2.0 per cent of total municipal expenditure, was spent on improvement of urban slums in the district during 1980-98. More than 50 thousand population identified as slum-dwellers in the district benefited from this amount. Roughly, it came to Rs. 509 per slum-dweller during 1980-98. Pavement of streets, construction of drains, water supply, sewerage disposal, construction of roads and street lighting were the schemes on which expenditure was made by the municipality for improvement of slums. On the whole, capital works received priority in implementation of the programme in towns of Bathinda district.
- Three towns of Goniana Mandi, Bhucho Mandi and Bathinda shared a much higher proportion of total municipal expenditure of the district on slum improvement than their respective shares in total slum population in the district. The reverse is the case of Maur Mandi, Raman Mandi and Kot Fatta towns. However, the expenditure on slum improvement in a town does not find an association with its share in slum population and size category of the town.
- On per captia basis, Goniana Mandi was the top with Rs. 65 per anum and Maur Mandi at the bottom, with Rs. 9. Inter-minicipal variations in per capita expenditure on slum improvement were lower than the share of aggregate

municipal expenditure on slum improvement in the district. The maximum per captia expenditure on slum improvement was higher by about seven times than the minimum. The highest and the lowest proportional share of per annum expenditure by municipalities on slum improvement programme differed by 25 times.

- An element of political favour in declaration of any locality as slum area and in allocation of funds for environmental improvement of slums has been observed. Some of the localities were allocated more funds than others in each of the eight towns in the district.
- The expenditure on the 'Environmental Improvement of Slums' makes a positive change in the quality of life in these localities, but does not yield any returns in reverse terms for the municipal government. It therefore, becomes a case of hundred per cent subsidy.

RECREATIONAL FACILITIES

To harness the productive capabilities of city-dwellers, it is essential that they stay physically and mentally fit. It is therefore, important to plan and maintain recreational facilities properly so that residents in urban areas utilize their leisure time enjoyably and conveniently. This has become all the more important in the context of increased tension and pressure of modern life in urban centres. That is why the provision of recreational facilities, such as public parks, community halls, gardens, libraries and museums, is one of the discretionary functions of municipal bodies in India. In the following, the pattern of expenditure and subsidy on recreational services provided by municipalities in Bathinda district has been analysed for different municipalities for the period 1980-98.

Expenditure: Pattern and Change

Before analyzing the municipal expenditure on recreational services by municipalities in the district, it would be imperative to have a brief discussion on the availability of this service in different towns of the district. There are in all eight municipal towns in the district. Three of these, namely, Maur Mandi, Kot Fatta and Sangat Mandi do not provide this facility to their residents. In Rampura Phul, this service was started in the financial year 1984-85. In Raman Mandi, it started as late as in 1990-91. Hence, there are three municipal towns, namely, Bathinda, Goniana Mandi and Bhucho Mandi which incurred expenditure on this count regularly during 1980-98. Another interesting feature of this service in the district is that it is only the Bathinda municipality that earns some income from this service. Rest of the municipalities, providing this service, do not get any penny in return. Hence, it is a highly subsidized municipal service in the district.

During 1980-98, an average annual amount of Rs. 22.17 lakh was incurred by municipalities in Bathinda on recreational service (Table 6.2). It made less than 3 per cent in total municipal expenditure in the district on urban services during the period. Of this amount, Bathinda municipality alone incurred Rs. 19.73 lakh or 89 per cent, followed by Rampura Phul with Rs. 1.32 lakh or about 6 per cent. In this way, Rs. 95 out of every Rs. 100 spent by municipalities in the district on recreational services, on an average annual basis, were shared by two of the largest municipal towns of Bathinda and Rampura Phul. The remaining three towns namely, Raman Mandi, Goniana Mandi and Bhucho Mandi, together, shared only about 5 per cent of the total municipal expenditure in the district on recreational services. Raman Mandi incurred the lowest amount of Rs. 6000 per annum during 1980-98.

In proportional terms, it ranged from a high 3.4 per cent in Bathinda municipal to a low of only 0.2 per cent in Raman Mandi during 1980-98. Bhucho Mandi, a Class IV town, incurred 2.1 per cent in its total municipal expenditure on this count. Definitely, the expenditure share incurred by municipalities in Bathinda on recreational facilities was not only low but also differed widely among the municipalities. Bathinda municipal town, which incurred nearly nine-tenth of the total municipal expenditure on recreational services in the district, maintains more than 25 parks, one rose garden and one swimming pool. No other town matches Bathinda in this regard. Rampura Phul, the second largest town in the district, was far behind Bathinda city in this regard as it developed parks for the first time in 1984-85.

TABLE 6.2

Bathinda District: Expenditure on Recreational Facilities as Percentage of Total Municipal Expenditure on Services, 1980-98

(*Rs. in lakhs*)

Name of Town	*Civic status*	*1982-83**			*1987-88**			*1992-93**			*1996-97**			*1980-98**		
		Aggregate expenditure	*Expenditure on recreational service*	*Percentage of aggregate expenditure*	*Aggregate expenditure*	*Expenditure on recreational service*	*Percentage of aggregate expenditure*	*Aggregate expenditure*	*Expenditure on recreational service*	*Percentage of aggregate expenditure*	*Aggregate expenditure*	*Expenditure on recreational service*	*Percentage of aggregate expenditure*	*Aggregate expenditure*	*Expenditure on recreational service*	*Percentage of aggregate expenditure*
1	*2*	*3*	*4*	*5*	*6*	*7*	*8*	*9*	*10*	*11*	*12*	*13*	*14*	*15*	*16*	*17*
Bathinda	I	207.10	2.72	1.31	456.43	14.40	3.15	755.21	30.62	4.05	1135.78	37.99	3.34	583.39	19.73	3.38
Rampura Phul	III	34.62	3.22	9.30	55.62	0.57	1.02	104.96	0.51	0.49	162.77	0.78	0.48	81.35	1.32	1.62
Raman Mandi	IV	12.20	Nil	Nil	28.50	Nil	Nil	53.35	0.10	0.19	85.41	0.18	0.21	40.36	0.06	0.15
Goniana Mandi	IV	14.30	0.05	0.35	28.70	0.13	0.45	41.46	0.21	0.51	54.33	0.37	0.68	32.52	0.17	0.52
Bhucho Mandi	IV	18.04	0.11	0.61	39.60	0.09	0.23	42.47	1.60	3.77	90.16	2.32	2.57	42.84	0.89	2.08
Aggregate Expenditure		286.26	6.10	2.13	608.85	15.19	2.49	997.45	33.04	3.10	1528.45	41.64	2.72	786.46	22.17	2.82
C.V.		1.32	0.95		1.38	1.61		1.40	1.82		1.36	1.78		1.37	1.73	

*Annual averages.

Notes: C.V. stands for Coefficient of Variability.

Source: Data calculated from *Classified Abstracts* of different municipalities for various years.

The municipal expenditure on recreational facilities has gone up during 1980-98. It has grown to Rs. 41.64 lakh in 1996-97 from Rs. 6.10 lakh in 1982-83, registering an increase of 583 per cent. There have been wide inter-municipal differentials in this context. While the expenditure in Bhucho Mandi town increased by more than twenty times, it recorded a sharp decline in the case of Rampura Phul town during the same period. In latter case, the amount of expenditure on recreational facilities was reduced to about one-fourth in 1996-97 from 1982-83. In Goniana Mandi the expenditure rose by about 640 per cent and Raman Mandi was not regular in spending on this count.

In 1982-83 when the expenditure on recreational facilities for all the four municipalities, providing these facilities, was Rs. 6.10 lakh, Rampura Phul shared more than half or about 53 per cent of the total municipal expenditure on these facilities. Bathinda municipality shared another 45 per cent. In this way, 97 per cent of the total municipal expenditure on recreational facilities was shared by the two largest towns in the district. The combined share of remaining two municipalities, namely, Goniana Mandi and Bhucho Mandi was only about 3 per cent. It is to be noted here that Rampura Phul introduced this facility from the financial year of 1984-85 when it developed parks in different parts of the town and the municipal administration had to make a large initial investment. Inter-municipal disparities in expenditure were quite high because the co-efficient of variability (C.V.) index was as high as 0.95.

In 1987-88, the municipal expenditure on recreational services increased to Rs. 15.2 lakh, registering an increase of 149 per cent. There were, however, wide inter-municipal variations in this regard. Nearly, 95 per cent of this increase was shared by Bathinda city where expenditure rose to Rs. 14.40 lakh in 1987-88 from only Rs. 2.72 lakh in 1982-83. Against this, Rampura Phul town recorded a sharp decline in its expenditure on this count, as the absolute amount of expenditure came down to only Rs. 52 thousand in 1987-88 from Rs. 3.32 lakh in 1982-83. Bhucho Mandi town also recorded an absolute decline in its expenditure on recreational facilities. It was only in Goniana Mandi town that expenditure on recreational facilities increased from five thousand in 1982-83 to 13 thousand in 1987-88 and Raman Mandi town was yet to enter in this arena. Evidently, the enrichment of the quality of life in towns of Bathinda district was highly neglected, except in the case of Bathinda city.

In proportional terms, expenditure in Bathinda town increased from 1.31 per cent to 3.15 per cent, while it declined to about one per cent in Rampura Phul from 9.3 per cent between 1982-83 and 1987-88. Proportional share of Bhucho Mandi town also registered decline, where as the share of Goniana Mandi town recorded a marginal increase. Inter-municipal disparities further grew as C.V. index rose to 1.61 in 1987-88 from 0.95 in 1982-83 (Table 6.2).

Bathinda town where municipal expenditure on recreational services increased by 429 per cent between 1982-83 and 1987-88, an ambitions plan of developing a rose garden in the town was initiated and parks developed in new localities. This was the reason that Bathinda municipality incurred 95 per cent of the total municipal expenditure in the district on recreational facilities in 1987-88. The rose garden stretches along the tributary of the Sirhind Canal and covers an area of 22 acres. It is meant as a recreational site for the city residents and also is a tourist attraction. It has features like children traffic park, Manmohni hill, open air theatre, Rose bud canteen, fountains and lights, 35 varieties of flowers, ornamental trees and bushes, some caged animals, an ornamental bridge, a fountain and swings for children. While Rs. 15 lakh were spent on its development Rs. 3 lakhs are spent on its maintenance, annually.

In 1992-93 the municipal expenditure on recreational facilities in the district rose to Rs. 33.04 lakh from Rs. 15.2 lakh in 1987-88, registering an increase of 118 per cent. There were, however, wide inter-municipal differentials in this regard. Once again, Bathinda municipality incurred the dominant share of 93 per cent in total municipal expenditure in the district on recreational facilities. Its expenditure on this facility rose to Rs. 30.62 lakh in 1992-93 from Rs. 14.40 lakh in 1987-88, registering an increase of 113 per cent. During this period, the municipality developed not only more parks in new localities but also further expanded the rose garden project. The second highest expenditure on recreational facilities in this period was incurred by Bhucho Mandi, spending Rs. 1.60 lakh. Raman Mandi, which incurred expenditure for the first time on recreational facilities, spent an amount of Rs. 10 thousand. The combined expenditure of remaining two municipalities, namely, Rampura Phul and Goniana Mandi made up Rs. 72 thousand, coming to about 2 per cent of total municipal expenditure on recreational facilities in

1992-93. There has been a further increase in inter-municipal disparities in expenditure on recreational facilities as C.V. index value rose to 1.82 in 1992-93 from 1.61 in 1987-88.

In 1996-97 when municipal expenditure on recreational facilities in the district rose to Rs. 41.64 lakh from Rs. 33.04 lakh in 1992-93, it registered an increase of 26 per cent. Earlier, during 1987-88 1992-93 this increase had been 118 per cent. Evidently, growth of municipal expenditure on recreational service in the district slowed down considerably after 1992-93. In proportional terms also, it came down to 2.72 per cent in 1996-97 from 3.10 per cent in 1992-93. The respective shares of three of the five municipalities, incurring expenditure on this count registered a decline. Nevertheless, none of the municipal towns registered decline in absolute amount of expenditure on recreational facilities in the district, but expenditure grew quite slowly. The growth rate for all the municipalities has been only 26 per cent. Bathinda, the largest town in the district, recorded the lowest growth rate of 24 per cent and the highest growth rate was (80%) experienced by Raman Mandi. Bhucho Mandi, the second highest spending town on this count, recorded a growth rate of 45 per cent.

Once again Bathinda municipality, which incurred the largest amount of Rs. 38 lakh, shared more than nine-tenth of the total municipal expenditure on recreational facilities in the district in this year. This was followed by Bhucho Mandi with Rs. 2.32 lakh. Against this, Raman Mandi incurred the smallest amount of Rs. 18,000.

Briefly, as revealed from expenditure on and availability of recreational facilities in municipal towns of Bathinda district, this is one of the least cared urban services in the district. It means that the enrichment of cultural life is not receiving the desired attention from the municipal administration in the district. The municipal expenditure on this service was not only low but also declining over the period both in proportional as well as incremental terms. There are only three out of eight municipal towns in the district which have been providing this facilities on regular basis during 1980-98.

Income: Pattern and Change

As stated in the beginning, there is only one municipality of Bathinda which receives some revenue income from this service. Rest of the municipalities, namely, Rampura Phul, Raman Mandi,

Goniana Mandi and Bhucho Mandi, which also provide this service to their residents, do not get a single penny in return from this facility. In this way, recreational facilities are among the highly subsidized urban services in the district.

Even in case of Bathinda municipality, the revenue earnings from these facilities started after 1984-85. The main source if income are the bidding of contracts for the Blue Fox, a restaurant adjacent to the Rose Garden, a Canteen inside the Rose Garden and the parking lots along with the fee charged on the stalls put up by the vendors near the entry gates of the Rose Garden. In 1988-89, an income of Rs. 42 thousand was earned by the municipality through contracting out the canteen, the parking space and the photography service. A swimming pool, in the Civil Lines area, charges a fee of Rs. 40 per month from those using this facility. It covers an area of 1.5 acres and is equipped with modern facilities. School boys and college students enjoy concessional rates. The services of a coach of international standards are available here for training purposes. On an average, Bathinda municipal town earned an amount of Rs. 2.56 lakh per annum from recreational facilities during 1980-98 (Table 6.3). This made up about 13 per cent of its average annual expenditure (Rs. 19.73 lakh) on recreational facilities during 1980-98.

TABLE 6.3

Bathinda District: Income Earned from Recreational Facilities, 1980-98

(Rs. in lakhs)

Years	*Expenditure*	*Income*	*Income/expenditure (in %)*	*Per capita income (in Rs.)*
1982-83*	2.72	—	—	—
1987-88*	14.40	1.39	9.65	1
1992-93*	30.62	2.62	8.56	2
1996-97*	37.99	4.44	11.69	4
1980-98*	19.73	2.56	12.98	2

*Annual averages.

Notes: 1. No income was earned through this service by other seven municipalities.

2. Per capita subsidy has been calculated on the basis of 1981 Census data. In case of Bathinda population figures used for calculation of subsidy confined to areas falling under the jurisdiction of Bathinda Municipal Committee. Two public sector units, Fertilizer and Thermal Plant make their own arrangement for provision of services, provided to their residents. Hence excluded from the calculations.

Source: Data calculated from *Classified Abstracts* of different municipalities for various years.

In other words, Bathinda municipal town earned 13 rupees out of every 100 rupees it spent on recreational facilities during 1980-98. The remaining Rs. 87 comprised the subsidy element on this service. Obviously, recreational facilities were a highly subsidized service in Bathinda town. In 1982-83, Bathinda municipal town did not earn a single penny out of its expenditure of Rs. 2.72 lakh. In this way, the whole amount was the subsidy. Coming to 1987-88, it earned Rs. 1.39 lakh from an expenditure of Rs. 14.40 lakh. The income from recreational facilities made less than one-tenth of the municipal expenditure on this service. In 1992-93, when the income from recreational facilities to Bathinda municipality rose to Rs. 2.62 lakh, it made less than 9 per cent in total municipal expenditure of Rs. 30.62 lakh. In this way, the income, though increased by about 90 per cent but as a proportion of expenditure it registered a decline.

However in 1996-97, when expenditure was Rs. 37.99 lakh, income had been Rs. 4.44 lakh, making about 12 per cent of municipal expenditure on this count. In this way, the municipal income grew only in terms of proportional share of its expenditure on recreational facilities but also in growth terms. Income increased by 69 per cent between 1992-93 and 1996-97. Against this, expenditure on recreational facilities increased by only 24 per cent during the same period. In this way, income from recreational facilities, though making up only a small share of total expenditure of Bathinda municipality on this count, has been growing faster than municipal expenditure on this count.

Briefly, of all the municipal towns in the district Bathinda municipal town is the only town which earns from its recreational facilities. Rest of the municipalities do not earn a single penny on account of this. The municipal income from recreational services made for only a small proportion of its expenditure on the service. However, the municipal income from recreational facilities has been growing faster than the municipal expenditure on this count.

Subsidy: Pattern and Change

As stated earlier, Bathinda is the only municipal town in the district which earns some revenue from recreational facilities. The Rose Garden is the main source of revenue income generation. Parks, swimming pool, libraries, children parks, fountains, etc.

developed by different municipal towns under their jurisdictions fetch no income to municipalities. There is no entry fee imposed at all such places. In other words, recreational facilities in all the towns, except Bathinda, are fully subsidized. Five out of eight municipal towns in the district provide recreational facilities and four of them render these facilities free of charge. In the following, the pattern and change in subsidy component is examined and compared.

During 1980-98, municipalities in Bathinda district provided an amount of Rs. 19.61 lakh, on average annual basis, as subsidy on recreational facilities (Table 6.4). This made more than 88 per cent in total municipal expenditure (Rs. 22.17 lakh) incurred by five municipal towns in the district on average annual basis. In other words, 88 rupees out of every 100 rupees incurred by municipal towns in the district on recreational facilities made the subsidy component on this service. It is to be noted here that the 12 rupees, which is an income on every 100 rupees expenditure on this service in the district, was earned by only the Bathinda municipality.

There are wide inter-municipal variations in this regard. More than 87 per cent of total municipal subsidy in the district on this service was provided by Bathinda municipality. Rampura Phul, the second largest municipal town in the district, provided another about 7 per cent. In this way, the combined share of these two municipal towns made more than 94 per cent of total municipal subsidy on recreational services in the district. If the subsidy share of Bhucho Mandi is also added to this, it goes to about 99 per cent of total municipal subsidy on this account in the district. In other words, Raman Mandi and Goniana Mandi towns provide a negligible amount on this count. Raman Mandi, which provides the lowest share of the total subsidy in the district on recreational facilities, incurred only Rs. 6000 on annual average basis during 1980-98. It is to be noted further that Raman Mandi was not regular in spending on this count.

In per capita terms, municipal subsidy on recreational service was Rs. 11 for 1980-98. Among municipalities, Bathinda was again at the top with Rs. 15 per capita and Raman Mandi at the bottom with only 40 paisa. Bathinda municipality was closely followed by Bhucho Mandi, a Class IV town, with Rs. 11 per capita. Rampura Phul, the second largest town in the district, provided

TABLE 6.4

Bathinda District: Per Capita Subsidy on Recreational Facilities by Municipalities, 1980-98

Name of town	*1982-83**		*1987-88**		*1992-93**		*1996-97**		*1980-98**	
	Subsidy (Rs. in lakhs)	*Subsidy Per capita (in Rs.)*	*Subsidy (Rs. in lakh)*	*Subsidy Per capita (in Rs.)*	*Subsidy (Rs. in lakhs)*	*Subsidy Per capita (in Rs.)*	*Subsidy (Rs. in lakhs)*	*Subsidy Per capita (in Rs.)*	*Subsidy (Rs. in lakhs)*	*Subsidy Per capita (in Rs.)*
Bathinda	2.72 (44.59)	2	13.01 (94.28)	11	28.0 (92.04)	24	33.56 (90.19)	29	17.17 (87.56)	15
Rampura Phul	3.22 (52.79)	10	0.57 (4.13)	2	0.51 (1.68)	2	0.78 (2.10)	2	1.32 (6.73)	4
Raman Mandi	Nil	—	Nil	—	0.10 (0.33)	1	0.18 (0.48)	1	0.06 (0.31)	0.4
Goniana Mandi	0.05 (0.82)	1	0.13 ((0.94)	2	0.21 (0.69)	2	0.37 (0.99)	4	0.17 (0.87)	2
Bhucho Mandi	0.11 (1.80)	1	0.09 (0.65)	1	1.60 (5.26)	20	2.32 (6.23)	30	0.89 (4.54)	11
All Towns	6.10 (100)	4	13.80 (100)	8	30.42 (100)	17	37.21 (100)	21	19.61 (100)	11

*Annual averages.

Notes: (i) Figures in parentheses indicate to percentage share in total.

(ii) Per capita subsidy has been calculated on the basis of 1981 Census data. In case of Bathinda population figures for calculating of subsidies confined to areas falling under the Bathinda M.C. jurisdiction. Two public sector units, Fertilizer and Thermal Plant make their own arrangements and have been excluded from the calculations/computations.

Source: Data calculated from *Classified Abstracts* of different municipalities for various years.

only Rs. 4 on per capita basis. In this way, it is only in Bathinda and Bhucho Mandi towns where municipal administration showed concern about the enrichment of the cultural life of their residents.

In 1982-83, when municipal subsidy on recreational facilities made Rs. 6.10 lakh, Rampura Phul topped the list with Rs. 3.22 lakh or about 53 per cent of the total municipal subsidy on this count in the district. Then too only four out of eight municipalities in the district provided this service and the total expenditure on this count was the subsidy as none of the municipalities, including Bathinda, earned any revenue income from this service. Rampura Phul, where this service was introduced in 1984-85, incurred heavy initial expenditure on the development of parks in the town. This explains the reason for its being on the top among all the municipalities. Bathinda municipality shared another about 45 per cent or Rs. 2.72 lakh, both, in combination sharing more than 97 per cent of total municipal subsidy in the district on this service. In per capita terms, against the average of Rs. 4 per person, Rampura Phul provided Rs. 10 and Bathinda only Rs. 2. Bhucho Mandi and Goniana Mandi provided one rupee each. Raman Mandi town did not spend any amount on this count.

Coming to 1987-88, when the amount of subsidy on this count rose to Rs. 13.80 lakh, it registered an increase of 126 per cent. Bathinda municipality shared more than 94 per cent or Rs. 13.01 lakh of the total municipal subsidy on this count. During this period, Bathinda municipality initiated its ambitious plan of developing the Rose Garden. It incurred an expenditure of Rs. 14.40 lakh, on annual average basis, to earn Rs. 1.39 lakh. The remaining amount of Rs. 13.01 lakh, was thus, the subsidy element on this count. Rampura Phul, though far behind provided the second highest amount, Rs. 57,000 on this account. Bhucho Mandi provided the lowest amount of Rs. 9,000 only. In per capita terms, Bathinda provided Rs. 11, against the average amount of Rs. 8. Against this, Bhucho Mandi provided only one rupee per head. Raman Mandi did not spend a single penny on recreational facilities.

In 1992-93, the amount of subsidy on recreational facilities rose to Rs. 30.42 lakh from Rs. 13.80 lakh in 1987-88 (Table 6.4). It registered an increase of 120 per cent against 126 per cent earlier between 1982-83 and 1987-88. Obviously, there has been a slow growth of subsidy during this period comparatively. Once again, Bathinda municipality shared the dominant proportion of 92 per cent. It's share earlier in 1987-88 made 94 per cent in total amount of subsidy on recreational service in the district. Bhucho Mandi was next to Bathinda with more than 5 per cent of total subsidy. Rampura Phul, the second largest town in the district, was now relegated to third position. It shared less than two per cent of total subsidy amount on recreational facilities in the district in 1992-93. On the other side of the scale, Raman Mandi provided the smallest amount of Rs. 10 thousand, making for less than half of a per cent in total amount of subsidy. Notably, it was for the first time that Raman Mandi made an investment in recreational facilities. In per capita terms, inter-municipal disparities in subsidy amount were still larger. It varied from a high of Rs. 24 per capita in Bathinda city to a low of one rupee only in Raman Mandi, Bhucho Mandi, a Class IV town, ranked second after Bathinda city. Rampura Phul, second largest town in the district, provided only Rs. 2 per head per annum. The average for all the five municipalities was Rs. 17.

In 1996-97, when the municipal subsidy on recreational services rose to Rs. 37.21 lakh, the annual increase in subsidy came down to only 22 per cent. Earlier, between 1987-88 and 1992-93 subsidy on this service increased by 120 per cent. Evidently, the increase in subsidy on recreational facilities has been slowing down over the period after attaining its peak between 1982-83 and 1987-88. It shows that the municipal expenditure on recreational facilities slowed down in the nineties as compared to the eighties. In the nineties, the municipalities began facing a resource crunch, as the state and central governments were reducing their expenditures after the initiation of new economic policies. Recreational facilities, not being in the priority list of municipal governments, suffered greatly in this regard (Fig. 6.1).

There has been wide inter-municipal variation in share of subsidy amount on recreational facilities. It varied from a high of more than 90 per cent of total subsidy amount for all the five municipalities to a low of less than half of a per cent in Raman Mandi town. Bhucho Mandi, a Class IV town, was distantly behind Bathinda town with more than 6 per cent. Rampura Phul, a Class III town and second largest town in the district shared only about two per cent of total subsidy amount. Though the

Fig 6.1

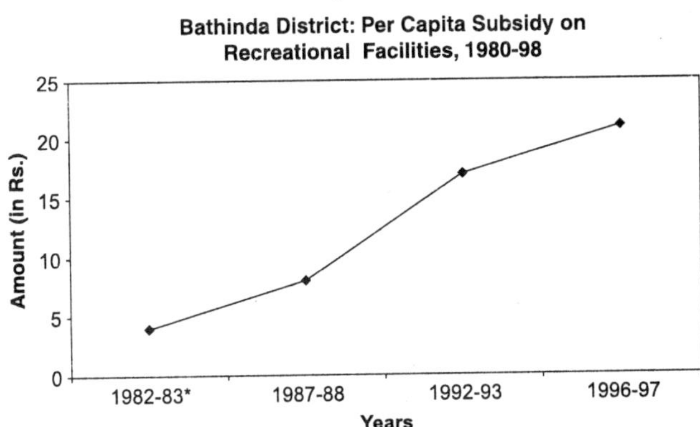

*Annual averages, calculated at the mid-year. For example, subsidy amount from 1980 to 1985 has been used to calculate per capita subsidy in 1982-83 and so on.

subsidy amount given by Bathinda municipality increased by 20 per cent between 1992-93 and 1996-97, its share in total subsidy amount on recreational facilities came down to 90 per cent from 92 per cent during the same period. Its share in total subsidy amount on recreational facilities gradually came down. This was mainly due to substantial increase in the amount of subsidy by other municipal towns.

In per capita terms, it varied from a high Rs. 30 per capita in Bhucho Mandi town to a low of only rupee one in Raman Mandi town (Table 6.4). For the first time, Bhucho Mandi town reached the top relegating Bathinda city to the second position with Rs. 29 per capita per annum. The third position was held by Goniana Mandi town with Rs. 4 per capita and Rampura Phul, the second largest town in the district, was at fourth rank with Rs. 2 per capita.

Spatial Discrimination in Subsidy on Recreational Facilities

Old and congested parts in all the towns in Bathinda district suffer badly on this count. In their distribution, the parks are generally located in new localities developed under the urban planning schemes or as part of the planned housing colonies by the Indian Railways, Fertilizers Corporation of India and other Central organisations for their employees. The parks have been developed along the major highways at the intersections of major transport routes, and near government offices and industrial establishments.

There are hardly any such parks in the old parts of these towns. For example, there is no park in the old parts of Bathinda town. More than 25 parks in the city are confined mainly to more open areas or institutional complexes. During the summer season, particularly in the months of May, June and July, the residents living in the old congested localities in the inner parts of the city have to stay inside their houses in scorching heat in the absence of parks in their surroundings. Against this, residents in Civil Lines or those living in localities adjoining the Rose Garden enjoy open air and relatively cool breeze during the summer months. In addition, there is a children park in the Civil Lines area and the Rose Garden is blessed with multiple facilities of a high standard. Civil Lines has a swimming pool also, fitted with modern facilities. It spreads over 1.5 acres of land and was constructed at the cost of Rs. 20 lakh.

Located along the branch of Sirhind canal on 22 acres of land, the Rose Garden has the children traffic park, Manmohni hill, open air theatre, Rose bud canteen, fountains and lights, a large variety of flowers, ornamental trees and bushes and swings for children. It was developed at the cost of Rs. 15 lakh and more than Rs. 3 lakh are annually spent on its maintenance.

Obviously, the subsidy on recreational facilities is generally enjoyed by the residents of those parts of the towns where these are located. The residents in the old and congested parts of the towns remain deprived of the subsidy element on recreational facilities. The old, congested and poor income group localities in different towns in the district are at a disadvantage in this regard.

Main Highlights

- Notwithstanding the significance of recreational facilities in enrichment of cultural life in towns and to keep residents physically and mentally healthy, these services are generally neglected by municipalities in Bathinda district. There are only four out of eight municipal towns in the district which were regularly spending on recreational facilities during 1980-98. Raman Mandi has been irregular and Maur Mandi, Sangat Mandi and Kot Fatta did not provide recreational facilities to their residents. It is mainly Bathinda and Bhucho Mandi which maintain a good network of parks, gardens, etc. as recreational facilities for their residents.

- During 1980-98, municipalities in Bathinda district incurred an amount of Rs. 22.17 lakh on annual average basis on recreational facilities. This amount made up only 2.82 per cent of total average annual municipal expenditure on urban services in the district. About nine-tenths of this amount was shared by Bathinda municipality. Bathinda alongwith Rampura Phul and Bhucho Mandi towns incurred about 99 per cent of the total municipal expenditure on recreational facilities in the district. It shows that recreational services exist just in name in other towns except in Bathinda, Rampura Phul and Bhucho Mandi towns.

  Bathinda municipal town, which is the largest town in the district and maintains more than 25 parks, one Rose Garden and one Swimming pool as recreational facility, shared the largest amount of total municipal expenditure on this count in the district during 1980-98. Its share varied from a minimum of 45 per cent in 1982-83 to a maximum of 95 per cent in 1987-88. Over the period, its share in total municipal expenditure in the district on recreational facilities recorded a decline with increased amount of expenditure by other municipalities.
- Municipal expenditure on recreational services has been growing during 1980-98, but with a slowed down growth rate. While the municipal expenditure on recreational facilities increased by 149 per cent between 1982-83 and 1987-88, it increased by only 26 per cent between 1992-93 and 1996-97. This indicates how recreational facilities fell victim to the financial resource crunch which the municipal administration had been facing after the policy of cuts in public expenditure followed in the post-economic reform period in India.
- There has been wide inter-municipal variation in growth of municipal expenditure on recreational facilities. During 1980-98, Bhucho Mandi town municipality recorded the highest increase of more than 20 times in its expenditure on recreational facilities. It was followed by Bathinda city with about 13 times increase. In contrast, Rampura Phul registered

a sharp decline in expenditure on recreational facilities. Raman Mandi was not regular in spending on this count.

- Of all the five towns, which were spending on recreational facilities, Bathinda has been the only town that earned some income from this service. In rest of the municipal towns, this service was provided free of cost. Bathinda town, which started the revenue income from this service after 1984-85, earned an average annual income of Rs. 2.56 lakh by way of bidding of contracts for Blue Fox restaurant, adjacent to the Rose Garden, a canteen, parking fee from parking lots near the Rose Garden and swimming pool in the Civil Lines. Income from all such sources made only 13 per cent of its total expenditure on recreational facilities during 1980-98. This shows that the recreational facility in towns of Bathinda district has been highly subsidized.
- On annual average basis, municipalities in Bathinda provided an amount of Rs. 19.61 lakh as subsidy on recreational facilities during 1980-98. This amount made more than 88 per cent of the total municipal expenditure in the district on this service annually. In other words, municipalities in Bathinda district recover only less than Rs. 12 out of every Rs. 100 incurred as expenditure on recreational facilities. More than 87 per cent of this subsidy amount was shared by Bathinda city alone. Bathinda along with Rampura Phul and Bhucho Mandi towns shared nearly 99 per cent of total subsidy amount provided by five municipalities in the district.
- On per capita basis, municipalities in Bathinda district provided Rs. 11 as subsidy on recreational facility, on average annual basis, during 1980-98. There are wide inter-municipal disparities in this regard. It varied from a high of Rs. 15 in Bathinda municipality to a low of only forty paisa in Raman Mandi. The latter is not regularly spending on this count. Bhucho Mandi, a Class IV town, was next to Bathinda city with Rs. 11 per capita during the same period. Rampura Phul, the second largest town in the district, provided only Rs. 4 on this count. However, in 1982-83 Rampura Phul was at the top with Rs. 10 per capita. The same place of pride was available to Bhucho Mandi town in 1996-97 when it registered the highest per capita amount of Rs. 30 as subsidy on recreational facilities.

- Although the per capita amount of subsidy on recreational facilities has increased over the period in the district, but its growth has been slowing down over the period. While, it grew by about 113 per cent between 1987-88 and 1992-93, the growth rate came down to only about 24 per cent during 1992-93 – 1996-97. It seems that the resource crunch which the municipal administration faced in the nineties under the economic reforms programme, where cut in public expenditure had been one of the important measures, hit hard the provision of recreational facility rendered by the municipal administration to its residents in all the towns.
- There has been wide intra-town discrimination in distribution of subsidy on recreational facilities in towns of Bathinda district. In all the urban centres in the district, these facilities are generally located in the newly planned or high income localities. The institutional enterprises also have these facilities in their proximity. The old congested localities, mostly in inner parts of all the towns in the district, are at a disadvantage in this regard.

SECTION III

7

Subsidy Component in Urban Services

This chapter presents a consolidated picture of the subsidy element in urban services arrived at in the preceding chapters. In this regard, the following important questions have been probed:

1. What is the aggregate amount of subsidy that the municipal bodies in Bathinda district pass on to their residents in the process of providing different urban services to them?
2. What has been the trend in subsidy component?
3. What are the inter-municipal variations in the distribution of subsidy?
4. Which of the urban services are highly subsidized and which are not? and
5. If the subsidy component is high in urban services, how can it be rationalized?

For understanding spatial discrimination in distribution of subsidies within towns, the availability, quality and spatial spread of different urban services have been mapped. In addition, extensive fieldwork was undertaken to observe the socio-economic gradient in different towns. Four towns, namely, Bathinda, Rampura Phul, Bhucho Mandi and Sangat Mandi have been picked up for a detailed examination, as the representatives of Class I, Class III, Class IV and Class VI towns respectively in the district.

Spatial organisation of different urban services and temporal changes therein have been mapped to understand the gaps in their spatial coverage and quality of services available.

AGGREGATE AMOUNT OF SUBSIDY

During 1980-98, eight municipalities in Bathinda district provided an aggregate amount of Rs. 928.3 million as subsidy on major urban services. This amount excludes municipal expenditure on slum improvement, being a location specific and irregular expenditure. It makes up about 92 per cent of the total municipal expenditure of Rs. 1009.98 million incurred on major urban services by different municipal towns in the district. On an annual average basis, subsidy amount comes to Rs. 51.6 million or Rs. 31 per capita during 1980-98 (Table 7.1). An average amount of about Rs. 4.54 million per annum is the income to municipalities from the urban services rendered by them to their residents. In other words, Rs. 92 out of each Rs. 100 incurred by different municipalities in the district goes as a subsidy element. Evidently, urban services in the district are highly subsidized.

The amount of subsidy on urban services in the district has been growing over the period. While it was only Rs. 18.25 million, on annual average basis, in 1982-83, it rose to Rs. 107.22 million in 1996-97, recording an increase of 488 per cent in 18 years. In per capita terms, it increased to Rs. 65 from Rs. 11 during the same period. Growth of subsidy had, thus, been slower in per capita terms in comparison to aggregate amount (Fig. 7.1). Another notable fact about subsidy amount is that the growth of subsidy amount has been slowing down over the years. This is true both in terms of aggregate as well as per capita amount. Aggregate amount of subsidy increased by 94 per cent between 1982-83 and 1987-88, when it rose to Rs. 35.39 million in 1987-88 from Rs. 18.25 million in 1982-83. It further increased by 102 per cent between 1987-88 and 1992-93. But the growth came down to only about 50 per cent between 1992-93 and 1996-97. Similarly, per capita amount increased by 100 per cent between 1982-83 and 1987-88, but came down to only about 48 per cent between 1992-93 and 1996-97 (Table 7.2).

It is to be noted here that in July 1991, the Indian government initiated economic reforms to curtail public expenditure and reduction in subsidies on public goods and services had been one of the major objectives. The decline in rate of increase in municipal subsidies on urban services after 1992-93 in Bathinda district indicates that even the municipal subsidies could not

TABLE 7.1

Bathinda District: Distribution of Subsidy on Different Urban Services, 1980-98

Name of urban services	*1982-83**		*1987-88**		*1992-93**		*1996-97***		*1980-98**	
	Subsidy (Rs. in lakhs)	*Subsidy Per capita (Rs.)*	*Subsidy (Rs. in lakhs)*	*Subsidy Per capita (Rs.)*	*Subsidy (Rs. in lakhs)*	*Subsidy Per capita (Rs.)*	*Subsidy (Rs. in lakhs)*	*Subsidy Per capita (Rs.)*	*Subsidy (Rs. in lakhs)*	*Subsidy Per capita (Rs.)*
Water supply	13.80 (7.56)	7	21.52 (6.16)	11	54.50 (7.62)	27	78.98 (7.57)	38	38.67 (7.50)	19
Sewerage	42.27 (23.16)	21	76.12 (21.41)	37	173.82 (24.30)	85	196.57 (18.33)	95	113.88 (22.08)	58
Drainage	23.76 (13.02)	12	35.85 (10.12)	17	40.12 (5.61	20	73.27 (6.83)	36	39.92 (7.74)	19
Roads	39.89 (21.85)	19	77.30 (21.83)	38	134.92 (18.87)	66	235.89 (22.0)	115	109.34 (21.20)	53
Street Lighting	11.23 (6.15)	5	23.15 (6.54)	11	54.92 (7.68)	27	74.82 (6.98)	36	26.69 (5.18)	13
Health and Sanitation	42.77 (23.43)	21	95.44 (26.95)	46	205.96 (28.80)	100	344.45 (32.13)	167	153.00 (29.66)	75
Fire Brigade Service	2.72 (1.49)	1	10.67 (3.01)	5	20.54 (2.87)	10	31.01 (2.89)	15	14.61 (2.83)	8
Recreational Facilities	6.10 (3.34)	3	13.80 (3.90)	7	30.42 (4.25)	15	37.20 (3.47)	18	19.61 (3.80)	11
All facilities	182.54 (100)	11	353.85 (100)	22	715.20 (100)	44	1072.19 (100.0)	65	515.72 (100)	31

*Quinquennial averages. ** Triennium average.

Notes: (i) Figures in parentheses indicate to percentage share in total.

(ii) Per capita subsidy has been calculated on the basis of 1981 Census data. In case of Bathinda population figures for calculating subsidies confined to areas falling under the Bathinda M.C. jurisdiction. Two public sector units, Fertilizer and Thermal Plant make their own arrangements and have been excluded from the calculations/computations.

Source: Data calculated from *Classified Abstracts* of different municipalities for various years.

Fig. 7.1

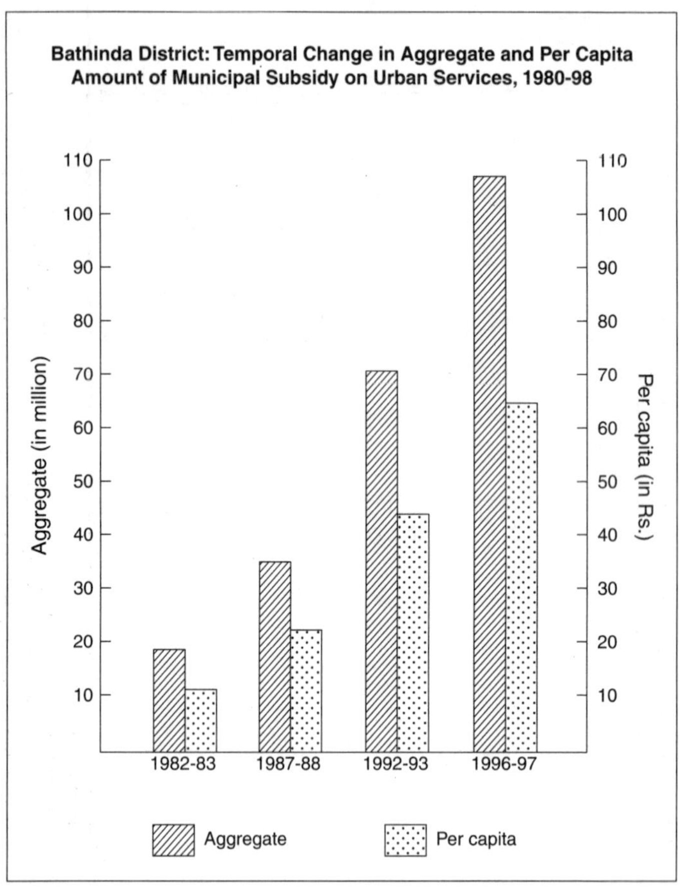

TABLE 7.2

Bathinda District: Temporal Change in Aggregate and Per Capita Amount of Municipal Subsidy on Urban Services, 1980-98

Subsidy Amount	*1982-83*	*1987-88*	*Change in %*	*1992-93*	*Change over 1987-88*	*1996-97*	*Change over 1992-93*
Aggregate (in million)	18.25	35.39	93.9	71.52	102	107.22	50.0
Per capita (in Rs.)	11	22	100	44	100	65	48

escape from the effect of the reforms agenda, initiated at the national level. It is, however to be remembered that the subsidy element in urban services directly depended upon municipal expenditure on various urban services. Here, the sharp decline in growth rate of subsidy on urban services in Bathinda district after 1992-93 indicated a slowing down of municipal expenditure on different urban services in the district and hence involved a compromise on the available quality of urban services in towns of the district.

INTER-SERVICE VARIATIONS IN SUBSIDY

Of all the municipal services, health and sanitation received the highest amount of the total subsidy provided by the municipalities in Bathinda district, on average annual basis, during 1980-98. On this service, municipalities provided an amount of Rs. 15.30 million or 29.70 per cent of total average annual subsidy in the district (Table 7.1). This was followed by the subsidy on sewerage with Rs. 11.39 million or 22 per cent and then by the construction and maintenance of municipal roads with Rs. 10.93 million or 21.2 per cent. In this way, nearly three-fourth or 72.9 per cent of total subsidy has gone to three services of health and sanitation, sewerage and maintenance of municipal roads.

On the other side of the scale, fire brigade service, concerned with public safety, received only an amount of Rs. 1.46 million or 2.83 per cent, the lowest for any of the eight services included here. Water supply, an important component of public health, received about Rs. 3.9 million or 7.6 per cent. Drainage, open and underground, received another Rs. 4 million or 7.75 per cent. Recreational facilities, considered important in the context of present day urban life, received only Rs. 1.96 million or 3.80 per cent. Distribution of aggregate amount of subsidy on different municipal services goes hand in hand with per capita amount of subsidy. In other words, higher the aggregate amount of the subsidy on a municipal service, higher is the per capita amount of subsidy on that service and *vice versa*.

Over the period, the subsidy amount has been growing. However, the growth in subsidy amount has been different for different services. For example, not only the amount of subsidy but also its growth has been faster in case of sewerage, municipal roads, health and sanitation. The growth of subsidy amount has been much faster, in their case, between 1987-88 and 1992-93. In consonance with municipal expenditure on urban services, growth in subsidy amount for all services has been the fastest between 1987-88 and 1992-93 and the slowest between 1992-93 and 1996-97. However, slowing down the growth in subsidy amount has been gradual in case of health and sanitation and maintenance of municipal roads but sharp in all other services.

During 1982-83, Rs. 18.25 million has been the average annual amount of subsidy on urban services. The highest amount (Rs. 4.28 million) was given on health and sanitation, making 23.4 per cent of the total subsidy amount. This was followed by sewerage with Rs. 4.23 million or 23.2 per cent. Both the services, in combination, received nearly Rs. 8.5 million or more than 46 per cent of the total subsidy amount by all the municipalities. Construction and maintenance of municipal roads is the third highest gainer in this regard. It received about Rs. 4 million or 22 per cent. In this way, the combined subsidy share of three services of health and sanitation, sewerage and municipal roads comes to about 68 per cent or more than two-thirds in total subsidy amount during 1982-83. If the drainage is also added to this list, these four services, in combination, share more than four-fifths of the total subsidy on urban services in Bathinda district.

In contrast, the combined share of the fire brigade and recreational facilities made only about 5.0 per cent of the total subsidy amount. Individually, the share of recreational services comes to only 3.3 per cent in total. Since, the subsidy element in an urban service is strongly associated with the municipal expenditure on that service, it is not difficult to estimate the plight of recreational services like parks, play grounds, and green belts in towns of Bathinda district.

During 1987-88, when the average amount of subsidy rose to Rs. 35.39 million from Rs. 18.25 in 1982-83, health and sanitation further consolidated its position by cornering about 27 per cent of the total subsidy amount provided by all municipal towns in the district. Earlier in 1982-83, it shared only 23.4 per cent. Against this, the subsidy share on sewerage, the second largest subsidy provided to an urban service, declined to 21.4 per cent from 23.2 per cent in 1982-83. The subsidy share on drainage registered further decline from its previous share (10.1 per cent from 13.0 per cent). However, the share of construction and maintenance of municipal roads in total subsidy amount remained almost at the same level. On the whole, four services, namely, health and sanitation, sewerage, municipal roads and drainage cornered more than four-fifths of the share, which was equal to their combined share in 1982-83. In this way, losses to drainage and sewerage were compensated by the gains experienced in the case of health and sanitation.

After health and sanitation, another notable increase in subsidy share was experienced by the fire brigade service, whose share increased by 1.52 per cent. The share of recreational facilities also registered a marginal gain. In contrast, like sewerage, water supply also registered a decline in its share to 6.16 per cent from 7.56 per cent between 1982-83 and 1987-88. On the whole, four services such as health and sanitation, sewerage, drainage and municipal roads continued to maintain their dominance in total subsidy amount on urban services in the district, health and sanitation recorded the highest gain and sewerage the maximum loss. Other important losers and gainers were water supply and fire brigade services, respectively.

In 1992-93, when average annual subsidy amount increased to Rs. 71.43 million from Rs. 35.39 million in 1987-88, health and sanitation further consolidated its position, as its share rose to about 29 per cent from about 27 per cent in 1987-88. This was followed by sewerage with more than 24 per cent. Earlier in 1987-88, sewerage shared little over 21 per cent. Their combined share was now more than half (53.1 per cent) the total, against about 48 per cent earlier in 1987-88. In contrast, municipal roads and drainage, the third and fourth ranking services in terms of subsidy share, recorded significant decline in their respective shares. The share of the former declined to about 19 per cent from 22 per cent and of the latter to 5.61 per cent from 10.12 per cent between 1987-88 and 1992-93. Their combined share, thus, came down to less than 25 per cent from about 32 per cent during this period. The sharpest decline has been in the case of drainage whose share declined by about 5 per cent from 10.12 per cent to 5.61 per cent. This was by far a significantly large decline in the shares of drainage and roads that the combined share of the four highly subsidized urban services came down to about 78 per cent from more than 80 per cent in 1988-87.

On the other hand, most of the low subsidized urban services recorded an increase in their respective shares. Particularly, water supply registered an increase of 1.42 per cent in its share during the period. Recreational facilities also recorded a considerable increase in share, from 3.90 per cent in 1987-88 to 4.25 per cent in 1992-93. The decade of the 1980s was declared as the International Decade for Water Supply by the World Health Organisation. At the same time, at the national level, the Government of India decided to get rid off the night-soil disposing system (whereby it was manually disposed off by carrying on the head) from urban areas in a phased manner, by expanding the underground sewerage system in urban centres. These factors, together provided a boost to the expenditure on water supply and sanitation.

In 1996-97, annual average amount of subsidy rose to Rs. 107.22 million from Rs. 71.52 million in 1992-93. With this increase, the share of health and sanitation further rose to 32.13 per cent from 28.80 per cent in 1992-93. Sewerage, second ranking during the earlier periods, was pushed to the third position by construction and maintenance of municipal roads which was holding the third position till now. While, health and sanitation and roads recorded increase in their respective shares between 1992-93 and 1996-97, sewerage recorded a sharp decline. Another notable fact was a big difference in the proportional shares of the highest and the second highest subsidy shares. The subsidy share of health and sanitation, the highest share, and municipal roads, the second highest share, differed by more 10 per cent.

However, the combined share of three top-most subsidy providing urban services, namely, health and sanitation, municipal roads and sewerage recorded a slight increase from 71.97 in 1992-93 to 72.46 per cent in 1996-97. In fact, the combined increase in shares of health and sanitation and municipal roads was higher than the decline witnessed by sewerage. Municipal bodies do earn some income from sewer connections, while health and sanitation and municipal roads are among the free of charge municipal services. Firstly, there is an effort, at all the spatial scales of administration in India, to reduce the burden of subsidies on public goods and services. Secondly, there has been very little expansion in sewer system in towns of Bathinda district after 1995. It is the combined effect of these two factors that has been responsible for a sharp decline in the share of subsidy on sewerage.

The share of drainage in total subsidy amount, which sharply declined between 1987-88 and 1992-93, had recovered to record an increase of more than 1.0 per cent. Against this, street lighting and recreational services recorded a decline in their respective shares.

GROWTH OF SUBSIDY AMOUNT

In the preceding discussion, we examined percentage share of different urban services in total amount of subsidy amount and the change during 1980-98.

The temporal change in proportional share presents a confusing picture when there is a negative change in proportional share. In fact, the subsidy amount might be growing even if there is a negative change in proportional terms. Therefore, it was thought better to examine the subsidy amount in terms of its growth during 1980-98. Annual compound growth rates have been calculated for quinquennial average amounts of subsidy on different urban services.

During 1980-98, subsidy amount on all the eight urban services grew on annual compound growth rate of more than ten percent (10.33 per cent). Against this, growth rate has been as high as 14.48 per cent for fire brigade service and as low as only 6.45 per cent for drainage (Table 7.3). Sewerage, on which the municipalities in the district provided the second highest amount as well as proportional share of aggregate subsidy amount, recorded the second lowest growth (8.91 per cent). In this way, sewerage and drainage, two of the four top ranking services in subsidy amount and share, have registered the lowest growth rates during 1980-98. Against this, health and sanitation recorded not only the highest amount as well as the share in total subsidy amount but also registered the second highest growth rate (12.28 per cent). Construction and maintenance of municipal roads, the third ranking in proportional share of subsidy amount, recorded a growth rate that was higher than the average for all urban services. In general, services which shared relatively low proportion in total subsidy amount on different services registered growth rate of subsidy higher than the average growth (10.33 per cent) for all services. While the majority of urban services, that shared relatively higher share registered lower or almost equal to the average growth rate during 1980-98. Health and sanitation service was the only exception, recording higher than the average growth rate along with higher than average share in total subsidy amount.

TABLE 7.3

Bathinda District: Growth of Subsidy on Different Urban Services 1980-98

Name of urban service	*Subsidy amount (Rs. in lakh)*				*Annual compound growth rate (in percentage)*			
	1982 -83	*1987 -88*	*1992 -93*	*1996 -97*	*1982-83 over 1987-88*	*1987-88 over 1992-93*	*1992-93 over 1996-97*	*1980 -98*
Water supply	13.80	21.52	54.50	78.98	9.29	20.42	7.70	10.17
Sewerage	42.27	76.12	173.82	196.57	12.48	17.95	2.49	8.91
Drainage	23.76	35.85	40.12	73.27	8.57	2.28	12.80	6.45
Roads	39.89	77.30	134.92	235.89	14.15	11.78	11.82	10.38
Street Lighting	11.23	23.15	54.92	74.82	15.57	18.86	6.38	11.10
Health and Sanitation	42.77	95.44	205.96	344.45	17.41	16.63	10.83	12.28
Fire Brigade Service	2.72	10.67	20.54	31.01	31.44	14.00	8.59	14.48
Recreational Facilities	6.10	13.80	30.42	37.20	17.73	17.13	4.10	10.56
All Facilities	182.54	353.85	715.20	1072.19	14.15	15.11	8.43	10.33

On the whole, two (sewerage and drainage) of the three important urban services (sewerage, drainage and health and sanitation), having significant bearing on quality of urban life, have recorded the slowest growth rates of subsidy amount during 1980-98. Notably, the subsidy element on different urban services in the district has been a function of the municipal expenditure on them. Obviously, there has been slow growth in municipal expenditure on important urban services such as sewerage and drainage in the district.

The growth rates of subsidy amount have been changing fast over the period. For all the services, while the growth of subsidy has been the highest (15.11 per cent) between 1987-88 and 1992-93, and the lowest (8.43 per cent) between 1992-93 and 1966-97. It shows that the subsidy component has been growing slowly, increasing steadily during the 1990s.

Among all the urban services, health and sanitation is one such service where growth of subsidy has always been higher than the average for all the services. While, the reverse is not true for any of the services. Between 1982-83 and 1987-88, the fire brigade service recorded the highest growth (31.44 per cent) against the lowest (8.57 per cent) in the case of drainage. Five of the eight services included in the analysis, recorded a growth rate which was higher than the average for all (14.15 per cent). Between 1987-88 and 1992-93, when average growth had been 15.11 per cent, it ranged from a high of 20.43 per cent in water supply to a low of 2.28 per cent in drainage. Notably, growth of subsidy on drainage had been the lowest earlier too. Once again, majority of services recorded a higher growth of subsidy than the average. Nevertheless, there were only three services where growth rate of subsidy amount has been higher this time as compared to earlier. During 1992-93 to 1996-97 when overall growth of subsidy on urban services dipped to only 8.43 per cent from 15.11 per cent earlier, it ranged from a high of 12.80 per cent in drainage to a low of 2.49 per cent in sewerage. Except in the case of drainage and roads, growth rate of subsidy has been lower during this period in comparison to the earlier period. Notably, growth rate of subsidy amount has been the lowest in case of both drainage and roads earlier, during 1987-88 to 1992-93. In a way, the period from 1992-93 to 1996-97 has been a period of slow growth in subsidy amount on urban services in the district.

INTER-MUNICIPAL DISPARITIES IN DISTRIBUTION OF SUBSIDY

After an examination of inter-service variations in distribution of subsidy, we analyse here the inter-municipal variations in distribution of subsidy on different urban services in the district. As stated earlier, municipalities in Bathinda district incurred an amount of Rs. 561.1 lakh per annum on eight major urban services[1]

1. Eight urban services include water supply, sewerage, drainage, roads, street lighting, health and sanitation, fire brigade service and recreational facilities. Environmental improvement of slums, which has also been studied in this dissertation, has been excluded here for two reasons: (i) expenditure on slums improvement is not regularly spent by municipalities, and (ii) expenditure under this head is specific to target areas and target population. However, an aggregate amount of Rs. 266.13 lakh was spent by all municipalities on slum improvement during 1980-98.

during 1980-98. An amount of Rs. 515.72 lakh or about 92 per cent has been the subsidy element. In this way, municipal administration in the district gets back only a meagre amount of Rs. 45.38 lakh or about 8 per cent of it on annual average basis. There were, however, wide inter-municipal variations in this regard.

The subsidy share ranged from a high of about 94 per cent in Bathinda city to a low of 79 per cent in Sangat Mandi town (Table 7.4). The former is the largest and the latter the smallest, in population size, in the district. However, the share of subsidy of different towns in the district does not find one to one correspondence. Kot Fatta, a Class V and the second smallest population size town in the district, had the second highest share (93.22 per cent) after Bathinda city. Similarly, Bhucho Mandi, a Class IV and the third smallest town in the district, recorded the third highest share. It is interesting to note that Kot Fatta, which provide only four out of eight urban services to its residents, recorded the second highest subsidy share after Bathinda city, which was rendering all the eight services. In fact, average annual expenditure of Kot Fatta on urban services was only Rs. 2.36 lakh. This amount was not only the lowest for any of the eight towns in the district but also only about half a per cent (0.57 per cent) of total annual expenditure incurred by Bathinda city. Of the four urban services, public health and sanitation, roads, drainage and water supply, it is only the water supply service from which Kot Fatta earns some income. The remaining three services are provided free of cost by all the municipalities including Kot Fatta.

Urban services, such as sewerage, recreational facilities and fire brigade, which are priced services, have not been provided by Kot Fatta. This explains the high proportional share of subsidy element on urban services in the case of Kot Fatta town. On the other side of the scale, Bhucho Mandi town, which provided the third highest percentage share of subsidy in the district, is the richest of all the municipal towns in the district. It receives the highest per capita income and provides seven out of the eight services included in the study. Not only is the quality of services, which it provides to its residents, quite good but also there is little spatial discrimination in distribution of services. Perhaps, the criterion of economic efficiency is found difficult to respect

TABLE 7.4

Bathinda District: Aggregate Distribution of Subsidy on Urban Services in Different Towns, 1980-98

Name of tou	*Civic status*	*Expenditure on urban services*			*Subsidy on urban services*			*Subsidy as% of expenditure*
		Total (Rs. in lakh)	*%age*	*Per capita (Rs.)*	*Total (Rs. in lakh)*	*%age*	*Per capita (Rs.)*	
Bathinda	I	414.48	73.87	358	388.31	75.30	333	93.69
Rampura Phul	III	50.80	9.05	159	44.89	8.70	141	88.37
Maur Mandi	III	24.40	4.35	129	21.22	4.11	113	86.97
Raman Mandi	IV	21.61	3.85	151	18.55	3.60	130	85.84
Goniana Mandi	IV	19.79	3.52	230	15.94	3.09	187	80.55
Bhucho Mandi	IV	25.28	4.50	323	22.72	4.40	291	89.87
Kot Fatta	V	2.36	0.42	47	2.20	0.43	44	93.22
Sangat Mandi	VI	2.38	0.42	83	1.89	0.37	66	79.41
All Towns		561.10	100.00	279	515.72	100.00	256	91.91

fully by the municipal administration in Bhucho Mandi town, while taking into account the quality of services and spatial justice in their distribution. This is perhaps a reason for the high share of subsidy component of Bhucho Mandi town.

Sangat Mandi town, which provided the lowest share of subsidy on urban services in the district, gave only five of the eight urban services being studied. Secondly, its income from water supply service has been relatively higher in comparison to other towns.

More than three-fourths (75.3 per cent) of the total average annual subsidy is provided by a single municipality of Bathinda city. Against this, Bathinda city shares only about 60 per cent of the total urban population and about 74 per cent of the total municipal expenditure on urban services in the district. In contrast, Rampura Phul and Maur Mandi towns, two Class III towns in the district, shared, in combination, 12.81 per cent of the total annual average subsidy amount against 13.4 per cent expenditure on urban services in the district. Similarly, Goniana Mandi town's share in total municipal expenditure is also higher (3.52 per cent) than its share in the subsidy amount (3.1 per cent).

In per capita terms, inter-municipal disparities in subsidy amount were still sharp. It ranged from a high of Rs. 333 per capita in Bathinda City to a low of only Rs. 44 in Kot Fatta. The average for all municipal towns had been Rs. 256 per capita. Kot

Fatta municipality provides only four out of eight urban services to their residents. Secondly, its per capita expenditure on urban services has also been one of the lowest of all the towns in the district.

Bhucho Mandi town needs special mention for providing the second highest (Rs. 291) per capita amount of subsidy despite being a Class IV town and sixth ranking in population size. It has one of the highest per capita incomes in the district. Naturally, the administration here has been in a position to provide large number of urban services and also maintain them well. Infact Municipal expenditure on urban services and the subsidy element finds a strong positive association. Higher the expenditure on a service in a town, higher is the subsidy element in that service. For example, both the per capita expenditure and per capita subsidy by Kot Fatta town were lowest among all the towns in the district.

Rampura Phul and Maur Mandi towns, two Class III towns in the district, provided relatively low per capita amount of subsidy on urban services in comparison to Goniana Mandi and Bhucho Mandi towns, both Class IV towns in the district. In brief, towns which incurred higher expenditure on urban services by virtue of higher income, were able to provide higher amount of subsidy both in aggregate and per capita terms. While there has been a broad conformity between the civic status of a town and its proportional share of subsidy on urban services, this was all the more true of per capita amount of subsidy. Class III towns, in general, provided lesser amount of per capita subsidy on urban services in comparison to Class IV towns in the district.

In the following is an examination of the inter-municipal differentials in subsidy component on urban services.

INTER-MUNICIPAL DIFFERENTIALS IN SUBSIDY ON SERVICES

Notably, four out of the eight services examined here are provided free of charge to their residents by the towns in the district. Such services include public health and sanitation, drainage, street lighting and maintenance of municipal roads. An amount of Rs. 328.95 lakhs, making about 64 per cent in total subsidy amount (Rs. 515.72 lakh), on average annual basis during

1980-98, went as subsidy on these four services. Of the remaining four, which fetch some income to the municipalities, recreational services are charged only in Bathinda city. Here, the municipality earned income from the auctioning off of conveniences like the restaurant inside the Rose Garden in the city, parking lots and stalls. In other towns, recreational facilities mainly as parks are provided free of cost to the residents. Fire brigade, another facility, though chargeable in certain cases, had hardly any income to its credit in any of the four towns that had been rendering this service during 1980-98. Hence, it is only water supply and sewerage services which fetch some income in all the municipalities in the district.

This explains the high subsidy component in urban services in the district. However, the amount of subsidy on urban services differs widely from service to service and municipality to municipality.

On public health and sanitation, which is an entirely subsidized urban service in the district, municipalities provided an aggregate amount of Rs. 153.0 lakh as subsidy on average annual basis during 1980-98. This amount made up nearly 30 per cent in aggregate amount of subsidy. Of this amount, more than two-thirds or 67 per cent was shared by Bathinda municipal town alone (Table 7.5). Another 13 per cent was shared by Rampura Phul, the second largest town in the district. Against this, their combined population made up 73 per cent of the total urban population in the district in 1991. It is, however, notable that subsidy on public health and sanitation made only 26.4 per cent in total amount of subsidy. While this share was as high as 44.5 per cent in Rampura Phul. The share of subsidy on public health and sanitation ranged from a low of about 11.0 per cent in Kot Fatta to a high of about 50 per cent in Maur Mandi town, with 30 per cent being the average for all towns. Half the municipalities provided for higher than this share.

Sewerage, which accounts for more than half (22.1 per cent) of the aggregate annual (average) subsidy amount on all major urban services in the district, recorded much wider differentials in distribution of subsidy on this account. Firstly, two of the smallest population sized towns, Kot Fatta and Sangat Mandi, did not provide this facility to their residents. Secondly, more than nine-tenths (92.2 per cent) of the total subsidy on this count was shared

TABLE 7.5

Bathinda District: Distribution of Subsidy by Urban Services in Different Towns, 1980-98

(Amount in lakh rupees)

Name of town	*Name of the service*																	
	Public health and sanitation		*Sewerage*		*Roads*		*Drainage*		*Water supply*		*Street lighting*		*Recreational facilities*		*Fire services*		*All services*	
	Amount	*%*	*Amount*	*%*	*Amount*	*%*	*Amount*	*%*	*Amount*	*%*	*Amount*	*%*	*Amount*	*%*	*Amount*	*%*	*Amount*	*%*
Bathinda	102.45	67	105.01	92.2	79.54	72.7	30.70	76.9	26.50	68.5	17.29	64.8	17.17	87.6	9.65	66.0	388.31	75.3
	(26.4)		(27.0)		(20.5)		(7.9)		(6.8)		(4.5)		(4.4)		(2.5)		(100.0)	
Rampura Phul	19.96	13	4.07	3.6	9.18	8.4	2.99	7.5	1.68	4.3	3.21	12.0	1.32	6.7	2.48	17.0	44.89	8.7
	(44.5)		(9.0)		(20.4)		(6.7)		(3.7)		(7.2)		(2.9)		(5.6)		(100.0)	
Maur Mandi	10.54	6.9	0.63	0.6	4.28	3.9	1.57	3.9	1.16	3.0	1.80	6.7	—	—	1.24	8.5	21.22	4.1
	(49.67)		(3.0)		(20.1)		(7.5)		(5.5)		(8.6)				(5.8)		(100.0)	
Raman Mandi	7.11	4.6	0.89	0.8	4.02	3.7	1.18	3.0	2.51	6.5	1.54	5.8	0.06	0.3	1.24	8.5	18.55	3.6
	(38.3)		(4.8)		(21.7)		(6.4)		(13.5)		(8.3)		(0.3)		(6.7)		(100.0)	
Goniana Mandi	6.44	4.2	0.53	0.5	4.01	3.7	0.82	2.1	2.80	7.2	1.17	4.4	0.17	0.9	—	—	15.94	3.1
	(40.4)		(3.3)		(25.2)		(5.1)		(17.6)		(7.3)		(1.1)				(100.0)	
Bhucho Mandi	5.76	3.8	2.75	2.3	7.57	6.9	1.39	3.5	2.86	7.4	1.50	5.6	0.89	4.5	—	—	22.72	4.4
	(25.4)		(12.1)		(33.3)		(6.1)		(12.6)		(6.6)		(3.9)				(100.0)	
Kot Fatta	0.24	0.2	—	—	0.24	0.2	0.82	2.1	0.90	2.3	—	—	—	—	—	—	2.20	0.4
	(10.9)				(10.9)		(37.3)		(40.9)								(100.0)	
Sangat Mandi	0.50	0.3	—	—	0.50	0.5	0.45	1.0	0.26	0.8	0.18	0.7	—	—	—	—	1.89	0.4
	(26.5)				(26.5)		(23.8)		(13.8)		(9.4)						(100.0)	
All towns	153.00	100	113.88	100	109.34	100	39.92	100	38.67	100	26.69	100	19.61	100	14.61	100	515.72	100
	(29.67)		(22.1)		(21.3)		(7.7)		(7.6)		(5.2)		(3.8)		(2.8)		(100.0)	

Note: Figures in the parenthesis indicates to percent in total amount of subsidy on all services by a town.
Source: Data calculated from *Classified Abstracts* of different municipalities for various years.

by Bathinda city alone (Fig. 7.2). Another about four per cent (3.6 per cent) was shared by the second largest town of Rampura Phul. Bhucho Mandi, the sixth ranking and a Class IV town in the district, shared another 2.3 per cent of the total subsidy. In this way, more than 98 per cent of the total subsidy amount was shared by three of the eight towns in the district. The respective shares of their combined population and area being 77 per cent and 84 per cent. Not only that, subsidy element in this service was not uniformly enjoyed by all residents of the respective towns. As already stated in an earlier chapter on sewerage, only 56 per cent of the population of Bathinda city, 41 per cent of Rampura Phul and 60 per cent of Bhucho Mandi town was covered under sewerage facility. In this way, there has been wide inter and intra-town discrimination in distribution of subsidy on sewerage service in Bathinda district.

Subsidy share on sewerage varied from a minimum of 3 per cent in Maur Mandi town to a maximum of 27 per cent in Bathinda City. Bhucho Mandi, a Class IV and sixth ranking town among the eight towns studied in the district, was placed next only to Bathinda City, a Class one town in the district, with 12.1 per cent. In remaining towns the subsidy share had been less than 10 per cent.

Municipal roads shared another 21.3 per cent of total subsidy on urban services in the district. Bathinda City shared nearly 73 per cent of the total subsidy on this count. Against this, Kot Fatta, a Class V town, shared only a fraction of a per cent (0.2 per cent) in total. In general, the population size and the civic status of towns in the district found positive association with their respective shares in aggregate subsidy amount on municipal roads. Bhucho Mandi, a Class IV town in the district, shared about 7 per cent of the total subsidy amount. Its share was the third highest after Bathinda and Rampura Phul towns, the two largest towns in the district. Against its third rank in subsidy share, Bhucho Mandi ranked sixth in population size among the eight towns in the district.

As regards the share of subsidy on roads, Bhucho Mandi was at the top with more than one-third (33.3 per cent) of its total subsidy amount provided on all urban services. This was not only the highest share among all the towns in the district, but also the highest subsidy share, provided by Bhucho Mandi town

Fig. 7.2

Bathinda District: Temporal Change in Aggregate and Per Capita Amount of Municipal Subsidy on Urban Services, 1980-98

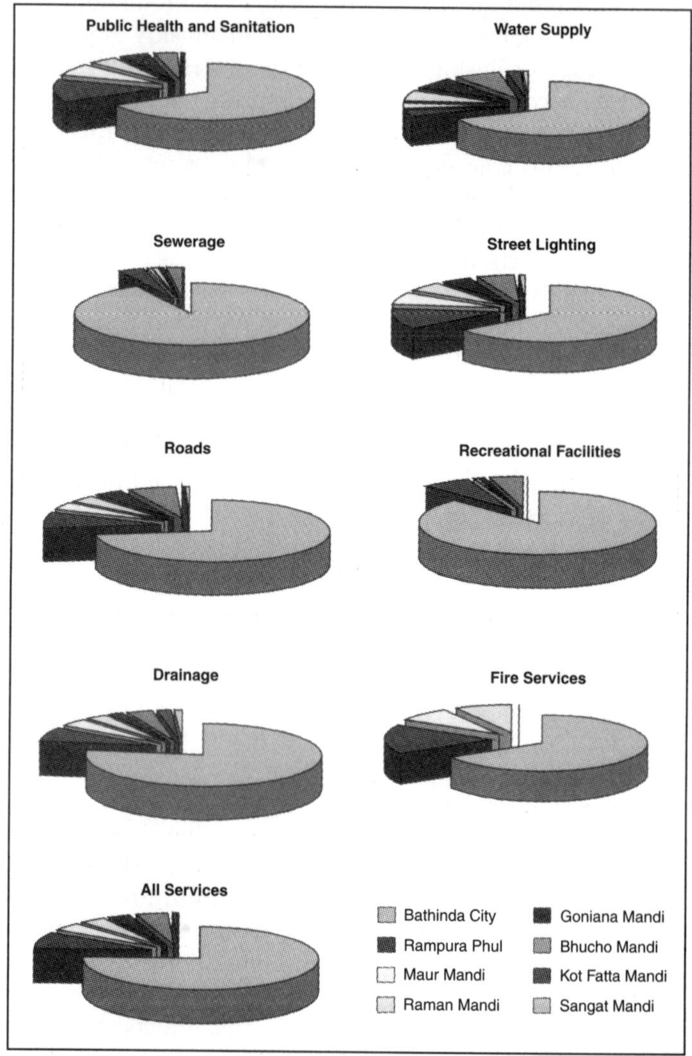

on any of the urban services it provides. This indicates that municipal roads have been receiving top priority from the municipal administration in Bhucho Mandi town.

Bhucho Mandi town was followed by Sangat Mandi, a Class VI and the smallest town in the district, with 26.5 per cent share of its total subsidy amount. Sangat Mandi town provides only five out of the eight services included in the analysis. Secondly, the absolute amount of subsidy provided by Sangat Mandi town on this service was only Rs. 50,000 on average annual basis. Further, the entire township has been declared as a slum area under the slum improvement scheme. Hence, there is hardly any significance attached to a high proportional share of subsidy in the case of Sangat Mandi town. Goniana Mandi town, a Class IV town like Bhucho Mandi, provides a share of 25.2 per cent of its total subsidy amount to roads.

Bathinda City, a Class I town and providing about 73 per cent of total subsidy amount by all municipalities on this service, provided only 20.5 per cent of its total subsidy amount to roads. Almost the same share is provided by Rampura Phul, the second largest town in the district. Half of the towns recorded a share higher than average for all (21.3 per cent). Kot Fatta, a Class V town in the district, provided the lowest share (10.9 per cent), which was nearly half the average share. On the whole, with the exception of Kot Fatta, small-sized municipal towns provided the higher share of subsidy out of their total subsidy amount on all urban services in comparison to the large-sized municipal town. However, in case of share in total subsidy amount on construction and maintenance of municipal roads, the reverse was true.

Subsidy on drainage, which accounts for 7.7 per cent of the total subsidy amount on all urban services ranged from a maximum of 37.3 per cent in Kot Fatta town to a minimum of 5.1 per cent in Goniana Mandi town. There has been hardly any association between the civic status or population size of a town and its subsidy share on drainage.

Of course, there have been wide inter-municipal variations in share of subsidy amount on drainage. There has been a broad association between the town-size category and share of subsidy amount on drainage. Bathinda City alone shared nearly 77 per cent of total subsidy on drainage and Sangat Mandi town shared only 1.0 per cent. Rampura Phul, a Class III and the second largest town in the district, recorded a share of only 7.5 per cent, the second highest share after Bathinda City. Maur Mandi town, another Class III and the third ranking town in the district, shared 3.9 per cent. In this way, three of the top-most towns shared more than 88 per cent of the total subsidy amount on drainage. It is, however, notable that Bhucho Mandi, though smallest of all the three towns in the district, falling in Class IV category of towns, shared the highest percentage share of 3.5 per cent, placing it fourth after Bathinda, Rampura Phul and Maur Mandi towns in terms of the share in total amount of subsidy. This is mainly because it has the most dense network of the drainage system in the district. Its capacity to generate high income from its own revenue sources has been mainly responsible for this.

The share of water supply in total amount of subsidy has been almost the same (7.6 per cent) as drainage (7.7 per cent). Nearly 69 per cent of total subsidy amount was shared by Bathinda municipal town alone. Against this, its share in total urban population in the district has been about 60 per cent. Bathinda City, which is the district headquarters, has to place a number of stand posts at public places for the public. Drinking water supplied through stand posts is free of charge. In addition, the city has a large slum population that is also supplied drinking water free of cost. For these reasons, Bathinda City has to invest more yet earns less from the water supply service. Against this, Rampura Phul, the second largest town, shared only 4.3 per cent of the total subsidy. Bhucho Mandi, a Class IV and sixth ranking town in the district, shared the second highest proportional share (7.4 per cent) in total subsidy.

In case of Class III towns in the district, namely, Rampura Phul, Maur Mandi, and Raman Mandi, water taps dominated the water supply service. The water tap is, in general, a charged service. Hence, municipalities earn revenue from this service, to reduce the burden of subsidy on account of water supply.

Kot Fatta municipal town shared only 2.3 per cent of the total subsidy, yet it made up nearly 41 per cent of the total subsidy amount it provided on all urban services. In contrast, this share made up only less than 4 per cent in Rampura Phul town and less than 7 per cent in case of Bathinda City.

Street lighting, one of the entirely subsidized urban services in the district, shared another 5.2 per cent of total subsidy amount. Bathinda City shared nearly 65 per cent of the total. This share is roughly equal to its area share in total geographical area of urban centres in the district. Rampura Phul, the second largest town in the district, shared another 12 per cent. Their combined share made for more than three-fourths in total subsidy amount on street lighting in the district. Kot Fatta, a Class V town in the district, did not provide this service to its residents, while Sangat Mandi, the smallest town in the district, shared less than one per cent in the total subsidy amount.

Subsidy on street lighting made up as high as about 17 per cent in total subsidy amount provided by Bhucho Mandi town on urban services but as low as less than 5 per cent in Bathinda City, the largest town in the district. Recreational services, provided by only five out of the eight towns in the district, is a charged service only in the case of Bathinda City. Rest of the four towns provide this service free of cost. Bathinda shared nearly 88 per cent of the subsidy amount provided by all the towns in the district on this count. Another about 7 per cent was shared by Rampura Phul, the second largest town in the district. In remaining less than 6 per cent, 4.5 per cent was shared by Bhucho Mandi and the remaining 1.2 per cent was shared between Raman Mandi and Goniana Mandi towns. In the name of recreational services, there were parks developed by different towns, except in Bathinda City which has developed a huge Rose Garden and a restaurant inside the Rose Garden along with several parks in its different parts.

Fire Services, though a charged service, yet hardly earned any income for towns in the district, is rendered by only four towns in the district. These are Bathinda, Rampura Phul, Maur Mandi and Raman Mandi towns. The latter three towns run this service on shared basis. Subsidy amount on fire services made up only about 3 per cent of the total amount of subsidy. This is the lowest share of subsidy for any of the eight services studied here. Two-thirds of the total subsidy amount on this service was shared by Bathinda City. Of the remaining one-third, one-half was shared between Rampura Phul and remaining one-half was equally shared by Maur Mandi and Raman Mandi towns.

INTER-MUNICIPAL DISPARITIES IN PER CAPITA SUBSIDY

Inter-municipal disparities in distribution of subsidies provides not only a more realistic picture of the subsidy element but also of variations in their distribution. Higher per capita amount of subsidy provided by municipal town indicates a variety of factors depicted as follows:

1. Since most of the urban services are highly subsidized, higher the per capita amount of subsidy by a town means higher per capita expenditure on such services, reflecting, in turn, on quality of life in a town;
2. In contrast to above, higher per capita subsidy meant little income from services to a town. The revenue loss to a municipality in the process left it with little for further investment for maintenance and expansion of different urban services; and
3. Lower income to a municipal body from its own sources increases its dependency on grants from the state government, which are, in general, irregular and at times tied up with pre-conditions, leaving little freedom with the municipality to use such amounts in accordance with their own priorities.

In the following an attempt will be made to examine inter-municipal variations in distribution of per capita amount of subsidy on urban services in Bathinda district during 1980-98. In addition, an attempt will also be made to know the highest and the least subsidized urban services in the district and towns.

During 1980-98, all towns in the district spent an annual average amount of Rs. 278 per capita on urban services (Table 7.6). Of this amount, Rs. 256 or 92 per cent was the subsidy element. There are, however, wide inter-municipal variations in this regard. The amount varied from a high of Rs. 333 per capita in Bathinda City to a low of Rs. 44 in Kot Fatta town, making a ratio of 1:7.6 between the two. In other words, residents of Bathinda City received an amount of Rs. 333 per capita as subsidy on different urban services, against only Rs. 44 received by the residents of Kot Fatta town. While Bathinda City provided all the eight services included in the analysis here, Kot Fatta provided only four of them.

TABLE 7.6

Bathinda District: Distribution of Average Annual Per Capita Subsidy by Urban Services in Different Towns, 1980-98

(Figures in Rupees)

Name of municipal town	*Name of the service*								
	Public health and sanitation	*Sewerage*	*Roads*	*Drainage*	*Water supply*	*Street lighting*	*Recreational facilities*	*Fire services*	*All services*
Bathinda	88	91	69	26	23	15	15	8	333
	(88)	(96)	(69)	(26)	(37)	(15)	(17)	(8)	(356)
Rampura Phul	63	13	29	9	5	10	4	8	141
	(63)	(15)	(29)	(9)	(22)	(10)	(4)	(8)	(158)
Maur Mandi	56	3	23	8	6	10	-	7	113
	(56)	(6)	(23)	(8)	(21)	(10)		(7)	(131)
Raman Mandi	50	6	28	8	18	11	0.4	9	130
	(50)	(10)	(28)	(8)	(36)	(11)	(0.4)	(9)	(152.4)
Goniana Mandi	75	6	47	10	33	14	2	—	187
	(75)	(23)	(47)	(10)	(60)	(14)	(2)		(231)
Bhucho Mandi	74	35	97	18	37	19	11	—	291
	(74)	(41)	(97)	(18)	(63)	(19)	(11)		(323)
Kot Fatta	5	—	5	16	18	—	—	—	44
	(5)		(5)	(16)	(21)				(47)
Sangat Mandi	17	—	17	16	9	6	—	—	66
	(17)		(17)	(16)	(26)	(6)			(82)
All towns	75	58	53	19	19	13	11	8	256
	(75)	(63)	(53)	(19)	(35)	(13)	(12)	(8)	(278)

Note: Figures in parentheses indicate per capita average annual expenditure of municipalities on urban services

Bhucho Mandi, a Class IV and sixth ranking town in the district, provided the second highest subsidy amount of Rs. 291 per capita. The third highest subsidy amount of Rs. 187 was provided by Goniana Mandi town, which is also a Class IV town in the district.

Rampura Phul, a Class III and second largest town in the district, provided only Rs. 141 per capita, the fourth highest subsidy amount and it was followed by Raman Mandi, a Class IV town, with Rs. 130 per capita. In all, two municipal towns of Bathinda and Bhucho Mandi provided an amount of subsidy which was higher than the average (Rs. 256) for all the municipalities. Further in per capita amount of subsidy the Class I towns were followed by Class IV towns in the district. The lowest amount was provided by the Class V towns. However, the lowest amount of subsidy by Class V towns was provided not because of high recovery rates in such towns but due to lesser number of urban services provided by these towns as well as the low amount of expenditure on urban services therein.

There has been wide inter-municipal variation in distribution of per capita subsidy on urban services. In the case of public health and sanitation service, which was not only fully subsidized but also the most subsidized urban service in the district, the per capita subsidy amount varied from a high of Rs. 88 in Bathinda City to a low of Rs. 5 in Kot Fatta town. An amount of Rs. 75 was the average for all towns. The highest subsidy amount differed by about 18 times from the lowest.

Goniana Mandi, a Class IV town in the district, provided the second highest amount of Rs. 75 per capita, which was closely followed by Bhucho Mandi town, another Class IV town, with Rs. 74. However, Rampura Phul, a Class III and the second largest town in the district, provided only Rs. 63, which was lower than the average. The Class IV towns, as a category, provided higher per capita amount (Rs. 66) than Class III towns (Rs. 60). Since public health and sanitation is an entirely subsidized urban service, per capita subsidy and per capita expenditure are one and the same thing. This meant that Class V and VI towns invested relatively less in public health and sanitation services, reflecting on the environmental conditions in such towns.

Sewerage, which ranks second after public health and sanitation in terms of per capita amount of subsidy, is only a partially subsidized service. On this account, towns in the district earn Rs. 5 per capita against an expenditure of Rs. 63 per capita. In this way, remaining amount of Rs. 58 per capita was the subsidy element on this service.

Like public health and sanitation, there were wide inter-municipal variations in distribution of per capita subsidy on sewerage also. It ranged from a high of Rs. 91 per capita in Bathinda City to a low of only Rs. 3 in Maur Mandi town. In this way, the highest and the lowest amounts differed by more than 30 times. Earlier in public health and sanitation, this difference was 18 times. Further, it is also to be noted that two municipalities of Kot Fatta and Sangat Mandi were not rendering this service to their residents.

Bhucho Mandi town, providing the second highest amount of Rs. 35 per capita on sewerage, was distantly placed in comparison with Bathinda City. Per Capita subsidy on sewerage provided by Bathinda City was higher by 2.6 times than that of Bhucho Mandi town. Rest of the towns provided a very low amount of subsidy on this count. Rampura Phul, a Class III and the second largest town in the district, provided only Rs. 13 per capita, which was lower by 7 times than the amount provided by Bathinda City.

Municipal roads, which get the third highest amount of subsidy among all the urban services in the district, was a fully subsidized service. Hence, per capita subsidy and expenditure were considered one and the same. The subsidy amount ranged from a high of Rs. 97 in Bhucho Mandi town to a low of only Rs. 5 in Kot Fatta, Rs. 53 being the average. The highest and the lowest amount differed by more than 19 times. In this way, inter-municipal differences in subsidy amount were, though significantly lower than in sewerage, but higher than public health and sanitation. Notably, Bhucho Mandi town, a Class IV town and ranking at sixth place among eight towns in the district in population size, was placed at the top and Bathinda, a Class I town in the district, placed second with only Rs. 69 per capita. Rest of the towns including Rampura Phul, the second largest town in the district, fared far below the average amount for all towns. Per capita subsidy on this count by Rampura Phul municipality (Rs. 29) was nearly one-half of the average for all towns. In fact, Goniana Mandi, a Class IV town, provided subsidy (Rs. 47) that was higher by more than 60 per cent than that provided by Rampura Phul municipality. Class IV towns, as a group, fared very well in this context.

Like roads, drainage is also a fully subsidized urban service. In this way, recovery rate on drainage service is nil. On an average, Rs. 19 per capita was provided as subsidy on drainage per annum during 1980-98. Among municipalities, it ranged from a high of Rs. 26 in Bathinda City to a low of Rs. 8 in Maur Mandi and Raman Mandi towns. The highest and the lowest amount of subsidy differed by more than three times. This is one of the lowest differentials between the two extremes. This service seems to be more or less universal in nature, hence inter-municipal differentials are quite low. It is quite interesting to note that small area and population sized Class V and Class VI towns, fared well in this context. Kot Fatta and Sangat Mandi towns, the two smallest population sized towns, provided an amount (Rs. 16) which was higher by two times of the amount provided by Maur Mandi and Raman Mandi towns, Class III and IV towns, respectively.

Water supply, a partially paid service, incurred a per capita municipal expenditure of Rs. 35. Out of this amount, Rs. 19 or more than 54 per cent was the subsidy element. This is the lowest share of subsidy on any of the eight services included in the analysis. At the municipal level, subsidy amount ranged from a high of Rs. 37 in Bhucho Mandi town to a low of only Rs. 5 in Rampura Phul, two amounts differing by more than seven times. Notably, per capita subsidy was the lowest (Rs. 5.50) for Class III towns and the highest for Class IV towns (Rs. 29), as a group. Water supply sources played a crucial role in this context. In municipal towns, where tap water supply sources dominated among the methods of water supply, provided the lower amount of subsidy in comparison to those towns where the use of posts was wide spread because this is a free source of water supply.

Street lighting, which is again a free of cost urban service, gets another Rs. 13 per capita subsidy. Per capita subsidy on this service varied from a high of Rs. 19 in Bhucho Mandi town to a low of Rs. 6 in Sangat Mandi town, both differing by more than three times. Kot Fatta, a Class V town in the district, did not provide this service to their residents. Bathinda City was placed second after Bhucho Mandi town with Rs. 15 per capita. This was closely followed by Raman Mandi town, a Class IV town, with Rs. 14 per capita. Against this, Class III towns in the district provided Rs. 10 per capita on this account.

Recreational facilities, which have gained importance in modern day city life, received Rs. 11 per capita amount of subsidy during 1980-98. This service however, was provided by only five out of eight towns in the district. Further, it was a free of cost service in all towns except in Bathinda City. Per capita amount ranged from a high of Rs. 15 in Bathinda City to a low of only forty paisa in Raman Mandi town. The highest and the lowest amounts differed by more than 37 times from each other. This is one of the highest differences among all the urban services. Bhucho Mandi, a Class IV town in the district, was placed next only to Bathinda City. Against this, Rampura Phul, a Class III and the second largest town in the district, was placed third with Rs. 4. This amount made up about one-third that of Bhucho Mandi and about one-fourth of Bathinda City.

Fire services, a partially paid service, but hardly accruing any income in the district, received another Rs. 8 per capita subsidy amount during 1980-98. This service is jointly run by Rampura Phul, Maur Mandi and Raman Mandi towns on shared basis, while Bathinda City runs it independently. However, fire brigade is the only one, among the urban services analysed here, that is provided on request to any of the towns not only within the district but also in other towns of the surrounding districts in the State. There has been little inter-municipal differential in per capita subsidy amount on this count, as per capita subsidy amount varied from a low of Rs. 7 in Maur Mandi town to a high of Rs. 9 in Raman Mandi town. In this way, there has been the least inter-municipal differential in distribution of subsidy amount in case of fire services, against the maximum in the case of recreational services. While in case of former services, it differed by more than one time and in the latter case it differed by more than 37 times.

In brief, of all the eight urban services included here in the analysis public health and sanitation received the highest and fire brigade services received the lowest amount of subsidy. Further, six out of the eight urban services were fully subsidized, while remaining two were partially subsidized. There have been wide inter-municipal variations in distribution of subsidy amount on different urban services. Inter-municipal differentials in subsidy amount ranged from a high of more than 37 times in the case of recreational services to a minimum of more than one time in fire services. Also, there have been wide inter-municipal variations in the case of sewerage, municipal roads and public health and sanitation. While public health and sanitation was the most subsidy receiving urban service in majority of the towns in the district, it was sewerage in the case of Bathinda City, municipal roads in Bhucho Mandi town, and water supply in Kot Fatta town. Against this, recreational facilities received the least amount of subsidy in half the towns, fire services in the case of Bathinda City and sewerage in Maur Mandi town (Fig. 7.3).

Fig. 7.3

Most and Least Amount Receiving Urban Services in Different Towns of Bathinda District

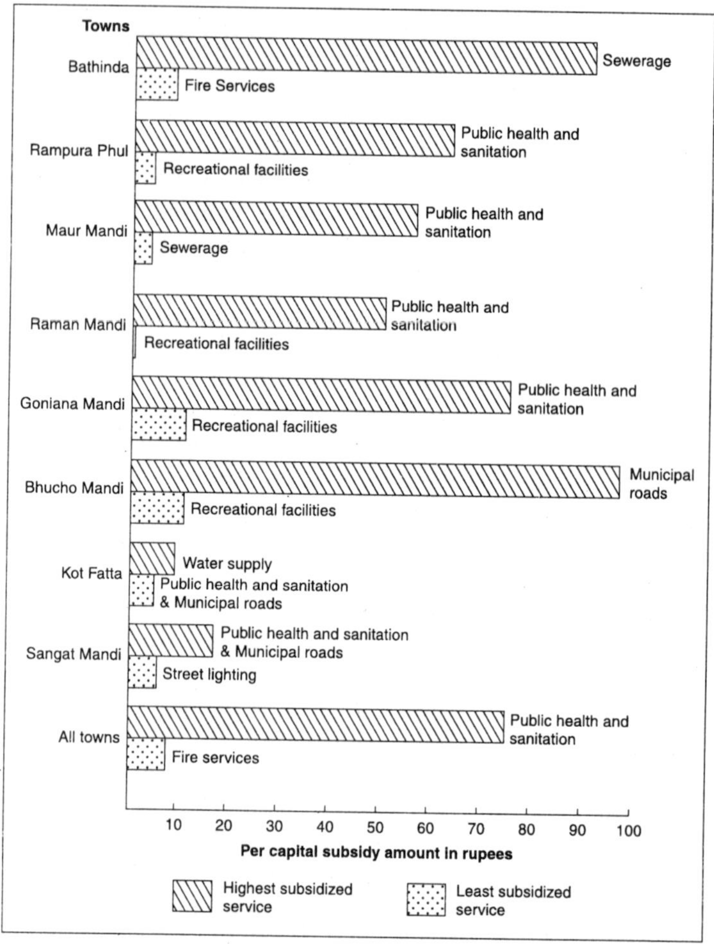

RECOVERY RATES: INTER-SERVICE AND INTER-MUNICIPAL DIFFERENTIALS

Four of the eight services included here are fully subsidized. Fire services, although a partially charged service, received hardly any amount during the study period. The remaining three services, which are partially subsidized, received little in terms of per capita. As a result, recovery rate, on average annual basis, has been less than 8.0 per cent during 1980-98 (Table 7.7).

TABLE 7.7
Bathinda District: Inter-service Differentials in Recovery Rates, 1980-98

Name of the urban service	*Per capita expenditure (in Rs.)*	*Per capita revenue income (in Rs.)*	*Recovery rates (in %)*
1	2	3	4
1. Public health and sanitation	75	Nil	Nil
2. Sewerage	63	5	7.9
3. Municipal Roads	53	Nil	Nil
4. Drainage	19	Nil	Nil
5. Water Supply	35	16	45.7
6. Street Lighting	13	Nil	Nil
7. Recreational Facilities	12	1	8.3
8. Fire Services	8	Nil	Nil
All Services	278	22	7.9

Municipalities incurred an average per capita amount of Rs. 278 per annum on eight urban services in the district to get only Rs. 22 per capita, with the remaining amount of Rs. 256 being the subsidy element. Since no amount was recovered from rendering the urban services such as public health and sanitation, municipal roads, drainage, street lighting, and fire brigade services, there is hardly any need to discuss recovery rates on these services. These are completely subsidized services.

Of the remaining services, water supply service needs the first attention for its highest recovery rate. It recovered Rs. 16 per capita against expenditure of Rs. 35, with the recovery rate coming to about 46 per cent. However, there have been wide inter-municipal differentials in this regard. Recovery rates varied from a high of more than three-fourths (77 per cent) in the case of Rampura Phul to a minimum of 14 per cent in the case of Kot Fatta town (Table 7.8). Recovery rates were 50 per cent or more in four towns, namely, Rampura Phul, Maur Mandi, Raman Mandi and Sangat Mandi towns. On the other side of the scale, the recovery rate was less than one-fourth in Kot Fatta town. Notably, the recovery rate of Bathinda City was the second lowest after Kot Fatta. The recovery rate was exceptionally high in the case of Class III towns, while Class V and Class VI towns presented a contrasting picture. Kot Fatta, a Class V town recovered only 14 per cent, while Sangat Mandi, a Class VI town recovered as high as 65 per cent of its expenditure on water supply.

TABLE 7.8
Bathinda District: A Comparison of Recovery Rates on Different Urban Services, 1980-98

Name of town	*Water Supply*			*Sewerage*			*Recreational facilities*		
	Per capita (in Rs.)			*Per capita (in Rs.)*			*Per capita (in Rs.)*		
	Expenditure	*Income*	*Recovery rate (%)*	*Expenditure*	*Income*	*Recovery rate (%)*	*Expenditure*	*Income*	*Recovery rate (%)*
Bathinda	37	14	38	96	5	5	17	2	12
Rampura Phul	22	17	77	15	2	13	4	—	—
Maur Mandi	21	15	71	6	3	50	—	—	—
Raman Mandi	36	18	50	10	4	40	0.4	—	—
Goniana Mandi	60	27	45	23	17	74	2	—	—
Bhucho Mandi	63	26	41	41	6	15	11	—	—
Kot Fatta	21	03	14	—	—	—	—	—	—
Sangat Mandi	26	17	65	—	—	—	—	—	—
All towns	35	16	46	63	5	8	12	1	8

The recovery rate was in general high in towns where the domestic water taps dominated the water supply sources and the collection of water bills was regularly efficient. Domestic tap connection, which is demand based, is the main source of income for municipal bodies apart from water supply service. In towns such as Rampura Phul and Maur Mandi domestic tap connections were the dominant source of water supply.

The recovery rate from sewerage is barely 8 per cent. In other words, the municipality in Bathinda district earns only Rs. 8 from sewerage service against an expenditure of Rs. 100. Two municipal towns of Kot Fatta and Sangat Mandi were not providing this service to their residents. Among the remaining six towns, recovery rates varied from a high of 74 per cent in Goniana Mandi town to a low of Rs. 5 in Bathinda City, differing by about 15 times from each other. Goniana Mandi municipality has imposed higher rates per toilet seat than the other towns in the district. It charges Rs. 12 per toilet seat in comparison to Rs. 10 by other municipalities in the district. Recovery rates are also high in case of Maur Mandi and Raman Mandi towns. Against this, recovery rate is the lowest of all in the case of Bathinda City, a Class I town and the district headquarters because it has to construct a number of toilets and extend sewerage lines to public places. This results in increase of expenditure without any increase in revenue income.

Recreational facilities is the last service against which municipalities in the district earn some income. Recovery rates, however, are not only low but recovered only in Bathinda City. Bathinda municipality, which has constructed a huge Rose Garden in the City earns some income from the auction of a restaurant inside the garden and parking lots near it as well as imposition of fee on stalls placed near the gates of the garden. Rest of the municipalities have constructed only parks where there is no entry fee. The recovery rate in Bathinda City is only 12 per cent. In this way, with the exception of Bathinda City recreational facilities are provided by municipalities in the district free of cost. In fact, there are three such towns, namely, Maur Mandi, Kot Fatta and Sangat Mandi which are not providing this service to their residents.

Briefly, five of the eight urban services in Bathinda district selected for study here are fully subsidized services. Three services, from which municipalities do get some revenue income, are also heavily subsidized. Hence, the recovery rates are as low as 8 per cent. There are, however, wide inter-service and inter-municipal variations in recovery rates. Recovery rate varied from a high of about 46 per cent in case of water supply service to a low of less than 8 per cent in sewerage service. Among municipalities, recovery rates on water supply varied from a high of 77 per cent in Rampura Phul to a low of only 14 per cent in Kot Fatta.

Inter-municipal differentials in recovery rates have been the maximum in sewerage. Whereas recreational facilities recovery was viable only in Bathinda City.

CORRELATES OF SUBSIDY ELEMENT

In the following, an attempt has been made to examine the nature and degree of association between absolute (annual average) and per capita amounts of subsidy and some of the attributes of towns in Bathinda district, including town status, administrative status, year of establishment of municipal body, area and population sizes, annual growth of population, and the absolute (annual average) and per capita amount of expenditure on different urban services. Functional characteristic of towns should also be included in these attributes, but all towns in the district are market towns, as marketing agricultural produce has been the main function. Hence, functional status of towns has been excluded from the analysis here.

Notably, some of the attributes are quantifiable while others are non-quantifiable. Therefore, we will use quantitative techniques to handle association with quantitative attributes and make grassroots level observations in the case of non-quantifiable attributes.

A. Subsidy Element and Non-quantitative Attributes of Towns

Beginning with non-quantifiable attributes, such as civic status and administrative status of towns and year of establishment of municipal bodies, we start with the examination of associations between civic status of towns and subsidy amount both in absolute and per capita term, followed by other attributes in sequential order.

Civic status of towns in the district finds a broad positive association with absolute amount (average annual) of subsidy. Higher the civic status of a town higher the amount of subsidy it provides on urban services. Bhucho Mandi town defies this broad generalization. It is the smallest town in the category of Class IV towns, but provides an amount of subsidy that is not only higher than the two other Class IV towns but also higher than that of Maur Mandi, a Class III town in the district (Table 7.9).

As regards the association between civic status of a town and per capita amount of subsidy it provides on urban services, no such association was found. Class IV category of towns, as a category, provided a higher per capita subsidy (Rs. 203) than

TABLE 7.9

Bathinda District: Association between Civic Status and Administrative Status of Towns and Year of Establishment of Municipal Bodies and Subsidy Element

Name of town	*Civic status*	*Administrative status*	*Year of establishment*	*Subsidy element (annual average)*	
				Absolute amount (Rs. in lakh)	*Per capita (in Rs.)*
Bathinda City	I	District HQS	1945	388.31	333
Rampura Phul	III	Sub-divisional HQS	1950	44.89	141
Maur Mandi	III	Block HQS	1951	21.28	113
Raman Mandi	IV	**	1956	18.49	130
Goniana Mandi	IV	**	1952	15.94	187
Bhucho Mandi	IV	**	1952	22.72	291
Kot Fatta	V	**	1957	2.20	44
Sangat Mandi	VI	Block HQS	1956	1.89	66

**No Administrative Status.

Class III towns (Rs. 127) in the district. Similarly a Class VI town (Sangat Mandi, Rs. 66) provided higher per capita amount than a Class V town (Kot Fatta, Rs. 44) in the district.

Administrative status of a town finds a strong positive association with absolute as well as per capita amount of subsidy on urban services in the district. Bathinda City, which functions as a district HQ, surpasses all the towns both in absolute as well as per capita subsidy. This is followed, though, distantly, by Rampura Phul town, functioning as sub-divisional headquarters. Maur Mandi town, functioning as a block headquarters has been placed at third rank. There are, however, four towns, which do not have any administrative status but provide fairly high per capita amount of subsidy. Two such towns, namely, Goniana Mandi and Bhucho Mandi provide a per capita amount of subsidy which is much higher than that provided by Rampura Phul, having sub-divisional status.

First municipality in the district was established in 1945 at Bathinda town and the last in 1957 at Kot Fatta town. It took 13 years to complete full circle but the circle by now is more than 45 years old. It is expected that older municipal towns will provide higher amount of subsidy both in absolute as well as per capita terms. Bathinda municipality, which was first to be established, provided the highest amount of subsidy both in absolute as well as per capita terms. But the same is not true of other municipal towns. In Bhucho Mandi, where the municipality was established in 1952, provided the second highest per capita amount of subsidy, whereas Rampura Phul, established in 1950, provided less than half per capita subsidy amount of Bhucho Mandi town. Similarly, Maur Mandi, where the municipality was established in 1951, provided much lower per capita subsidy than Raman Mandi established in 1956.

Briefly, thus, while civic status and administrative status of towns in the district find somewhat broad association with absolute as well as per capita amount of subsidy on urban services, no such association was observed between the number of years of establishment of municipal bodies and the subsidy amount they provided on urban services.

B. Subsidy Element and Quantitative Attributes of Towns

As expected, absolute amount of subsidy finds a high positive association with area (r = 0.996) and population (r = 0.996) sizes of towns and absolute amount of expenditure on urban services (Table 7.10A & 7.10B). Its association with per capita amount of expenditure was also quite strong, but was weak with growth rate of population (r = 0.491).

Per capita amount of subsidy on urban services recorded strong positive association with all the attributes, but association was exceptionally strong with growth rate of population and per capita amount of expenditure. In other words, rapidly growing and high per capita spending towns provided very high per capita amount of subsidy on urban services. Large area and population size municipal towns also provided high per capita amount of subsidy but in lesser degree.

RATIONALISATION APPROACH TO SUBSIDY ELEMENT

It is evidently clear from the above discussion that urban services in the district are highly subsidized though somewhat unequally. Some are more subsidized than the others. In addition, there is spatial discrimination in distribution of the subsidy

TABLE 7.10

A. Bathinda District: Association between Area and Population Size, Growth Rate of Population, Expenditure on Urban Services and Subsidy Element

Name of municipal town	*Area (in km^2) 2001*	*Population (in numbers) 2001*	*Annual growth rate of population 1971-01 (in %age)*	*Annual average expenditure on urban services*		*Subsidy (annual element average)*	
				Absolute amount (in lakh Rs.)	*Per capita amount*	*Absolute amount (in lakh Rs.)*	*Per capita amount*
1	2	3	4	5	6	7	8
Bathinda	110	217387	4.1	414.48	355	388.31	333
Rampura Phul	18	44661	2.2	50.80	159	44.89	141
Maur Mandi	4.8	27531	2.4	24.40	129	21.28	113
Raman Mandi	9.9	19549	1.8	21.61	151	18.49	130
Goniana Mandi	8.0	12812	2.3	19.79	230	15.94	187
Bhucho Mandi	2.2	13183	5.1	25.28	323	22.72	291
Kot Fatta	1.6	6493	1.4	2.36	47	2.20	44
Sangat Mandi	1.3	5396	1.4	2.38	83	1.89	66
All towns	155.8	347014		561.10		515.72	256

B. Bathinda District: Correlation Matrix between Attributes of Municipal Towns and Subsidy Element in Urban Services

Subsidy element	*Attributes of towns*				
	Area size	*Population size*	*Growth rate of population*	*Absolute amount of expenditure*	*Per capita amount of expenditure*
1. Absolute amount	0.996	0.996	0.491	0.999	0.659
2. Per capita amount	0.675	0.677	0.919	0.704	0.996

component. Hence, the question arises, as to what should be the rational approach to the subsidy component on urban services.

The issue of subsidy element is associated with a variety of factors. Some of these are: (i) What procedure is adopted to fix the rates of urban services?, (ii) Which cost of urban services is recovered?, (iii) What is the trade-off between free and priced supply of different urban services?, (iv) What should be the interval to revise rates? and (v) How to ensure full recovery of bills?

The common experience is that the elected representatives go by populist measures. They would favour the soft option of keeping the services subsidized. Bureaucrats believe, in general, in simplifying things to their convenience in place of following a rigorous practice. Technocrats are likely to assess the cost of urban services rather liberally. They may end up by suggesting very high rates. The professionals, who can deliver the goods, are the financial experts. In this task, they may be assisted by a team of planners, sociologists, economists and geographers who understand the intricacies of the matter.

Theoretically speaking, a welfare state is obliged to provide a service at a subsidized rate, even if it amounts to low recoveries resulting in poor supply of the service. The fact that the consumer may be willing to pay higher if quality of the service is improved does not receive due consideration. This mindset needs to be changed now.

For example, there has always been, in the case of water supply, a provision for charging water on flat rate basis alongwith the charges for metered connection. Flat rate method is well known for its disadvantages, yet popular with municipal administration in the district as well as other parts of the state. The plea given is that water meters give incorrect readings either due to tampering or at times because they are faulty. An implicit consideration here is that it simplifies the billing procedure for the authority. There have been other methods, adopted by municipalities, to simplify the procedure. The rates were differentiated on the basis of *Kutcha* and *Pucca* form of residence. All this hints at the lack of a sound financial management culture.

Considering the small duration of supply hours of water or electricity, flat rates could be turned into a gainful proposition for the municipal administration. But then it is at the cost of the quality of service being rendered to the consumer. One positive outcome of high flat rates might be that consumers are impelled to go in for metered connections.

Issue of determining an appropriate interval at which rates of urban services should be revised is no less important. Rates are revised after long durations. In the meantime, inflation rate neutralizes the whole effect of increase in the service rates. According to a study, conducted on pricing of water supply in Ludhiana City (Krishan and others, 1994, p. 61), first revision in water rates, done after 1960, was at a gap of 14 years in 1974. The latest revision done in 1993, took nineteen years. General price rise is enormous during any such span. And yet when water rates are raised, even after long intervals even at a rate lower than that of inflation, these come as a shock to the people. Smaller doses of rate increase at shorter intervals are likely to be more acceptable to consumers.

In addition, rational pricing of urban services must be accompanied by full collection of bills. Bills remain uncollected for long durations. The defaulters are mostly from two types of consumers, either the slum-dwellers or the influential industrial enterprises. As regards the slum-dwellers, who may not perhaps be in a position to afford the payment of different urban services, the important issue, needing attention of decision-makers is: how to combine economic efficiency with social justice?

Another aspect pertaining to the pricing of urban services, having a close connection with subsidy element, is the question of affordability. While too low or subsidized rates may lead to excessive use and wastage of water. Against this, too high rates may discourage people from using even that amount which is necessary.

A project report of a survey conducted for Human Settlement Management Institute on issues of pricing of water supply in Ludhiana city reported a sampled household field survey covering 500 households to assess the question of affordability of city residents in paying higher price for water so as to reduce the subsidy in provision of this service and raise additional resources for improving the system. Slum localities were kept out of this survey by the authors of the report (Krishan and others, 1994).

The survey found that 60 per cent of the total population in the main city had installed private handpumps/borewells, almost 70 per cent had installed booster pumps either on the water supply lines or hand pump tubewells. This involved a handsome amount. The median cost at the time of installing a handpump/borewell, was estimated as Rs. 1600 and of a booster more than Rs. 2000. The running and maintenance cost of booster and handpumps was estimated to be about Rs. 40 per month. In addition, these households were paying regular water bills against piped water supply, however inefficient it may have been. The survey revealed that two-thirds of the respondents did not assess the prevailing water rates as inordinately overpriced, showing the awareness of the benefit they were enjoying in respect of the price of water. After examining the whole issue, the study concluded that 'affordability is not that critical an issue as it is often made out to be. The most critical issue relates to availability and quality of service' (Krishan and others, 1994, p. 71). In fact people were already spending a sizeable additional amount on installation of booster pumps and handpumps/borewells to augment their water supply, they were ready to pay the higher amount for quality service and a majority favoured the deposit of a large lump sum amount, if spared off from paying small bills frequently.

If affordability exists among the urban households, as proved by the study conducted on the issue of water supply in Ludhiana city, one is inclined to think in terms of following issues: (i) How the dwellers can be made aware of the fact that their real and hidden expenditures are a lot more on procuring urban services than what they are paying in the form of bills to the municipal administration? How the municipal bodies can convince people that the administration can improve the quality of urban services if they are ready to pay higher? How the municipal bodies, on their part, can work out an appropriate balance between the quality and price of services they can possibly offer?

In the final analysis, the immediate solution that comes to mind is a hike in the tariff structure of urban services. This can be achieved in a phased manner. In the first phase, at least the cost of running an urban service should be charged from the consumers. Later on, they may be asked to pay more depending on availability and quality of different urban services. It is, however, true that things are not as simple as they seem, as revision of tariff is linked with several other issues. These revolve around various entities and ideas including the 'consumer', the 'administrator', the 'decision-maker', the 'ruling paradigm' and 'futuristic possibilities'.

As regards the consumer, the main issue relates to the question of increase in the coverage and quality of urban services. Only then, he will agree to pay more for the urban services. That would require the agency/agencies responsible for providing service/service to establish their credibility in the eyes of the consumers. Before initiating a price hike should they be made to realise that they are enjoying highly subsidized services?

On the part of the administrator, the major concern is how best to recover the costs incurred by the system? For this what would be the right kind of mechanism for pricing of urban services? What kind of costs should be included? What is the ideal number of agencies that should be included and how could their roles be best determined? At the level of the decision-maker, the main point of debate is the ideology that should govern the fixing of tariff. Should one be content with the ideology of subsidization? Should cost recovery be a goal? In addition, who could best decide the amount of tariff to be imposed? Should it be left to the politician or bureaucrats or technocrats or financial management experts? What could be the ideal interval for raising tariffs.

Additionally, there are important issues such as: (i) social justice *vs.* economic efficiency, and (ii) possibilities of including the private sector in the provision of urban service. The introduction of new economic policy in 1991 has brightened the chances of inducing the private sector in all sectors of Indian economy including urban services. The evolving paradigm in the field of urban services in India is, among others, to involve urban residents in management of urban services and introduce the private sector on selective basis.

Finally, some of the core issues are: (i) How to convince the people that they are getting highly subsidized urban services; that the poor quality of services being rendered is related to this fact; and that they must pay for these adequately?, (ii) How to work out a scenario in which the consumer is convinced that it is not the administrative mismanagement but the financial crunch which is more responsible for the prevailing situation?, and (iii) How to prepare the local politician in resisting the tendency towards populism by opposing any rationalization of pricing of urban services? On the whole, the situation is more favourable now than ever before. Already, there is a trend in favour of rationalizing the prices of urban services so as to ensure adequate availability and good quality of urban services. The urban-dwellers have also started getting a feel of it. Their mindset is now changing to accommodate emerging realities.

MAIN HIGHLIGHTS

- Urban services in the district are highly subsidized. An amount of Rs. 92 out of each Rs. 100 incurred as expenditure on urban services by the municipalities in the district goes as subsidy element. During 1980-98, on average annual basis municipalities in the district incurred an amount of Rs. 56.11 million to get a meagre amount of Rs. 4.54 million as income from urban services, giving, thus, an amount of Rs. 51.6 million in subsidy on average annual basis.

- Over the period, this amount of subsidy on urban services had been growing in the district. It increased to Rs. 107.22 million in 1996-97 from Rs. 18.25 million in 1982-83, on annual average basis, recording an increase of 488 per cent or about five times. However, in per capita terms it increased to Rs. 31 from Rs. 11 during the same period, showing a slower growth in per capita terms than in absolute amount.
- Happily, subsidy element in urban services is slowing down over the period both in absolute as well as in per capita terms. While the subsidy amount grew by 94 per cent between 1982-83 and 1987-88, the growth came down to about 50 per cent between 1992-93 and 1996-97. Similarly, per capita amount of subsidy grew by 100 per cent between 1982-83 and 1987-88, but came down to only 48 per cent during 1992-93 and 1996-97. Since the subsidy element finds a highly positive association with municipal expenditure on urban services, it definitely involves deterioration in quality of available urban services in different towns in the district.
- The subsidy element differed widely from service to service and time to time. Of the eight urban services, public health and sanitation received the highest amount of Rs. 15.30 million or about 30 per cent of total subsidy amount during 1980-98 in the district. Against this, fire brigade service, received only Rs. 1.46 million or less than 3 per cent. In all, three urban services of public health and sanitation, sewerage and roads cornered nearly 73 per cent of total subsidy amount during the period. Fire brigade services recorded the highest compound annual growth rate in its subsidy component between 1982-83 and 1987-88, water supply between 1987-88 and 1992-93, and drainage between 1992-93 and 1996-97.
- Also the subsidy element in urban services differed widely among municipalities. Against an average of 92 per cent for all the municipalities it ranged from a high of 94 per cent in

Bathinda City to a low of 79 per cent in Sangat Mandi town. The former is the largest and the latter the smallest town in population size, yet no relation between the population size and subsidy share of different towns in the district is apparent. In absolute terms, Bathinda City provided more than three-fourths of total subsidy amount of all municipalities. Against this, Sangat Mandi town's share was a mere less than half a per cent.

In per capita amount of subsidy, inter-municipal disparities were still larger. It varied from a high of Rs. 333 per capita in Bathinda City to a low of only Rs. 44 in Kot Fatta. Municipal expenditure on a service provided and its subsidy element found a positive association in the district.

- Of all the eight urban services, public health and sanitation received the highest and fire brigade services received the lowest amount of subsidy. Further, five of the eight urban services were fully subsidized, while remaining three were partially subsidized. There have been wide inter-municipal variations in distribution of subsidy amount on different urban services. Inter-municipal differentials in subsidy amount ranged from a high of more than 37 times in the case of recreational services to a minimum of more than one time in fire services. Also, there have been wide inter-municipal variations in the case of sewerage, municipal roads and public health and sanitation. While public health and sanitation was receiving the most subsidized status in majority of towns in the district, it was sewerage in the case of Bathinda City, municipal roads in Bhucho Mandi town, and water supply in Kot Fatta town that had a similar position. Against this, recreational facilities received the least amount of subsidy in half the towns, with fire services in Bathinda City and sewerage in Maur Mandi town having the same status.
- Five of the eight urban services in Bathinda district selected for study here are fully subsidized services. Three services, from which municipalities obtained some revenue income, were also heavily subsidized. Hence, recovery rates are as low as 8 per cent. There are, however, wide inter-service and inter-municipal variations in recovery rates. Recovery rate varied from a high of about 46 per cent in case of water

supply service to a low of less than 8 per cent in sewerage service. Among municipalities, recovery rates on water supply varied from a high of 77 per cent in Rampura Phul to a low of only 14 per cent in Kot Fatta.

Inter-municipal differentials in recovery rates have been the maximum in sewerage. Whereas recreational facilities made any sort of recovery only in Bathinda City.

- While civic status and administrative status of towns in the district find a broad association with absolute as well as per capita amount of subsidy on urban services, no such association was observed between the year of establishment of municipal bodies in terms of number of years of existence and the subsidy amount they provided on urban services.
- Absolute amount of subsidy finds a high positive association with area (r=0.996) and population (r=0.996) sizes of towns and absolute amount of expenditure on urban services. Its association with per capita amount of expenditure was also quite strong, but was weak as compared to growth rate of population (r=0.491).

  Per capita amount of subsidy on urban services recorded strong positive association with all the attributes, but association was exceptionally strong with growth rate of population and per capita amount of expenditure. In other words, rapidly growing and high per capita spending towns provided very high per capita amount of subsidy on urban services. Large area and population size municipal towns also provide high per capita amount of subsidy but to a lesser degree.
- The immediate solution that comes to mind is a hike in the tariff structure of urban services. This can be achieved in a phased manner. In the first phase, at least the cost of running an urban service should be charged from the consumers. Later on, they may be asked to pay more depending on the availability and quality of different urban services. It is, however, true that things are not as simple as they seem, as revision of tariff is linked with several other issues. These revolve around various entities and ideas including the 'consumer' the 'administrator', the 'decision-maker', the 'ruling paradigm' and 'futuristic possibilities'.

- Some of the core issues are: (i) How to convince the people that they are getting highly subsidized urban services; that the poor quality of services being rendered is related to this fact; and that they must pay for these adequately?, (ii) How to work out a scenario in which the consumer is convinced that it is not the administrative mismanagement but the financial crunch which is more responsible for the prevailing situation?, and (iii) How to prepare the local politician for resisting the tendency towards populism opposing any rationalization of pricing of urban services? On the whole, the situation is more favourable now than ever before. Already, there is a swing in favour of the municipal service provider. The consumer, now exposed to better quality services in other towns like Chandigarh etc. may be willing to pay more, in various modes either one time or over a period of time, to be able to get for himself the best that can be offered by the municipality.

8

Summary and Conclusions

A geographic study of the subsidy element in the provision of urban services in Bathinda district of Punjab was the focus of the present research work. This involved gaining a knowledge of the number and nature of services provided by the municipal bodies in the district—an understanding of the subsidy element in the provision of urban services and an examination of the inter-service and inter-municipal variations in it as well as an identification of spatial discrimination, if any, in the distribution of subsidy on different urban services and suggesting an approach for rationalization of the subsidy element in urban services. A number of research questions raised in this context included: What is the role of location, size and functions in differentiating expenditure pattern of municipal bodies on various urban services? How the role of location differs from that of size and function? How the municipal expenditure on, income from and subsidy element in urban services differed within the district? How it differs within the towns? The entire empirical exercise carried out was within the purview of Urban Geography, wherein there virtually has been a complete dearth of systematic studies on the availability and extent of the subsidy element in the provision of urban services.

Different methodological tools were used to meet the requirements of varying research themes. Information on municipal income and expenditure, available from the offices of the eight Municipal Committees in the district was analysed to ascertain the patterns and changes in income, expenditure and the subsidy component in urban services. Wherever necessary, the processed data was presented through maps and diagrams. Extensive fieldwork was conducted to map the spatial coverage of different urban services for all towns and to demarcate various phases of the coverage. The objective was to know the spatial discrimination discernible in the distribution of the subsidy component.

For examining the nature of association between different qualitative and quantitative attributes of towns in the district and the subsidy component in urban services, appropriate statistical techniques were applied. The selection of a technique was guided by its own underlying philosophy and its capacity to handle a particular point of enquiry.

The study covered a period of little under two decades (18 years) from 1980 to 1998. The information on municipal finances was considered from 1980-81 continuously and 1997-98 was the latest year for which the information was available at the time of initiation of this study. Four sub-periods of five years each: 1980-85, 1985-90, 1990-95 and 1995-98* were identified to re-arrange the information so as to calculate annual averages for each of the sub-periods. Annual averages for five year sub-periods were calculated by making the mid-year as the base year. The objective was to minimize the effect of annual fluctuation in municipal expenditure on different urban services.

The study was also intended to test a number of hypotheses:

(i) The administrative and civic status of a town plays a significant role in the generation of municipal income and its spending on various urban services. For their higher spending capacity, larger civic and administrative towns provided higher amount of subsidy on urban services. Hence, higher the status of a town greater would be the amount and share of subsidy element in urban services provided to its residents.

(ii) The component of subsidy on urban services would differ from service to service and town to town. Services such as street lighting and sanitation would be more subsidized than water supply and sewerage. Similarly, fast growing and dynamic towns would provide higher amount of subsidy on services than the slow growing and stagnant ones.

*Last sub-period is of three years duration as the study period extends only upto 1998.

(iii) There would be inter and intra-municipal town discriminations in distribution of subsidy on various urban services. Localities having central location and resided in by higher economic, political and social status citizens would benefit more from the subsidies than those having peripheral locations and resided in by the socio-economically and politically weaker sections of humanity. However, such a discrimination would be more in the case of big towns in comparison to smaller towns.

MUNICIPAL INCOME AND EXPENDITURE IN PUNJAB: AN OVERVIEW

The major sources of municipal income in Punjab include octroi, house and land tax, and grants from the government. On the other hand, the main expenditure heads include the establishment, salary of the municipal staff, municipal services such as water supply, electricity supply, sanitation, construction and maintenance of roads, parks, etc. and the repayment of loans and interest on loans. In the financial year 1997-98, total municipal income in Punjab had been Rs. 4188.01 million, against an expenditure of Rs. 3996.23 million. Earlier in 1965-66, total municipal income had been Rs. 144.85 million, against an expenditure of Rs. 136.90 million indicating a tradition of the municipal administration to keep a surplus budget.

Aggregate municipal income, from all sources, increased by more than eight times (8.27 times) during 1980-98 in the state. Against this, increase in expenditure was less than eight times (7.57 times) during the same time. It seems that the tendency to keep a surplus budget has been responsible for this. Increase in municipal income and expenditure, if seen in per capita terms, is rather disappointing. In per capita terms, income increased by about six times (5.87 times) and expenditure by 5.37 times during 1980-98. During this period, wholesale price index (WPI) increased by about four times.

The quantum of grants from the government has increased substantially after 1992-93. Per capita municipal income which was Rs. 395 in 1992-93 increased to Rs. 497 in 1993-94 and to Rs. 612 in 1994-95. It rose to Rs. 687 in 1997-98. Similarly, per capita expenditure rose from Rs. 383 to Rs. 475, then to Rs. 595

and finally to Rs. 655 during the same period. Municipal budgets recorded the maximum surplus in 1997-98 against a maximum deficit in 1982-83.

Like the municipal income, municipal expenditure too differed widely among the districts. It ranged from a high of Rs. 1510 in Fatehgarh Sahib district to a low of Rs. 373 in Mansa district, giving a difference of 4 times, i.e. a ratio of 1:40. Earlier, in the case of municipal income this ratio was slightly higher (4.24 times) than that of expenditure. Bathinda district with a per capita municipal expenditure of Rs. 670 was placed fifth from the top among all the seventeen districts in the state. In line with its position among top five municipal income districts in the state it was again placed in five top districts of Fatehgarh Sahib, Rupnagar, Ludhiana, Jalandhar and Bathinda.

Octroi is the major source of municipal income in Punjab. In 1997-98, nearly 58 per cent of total municipal income came from this source. There were, however, wide inter-district variations. It varied from a high of about 80 per cent in Rupnagar district to a low of about 37 per cent in Muktsar district. In Bathinda district, octroi contributed two-thirds or 66.7 per cent of the total municipal income. The share of octroi in income of municipalities in Bathinda district has been higher than the state average. In fact, Bathinda ranks next only to Rupnagar, the highest ranking district in this context. There are seven other districts, including Bathinda district, where octroi contributes higher than the state average.

Urban services including public health, public works and public safety consumes the dominant share of municipal expenditure in Punjab. The combined share of these services made up for three-fourths of the total municipal expenditure. Public health, water supply and convenience alone consume nearly 45 per cent. Another 22 per cent goes to public works. Public safety consumes remaining 9 per cent. General administrative services consume about 16 per cent of the total municipal budget. It includes salaries only to general staff of municipalities as well as maintenance of building, payment of rent on land and building and maintenance of vehicles. The salaries of municipal staff employed for various urban services such as water supply, sanitation, street lighting, etc. are not included.

Three of eight towns in Bathinda district fall in the 'low' or 'very low' category of per capita municipal expenditure. Earlier, the same pattern was observed in the case of per capita municipal income. Bhucho Mandi, which was in the 'moderate' category of per capita income and had moved up to the 'moderately high' category of per capita expenditure, was the only exception.

During 1995-98, on average annual basis municipal bodies in Punjab incurred an amount of Rs. 2239.03 million on urban services, making up more than 57 per cent of the total municipal expenditure (Rs. 3925.6 millions) during this period. In other words, fifty-seven paisa out of every rupee spent by municipalities in Punjab went to urban services. Rest of the money was incurred on the maintenance of establishment, payment of salaries to the staff, repayment of loans, interest on loans and other miscellaneous items. In this way, while the major share of the municipal expenditure in Punjab went into running and maintaining of urban services, the share and amount of non-developmental expenditure, incurred on establishment, salaries of staff and repayment of loans and interests was no less significant.

Urban services in Punjab are highly subsidized. Only an amount of Rs. 321.8 million, making up only 8.0 per cent of total municipal expenditure (on average annual basis) and less than 15 per cent of total municipal expenditure on urban services, is recovered by the municipalities. In other words, 85 paisa out of each rupee spent by municipal bodies on urban services goes in as subsidy. However, there were wide inter-district variations in this regard. In general, municipal bodies in districts falling in South-West Punjab provided higher proportion of subsidy on urban services. For ecological reasons, per head cost of providing urban services, which in turn are highly subsidized, are much higher in this part of the state. Bathinda district is ranked second among the 17 districts in the state in terms of the subsidy element in urban services.

Inter-district disparities in subsidy element on urban services gets more accentuated in per capita terms than in proportional share. Against the state average of Rs. 315 per capita per annum subsidy on urban services, it ranged from a high of Rs. 659 in Fatehgarh Sahib district to a low of only Rs. 145 in Mansa district. It gave a ratio of 1:4.5 between the highest and lowest values. Earlier, this ratio was only 1:1.3 in case of proportional share of subsidy on various urban services.

Per capita amount of municipal subsidy on urban services in the district finds a strong positive association with the development of the districts. In developed districts, municipalities tend to generate high income from their own income sources which enhance their capacity to spend on urban services. Since most of the urban services are highly subsidized, the amount of subsidy, both in proportional and per capita terms, gets increased in such districts. This is probably the reason why there is a still higher association between the per capita municipal expenditure and per capita municipal subsidy of districts in the state.

Water Supply

Owing to the peculiar geographical conditions and the poor ground water quality in Bathinda district, the supply of safe drinking water is the most essential obligation for the local bodies in towns of the district. The ground water quality is poor, hence the surface water, mainly the canal water, is the main source of water supply in the towns of Bathinda, using both the piped and non-piped modes for this purpose.

About Rs. 71 lakh making up 9 per cent of the total municipal expenditure in the district was annually incurred on water supply during 1980-98. In other words, water supply received nearly Rs. 11 out of every Rs. 100 spent on various services. However, there were wide inter-municipal and temporal variations in this regard.

The larger municipal towns incurred much higher amounts, in absolute terms, on water supply than the small-sized towns in the district. The average annual expenditure on water supply of Bathinda municipality, during 1980-98 was about 58 times higher than that of Sangat Mandi, the smallest town in the district. However, in proportional terms Bathinda incurred only about 7 per cent and Kot Fatta, another small-sized municipality, about 24 per cent of its total annual expenditure on this account. **Obviously, the large towns were guided by the principle of economic efficiency in spending on the water supply in comparison to small municipalities, where the concept of equity prevailed over the efficiency criterion.**

Per capita expenditure, a more realistic measure of municipal expenditure on water supply, revealed that the small-sized towns spent more in per capita terms than the large-sized ones. However, there were wide inter-municipal disparities in this regard, which kept on widening between 1980 and 1990, although there had been a tendency towards narrowing these down in recent years. Higher growth in per capita expenditure of municipalities spending less earlier was largely responsible for this. On the whole, the small-sized municipalities incurred higher per capita expenditure on water supply than the large-sized municipalities in the district during the study period.

An amount of almost Rs. 33 lakh per annum, making up nearly 4 per cent in average annual income from different sources, was the income from water supply during 1980-98. In other words, four out of every hundred rupees earned by municipalities came from water supply.

Municipal income from water supply grew about seven times between 1982-83 and 1996-97, from Rs. 11 lakh to Rs. 79 lakh. More than half the total municipal income from water supply in the district was earned by the single municipality of Bathinda. Against this, four municipalities, in combination, earned less than one-sixth of this income. This income contributed more than one-tenth of the total annual income of Sangat Mandi municipality. Against this, water supply contributed only one-fortieth of the income of Bathinda town. Over the period, three municipalities of Bathinda, Goniana Mandi and Sangat Mandi registered a decline in the shares of their income from the water supply, while the remaining five recorded an increase.

During 1980-98, municipalities in Bathinda district earned an average annual amount of Rs. 16 per capita from the water supply. During this period, while the per capita income in absolute terms maintained an incremental trend, the growth in per capita income kept on declining to the extent of becoming almost marginal towards the end of the study period. Broadly, a correspondence was noticed between the per capita expenditure and the per capita earnings of municipalities from the water supply in the district.

A major share of the municipal expenditure on water supply goes as subsidy. On an average, municipalities provided an amount of about Rs. 39 lakh or more than 54 per cent of their total expenditure annually as subsidy on water supply during 1980-98.

More than two-thirds of the total subsidy on water supply was the share of Bathinda municipality. On the other side of the scale, the combined share of the four municipalities made up only about one-tenth of the total. Rampura Phul, the second largest municipal town in the district, shared only about 4 per cent. Class IV, V and VI towns provided higher proportion of their expenditure as subsidy on water supply than the Class III municipal towns. Kot Fatta, a Class V category of town, provided as high as 85 per cent of its expenditure as subsidy.

On an average, Rs. 19 as per capita was the subsidy on water supply annually during 1980-98, varying from a low of Rs. 5 in Rampura Phul to a high of Rs. 37 in Bhucho Mandi. Per capita amount of subsidy on water supply kept on growing over the period but its growth has been the highest between 1987-88 and 1992-93 when per capita amount increased more than two times. Against this, per capita subsidy amount increased by only 40 per cent during 1992-93 to 1996-97.

Inter-municipal variations in per capita amount of subsidy on water supply find a negative relationship with rise in amount of per capita subsidy. In 1996-97, when per capita subsidy rose to its peak level of Rs. 38, inter-municipal variations were the least. It seems that there is a threshold point beyond which the growth of subsidy has to be kept within limit. This may be the reason for decline in inter-municipal disparities in per capita amount of subsidy on water supply after it attained a reasonably high level in 1992-93.

There has been wide inter-town and intra-town spatial discrimination in distribution of subsidy component in water supply. Tap water supply, as a source of water supply, was introduced as late as in 1994-95 in Kot Fatta, whereas it was introduced long back in Bathinda City. Further, canal water which is sweet to drink is supplied in central parts of the city, while peripheral areas have to depend on hand-pumps as the main source of water supply.

Sewerage

An average amount of Rs. 114 lakh per annum, making about 92 per cent in total expenditure on sewerage and 14 per cent in aggregate municipal expenditure in the district, was the subsidy component on this service during 1980-98. In other words, Rs. 14 out of every Rs. 100 incurred annually by municipalities on various services and Rs. 92 out of every Rs. 100 spent on sewerage systems was the subsidy component on sewerage in the district.

During 1980-98, subsidy varied from a high of 18 per cent of total expenditure in Bathinda town to a low of less than 2 per cent in Maur Mandi. During the same period, the subsidy component was a maximum of about 94 per cent of total expenditure on sewerage in Bathinda town and a minimum of 27 per cent in Goniana Mandi.

In relative terms, the small-sized towns earned higher shares of income from sewerage services than did the large sized towns. The combined income share of the five small-sized towns became quite high (34 per cent) in total income from sewerage than their combined share in total subsidy (18 per cent) on this account during 1980-98. Notably, Goniana Mandi, one of the small-sized towns, earned 14.2 per cent of the aggregate income from sewer connections, in comparison to its share of less than one per cent in total amount of subsidy by all towns. Against this, Bathinda, the largest town earned only 66 per cent of the total income from this source in comparison to imparting subsidy to the tune of 92 per cent in aggregate amount of subsidy. Evidently, the small-sized municipalities earned more than they spent on this facility.

Per capita amount of subsidy differed widely among municipalities. Against the average per capita subsidy of Rs. 58 during 1980-98, it varied from a high of Rs. 91 in Bathinda municipality to a low of Rs. 3 in Maur Mandi. Majority of the small-sized towns provided low per capita subsidy in comparison to large sized towns. **Differential rates charged by municipalities on per toilet seat basis at the time of sewer connections was one of the important factors in the wide inter-municipal variations in subsidy on and income from sewerage service.**

Per capita amount of municipal subsidy on sewerage has been growing in the district during 1980-98. However, the growth rate has slowed down in recent years. Increase in proportional terms has declined to about 13 per cent between 1992-93 and 1996-97, from about 126 per cent during 1987-88 and 1992-93. **In addition to change in macro-level policies, emphasizing on reduction of subsidies in public goods and services, factors such as low and stagnating rates charged on sewer connections for popularistic**

reasons, and an inefficient system for collecting water and sewerage bills played an important role.

There has been wide spatial discrimination in availability and quality of sewerage and drainage facilities in different towns of the district. **While, more than half of the total urban population in the district was yet to avail themselves of the facility of sewerage, peripheral localities in all the towns were yet to get any of the two facilities of sewerage and drainage. In Bathinda town, the largest urban centre in the district, 90 per cent of the sewerage system was confined to localities falling East of the railway line. Whereas in Rampura Phul, twin towns, Phul township was completely devoid of sewerage facility.** Hence, the subsidy given on sewerage facility by Rampura Phul municipality was completely enjoyed by the residents of Rampura township alone.

Drainage

On an average, municipalities in Bathinda district incurred nearly Rs. 40 lakh per annum on drainage during 1980-98. Since, the municipalities in the district provided this service free of any charges the entire amount automatically became the subsidy element. Hence, on an average Rs. 40 lakh were transferred as subsidy on drainage to their residents by the municipalities in Bathinda, annually.

There were wide inter-municipal variations in this regard. Bathinda municipality, which has only about 60 per cent of total urban population in the district, provided nearly 77 per cent of the subsidy amount on an annual basis.

Notwithstanding an increase of more than 200 per cent in absolute amount of subsidy on drainage in the district, its share in aggregate municipal expenditure declined by about half, from about 8 per cent in 1982-83 to less than 5 per cent in 1996-97. Further, **there were wide inter-municipal variations in proportional share of municipal expenditure on drainage, which were widening over the period. The ratio between the highest and the lowest shares which was 3:1 in 1982-83 rose to 26:1 in 1987-88. After this it came down gradually but remained much higher than the 1982-83 level.** Notably, however, this ratio was much higher in the case of absolute amount of subsidy on drainage.

No definite trend has been noticed in municipal expenditure/ subsidy on drainage in the district. It has been changing frequently in time and space. In relative terms, fluctuations have been minimum in the case of Bathinda municipality and maximum in Rampura Phul. In a temporal context, it has been the minimum in 1996-97 and the maximum in 1987-88. Further, no association has been found between the civic status of a town and its expenditure/subsidy on drainage. **In general, Class III towns in the district provided lower amount as well as proportional subsidy on drainage, the Class I and Class IV, V towns were providing more.**

On an average, the municipalities in Bathinda district provided an annual amount of Rs. 19 as subsidy on drainage during 1980-98. This amount increased by more than 200 per cent between 1982-83 and 1996-97, recording the sharpest increase between 1992-93 and 1996-97. There were, however, wide inter-municipal disparities in this context. During 1980-98, it varied from a high of Rs. 26 per capita in Bathinda municipality to a low of Rs. 8 in Raman Mandi and Maur Mandi towns. The disparities in per capita amount of subsidy were the highest in 1987-88 and the lowest in 1996-97.

Per capita subsidy on drainage finds no association with either the civic status or population size of a town. Towns with lower civic status and population were providing high per capita subsidy at par with the high civic status and population size towns. Bhucho Mandi, a Class IV town with second lowest population size town in the district, recorded the second highest per capita subsidy after only Bathinda town on drainage. Against this, Rampura Phul, a Class III and second largest town, provided the lowest amount of subsidy on this count. In fact, per capita subsidy finds a strong positive association with per capita municipal expenditure, on drainage in turn was positively associated with per capita municipal income. **Per capita municipal subsidy on this service finds a strong positive association with per capita municipal income and expenditure.**

Public Health and Sanitation

During the period 1980-98, municipalities in Bathinda district incurred an annual average expenditure of Rs. 153 lakh on public health and sanitation, making up more than 18 per cent of the total municipal expenditure on different services. There are, however, wide inter-municipal variations. It varied from a high of 26 per cent in Maur Mandi, a Class III town, to a low of 5 per cent in Kot Fatta town. Relatively large population-sized 'Mandi' towns along with Bathinda, which functions as the district headquarters and is the only Class I town in the district, incurred higher shares in proportion to their aggregate expenditure on sanitation.

The entire municipal expenditure on public health and sanitation in the district was actually the subsidy element on this service, as the municipalities provided this facility to their residents free of charge.

There were wide spatio-temporal variations in the distribution of subsidy on sanitation. In aggregate terms, three of the largest municipalities viz., Bathinda, Rampura Phul and Maur Mandi, shared 87 per cent of the total expenditure on sanitation in the district during 1980-98. Their combined population made up 81 per cent of the total urban population in 1991. Against this, five small-sized towns shared only 13 per cent of subsidy but had about 20 per cent of the total urban population. Bathinda town alone has more than two-thirds of total subsidy on this service, against its share of about three-fifths in the total urban population. In contrast, Kot Fatta shares less than 0.2 per cent of the total urban population. In 1982-83, Bathinda provided 14 per cent of total average annual expenditure on different services as subsidy on sanitation, which increased to about 21 per cent in 1996-97. In contrast, Kot Fatta, the second smallest town, recorded a decrease of about 6 per cent in 1996-97 from about 11 per cent in 1982-83. **Inter-municipal disparities in subsidy on sanitation, in absolute as well as proportional terms, were very wide but showed a mixed trend. Disparities widened between 1982-83 and 1987-88, but declined marginally between 1987-88 and 1992-93. The disparities, however, increased again between 1992-93 and 1996-97.**

Composition of expenditure/subsidy on sanitation has been highly revealing. **During 1980-98, more than nine-tenths of total municipal expenditure in the district on sanitation went into paying salaries to sanitary staff, leaving only less than one-tenth for purchase and maintenance of equipment etc. for the**

purpose. The share rose to more than 95 per cent of total municipal expenditure on sanitation in 1997-98 from 83 per cent in 1982-83. Implementation of Fifth Pay Commission's recommendations by the Punjab Government in 1988 resulted in a hefty increase in the salaries of government and semi-government employees. As a result, the share of salary component in municipal expenditure rose from 85.6 per cent in 1987-88 to 95.3 per cent in 1996-97. This left very little with the municipalities to invest in building and maintaining infrastructure for public health and sanitation work. **Small sized, low income municipalities were the hardest hit in this regard. The entire municipal expenditure on sanitation work in Kot Fatta, the second smallest municipal town in the district, was consumed with paying the salary of sanitary staff; leaving nothing at all for the purchase of even a broom. This had serious implications for public health and sanitation conditions in some towns of Bathinda district.**

Per capita municipal subsidy on sanitation has been growing over the period in the district. However, the fastest growth in per capita subsidy amount was recorded between 1987-88 and 1992-93. **Notably, this growth in subsidy amount was marked with reduction in inter-municipal disparities in per capita subsidy on sanitation. Hence, it may be called a period of growth with spatial justice. After 1992-93, the growth of per capita subsidy amount on sanitation slowed down, but the inter-municipal disparities in per capita amount of subsidy on sanitation marginally widened. Nevertheless, the trend in disparities undulated during the period 1980-98.**

There has been inter and intra-town discrimination in distribution of subsidy on public health and sanitation. While, there was not a single sweeper to sweep the roads and the drains of Kot Fatta town, there was one sweeper after each about 250 persons in Bathinda City and within Bathinda City localities inhabited by the high income group people and/or the government officials and special bazars were given greater attention at the cost of low income localities.

Fire Brigade

On average annual basis, municipalities in Bathinda district spent Rs. 14.61 lakh on fire brigade service during 1980-98.

Bathinda municipality shared two-thirds of this expenditure and remaining one-third was shared by Rampura Phul alongwith Maur Mandi and Raman Mandi towns.

Municipal expenditure on fire brigade service has been growing over the period. It increased to Rs. 31.01 lakh in 1996-97 from Rs. 2.72 lakh in 1982-83, on an average annual basis. However, the growth rate of expenditure on fire service has been slowing down over the period. It came down to 51 per cent between 1992-93 and 1996-97 from about 300 per cent during 1982-83 and 1987-88.

While the expenditure on fire brigade service has been mounting regularly, there is hardly any regular income from this service. Evidently, a very large component of subsidy was involved.

Roads

Municipalities in Bathinda district incurred an amount of Rs. 197 million on construction and maintenance of municipal roads during 1980-98, giving an average annual amount of Rs. 109 lakhs per annum. In proportional terms, it made up 13 per cent of the total municipal expenditure.

The municipalities did not earn a single penny on the provision of roads. Hence, the entire municipal expenditure, making up 13 per cent of their aggregate expenditure, on this account ultimately turned into the subsidy component.

There are, however, wide inter-municipal and temporal variations in distribution of subsidies on this count. Of the average annual amount of more than Rs. 109 lakh, Bathinda municipality shared nearly 73 per cent of the total. Its share combined with that of Rampura Phul and Bhucho Mandi towns made up 88 per cent of the total. Against this, remaining five municipal towns of Maur Mandi, Raman Mandi, Goniana Mandi, Sangat Mandi and Kot Fatta, in combination, shared only 12 per cent of the total expenditure on this service.

Municipal expenditure/subsidy on the provision of roads as a share in their total expenditure has been changing over the period. However, the share has been ranging between 12 and 15 per cent, 1996-97 being a peak year and 1987-88 a sluggish year.

In general, the change in expenditure share on roads has been negative. Nevertheless, Bathinda and Goniana Mandi towns present a contrasting picture. The former recorded an increase and the latter a decrease in their respective shares during different sub-periods. **Of late, negative change in subsidy share for all the towns in the district indicated the reduced priority accorded to roads in overall context of municipal expenditure.**

Per capita expenditure on roads presents an interesting picture. One of the Class IV category of towns, Bhucho Mandi, provided the highest per capita amount of Rs. 97 during 1980-98. Bathinda, the largest and only Class I town in the district, ranked distantly second to it with Rs. 69 per capita. On the other extreme, Kot Fatta provided only Rs. 5 per capita. Trends in per capita expenditure indicate that it continued to grow over the period. The growth rate has been the highest between 1982-83 and 1987-88 and the lowest between 1987-88 and 1992-93. At the level of individual municipal towns the trend differed widely. It was only in the case of Bathinda municipal town where per capita amount of expenditure on roads has consistently been growing, though at different rates, but no consistent trend is observed in case of other towns. Kot Fatta and Sangat Mandi were, in fact, not consistent even in spending on this provision.

There has been wide spatial discrimination in distribution of municipal expenditure/subsidy on the provision of roads in different towns. The localities which were peripherally located and or resided in by low income and social status groups suffered the most, both in terms of availability and quality of roads. While the roads in the inner parts of the towns were not only black top roads but also maintained well, it was mostly the poorly maintained un-surfaced roads that were the lot of the peripheral and low socio-economic status localities. This was, however, more a distinctive feature of large towns such as Bathinda. In small towns like Kot Fatta and Sangat Mandi, it was apparently not so.

Street Lighting

Municipal towns in Bathinda district incurred nearly Rs. 480 lakh or more than 3 per cent of aggregate expenditure on street lighting during 1980-98. On an average, this came to about Rs. 27 lakh per annum.

Municipalities provided the street lighting facility to their residents free of cost. A considerable share of municipal expenditure on this count goes into installation of new light points or replacement of the old ones and on payment of electricity bills against street lighting.

There have been wide inter-municipal and temporal variations in distribution of expenditure on street lighting. Nearly two-thirds or 65 per cent of the total expenditure on this facility, on average annual basis, was incurred in Bathinda city. Rampura Phul, the second largest town after Bathinda, incurred another 12 per cent of such expenditure. In combination, these two topmost towns in the district spent more than three-fourths of the total. Expenditure share of Bathinda municipality has been as high as 77 per cent in 1992-93. Also, it was during this period that **three top spending municipalities, Bathinda, Rampura Phul and Bhucho Mandi, together incurred nearly nine-tenths or 90 per cent of the total expenditure on street lighting.** This took the inter-municipal disparities in expenditure on street lighting to the highest level in 1992-93. Inter-municipal disparities in expenditure on this account were the lowest, though still very high, during 1982-83.

Expenditure on this count has been growing fast over the period. On an annual average, it increased from Rs. 11.23 lakh in 1982-83 to Rs. 74.83 lakh in 1996-97, registering an increase of nearly six times. This increase has been as high as about seven times in Bathinda city and as low as less than one time in Sangat Mandi town. The former is the biggest and the latter the smallest town in the district. There has been no strong association between civic status and growth of expenditure of a town on street lighting. In general, Class IV municipal towns made much higher expenditure on street lighting than Class III towns in the district. Municipal expenditure on street lighting recorded the fastest growth between 1987-88 and 1992-93 and the lowest during 1992-93 and 1996-97.

On per capita basis, municipalities in the district incurred an amount of Rs. 13 on street lighting per annum during 1980-98. There were wide inter-municipal and temporal variations in this regard too. Bhucho Mandi, a Class IV town, incurred a per capita amount (Rs. 19) more than three times the expenditure (Rs. 6) made by Sangat Mandi, a Class VI town. Per capita expenditure on street lighting followed, in general, the same pattern as was the case of the total expenditure on this count. However, inter-municipal variations were quite low in per capita expenditure in comparison to total municipal expenditure on street lighting. Interestingly, however, inter-municipal disparities in per capita expenditure on this count were the highest in 1992-93 when it reached Rs. 27 for all the municipalities after recording the highest growth rate of 125 per cent between 1987-88 and 1992-93. **Per capita expenditure of Bathinda city on street lighting has been not only quite high but also grew the fastest during 1980-98. Sangat Mandi town represents the reverse case. In general, Class IV municipal towns in the district incurred much higher per capita expenditure on street lighting in comparison to Class III towns.**

There have been wide spatial discriminations both at inter-municipal and intra-municipal levels in distribution of subsidy on street lighting. **The residents of Bhucho Mandi town enjoyed the per capita subsidy on street lighting which was more than three times that of the residents of Sangat Mandi town. Even the residents of Kot Fatta towns were not getting the facility of street lighting. Further in all towns, the quality and maintenance of street lighting differed widely between the high income localities and low income and peripherally located ones. However, the spatial discrimination was more a marked feature of big towns such as Bathinda city than in small towns, such as Sangat Mandi.**

Slums

Of more than 52 thousand urban slum-dwellers in the district, about 37 thousand or 71 per cent were in three largest towns of Bathinda, Rampura Phul and Maur Mandi. **Broadly speaking, larger the population size of a town, larger the number of slum-dwellers in it. At the level of individual town, while the entire population of Sangat Mandi town was made up of slum-dwellers, it comprised only about 11 per cent in case of Bathinda city. Half the population of Bhucho Mandi and two-fifths of Kot Fatta also comprised slum-dwellers. However, no association was found between the class category of a town and the share of slum population in it. Hence, urbanisation in Bathinda district contradicts the validity of the all-India level proven**

hypothesis that class category of a town and the proportional share of slum population have a strong positive association.

Municipalities in Bathinda district did not spend regularly on slum improvement. It depended mostly on the grants received by the municipalities from different sources. Nevertheless, an aggregate amount of Rs. 266.13 lakh, making for less than 2.0 per cent of total municipal expenditure, was spent on improvement of urban slums in the district during 1980-98. More than 52 thousand population identified as slum-dwellers in the district benefited from this amount. Roughly, it came to Rs. 509 per slum dweller during 1980-98. **Pavement of streets, construction of drains, water supply, sewerage disposal, construction of roads and street lighting were the schemes on which expenditure was made by the municipality for improvement of slums. On the whole, capital works received priority in implementation of the programme in towns of Bathinda district.**

Three towns of Goniana Mandi, Bhucho Mandi and Bathinda shared a much higher proportion of total municipal expenditure of the district on slum improvement than their respective shares in total slum population in the district. The reverse is the case of Maur Mandi, Raman Mandi and Kot Fatta towns. However, **the expenditure on slum improvement in a town does not find an association with its share in slum population and size category of the town.**

On per capita basis, Goniana Mandi was at the top with Rs. 65 per annum and Maur Mandi at the bottom, with Rs. 9. Inter-municipal variations in per capita expenditure on slum improvement were lower than the share of aggregate municipal expenditure on slum improvement in the district. The maximum per capita expenditure on slum improvement was higher by about seven times than the minimum. The highest and the lowest proportional share of per annum expenditure by municipalities on slum improvement programmes differed by 25 times.

An element of political favour in declaration of any locality as a slum area and in the allocation of funds for environmental improvement of slums has been observed. Some of the localities were allocated more funds than others in each of the eight towns in the district.

The expenditure on the 'Environmental Improvement of Slums' makes a positive change in the quality of life in these localities, but does not yield any returns in reverse terms for the municipal government. It thus becomes a case of hundred per cent subsidy.

Recreational Services

During 1980-98, municipalities in Bathinda district incurred an amount of Rs. 22.17 lakh on annual average basis on recreational facilities. **This amount made up only 2.82 per cent of total average annual expenditure on urban services in the district. About nine-tenths of this amount was shared by Bathinda City. Bathinda alongwith Rampura Phul and Bhucho Mandi towns incurred about 99 per cent of the total expenditure on recreational facilities in the district. It goes to show that recreational services existed just in name in other towns except in Bathinda, Rampura Phul and Bhucho Mandi towns.**

Bathinda town, which is the largest town in the district and maintains more than 25 parks, one Rose Garden and one Swimming pool as recreational facility, shared the largest amount of total municipal expenditure on this count in the district during 1980-98. Its share varied from a minimum of 45 per cent in 1982-83 to a maximum of 95 per cent in 1987-88. Over the period, its share in total expenditure in the district on recreational facilities recorded a decline with increased amount of expenditure by other municipalities.

Expenditure on recreational services has been growing during 1980-98, but with a slowed down growth rate. While the expenditure on recreational facilities increased by 149 per cent between 1982-83 and 1987-88, it increased by only 26 per cent between 1992-93 and 1996-97. **This indicates how recreational facilities fell victim to the financial resource crunch which the municipal administration had been facing after the policy of cuts in public expenditure followed in the country in the post-economic reform period.**

Of all the five towns, which were spending on recreational facilities, Bathinda has been the only town that earned some income from this service. In the rest of the municipal towns, this service was provided free of cost.

On per capita basis, municipalities in Bathinda district provided Rs. 11 as subsidy on recreational facility, on average annual basis, during 1980-98. There are wide inter-municipal disparities in this regard. It varied from a high of Rs. 15 in Bathinda municipality to a low of only forty paisa in Raman Mandi. The latter did not spend regularly on this account. Bhucho Mandi, a Class IV town, was next to Bathinda city with Rs. 11 per capita during the same period. Rampura Phul, the second largest town in the district, provided only Rs. 4 on this count. However, in 1982-83 Rampura Phul was at the top with Rs. 10 per capita. The same place of pride was accorded to Bhucho Mandi town in 1996-97 when it registered the highest per capita amount of Rs. 30 as subsidy on recreational facilities.

Although the per capita amount of subsidy on recreational facilities has increased over the period in the district, its growth has been slowing down over the period. While, it grew by about 113 per cent between 1987-88 and 1992-93, the growth rate came down to only about 24 per cent during 1992-93 and 1996-97. It seems that the resource crunch which the municipal administration faced in the nineties under the economic reforms programme, where cut in public expenditure had been one of the important measures, hit hard the provision of recreational facility rendered by the municipal administration to its residents in all the towns.

There has been wide intra-town discrimination in distribution of subsidy on recreational facilities in towns of Bathinda district. In all the urban centres in the district, these facilities are generally located in the newly planned or high income localities. The institutional enterprises also have these facilities in their proximity. The old congested localities, mostly in inner parts of all the towns in the district, are at a disadvantage in this regard.

SUBSIDY ELEMENT: A CONSOLIDATION

An amount of Rs. 92 out of each Rs. 100 incurred as expenditure on urban services by the municipalities in the district goes as subsidy element. **During 1980-98, on average annual basis, municipalities in the district incurred an amount of Rs. 56.11 million to get a meagre amount of Rs. 4.54 million as income**

from urban services, giving thus an amount of Rs. 51.6 million in subsidy on average annual basis.

Over the period, this amount of subsidy on urban services had been growing in the district. It increased to Rs. 107.22 million in 1996-97 from Rs. 18.25 million in 1982-83, on annual average basis, recording an increase of 488 per cent or about five times. However, in per capita terms it increased to Rs. 31 from Rs. 11 during the same period, showing a slower growth in per capita terms than in absolute amount.

Subsidy element in urban services is slowing down over the period both in absolute as well as in per capita terms. While the subsidy amount grew by 94 per cent in between 1982-83 and 1987-88, the growth came down to about 50 per cent between 1992-93 and 1996-97. Similarly, per capita amount of subsidy grew by 100 per cent between 1982-83 and 1987-88, but came down to only 48 per cent during 1992-93 and 1996-97. **Since the subsidy element finds a highly positive association with municipal expenditure on urban services, it definitely involves deterioration in quality of available urban services in different towns in the district.**

The subsidy element differed widely from service to service and time to time. **Of the eight urban services, public health and sanitation received the highest amount of Rs. 15.30 million or about 30 per cent of total subsidy amount during 1980-98 in the district. Against this, the fire brigade services, received only Rs. 1.46 million or less than 3 per cent. In all, three urban services of public health and sanitation, sewerage and roads cornered nearly 73 per cent of total subsidy amount during the period.** Fire brigade service recorded the highest compounded annual growth rate in its subsidy component between 1982-83 and 1987-88, water supply between 1987-88 and 1992-93, and drainage between 1992-93 and 1996-97.

Also the subsidy element in urban services differed widely among municipalities. **Against an average of 92 per cent for all the municipalities it ranged from a high of 94 per cent in Bathinda City to a low of 79 per cent in Sangat Mandi town.** The former is the largest and the latter the smallest population size town in the district, yet there has not been a perfect relation between the population size and subsidy share of different towns in the district. In absolute terms, Bathinda City provided more than three-fourths of total subsidy amount by all municipalities.

Against this, Sangat Mandi town shares only less than half a per cent.

In per capita amount of subsidy, inter-municipal disparities were still larger. It varied from a high of Rs. 333 per capita in Bathinda City to a low of only Rs. 44 in Kot Fatta. Municipal expenditure on a service and the subsidy element in it find a positive association in the district.

Five out of the eight urban services were fully subsidized, while remaining three were partially subsidized. There have been wide inter-service differentials in distribution of subsidy on different urban services. It ranged from a high of more than 37 times in the case of recreational services to a minimum of more than one time in fire services. Also, there have been wide inter-municipal variations in the case of sewerage, municipal roads and public health and sanitation. **While public health and sanitation was the highest subsidy receiving urban service in majority of towns in the district, it was sewerage in the case of Bathinda City, municipal roads in Mandi town, and water supply in Kot Fatta town. Against this, recreational facilities received the least amount of subsidy in half the towns, fire services in the case of Bathinda City and sewerage in Maur Mandi town.**

Five of the eight urban services in Bathinda district selected for the study were fully subsidized services. Three services, from which municipalities did get some revenue income, were also heavily subsidized. The recovery rates were as low as 8 per cent.

There are, however, wide inter-service and inter-municipal variations in recovery rates. **Recovery rate varied from a high of about 46 per cent in case of water supply service to a low of less than 8 per cent in sewerage service. Among municipalities, recovery rates on water supply varied from a high of 77 per cent in Rampura Phul to a low of only 14 per cent in Kot Fatta.**

Inter-municipal differentials in recovery rates have been the maximum in sewerage. Whereas recreational facilities made a recovery concept case only in the case of Bathinda City.

While, civic status and administrative status of towns in the district found a broad association with absolute as well as per capita amount of subsidy on urban services, no such association could be established between the year of establishment of municipal bodies and the subsidy amount they provided on urban services.

Amount of subsidy found a high positive association with area and population sizes of towns and absolute amount of expenditure on urban services. Its association with per capita amount of expenditure was also quite strong, but it was weak with the growth rate of population in different towns.

Per capita amount of subsidy on urban services recorded strong positive association with all the attributes of towns, included in the analysis, but association was exceptionally strong with growth rate of population and per capita amount of expenditure. In other words, rapidly growing and high per capita spending towns provided very high per capita amount of subsidy on urban services. Large area and population size municipal towns also provided high per capita amount of subsidy but to a lesser degree.

In view of the high subsidy component in urban services, there is a need for rationalization. The immediate solution that comes to mind is a hike in the tariff structure of urban services. It is, however, true that things are not as simple as they seem, as revision of tariff is linked with several other issues. These revolve around various entities and ideas including the 'consumer' the 'administrator', the 'decision-maker', the 'ruling paradigm' and 'futuristic possibilities'.

Some of the core issues are:

(i) Convincing people of the fact that they are getting highly subsidized urban services and that the poor quality of services being rendered is related largely to this fact; consequently they must pay for these services adequately,

(ii) Working out a scenario in which the consumer is convinced that it is not the administrative mismanagement but the financial crunch which is more responsible for the prevailing situation, and

(iii) Preparing the local politician to cooperate by resisting the tendency towards populism and opposing it to encourage any rationalization of pricing of urban services. **On the whole, the situation is more favourable now than ever before. Already, a favourable wind is blowing towards rationalizing of the prices of urban services so as to ensure adequate availability and good quality of urban services. The urban-dwellers have also started getting a feel of it. Their mindset is now changing towards the context of emerging realities.**

A number of hypotheses formulated at the beginning of the study were vindicated by the empirical analysis. Higher administrative and civic status towns in the district provided the higher amount of subsidy on urban services due to their higher income generating and spending capacity. Analysis found that while the absolute amount of subsidy on different urban services was quite strongly associated with administrative and civic status of different terms, relationship between the subsidy share and civic status was not so strong.

The nature and requirement of various urban services in the district differed widely from each other. That is why urban services such as drainage, street lighting, public health, slum upgradation services, and maintenance of municipal roads were provided by the municipal administration in towns of Bathinda district completely free of charge. Against this, tap water supply service, sewerage, and fire brigade were partially charged. Whereas recreational services were free of charge in all the towns but not in Bathinda City.

Fast growing towns in the district such as Bathinda and Bhucho Mandi provided very high amount of subsidy, both in absolute and per capita terms, than the slow growing stagnating towns like Kot Fatta, Sangat Mandi and Maur Mandi. Bathinda City provided a per capita amount of subsidy of urban services that was more than eight times higher than that provided by Kot Fatta town.

There was wide inter-town and intra-town discrimination in distribution of subsidy element. While sewerage was yet to become a reality for the people living in towns of Kot Fatta and Sangat Mandi towns, it was available only to less than one-third population in Maur Mandi town. Also none of the towns could boast of full coverage under the sewerage system and peripheral localities and areas resided in by lower income groups suffered badly in all towns of the district. The sharpest contrast was observed in the twin towns of Rampura and Phul where more than two-thirds of population of Rampura township enjoyed sewerage facilities, there was none in Phul township. Discrimination in terms of quality of services was a marked feature of big towns in the district. In such towns localities resided in by government officials and high income category people were well served at the cost of peripheral and low income localities.

BATHINDA DISTRICT: MUNICIPAL FINANCE, 1980-98

(i) Bathinda Municipal Committee

(Figures in lakh Rs.)

Year	*Income*	*Expenditure*
1980-81	131.43	128.64
1981-82	155.05	143.65
1982-83	215.04	231.82
1983-84	261.51	237.90
1984-85	334.70	293.50
1985-86	419.45	361.78
1986-87	589.47	387.03
1987-88	586.22	459.70
1988-89	498.36	500.50
1989-90	499.12	573.14
1990-91	687.68	720.76
1991-92	624.05	778.38
1992-93	627.72	596.51
1993-94	756.19	770.39
1994-95	904.21	910.00
1995-96	1048.61	1028.65
1996-97	1190.11	1162.53
1997-98	1248.16	1216.16

(ii) Rampura Phul Municipal Committee

Year	*Income*	*Expenditure*
1980-81	23.14	25.65
1981-82	30.20	42.53
1982-83	34.08	31.01
1983-84	36.81	35.62
1984-85	38.44	37.27
1985-86	47.95	39.49
1986-87	52.47	48.10
1987-88	55.94	51.05
1988-89	67.08	64.91
1989-90	63.24	74.56
1990-91	85.49	81.20
1991-92	90.36	83.53
1992-93	91.83	103.87
1993-94	125.17	116.25
1994-95	116.14	139.94
1995-96	191.00	187.05
1996-97	159.62	158.37
1997-98	142.06	142.88

(iii) Maur Mandi Municipal Committee

Year	*Income*	*Expenditure*
1980-81	11.68	8.91
1981-82	13.54	13.41
1982-83	16.45	15.08
1983-84	16.01	16.57
1984-85	18.89	19.10
1985-86	26.76	19.15
1986-87	34.63	33.39
1987-88	24.89	28.65
1988-89	28.37	39.47
1989-90	35.06	38.37
1990-91	45.40	42.75
1991-92	44.46	40.45
1992-93	58.88	46.88
1993-94	64.57	65.82
1994-95	68.14	65.60
1995-96	78.51	73.27
1996-97	79.00	77.33
1997-98	78.03	80.72

(iv) Raman Mandi Municipal Committee

1980-81	10.01	10.12
1981-82	15.11	17.71
1982-83	11.95	10.03
1983-84	12.06	11.26
1984-85	16.38	11.90
1985-86	18.63	13.76
1986-87	26.56	20.50
1987-88	23.50	28.44
1988-89	39.06	44.84
1989-90	36.37	35.04
1990-91	40.71	40.01
1991-92	43.30	40.03
1992-93	42.40	47.47
1993-94	51.99	58.08
1994-95	87.57	81.18
1995-96	75.34	86.22
1996-97	74.47	85.00
1997-98	99.58	88.63

(v) Goniana Mandi Municipal Committee

Year	*Income*	*Expenditure*
1980-81	11.62	10.46
1981-82	12.72	14.18
1982-83	12.83	12.35
1983-84	14.35	15.99
1984-85	18.71	18.51
1985-86	27.62	28.89
1986-87	36.70	36.40
1987-88	20.19	24.67
1988-89	28.48	22.68
1989-90	31.12	30.71
1990-91	36.31	32.45
1991-92	40.62	34.43
1992-93	45.74	48.10
1993-94	49.83	44.39
1994-95	53.52	47.92
1995-96	52.80	53.50
1996-97	57.35	58.08
1997-98	54.03	51.60

(vi) Bhucho Mandi Municipal Committee

Year	*Income*	*Expenditure*
1980-81	11.70	9.05
1981-82	18.63	15.06
1982-83	19.75	26.00
1983-84	16.70	19.71
1984-85	19.78	20.42
1985-86	29.40	30.34
1986-87	27.26	27.85
1987-88	20.01	25.40
1988-89	26.47	30.77
1989-90	27.90	33.53
1990-91	28.38	31.31
1991-92	29.09	29.16
1992-93	32.55	31.49
1993-94	47.35	52.03
1994-95	67.08	68.38
1995-96	106.77	82.57
1996-97	84.45	110.94
1997-98	74.29	76.97

(vii) Kot Fatta Municipal Committee

Year	*Income*	*Expenditure*
1980-81	1.43	1.47
1981-82	0.51	0.96
1982-83	0.57	0.55
1983-84	1.76	1.65
1984-85	0.77	0.65
1985-86	8.78	9.01
1986-87	5.36	5.46
1987-88	1.64	1.59
1988-89	4.66	4.01
1989-90	2.69	3.31
1990-91	2.14	2.20
1991-92	2.21	2.15
1992-93	2.98	2.72
1993-94	4.85	17.01
1994-95	6.70	4.15
1995-96	7.81	6.87
1996-97	7.80	7.29
1997-98	7.80	8.88

(viii) Sangat Mandi Municipal Committee

1980-81	1.09	1.08
1981-82	1.15	1.31
1982-83	1.53	2.70
1983-84	1.41	1.46
1984-85	2.10	1.68
1985-86	2.77	2.28
1986-87	2.90	2.26
1987-88	2.85	2.89
1988-89	3.29	2.73
1989-90	4.64	4.41
1990-91	4.89	4.93
1991-92	4.81	5.15
1992-93	7.22	5.77
1993-94	9.94	15.56
1994-95	10.74	13.55
1995-96	15.44	14.87
1996-97	9.28	10.84
1997-98	10.50	10.73

BATHINDA DISTRICT: INCOME AND EXPENDITURE OF VARIOUS MUNICIPALITIES, 1980-98

(i) Bathinda City

(Figures in Lakh Rs.)

Year	*Income sources*				*Expenditure sources*			
	Octroi	*House tax & excise duty*	*Others*	*Total*	*Establishment*	*Development*	*Contingency & others*	*Total*
1980-81	86.42	17.42	27.59	131.43	63.53	60.67	4.44	128.64
1981-82	104.77	18.19	32.09	155.05	65.02	70.99	7.64	143.65
1982-83	155.75	19.44	39.85	215.04	75.96	149.85	6.01	231.82
1983-84	187.85	19.41	54.25	261.51	101.78	129.89	6.23	237.90
1984-85	246.14	20.38	68.18	334.70	127.10	153.80	12.60	293.50
1985-86	312.29	38.62	68.54	419.45	137.23	210.04	14.51	361.78
1986-87	397.87	50.15	141.45	589.47	137.46	230.77	18.80	387.03
1987-88	402.59	44.61	139.02	586.22	139.39	297.40	22.91	459.70
1988-89	339.25	64.97	94.14	498.36	140.63	337.21	22.66	500.50
1989-90	343.29	64.17	91.66	499.12	169.43	380.35	23.36	573.14
1990-91	429.84	165.88	91.96	687.68	151.57	540.20	28.99	720.76
1991-92	446.26	105.30	72.49	624.05	190.20	555.98	32.20	778.38
1992-93	457.16	96.63	73.93	627.72	232.84	326.47	37.20	596.51
1993-94	514.03	145.91	96.25	756.19	258.96	469.74	41.69	770.39
1994-95	667.11	163.84	73.26	904.21	280.50	591.62	37.88	910.00
1995-96	761.02	184.09	103.50	1048.61	327.42	656.49	44.74	1028.65
1996-97	881.10	210.90	98.11	1190.11	385.47	722.90	54.16	1162.53
1997-98	990.12	211.63	46.41	1248.16	472.74	686.27	57.15	1216.16

(ii) Rampura Phul

1980-81	14.86	2.20	6.08	23.14	12.25	11.36	2.04	25.65
1981-82	15.09	2.25	12.86	30.20	22.11	15.97	4.45	42.53
1982-83	16.10	3.90	14.08	34.08	8.89	19.06	3.06	31.01
1983-84	21.11	5.15	10.55	36.81	13.87	19.67	2.08	35.62
1984-85	24.19	4.92	9.33	38.44	19.10	15.65	2.52	37.27
1985-86	28.26	6.40	13.29	47.95	19.87	15.82	3.80	39.49
1986-87	30.35	9.29	12.83	52.47	20.21	24.94	2.95	48.10
1987-88	32.62	8.70	14.62	55.94	29.90	18.98	2.17	51.05
1988-89	35.33	13.48	18.27	67.08	40.71	22.02	2.18	64.91
1989-90	33.18	12.30	17.76	63.24	50.39	20.30	3.87	74.56
1990-91	33.64	17.32	34.53	85.49	50.06	26.92	4.22	81.20
1991-92	40.70	18.61	31.05	90.36	50.48	27.60	5.45	83.53

(Contd.)

(Contd.)

1992-93	37.45	23.96	30.42	91.83	63.75	35.95	4.17	103.87
1993-94	48.11	38.75	38.31	125.17	72.71	31.88	11.66	116.25
1994-95	51.42	31.13	33.59	116.14	58.90	65.15	15.89	139.94
1995-96	85.93	34.94	70.13	191.00	76.59	98.84	11.62	187.05
1996-97	68.72	33.57	57.33	159.62	94.40	55.63	8.34	158.37
1997-98	67.10	29.71	45.25	142.06	99.70	35.89	7.29	142.88

(iii) Maur Mandi

Year	*Income sources*				*Expenditure sources*			
	Octroi	*House tax & excise duty*	*Others*	*Total*	*Establish-ment*	*Develop-ment*	*Contin-gency & others*	*Total*
1980-81	7.15	1.01	3.52	11.68	5.63	2.35	0.93	8.91
1981-82	7.65	1.20	4.69	13.54	6.52	5.25	1.64	13.41
1982-83	8.10	1.70	6.65	16.45	7.69	6.59	0.80	15.08
1983-84	8.73	1.02	6.26	16.01	8.97	6.99	0.61	16.57
1984-85	11.96	1.03	5.90	18.89	10.36	7.24	1.50	19.10
1985-86	14.53	1.35	10.88	26.76	10.51	7.67	0.97	19.15
1986-87	14.06	3.17	17.40	34.63	12.46	19.31	1.62	33.39
1987-88	13.96	2.55	8.38	24.89	16.49	10.54	1.62	28.65
1988-89	15.29	4.77	8.31	28.37	23.59	14.05	1.83	39.47
1989-90	17.04	4.32	13.70	35.06	23.33	12.95	2.09	38.37
1990-91	19.04	8.11	18.25	45.40	27.44	12.82	2.49	42.75
1991-92	19.07	8.86	16.53	44.46	25.36	12.22	2.87	40.45
1992-93	20.30	12.08	26.50	58.88	32.05	12.28	2.55	46.88
1993-94	23.33	9.16	32.08	64.57	36.80	26.75	2.27	65.82
1994-95	28.37	9.65	30.12	68.14	42.60	18.97	4.03	65.60
1995-96	34.57	9.90	34.04	78.51	45.34	24.31	3.62	73.27
1996-97	42.27	10.68	26.05	79.00	45.32	27.71	4.30	77.33
1997-98	37.57	11.13	29.33	78.03	46.02	30.83	3.87	80.72

(iv) Raman Mandi

1980-81	5.35	1.03	3.63	10.01	5.91	1.98	2.23	10.12
1981-82	5.83	1.63	7.65	15.11	6.18	9.15	2.38	17.71
1982-83	5.32	2.11	4.52	11.95	7.15	1.49	1.39	10.03
1983-84	5.98	1.91	4.17	12.06	7.68	0.58	3.00	11.26
1984-85	9.67	2.09	4.62	16.38	8.55	2.28	1.07	11.90
1985-86	11.93	1.66	5.04	18.63	8.99	3.14	1.63	13.76
1986-87	15.38	2.32	8.86	26.56	9.46	9.72	1.32	20.50
1987-88	12.52	4.49	6.49	23.50	12.45	15.28	0.71	28.44
1988-89	16.59	4.76	17.71	39.06	15.61	27.88	1.35	44.84
1989-90	16.43	4.63	15.31	36.37	18.43	15.53	1.08	35.04

(Contd.)

(Contd.)

1990-91	15.61	6.65	18.45	40.71	19.19	19.54	1.28	40.01
1991-92	15.91	7.59	19.80	43.30	20.79	18.15	1.09	40.03
1992-93	17.11	7.49	17.80	42.40	22.60	23.41	1.46	47.47
1993-94	20.43	9.14	22.42	51.99	23.49	31.77	2.82	58.08
1994-95	27.62	10.17	49.78	87.57	27.39	51.05	2.74	81.18
1995-96	23.12	10.27	41.95	75.34	29.56	53.95	2.71	86.22
1996-97	24.31	11.03	39.13	74.47	28.20	52.29	4.51	85.00
1997-98	29.30	12.19	58.09	99.58	29.30	54.71	4.62	88.63

(v) Goniana Mandi

Year	*Income sources*				*Expenditure sources*			
	Octroi	*House tax & excise duty*	*Others*	*Total*	*Establish-ment*	*Develop-ment*	*Contin-gency & others*	*Total*
1980-81	7.11	0.89	3.62	11.62	4.25	4.55	1.66	10.46
1981-82	6.59	1.17	4.96	12.72	5.37	6.01	2.80	14.18
1982-83	7.23	1.00	4.60	12.83	5.73	4.69	1.93	12.35
1983-84	8.16	1.33	4.86	14.35	6.99	6.96	2.04	15.99
1984-85	11.57	1.01	6.13	18.71	7.80	8.39	2.32	18.51
1985-86	11.65	1.42	14.55	27.62	8.37	16.90	3.62	28.89
1986-87	10.65	3.05	23.00	36.70	8.38	26.02	2.00	36.40
1987-88	12.47	2.61	5.11	20.19	11.33	10.29	3.05	24.67
1988-89	14.00	4.00	10.48	28.48	12.73	6.39	3.56	22.68
1989-90	14.96	5.03	11.13	31.12	18.24	7.08	5.39	30.71
1990-91	13.84	9.68	12.79	36.31	17.18	13.50	1.77	32.45
1991-92	14.24	10.30	16.08	40.62	18.04	14.46	1.93	34.43
1992-93	15.19	11.04	19.51	45.74	22.67	23.28	2.15	48.10
1993-94	19.35	16.32	14.16	49.83	21.49	20.44	2.46	44.39
1994-95	24.54	10.49	18.49	53.52	22.12	21.15	4.65	47.92
1995-96	24.11	13.32	15.37	52.80	27.37	22.02	3.91	53.30
1996-97	23.77	13.95	19.63	57.35	28.06	26.46	3.56	58.08
1997-98	23.80	13.10	17.13	54.03	31.86	17.34	2.40	51.60

(vi) Bhucho Mandi

1980-81	4.35	0.71	6.64	11.70	2.48	5.21	1.36	9.05
1981-82	4.87	0.70	13.06	18.63	3.05	10.98	1.03	15.06
1982-83	5.13	0.63	13.99	19.75	3.38	16.96	5.66	26.00
1983-84	6.05	0.75	9.90	16.70	3.22	15.72	0.77	19.71
1984-85	7.72	0.77	11.29	19.78	5.23	10.72	4.47	20.42
1985-86	8.88	0.79	19.73	29.40	5.18	12.45	12.71	30.34
1986-87	10.48	1.07	15.71	27.26	5.17	10.63	12.05	27.85
1987-88	10.15	1.25	8.61	20.01	6.02	13.20	6.18	25.40
1988-89	12.42	1.28	12.77	26.47	9.63	15.51	5.63	30.77

(Contd.)

(Contd.)

1989-90	12.79	1.84	13.27	27.90	10.43	17.60	5.50	33.53
1990-91	12.27	1.85	14.26	28.38	12.43	15.32	3.56	31.31
1991-92	12.50	2.05	14.54	29.09	13.05	14.01	2.10	29.16
1992-93	12.45	3.55	16.55	32.55	14.61	13.77	3.11	31.49
1993-94	13.01	3.95	30.39	47.35	15.21	19.98	16.84	52.03
1994-95	14.43	4.31	48.34	67.08	16.32	35.30	16.76	68.38
1995-96	14.69	4.45	87.63	106.77	17.05	39.85	25.67	82.57
1996-97	16.01	4.89	63.55	84.45	17.98	45.10	47.86	110.94
1997-98	16.79	4.43	53.07	74.29	18.49	35.52	22.96	76.97

(vii) Kot Fatta Mandi

Year	*Income sources*				*Expenditure sources*			
	Octroi	*House tax & excise duty*	*Others*	*Total*	*Establishment*	*Development*	*Contingency & others*	*Total*
1980-81	0.19	0.12	1.12	1.43	0.25	0.16	1.06	1.47
1981-82	0.22	0.15	0.14	0.51	0.42	0.13	0.41	0.96
1982-83	0.28	0.18	0.11	0.57	0.43	0.07	0.05	0.55
1983-84	0.41	0.18	1.17	1.76	0.37	0.22	1.06	1.65
1984-85	0.43	0.18	0.16	0.77	0.32	0.26	0.07	0.65
1985-86	0.41	0.16	8.21	8.78	0.62	0.78	7.61	9.01
1986-87	0.25	0.62	4.49	5.36	0.36	0.29	4.81	5.46
1987-88	0.28	0.71	0.65	1.64	0.45	0.33	0.81	1.59
1988-89	0.27	0.87	3.52	4.66	0.51	2.53	0.97	4.01
1989-90	0.30	1.14	1.25	2.69	0.56	1.68	1.07	3.31
1990-91	0.28	1.20	0.66	2.14	0.94	1.10	0.16	2.20
1991-92	0.36	1.25	0.60	2.21	1.07	0.90	0.18	2.15
1992-93	0.58	1.65	0.75	2.98	0.95	1.48	0.29	2.72
1993-94	0.44	2.59	1.82	4.85	1.24	15.63	0.14	17.01
1994-95	0.69	2.41	3.60	6.70	1.32	1.99	0.84	4.15
1995-96	0.88	3.18	3.75	7.81	3.38	3.04	0.45	6.87
1996-97	0.42	2.55	4.83	7.80	1.97	5.00	0.32	7.29
1997-98	0.38	3.53	3.89	7.80	2.51	5.98	0.39	8.88

(viii) Sangat Mandi

1980-81	0.71	0.03	0.35	1.09	0.76	0.26	0.06	1.08
1981-82	0.85	0.03	0.27	1.15	0.95	0.24	0.12	1.31
1982-83	0.86	0.03	0.64	1.53	1.04	0.54	1.12	2.70
1983-84	0.96	0.03	0.42	1.41	1.08	0.28	0.10	1.46
1984-85	1.61	0.03	0.46	2.10	1.15	0.30	0.23	1.68
1985-86	2.13	0.03	0.61	2.77	1.41	0.70	0.17	2.28
1986-87	1.81	0.12	0.97	2.90	1.74	0.35	0.17	2.26
1987-88	1.85	0.15	0.85	2.85	1.99	0.72	0.18	2.89

(Contd.)

(Contd.)

1988-89	2.14	0.14	1.01	3.29	1.81	0.72	0.20	2.73
1989-90	2.97	0.16	1.51	4.64	3.35	0.84	0.22	4.41
1990-91	2.10	1.47	1.32	4.89	3.92	0.76	0.25	4.93
1991-92	1.60	1.75	1.46	4.81	4.22	0.50	0.43	5.15
1992-93	1.60	4.26	1.36	7.22	3.73	1.76	0.28	5.77
1993-94	2.15	3.34	4.45	9.94	4.43	9.93	1.20	15.56
1994-95	2.18	4.51	4.05	10.74	5.68	7.33	0.54	13.55
1995-96	3.08	2.94	9.42	15.44	4.95	8.24	1.68	14.87
1996-97	3.68	2.69	2.91	9.28	6.23	3.40	1.21	10.84
1997-98	3.68	2.88	3.94	10.50	5.22	3.84	1.67	10.73

Bibliography

Ahmed, V. (1984): "Management of Urban Services for the Poor in Pakistan", in G.S. Cheema (ed.), *Managing Urban Development Services for the Poor*, United Nations Centre for Regional Development, Nagoya.

Altarman, R. (ed.) (1988): *Private Supply of Public Services: Evaluation of Real Estate Exactions, Linkage, and Alternative Land Policies*, New York University Press, New York.

Arora, P.L. (1991): "Metering of Water Supply as a means of checking Wastage of Water", Paper presented in a Seminar on Water Conservation, New Delhi.

Bapat, M. (1987): "Inherent Limitations of the Scheme for Environmental Improvement of Slums in India", *TRIALOG*, No. 13/14, Darmstadt, pp. 52-56.

Barai, D.C. (1993): "The Augmentation of Water Supply to Meet the needs of Rapidly Growing Metropolitan Cities of India", In J. Diddee and V. Rangaswamy (eds.), *Urbanization: Trends, Perspectives and Challenges*, Rawat Publication, Jaipur, pp. 165-77.

Beier, G. *et. al.* (1976): "Task ahead for the Cities of the Developing Countries", *World Development*, Vol. 4, No. 5, pp. 363-69.

Bhargava, G. (ed.) (1981): *Urban Problems and Policy Perspective*, Abhinav Publications, New Delhi.

Bhattacharya, B. (1979): *Urban Development in India Since Prehistoric Times*, Shri Publishing House, New Delhi.

Bhattacharya, M. (1975): "Urbanisation and Urban Problems in India: Some Policy Issues", *Nagarlok*, Vol. 7, pp. 1-14.

Bhattacharya, M. (1976): "Distributive aspects of Urban Water Supply", *Nagarlok*, Vol. 8, pp. 1-16.

Bhattacharya, M.K. (1971): "Financing of Water Supply and Sewerage", *Nagarlok*, Vol. 3, pp. 65-72.

Bhourasarkar, K.M. (1954): *Municipal Finance in Certain Leading Indian States*, The All India Institute of Local Self-Government, Bombay, pp. 1-4.

Bijlani, H.K. (1987): *Solid Waste Management*, Arnold Publishers, New Delhi.

Bijlani, H.U. (1974): "Quality of Life in Cities", Paper presented in 3rd Conference of Mayors of Major Cities of World, Milan, Italy.

Bijlani, H.U. (1977): *Urban Problems*, Centre for Urban Studies, Indian Institute of Public Administration (IIPA), New Delhi.

Bonbright, J.C. (1961): *Principles of Public Utility Rates*, Columbia University Press, New York.

Bose, A. (1978): *India's Urbanisation: 1901-2001*, Tata McGraw Hill, New Delhi.

Breeze, G. (1963), "Urban Development Problems in India", *Annals of the Association of American Geographers*, Vol. 53, pp. 253-65.

Bulsara, J.F. (1964): *Problems of Rapid Urbanisation in India*, Popular Prakashan, Bombay.

Census of India (1991): *A Handbook of Population Statistics*, Government of India, New Delhi.

Census of India (1991): *District Census Handbook of Bathinda*, Government of Punjab Press, Chandigarh.

Census of India (1991): *Housing and Amenities, Paper-2 of 1993*, Government of India, New Delhi.

Central Pollution Control Board (1989): *Status of Water Supply and Waste Water Collection, Treatment and Disposal in Class I Cities*, CPCB, New Delhi.

Chatterjee, P.K. and A.K. Dutta (1982): "Water Pricing with Reference to Calcutta Metropolitan District", *Nagarlok*, Vol. 14, pp. 78-83.

Cox, J.L. (1967): *Metropolitan Water Supply: The Denver Experience*, University of Colarado, Colorado, p. 179.

Dabral, S. (1975): "Urbanisation and Urban Poor", *Link*, 9 February, pp. 24-26.

Dalal, C. (1953): *Municipal Finance*, The All India Institute of Local Self-Government, Bombay.

Dasgupta, M. *et. al.* (eds.) (1998): *Health, Poverty and Development in India*, Oxford University Press, New Delhi.

Datta, A. (1970): *Urban Government, Finance and Development*, The World Press Pvt. Ltd., Calcutta.

Datta, A. (1976): "Public Policy for Urban Utilities", *Nagarlok*, Vol. 8, pp. 14-18.

Datta, A. (1991): "Local Government Finance: Trends, Issues and Reforms", Paper Presented in NIUA Seminar on Urban Finance, New Delhi.

De Souza, A. (ed.) (1983): *The Indian City: Poverty, Ecology and Urban Development*, Manohar Publications, New Delhi.

Desai, A.R. and S.D. Pillai (1970): *Slums and Urbanisation*, Popular Parkashan, Bombay.

Dharmarajan, K. (1996): "The Integrated Development of Small and Medium Towns Programme in India", In Kulwant Singh *et. al.*, (eds), *Urban India in Crisis*, New Age International, New Delhi, pp. 213-32.

Dieterich, B.H. and J.M. Henderson (1963): *Urban Water Supply Conditions and Needs in Seventy-five Developing Countries*, W.H.O., Geneva.

Dillinger, W. (1994): *Decentralization and its Implications for Urban Services Delivery*, Urban Management Programme Publication No. 16, World Bank, Washington D.C.

Dresmond, J.M. (1951): *The Finance of Local Government, England and Wales*, George Allen and Unwin Ltd., London.

Dresmond, J.M. (1962): *The Finance of Local Government*, George Allen and Unwin Ltd., London.

Dutta, A. (1965): *Urban Community Development and Local Authorities*, Indian Institute of Public Administration, New Delhi.

Dyal, L. (1992): Slums in an Industrial City: A Case Study of Ludhiana, A Ph.D. dissertation submitted to Department of Geography, Panjab University, Chandigarh, p. 38.

Ganeshwar, V. (1995): "Urban Policies in India—Paradoxes and Predicaments", *Habitat International*, Vol. 19, No. 3, pp. 293-316.

Gaolladay, F.L. (1980): "Community Healthcare in Developing Countries", *Finance and Development*, Vol. 17, No. 3, pp. 35-39.

Gautam, S. (1972): "Water shortage in Urban Areas", *Economic Times*, 16 June, p. 5.

_________ "Urban Water Supply, Planning Better Management System", *Economic Times*, 17 June, p. 5.

Ghosh, A. *et. al.* (1995): *Basic Services for Urban Poor: A Study of Baroda, Bhilwara, Sambalpur and Siliguri*, Urban Studies, Series No. 3, Institute of Social Sciences, Concept Publishing Company, New Delhi, p. 305.

Ghosh, S. (1964): *Local Finance in Urban Areas,* New Age Publishers Pvt. Ltd., New Delhi.

Government of India (1962): *Report of the Committee on Water Supply and Sanitation,* New Delhi.

Government of India (1964): *Proceedings of Recommendation of Seminar on Financing and Management of Water and Sewerage Works,* New Delhi.

Government of India (1966): *Report on National Urban Water Supply and Sanitation Programme,* Committee on Plan Projects, New Delhi.

Government of India (1971): *Standards for Drinking Water,* Ministry of Health and Family Planning, New Delhi.

Government of India (1983): *National Master Plan : India, International Drinking Water Supply and Sanitation Decade, 1981-90,* Ministry of Works and Housing, New Delhi.

Government of India (1986): *National Water Policy (Draft),* Ministry of Water Resources, New Delhi.

Government of India (1988): *Report of National Commission on Urbanisation,* Vols. I and II, Ministry of Urban Development, New Delhi.

Government of India (1992): *The Constitution of the 74th Amendment Act, 1992 on Municipalities,* Ministry of Urban Development, New Delhi.

Government of India (1993): *Power to the People: Nagarpalika Act,* Ministry of Urban Development, New Delhi.

Government of India (2002): *National Human Development Report, 2001,* Planning Commission, New Delhi, pp. 40-41.

Government of Punjab (1953): *Punjab Municipal Act,* 1911, Government of Punjab Press, Chandigarh.

Government of Punjab (1994): *District Gazetteer of Bathinda,* Government of Punjab Press, Chandigarh.

Gugler, J. (1988), *The Urbanization of the Third World,* Oxford University Press, New York.

Hanumappa, H.G. (1981), *Urbanization Trends in India: A Case Study of a Medium Town,* Ashish Publishing House, New Delhi.

Hardoy, J.E. *et. al.,* (2001): *Environmental Problems in an Urbanizing World,* Earthscan Publication Ltd., London.

Harrington, J. *et. al.,* (2001): "Financing Basic Social Services", in : *Choices for the Poor: Lessons for National Poverty Strategies,*

United Nations Development Programme, New York, pp. 173-202.

Heggade, O.D. (1998): *Urban Development in India*, Mohit Publications, New Delhi.

Hetzel, B.S., (ed.) (1978): *Basic Healthcare in Developing Countries: An Epidemiological Perspective*, Oxford University Press, Oxford.

Hewett, P.C. and M.R. Montgomery (2001): *Poverty and Public Services in Developing Country Cities*, Population Council, Working Paper No. 154, New York.

HPIPA (1991): *Urban Basic Services for the Poor*, Himachal Pradesh Institute of Public Administration, Workshop papers, 15-19 July (unpublished), Shimla.

HSMI (1995): *Public-Private Partnerships for the Provisions of Urban Services*, Human Settlement Management Institute, New Delhi.

IIPA (1979): *Slum clearance and improvement*, Papers of the Seminar, Centre for Urban Studies, Indian Institute of Public Administration, New Delhi.

Inoguchi, T.E. *et.al.* (1999): *Cities and the Environment: New Approaches for Eco-Societies*, United Nations University Press, Tokyo.

Jagannadam, V. and M. Bhattacharya (1977): *Integrated Delivery System for Social Services*, Indian Institute of Public Administration (IIPA), New Delhi.

Kapoor, R.M. and P.B. Anand (1995): "Functional domain of Municipalities and the Municipal Finance Implications", Paper prepared for International IHSP Seminar on Integrated Urban Infrastructure Development, February 1-4, New Delhi.

Khosla, J.M. (1970): "Urbanisation in the Developing Countries and its Consequences for Local Government", *Nagarlok*, Vol. 2, pp. 23-27.

King, A.D. (ed.) (1996): *Re-presenting the City: Ethnicity, Capital and Culture in the Twenty-first Century Metropolis*, Macmillan Press Ltd., London.

Krishan, G. (1990): "Privatisation of Urban Service Provisions: The Case Study of India", A Resource Paper prepared for National Institute of Urban Affairs (NIUA), New Delhi.

Krishan, G. (1991): "Pricing of Water Supply: A Case Study", *Urban India*, Vol. II, pp. 69-87.

Krishan, G. (1996): "The Integrated Development of Small and Medium Towns in the Punjab", in Kulwant Singh *et. al.*, (eds), *Urban India in Crisis,* New Age International, New Delhi, pp. 233-42.

Krishan, G. (1998): "Is India Over-urbanized?", *Population Geography*, Vol. 8, pp. 76-81.

Krishan, G. *et. al.* (1994): *Issues in Pricing of Water Supply – A Case Study of Ludhiana City: A Draft Report,* A Project report submitted to Human Settlement Management Institute (HSMT), New Delhi.

Krishnaswamy, J. (1958): *Studies in Local Finance and Taxation with Special Reference to Madras State,* The All India Institute of Local Self Government, Bombay, pp. 1-6.

Kundu, A. (1992): *Urban Development and Urban Research in India,* Khanna Publishers, New Delhi.

_________ (1993): *In the Name of the Urban Poor: Access to Basic Amenities,* Sage Publication, New Delhi.

_________ (1996): "Access of Urban Poor to basic Services: The Changing Policy Perspective", In Kulwant Singh *et. al.*, (eds.), *Urban India in Crisis,* New Age International, New Delhi, pp. 198-206.

Maharashtra Water Supply and Sewerage Board (1988): *Annual Report, 1987-88,* MWSSB, Bombay.

Marshall, A.H. (1960): *Financial Administration in Local Government,* George Allen and Unwin Ltd. London.

Mathur, O.P. (1990): *Major Urban Issues and Research Responses,* National Institute of Urban Affairs, New Delhi.

Mathur, O.P. (1993): *The State of India's Urban Poverty,* National Institute of Public Finance and Policy, New Delhi.

Mehta, M. and V. Satyanarayana (1994): *Infrastructure Finance Gaps and Policy Issues,* Training Material on Infrastructure Finance and Planning, Mimeo.

Mishra, A. (1986): *Urban Government and Administration in India,* Anu Books, Meerut.

Mishra, G.K. and M.K. Narain (ed.) (1989): *Development Programme for Urban Poor,* Indian Institute of Public Administration, New Delhi.

Misra, S.P. (1970): "Problem of Financing and Management of Water Supply", *Nagarlok,* Vol. 2, pp. 31-35.

Mitsuhiko, H. (1984): "Urban services in Indonesia: a Focus on Kampong Improvement Programme", in G.S. Cheema (ed.)

Managing Urban Development Services for the Poor, United Nations Centre for Regional Development Nagoya.

Mohan, R. (1992): "Housing and Urban Development: Policy Issues for 1990s", *Economic and Political Weekly*, Vol. 27, No. 36, pp. 1913-20.

Mohanty, B. (ed.) (1993): *Urbanisation in Developing Countries: Basic Services and Community Participation*, Institute of Social Sciences, New Delhi.

Municipal Corporation of Delhi (1982): *Sanitary Disposal of City Garbage and Generation of Power*, MCD, New Delhi.

Nageswara Rao, M. (1985), *Studies in Urban Public Sector*, Ashish Publishing House, New Delhi.

NCAER (1980): *A Study of the Resources of Municipal Bodies*, National Council of Applied Economic Research, New Delhi.

NIUA (1986): *Management of Urban Services*, National Institute of Urban Affairs, New Delhi.

_________: *Urban Basic Service Programme—A Reference Manual*, National Institute of Urban Affairs, New Delhi.

_________ (1988): *Provision of Urban Water Supply: Institutional Options*, National Institute of Urban Affairs, New Delhi.

NIUA (1988a): *Upgrading Municipal Services—Norms and Financial Implications*, National Institute of Urban Affairs, Volume I, New Delhi.

NIUA (1988b): *Approach to Urban Poverty: A Positive Note*, Research Study Series No. 27, National Institute of Urban Affairs, New Delhi.

NIUA (1989): *Upgrading Municipal Services—Norms and Financial Implications*, Volume II, National Institute of Urban Affairs, New Delhi.

NIUA (1991): *Basic Services and the Urban Poor*, Study Series No. 46, National Institute of Urban Affairs, New Delhi.

NSSO (1999): *Drinking Water, Sanitation and Hygiene in India*, National Sample Survey Organisation, 54th Round (January-June 1998), Report No. 449, Department of Statistics, Government of India, New Delhi.

Operations Research Group (1989): *Delivery and Financing of Urban Services*, ORG, Baroda.

Pacy, A. (1978): *Sanitation in Developing Countries*, John Wiley and Sons Ltd., London.

Patra, G. (1991): "The Present Water Supply, Sewerage and Drainage System in Bhubaneswar", Unpublished paper presented in *the Seminar on Infrastructure for Urban Development,* held at Bhubaneswar.

Percy, S.L. (1984): "Citizen Participation in the Co-production of Urban Services", *Urban Affairs Quarterly,* Vol. 19, No. 4, p. 433.

Premi, M.K. (1991): "India's Urban Scene and its Future Implications", *Demography India,* Vol. 20, pp. 41-52.

Rajbala (1986): *Trends in Urbanisation in India,* Rawat Publishers, Jaipur.

Ramachandran, S.R. (1974): "Water Supply of Calicut", *Nagarlok,* Vol. 6, pp. 46-51.

Rana, P.S. (1996): "The Corridor Concept: Towards Integrated Infrastructure Development", In Kulwant Singh *et. al.,* (eds.), *Urban India in Crisis,* New Age International, New Delhi, pp. 99-108.

Roberts, B. (1978), *Cities of Peasants: The Political Economy of Urbanization in the Third World,* Edward Arnold, London.

Robson, W.A. (1954): *Great Cities of the World,* George Allen and Unwin Ltd., London.

Robson, W.A. (1966): *Local Government in Crisis,* George Allen and Unwin Ltd., London.

Roth, G. (1985): *Private Provision of Public Services in Developing Countries,* Economic Development Institute, World Bank, Washington, D.C.

Roth, G. (1987): *The Private Provision of Urban Services,* Oxford University Press, New York.

Roy, A.K. (1968): "Water Pollution and its Control in Uttar Pradesh", *Civic Affairs,* Vol. 16, No. 3, October, pp. 25-28.

Sachittanandan, A.N. (1998): "Chennai: Constraints of Public Amenities", in R.P. Misra and K. Misra (eds.), *Million cities of India,* Sustainable Development Foundation, New Delhi, pp. 276-95.

Saleth, R.M. (1997): *Satisfying Urban Thirst; Water Supply Augmentation and Pricing Policy in Hyderabad City, India,* World Bank, Washington, D.C., p. 39.

Sarma, S. and M. Jansen (1996): "Sanitation—Is there any Hope", In Kulwant Singh *et. al.,* (eds.), *Urban India in Crisis,* New Age International, New Delhi, pp. 133-44.

Schofield, F. (1975): "Health Planning in Developing Countries", *Impact of Science on Society,* Vol. 25, No. 3, pp. 181-92.

School of Hygiene and Public Health (2003): *Meeting the Urban Challenge: Population Reports,* John Hopkins University, Baltimore.

Sen, A. (1999), Health in Development, *Bulletin of the World Health Organization*, Vol. 77(8), WHO, Genava, pp. 619-23.

Seth, B. (1965): *Municipal Finance: Proceedings of the Seminar on Municipal Government in India*, Vol. II, Department of Public Administration, Panjab University, Chandigarh, pp. 2-19.

Shah, K.T. and G.J. Bahadurji (1925): *Constitution, Function and Finance of Indian Municipalities*, P.C. King & Co., London.

Sharp, E.B. (1980): "Toward a new understanding of Urban Services and Citizen Participation: The Co-production Concept", *Midwest Review of Public Administration*, Vol. 14, pp. 105-18.

Shordt, K. (2002): *Improving Sanitation Programming*, International Water and Sanitation Centre.

Short, J.R. (1996): *The Urban Order: An Introduction to Cities, Culture and Power*, Blackwell Publishers, Oxford.

Singh, A.M. and V. DeSouza (1980): *The Urban Poor: Slum and Pavement Dwellers in the Major Cities of India*, Manohar Publishers, New Delhi.

Singh, K. and Others (eds.) (1996): *Integrated Urban Infrastructure Development in Asia*, Oxford & IBH, New Delhi.

Singh, K. *et.al.*, (eds.) (1996): *Urban India in Crisis*, New Age International, New Delhi.

Singh, N. (1990): Subsidy Element in Urban Service Provision: A Case Study of Bathinda City, An unpublished M.Phil dissertation submitted to Department of Geography, Panjab University, Chandigarh.

Singh, N.K. (1966): "Some trends in Urbanization in India", *Economic Review*, Vol. 1, pp. 35-40.

Singh, S.N. (1977): "The Slums-clearance and Improvement", *Nagarlok*, Vol. 9, pp. 84-94.

Sirken, A.A. (1979): *The Pricing of Public Urban Services*, World Bank, Washington, D.C.

Sivaramakrishanan, K.C. (1978): *Indian Urban Scene*, Indian Institute of Advanced Studies (IIAS), Shimla.

Subramanian, D.K. (1987): "Banglore City's Water Supply: A Study and Analysis", *Essays on Bangalore*, KSCST (Bangalore), Vol. 4, pp. 51-147.

Tamta, B.R. (1979): "Delhi Water Supply: Pollution Problems", *Economic Times*, September 9, p. 5.

TCPO (1984): *Level and Cost of Selected Municipal Services—An Empirical Study*, Town and Country Planning Organisation, New Delhi.

TCPO (1991): *Environmental Improvement of Urban Slums Scheme: A Supplementary to the Annual Report, 1989-90,* Town and Country Planning Organisation, Ministry of Urban Development, Government of India, New Delhi.

Tewari, T.P. (1988): "Public Health Administration in Urban Areas", *Indian Journal of Public Administration,* Vol. 14, No. 3, pp. 709-15.

Tewari, V.K. *et. al.,* (1986): *Indian Cities: Ecological Perspective,* Concept Publishing Company, New Delhi.

UNDP (1991): *Cities, People & Poverty: Urban Development Cooperation for the 1990s,* United Nations Development Programme, New York.

UNFPA (1996): *The State of World Population,* United Nations Fund for Population Activities (UNFPA), New York, pp. 1-2.

United Nations (1991): *World Urbanisation Prospects, 1990,* Department of International Economic and Social Affairs, UN, New York.

Vandamme, J.M.G. (1973): *Needs and Problems in Water Supply in Developing Countries,* Loughborough University Conference, Loughborough.

Verma, G.D. (2002): *Slumming India: A Chronicle of Slums and their Saviours,* Penguin Books, New Delhi.

Wegelin, E.A. (1990): "New Approaches in Urban Services Delivery: A Comparison of Emerging Experiences in Selected Asian Countries", *Cities,* Vol. 7, No. 3, pp. 244-58.

Whitaker G.P. (1980): "Co-production: Citizen Participation in Service Delivery", *Public Administration Review,* Vol. 40, pp. 240-46.

World Bank (1993): *Annual Review of Portfolio Performance: Water Supply and Sanitation Sector, Transportation, Water and Urban Development,* World Bank, Washington, D.C.

World Bank (1994): *World Development Report: Infrastructure for Development,* World Bank, Washington, D.C., pp. 80-81.

World Health Organization (1973): *Community Water Supply and Sewerage Disposal in Developing Countries,* World Health Statistics Report, W.H.O., Vol. 26, No. 1, pp. 720-83.

Yeung, Y.M. and T.G. Mcgel (eds.) (1986): *Community Participation in Delivering Urban Services in Asia,* International Development Research Institute, Ottawa, Canada.

Zukin, S. (1997): *The Cultures of Cities,* Blackwell Publishers, Oxford.

Index